Beyond Berlin

Social History, Popular Culture, and Politics in Germany
Geoff Eley, Series Editor

Series Editorial Board
Kathleen Canning, University of Michigan
David F. Crew, University of Texas, Austin
Atina Grossmann, The Cooper Union
Alf Lüdtke, University of Erfurt, Germany / Hanyang University, Seoul, Korea
Andrei S. Markovits, University of Michigan

Recent Titles
Beyond Berlin: Twelve German Cities Confront the Nazi Past
 Gavriel D. Rosenfeld and Paul B. Jaskot, Editors
Consumption and Violence: Radical Protest in Cold-War West Germany,
 Alexander Sedlmaier
Communism Day-to-Day: State Enterprises in East German Society
 Sandrine Kott
Envisioning Socialism: Television and the Cold War in the German Democratic Republic
 Heather L. Gumbert
The People's Own Landscape: Nature, Tourism, and Dictatorship in East Germany
 Scott Moranda
German Colonialism Revisited: African, Asian, and Oceanic Experiences
 Nina Berman, Klaus Mühlhahn, and Patrice Nganang, Editors
Becoming a Nazi Town: Culture and Politics in Göttingen between the World Wars
 David Imhoof
Germany's Wild East: Constructing Poland as Colonial Space
 Kristin Kopp
Colonialism, Antisemitism, and Germans of Jewish Descent in Imperial Germany,
 Christian S. Davis
*Africa in Translation: A History of Colonial Linguistics in Germany and Beyond,
 1814–1945,* Sara Pugach
*Between National Socialism and Soviet Communism: Displaced Persons in
 Postwar Germany,* Anna Holian
Dueling Students: Conflict, Masculinity, and Politics in German Universities, 1890–1914,
 Lisa Fetheringill Zwicker
*The Golem Returns: From German Romantic Literature to Global Jewish Culture,
 1808–2008,* Cathy S. Gelbin
German Literature on the Middle East: Discourses and Practices, 1000–1989,
 Nina Berman
Franz Radziwill and the Contradictions of German Art History, 1919–45,
 James A. van Dyke
*Weimar through the Lens of Gender: Prostitution Reform, Woman's Emancipation, and
 German Democracy,* Julia Roos
Murder Scenes: Normality, Deviance, and Criminal Violence in Weimar Berlin, Sace Elde
*Changing Places: Society, Culture, and Territory in the Saxon-Bohemian Borderlands,
 1870 to 1946,* Caitlin E. Murdock
After the Nazi Racial State: Difference and Democracy in Germany and Europe, Rita Chii
 Heide Fehrenbach, Geoff Eley, and Atina Grossmann

For a complete list of titles, please see www.press.umich.edu

Beyond Berlin
Twelve German Cities Confront the Nazi Past

Gavriel D. Rosenfeld
Paul B. Jaskot
EDITORS

The University of Michigan Press

Ann Arbor

First paperback edition 2015
Copyright © by the University of Michigan 2008
All rights reserved
Published in the United States of America by
The University of Michigan Press
Manufactured in the United States of America
♾ Printed on acid-free paper

2018   2017   2016   2015   5   4   3   2

No part of this publication may be reproduced, stored in a retrieval system, or transmitted in any form or by any means, electronic, mechanical, or otherwise, without the written permission of the publisher.

A CIP catalog record for this book is available from the British Library.

Library of Congress Cataloging-in-Publication Data

Beyond Berlin : twelve German cities confront the Nazi past / Gavriel D. Rosenfeld, Paul B. Jaskot, editors.
    p. cm. — (Social history, popular culture, and politics in Germany)
    Includes index.
    ISBN-13: 978-0-472-11611-9 (cloth : alk. paper)
    ISBN-10: 0-472-11611-8 (cloth : alk. paper)
    1. Memorialization—Germany—History—20th century. 2. World War, 1939–1945—Social aspects—Germany. 3. Historic preservation—Germany—History—20th century. 4. War memorials—Germany. 5. Holocaust memorials—Germany. 6. Germany—History—20th century. 7. Collective memory—Germany. I. Rosenfeld, Gavriel David, 1967– II. Jaskot, Paul B., 1963–

D838.G3B49   2007
940.53'1—dc22   2007030968

ISBN 978-0-472-03631-8 (pbk. : acid-free paper)

To our teachers
Saul Friedländer, Peter Hayes, and O.K. Werckmeister

Contents

Acknowledgments — ix

Introduction:
Urban Space and the Nazi Past in
Postwar Germany
   Paul B. Jaskot and Gavriel D. Rosenfeld — 1

**PART 1: SITES OF RECONSTRUCTION:
BETWEEN RECLAIMING AND EVADING THE PAST**

The Politics of New Beginnings: The Continued Exclusion
of the Nazi Past in Dresden's Cityscape
   Susanne Vees-Gulani — 25

Reconciling Competing Pasts in Postwar Cologne
   Jeffry M. Diefendorf — 48

Evading What the Nazis Left Behind: An Ethnographic
and Phenomenological Examination of Historic
Preservation in Postwar Rostock
   Susan Mazur-Stommen — 67

**PART 2: SITES OF NEW CONSTRUCTION:
INDUSTRIAL CITIES AND THE EMBRACE
OF MODERNISM**

Memento Machinae: Engineering the Past in Wolfsburg
   Jan Otakar Fischer — 89

Inventing Industrial Culture in Essen
   Kathleen James-Chakraborty — 116

PART 3: PERPETRATOR SITES: REPRESENTING NAZI CRIMINALITY

The Reich Party Rally Grounds Revisited:
The Nazi Past in Postwar Nuremberg
Paul B. Jaskot — 143

Memory and the Museum: Munich's Struggle to Create a
Documentation Center for the History of National Socialism
Gavriel D. Rosenfeld — 163

Concrete Memory: The Struggle over Air-Raid and
Submarine Shelters in Bremen after 1945
Marc Buggeln and Inge Marszolek — 185

Restored, Reassessed, Redeemed: The SS Past at the
Collegiate Church of St. Servatius in Quedlinburg
Annah Kellogg-Krieg — 209

PART 4: JEWISH SITES: COMMEMORATING THE HOLOCAUST

The Politics of Antifascism: Historic Preservation,
Jewish Sites, and the Rebuilding of Potsdam's Altstadt
Michael Meng — 231

Marking Absence: Remembrance and Hamburg's
Holocaust Memorials
Natasha Goldman — 251

The New Börneplatz Memorial and the Nazi
Past in Frankfurt am Main
Susanne Schönborn — 273

Epilogue: The View from Berlin
Brian Ladd — 295

Contributors — 303

Index — 307

Acknowledgments

Over the course of conceiving and completing the present study, we have benefited from the aid and support of a variety of institutions and individuals whom we would like to take the opportunity to thank. First, we would like to thank the more than fifty respondents to our original call for papers in 2004. Although we unfortunately could not include all of them in the present volume, their interest in the project encouraged us as we developed it further and confirmed our sense of its timeliness. The volume's eventual contributors deserve our thanks for their receptivity to our editorial advice and their tolerance of our hectoring and admonitory e-mails about deadlines, formatting, and photo permissions. In addition, we are grateful to the participants and audiences at the conferences of the German Studies Association in 2003 and 2006, at which several versions of our contributor's papers were presented and critically discussed. Further thanks go to Academic Vice President Orin Grossman and Dean of the College of Arts and Sciences Timothy Snyder at Fairfield University and to the University Research Council at DePaul University for generously providing grants that helped to subsidize the reproduction and inclusion of photographs in the present study. We would also like to give special thanks to Geoff Eley and the anonymous readers for their excellent editorial suggestions, as well as to Jim Reische, Chris Hebert, and Christine Byks at the University of Michigan Press, all of whom were a pleasure to work with in preparing the volume for publication. Finally, we are extremely grateful to Jill Butler Wilson for her meticulous copyediting.

Introduction
Urban Space and the Nazi Past in Postwar Germany
Paul B. Jaskot and Gavriel D. Rosenfeld

Few themes have preoccupied recent scholarship on postwar Germany as much as the nation's long struggle to "come to terms" with its National Socialist past. During the last decade and a half, a massive flood of scholarly and journalistic studies has chronicled the evolution of this confrontation with the Nazi legacy (known in German as *Vergangenheitsbewältigung*) and has tried to evaluate its success.[1] In so doing, most of this literature has conceptualized the German attempt to wrestle with the past in collective national terms, as an attempt to contend with the specific crimes of the German nation during the years 1933–45. This broad view is perfectly sensible for many reasons, but it has largely overlooked the obvious fact that Germans have also confronted the legacy of the Nazi regime as the inhabitants of their respective localities. Ever since 1945, the process of *Vergangenheitsbewältigung* has unfolded within specific geographies and revolved around distinct sites with particular histories. It has involved debates about reconstructing East and West German cities following their wartime destruction; controversies surrounding the moral significance of traditional, modern, or postmodern styles of architecture for new construction projects; disagreements about whether to preserve or demolish National Socialist architectural remnants; and discussions about how to best commemorate the Nazi years with memorials, monuments, or museums.

Up until now, however, the varied social and spatial dynamics of how cities across Germany have pursued what might be called "urban *Vergangenheitsbewältigung*" have largely been ignored. It is true that scholars in recent years have done significant work in examining the confrontation with the Nazi era in the capital of Berlin.[2] Indeed, a good number of important academic studies have chronicled well-known debates over the "critical reconstruction" of the city's general urban fabric; the preservation of Nazi structures, such as the former Air Ministry; and the creation of monuments commemorating the Holocaust, such as the recently completed Memorial to the Murdered Jews of Europe. Yet no matter how valuable these studies of Berlin have been, their tendency to reproduce the national focus of postwar German scholarship on *Vergangenheitsbewältigung* and their attendant lack of a comparative perspective have left certain basic questions unanswered. Foremost among them is the question of the representativeness of Berlin's recent engagement with the Nazi past. While it is clear that the citizens of Berlin have displayed a strong commitment to confronting the legacy of the Nazi years, what about the inhabitants of other German towns and cities? How have they struggled to deal with their own local experiences under National Socialism? Do they collectively amount to a consistent national response to the past, as the scholarship on Berlin implies? Or are they all unique in their own ways? Certainly there have been a few studies (some by contributors to this volume) of how individual German cities have addressed their respective pasts. Up until now, however, the absence of a comprehensive analysis that addresses a variety of German localities has made it impossible to answer the comparative questions with any degree of certainty. As a result, it remains unclear whether Berlin's fervent engagement with the Nazi experience represents the rule or the exception within Germany's overall memory landscape.

In an effort to try and correct this state of affairs, this volume moves beyond Berlin and explores how other German cities have pursued the task of *Vergangenheitsbewältigung* during the postwar period. In particular, we examine how cities in both the East and the West pursued this task and how that process unfolded in the years before and after reunification in 1990. By analyzing a wide range of buildings, memorials, and urban spaces that have sparked heated debates over the Nazi past in various towns and cities outside of the German capital, we intend to develop a more nuanced understanding of the dynamic interaction between local and national trends within Germany's broader culture of memory. Put differently, it is our hope that by moving away from the center and toward the periphery, we can arrive at a more comprehensive awareness of the relationship between memory and the German built environment. In so doing, we seek a deeper understanding of how postwar German society has dealt with the Nazi legacy.

Memory and the Built Environment

For some time, scholars have been aware of the close ties between national history, collective memory, and urban space. As far back as the late eighteenth century, no less a figure than Goethe commented extensively on the intimate relationship between history and building, between memory and site, when he defended the essential Germanness of Strasbourg Cathedral and the positive associations of "German" Gothic.[3] Within Germany, Goethe's observations helped launch an extensive literature—produced by architects, philosophers, and politicians alike—that linked the German nation's character and its historical past to its legibility in built forms. Over the course of the nineteenth century, architects and scholars in Germany and throughout Europe typically conceived of architecture in nationalistic terms, seeing buildings and styles from the past as essentially expressive of their particular culture.[4] Of course, architecture was not the only area of interest among scholars who perceived a transparent relationship between national character and cultural expression. As is well known, linguistics, anthropology, and religious studies were some of the key fields that explored an increasingly racialized connection between culture and nation well into the twentieth century.[5] Significantly, this line of reasoning was readily embraced after 1933 by prominent figures in Nazi Germany, such as Paul Schultze-Naumburg, Heinrich Himmler, and Adolf Hitler, all of whom identified specific buildings and historical styles, whether the Gothic or the neoclassical, as repositories of the *Volk*'s racial essence.[6]

Predictably enough, the Nazi regime's ideological exploitation of architecture and urban space constituted a burdensome legacy that weighed heavily on the German built environment after 1945, in both the East and the West. As Germans faced the daunting prospect of rebuilding their war-damaged cities, they also faced a new challenge: namely, how to acknowledge the negative experience of a criminal past within the postwar urban environment when all available forms of commemoration were based on a positive view of the unity between a nation's political and architectural history. A positive association between culture and national style had developed and grown over centuries and been at the heart of many of the major German architectural debates. But Goethe could not have reckoned with the extremity of Nazi brutality when he formulated his thesis on the relationship between buildings and German identity. After the war, Germans confronted an entirely new situation in which they attempted to undo the connection between the nation's historical memory and its architectural or urban forms on both sides of the iron curtain, only to see such attempts challenged by the constantly resurfacing Nazi past.

This volume explores how postwar German cities dealt with the historical, conceptual, and aesthetic conundrums posed by the Nazi past. In doing so, it aims to reaffirm the importance of the built environment in the construction of public memory. To a degree, this reality has become obscured in recent years by the dramatic expansion of memory studies.[7] So dramatic has this expansion been that scholars from numerous academic disciplines have begun to detect the presence of mnemonic forces in such disparate cultural, social, economic, and political areas as tourism, human sexuality, corporate relations, and international diplomacy.[8] Such studies, to be sure, have been salutary in helping us to understand memory's broad reach, but they have brought with them a somewhat inflationary tendency to perceive memory at work everywhere and anywhere. The effect has partly been a dilution of the perceived significance of the built environment for memory. One indication of this trend is the increasing tendency of scholars to apply the term *site*—by definition a spatial concept—to fields of study that are utterly nonspatial in nature.[9] Parallel to this tendency, while the study of memory has expanded dramatically in art history and visual studies over the last decade, the majority of this work, outside of analyses of Berlin, has dealt with fine arts media or film and moved away from a systematic analysis of memory, architecture, and urban planning.[10] Against the backdrop of such trends, this volume argues that however much the expansion of memory studies is to be welcomed, the built environment deserves to retain a central place as an investigative realm within the field at large.

With this conviction in mind, it is useful to recall not only the precedent of Goethe but also the pioneering insights of the French sociologist Maurice Halbwachs, who, working from the premise that "every memory unfolds within a spatial framework," concluded that "we can understand how we recapture the past only by understanding how it is ... preserved in our physical surroundings."[11] It would be a mistake, of course, to take Halbwachs narrowly at his word and restrict the study of memory to the built environment. But it would be equally mistaken not to emphasize the important contributions that scholars of urban space have made to the field of memory studies over the course of the last generation. Emanating from a wide range of academic disciplines—cultural geography, architectural history, sociology, and history—these contributions have taken

Halbwachs's theoretical arguments and empirically extended them in a variety of significant case studies and comparative volumes. For example, broad-ranging works by such cultural geographers as David Lowenthal and Kenneth Foote have helped us understand how the field of historic preservation has shaped (and frequently distorted) the memory of the past at specific sites.[12] More theoretically informed works of architectural history by such scholars as Dolores Hayden have applied similar insights to the landscapes of marginalized social groups in the United States, while M. Christine Boyer has shown how a close analysis of visual and textual evidence helps to trace the ways in which historical time is conceptualized and presented in the spaces and buildings of the modern city.[13] Their work followed in the path of such architects as Aldo Rossi and Robert Venturi, who, rejecting the postwar claims of the anonymity and universality of modernism, began to theorize more specifically the important relationship between urban space and historical meaning.[14] More recently, finally, numerous sociologists, historians, and art historians have fruitfully collaborated on wide-ranging edited volumes that have featured a global, comparative approach to the intersection of memory and public space.[15] All of these works have sharpened our awareness of why controversies over the past erupt at specific sites and how corresponding shifts in historical memory condition the shift in the physical form of the urban landscape.

Equally important insights into the relationship between memory and the built environment have been made by scholars in the specific field of German studies. Beginning with Thomas Nipperdey's pioneering essay in the late 1960s on monuments in the Kaiserreich, German historians have become increasingly aware of the importance of specific physical sites for the constitution of historical consciousness and national identity.[16] More recent historical studies have continued and extended this national focus, most notably Rudy Koshar's comparative works *From Monuments to Traces* and *Germany's Transient Pasts,* both of which surveyed long-term shifts in Germany's memorial landscape and national identity from the Kaiserreich to the Federal Republic. Other studies have broadly explored such issues in individual cities, especially Berlin.[17] With respect to the Nazi period in particular, groundbreaking works of art and architectural history by such German scholars as Hans-Ernst Mittig in the 1970s helped pave the way for the important studies of Werner Durth, Niels Gutschow, and Winfried Nerdinger, which exposed the continuities of personnel and planning ideologies from the Nazi period into the postwar era and offered new ways of conceptualizing the evasion of memory in the urban environment.[18] Not long thereafter, studies of Holocaust monuments began to appear, such as James Young's pioneering work *The Texture of Memory* and Peter Reichel's comparative analysis *Politik mit der Erinnerung*.[19] Most recently, our understanding of the preservation and representation of the Nazi past at concentration camps has been advanced by the work of Harold Marcuse.[20]

Yet while this broad range of scholarship has increased our understanding of the relationship between memory and urban space in postwar Germany, questions remain. Those studies that have adopted a primarily national focus have preferred to concentrate on the long sweep of German history rather than on the confrontation with the Nazi period exclusively. As a result, the issue of the Germans' relative success or failure at pursuing the task of *Vergangenheitsbewältigung* has remained underdeveloped. Similarly, many studies of monuments related to the Nazi era have preferred to concentrate on their formal qualities and commemorative strategies and refrained from systematically chronicling the agency or institutions that conditioned their origins and the disputes they have engendered. Indeed, scholars have too often projected an abstract concept of mourning or melancholia onto the formed characteristics of buildings and memorials and have preferred general claims about postwar ideology to concrete investigations of the changing function and definitions of the cultural engagement with the Nazi past.[21] Moreover, while these works have frequently provided insightful discussions of individual cases, they have often failed to situate their objects of analysis into a given city's broader effort to deal with the Nazi legacy and have furthermore frequently neglected to discuss them within the significant scholarship on *Vergangenheitsbewältigung*. The result is that it is difficult for readers to gauge these monuments' representative value as expressions of memory. The same problem has defined works on individual cities. Up until now, very few studies have explored the struggle to confront the Nazi past outside of Germany's capital city of Berlin. Apart from recent studies on Munich and Hamburg, we know little about how the dynamics of remembrance have played themselves out in the wider German built environment.[22] Moreover, we do not have works that compare how eastern sites differed from western ones during the cold war era of national division. As a result, much of the literature on the German built environment has lacked a comparative basis from which to determine whether there has truly been anything like a cohesive national mnemonic response to the criminal past. This volume attempts to fill in the gaps that remain in an otherwise distinguished body of scholarship.

Germany's Nazi Past and Urban *Vergangenheitsbewältigung*

In the effort to realize this goal, it is necessary to establish a basis for evaluating the foundational concept of urban *Vergangenheitsbewältigung*. As with the issue of "coming to terms with the past" in general, standards of success and failure for urban *Vergangenheitsbewältigung* are difficult to determine. To begin with, it is arguable whether anything like a fully "mastered" past can ever be attained—especially if such a past is understood as an ideal construct of a historical legacy that allegedly can be teleologically pursued and eventually arrived at with a final sense of closure. After all, as long as the past remains an active social reference point, it will remain open to interpretation and subjected to discussion and debate. Still, even if scholars have abandoned the concept of a fully mastered past, they have become particularly adept at identifying the telltale signs of "unmastered" pasts. Such pasts are those that have become surrounded by discourses marked by silences and stigmas, debates and denials. Linking them all is the tendency to avoid guilt or responsibility for misdeeds committed in the past—a trend expressed in the effort to universalize or forcibly normalize the past in one way or another. Conversely, the more a society is willing to accept responsibility for the misdeeds of the past in a particular locality and to make amends to the victims (or their descendants)—whether in a legal, monetary, symbolic, or commemorative fashion—the more the society can be seen as having made significant strides toward eliminating the aura of uneasiness surrounding a given historical legacy.[23]

Within the realm of the built environment, the struggle to come to terms with a shameful past can manifest itself in numerous ways. In the most general sense, it finds expression in the terms that politicians, institutions, and citizens use to discuss (or refuse to discuss) whether particular parts of the built environment should reflect and communicate something about the past and how, in turn, the built environment is (or is not) physically shaped to serve this broader goal. Through this process of struggle, specific sites, buildings, monuments, and other physical aspects of urban geographies emerge as evolving material embodiments of memory. Many physical aspects of a city's urban space can become the object of historical controversy, all serving as arenas for debate and dispute.

In postwar Germany, debates have erupted in all of these areas. The symbolic meaning of architecture in West Germany after 1945, for example, was strongly influenced by the Nazi experience. Historicism in general and neoclassicism and the *Heimatstil* (vernacular style), in particular, came under fire for their embrace by the Nazi regime. Conversely, modernism was widely, if tendentiously, valorized for its "democratic" credentials. New buildings with steel and glass forms seemed to communicate a new kind of openness, at least to the major economic and political institutions that supported their construction.[24] In the realm of historic preservation, meanwhile, debates over how to reconstruct the countless ruins left by the war was another subject of great controversy. What to do with buildings erected or used by the Nazi regime also sparked debate, as did the proper ways to commemorate the events of 1933–45 with monuments and museums.

Throughout the postwar period, West and East Germans have displayed different tendencies in dealing with the legacy of National Socialism in the built environment. In the early decades after 1945, German localities in both the West and the East were generally inclined to evade guilt or responsibility for the past, whether by nostalgically and unselfconsciously reconstructing the ruins of prominent historic buildings, by refusing to document (or by simply demolishing) sites where crimes were committed, by erecting memorials with ambiguous or euphemistic texts in far-flung locations, or by celebrating an alternative history of antifascism that refused to acknowledge any ties with the immediate past. Local commemorative efforts were often limited to the sites of murder and death, most prominently in the former concentration camps in East and West Germany as well as in designated cemeteries with war dead and the remains of victims of Nazi persecution. Meanwhile, Berlin and its urban environment came to be identified more with the cold war than with the Third Reich, especially following the construction of the Berlin Wall in 1961 and competing housing developments in the years that followed. Beginning in the early 1980s, however, West as well as East Germans slowly began to develop a more systematic culture of remembrance by preserving sites of Nazi barbarism and commissioning ambitious memorials that forthrightly documented and accepted responsibility for the past. These different responses have long been known to scholars in the form of famous individual cases, whether the early postwar reconstruction of the

Goethe House in Frankfurt, the demolition of the Gestapo headquarters on the Prinz-Albrecht-Strasse in Berlin, or the erection of Jochen and Esther Gerz's vanishing "countermonument" in Hamburg.[25] Apart from such well-known examples, however, we still lack a comprehensive and systematic understanding of how urban *Vergangenheitsbewältigung* has been pursued within the less well-known and more ordinary spaces of the German built environment.

This lack of knowledge is especially unfortunate given the important transformations that have been taking place within German memory since the 1980s. During that decade, such notorious cold war episodes as the Bitburg Affair and the Historians' Debate revealed the West Germans to be bitterly divided about the proper place of the Nazi legacy in contemporary German consciousness. Regarding the latter, the attempts of conservative West German intellectuals and politicians to relativize the significance of the Nazi era in the effort to normalize German national identity sparked a fierce response from left-liberals who accused them of failing to honor the obligations of remembrance. Meanwhile, the GDR made only small token gestures toward an official policy of historical recognition of the Nazi era and for the most part stuck to the thesis that Communist East Germany had arisen untouched by the fascist past.[26] On the whole, German memory in the 1980s became increasingly defined by polarization and politicization.

Following the collapse of the Berlin Wall in 1989 and the completion of national reunification in 1990, however, German attitudes toward the Nazi legacy began to change. In the wake of reunification, West German conservatives no longer felt as compelled as they had been during the 1980s to normalize German national identity by relativizing the Nazi past.[27] With the collapse of Communism, East Germans found it more difficult to hide behind the myth of antifascism and evade a genuine reckoning with the Third Reich's legacy. The result was that in both the West and the East, the restoration of Germany's "normal" condition of unity facilitated the emergence of a greater willingness to accept the full weight of the Nazi experience and integrate it into contemporary German consciousness. Whether through President Roman Herzog's public remarks in support of remembrance on the fiftieth anniversary of the end of World War II in 1995, the mass public interest in the Crimes of the Wehrmacht exhibition in the late 1990s, or the creation of the Memorial to the Murdered Jews of Europe in Berlin in 2006, the willingness of Germans to confront the more painful aspects of their nation's past dramatically grew in the 1990s. Germans today have become more willing not only to accept the reality that

Nazi perpetrators came from their own midst and committed unprecedented crimes but also to accept the obligation to meditate on the significance of these facts for the foreseeable future. Indeed, growing numbers of Germans seem to have embraced a new national identity as a people that, despite being partly descended from perpetrators, has excelled at coming to terms with a painful past and become a moral beacon to other nations.[28] Gone at the official level are the previous declarations of the need for Germany to become a "normal" nation by putting the Nazi past behind it.

Yet while this trend represents a notable shift in official memory, signs of a restless counter-memory within German society remain. The controversial interchange in 1998 between writer Martin Walser and the president of the Central Council of Jews in Germany, Ignaz Bubis, about the right of Germans to stop feeling eternally burdened by Nazi crimes signaled the ongoing desire of some Germans to draw a line (*Schlussstrich*) under the past and end the obsessive fixation on the Nazi era. In a very different vein, but no less concerning to many observers, has been the more recent demand of other Germans to remain focused on the Nazi past—but now with an eye toward the suffering of German victims instead of the crimes of German perpetrators.[29] For example, since the turn of the millennium, considerable controversy has swirled around books describing the Allied bombing of German cities, such as W. G. Sebald's *Luftkrieg und Literatur* and Jörg Friedrich's *Der Brand,* along with works featuring other episodes of German suffering, such as Günter Grass's 2002 novel *Im Krebsgang* (which revived attention to the sinking of the *Wilhelm Gustloff,* a refugee-packed Nazi cruise ship, in January 1945) or the anonymously written diary posthumously published in 2005 as *Eine Frau in Berlin* (which chronicled the rape of German women by Soviet Red Army soldiers in the last weeks of World War II).[30] The effort in 2002 to open up the Center against Expulsion (*Zentrum gegen Vertreibung*), to trace the history of the deportation of millions of ethnic Germans during World War II within the modern history of ethnic cleansing and mass expulsion, has also been criticized as a method of masking a renewed effort to focus attention on German suffering behind a seemingly benign cloak of concern for universal human rights. Finally, neo-Nazism has remained a problem in scattered parts of the country (particularly the eastern states) and reflects—in addition to powerful economic and political grievances—the continued disaffection with postwar Germany's progressive efforts to contend with its Nazi past.[31]

In light of the apparent split between official memory and counter-memory in Germany, it is worth exploring whether a similar split has been mirrored in the German urban environment. German official memory has found its primary physical embodiment in Berlin, which has clearly served as unified Germany's public face to the outside world since the epochal events of 1989–90. Whether in the realm of architecture, historic preservation, or monuments, the city has served as the nation's showcase for urban *Vergangenheitsbewältigung*—so much so that it has recently begun to market its sites of memory as part of a larger "national memory district" or "memory mall."[32] This centralization of commemoration at the national level, however, raises obvious questions about the dynamics of remembrance in other regional centers in the German urban landscape. Has the centralization of memory sites in Berlin had a positive or negative impact on the previously decentralized reality of Germany's memorial landscape? Have the progressive trends visible in the nation's capital over the last decade found echo in Germany's many other important towns and cities? Or has the appearance of an official mnemonic consensus at the national level possibly obscured the existence of dissenting trends at the regional level?

German Cities beyond Berlin

To answer these questions, this volume has assembled twelve essays and an epilogue written by a range of scholars spanning multiple academic disciplines that examine various sites of contested postwar memory. It covers a geographically diverse selection of German cities and towns that have thus far not received sustained and comparative scholarly attention. The essays are grouped into four separate sections, each of which is defined by a common spatial or mnemonic theme. But all of the essays address the confrontation with the National Socialist past within specific urban contexts on the basis of particular sites that showcase the localized experience and interpretation of that past. Each of them attempts to cover a wide chronological range, moreover, and addresses trends from the early postwar period up to the present day. While diverse in their scope and conclusions, the essays offer important new observations about the Germans' successes and failures in dealing with the legacy of the Third Reich in the urban environment.

Part 1, "Sites of Reconstruction: Between Reclaiming and Evading the Past," explores how various German cities that experienced substantial wartime devastation went through the process of dealing with the burden of the Nazi legacy through the selective rebuilding of historic structures and the active obscuring of shameful sites. Susanne Vees-Gulani asserts in "The Politics of New Beginnings: The Continued Exclusion of the Nazi Past in Dresden's Cityscape," that Dresden officials and citizens used the built environment to deflect attention from their former cooperation with the Nazi regime by focusing on their victimization by the infamous Allied firebombing of the city on February 13, 1945. Vees-Gulani describes this process by comparing the postwar treatment of the ruin of the Frauenkirche with the recent construction of the architecturally ambitious new synagogue by the firm of Wandel, Höfer, Lorch, and Hirsch on the site of Gottfried Semper's famed temple destroyed on Kristallnacht in 1938. In "Reconciling Competing Pasts in Postwar Cologne," Jeffry M. Diefendorf similarly discusses evasion tactics by examining an era seldom explored in the literature on urban *Vergangenheitsbewältigung,* that of immediate postwar West Germany. Analyzing a range of Cologne's urban planning and architectural initiatives, such as the creative reuse of the remnants of the Church of St. Alban to commemorate German war dead, Diefendorf argues that the Nazi past was not so much repressed in the built environment as it was relegated to more minor and inconspicuous locations. Finally, Susan Mazur-Stommen's "Evading What the Nazis Left Behind: An Ethnographic and Phenomenological Examination of Historic Preservation in Postwar Rostock" concentrates on the selective remembering and forgetting of the past in the Hanseatic East German port city. Using an anthropological methodology, she shows that the casual conversations and discussions of her study group reveal how local citizens have worked to obfuscate the Nazi and Communist pasts at prominent historic sites throughout Rostock to create a workable present. In all three cases, a tendency to reclaim an idealized historical legacy in order to elude guilt from a more burdensome one is visible both in the early postwar era and since the 1990s.

Part 2, "Sites of New Construction: Industrial Cities and the Embrace of Modernism," investigates how certain German cities tried to free themselves of the Nazi era's stigmas by embracing modern architecture. Jan Otakar Fischer's "Memento Machinae: Engineering the Past in Wolfsburg" describes how one of Germany's most important industrial cities, Wolfsburg, shed its identity as Hitler's Stadt des KdF-Wagens (City of the KdF Car) after 1945 and reinvented itself as a showcase of modern architecture. Kathleen James-Chakraborty, in "Inventing Industrial Culture in Essen," analyzes a similar process in the equally important industrial center of Essen, focusing particularly on the city's pursuit of historic preservation status for the Zeche Zollverein Pithead XII. She shows how this Weimar landmark of modern architecture was appropriated by the Nazis as a symbol of industrial power in the 1930s but was selectively denazified and refashioned by city officials after 1945 into a progressive symbol of democratic ideals, despite having served an authoritarian regime during the years of the Hitler state. Both of these essays highlight the selective historical vision embedded within the otherwise praiseworthy attempt of German cities to shake off the ugly past and embrace a more progressive future.

Part 3, "Perpetrator Sites: Representing Nazi Criminality," examines how German cities with particularly burdensome Nazi legacies struggled to confront them during the postwar period. Paul Jaskot's "The Reich Party Rally Grounds Revisited: The Nazi Past in Postwar Nuremberg" analyzes the social and political dynamics at work in the expanded postwar use of a massive site known for National Socialist propaganda festivals. He focuses on how contemporary city policies in Nuremberg have attempted to resolve competing architectural and historical impulses, resulting in an attitude toward the past quite different from that in many other cities. In particular, a pragmatic politics of consensus about the use of the city's Nazi legacy has predominated among the various local liberal and conservative constituencies where one would expect ideological conflict, as still occurs in such symbolic centers as Berlin. Remaining in Bavaria, Gavriel D. Rosenfeld's "Memory and the Museum: Munich's Struggle to Create a Documentation Center for the History of National Socialism" examines the Bavarian capital's ongoing difficulty in acknowledging its identity as the former "capital of the movement" by exploring the reasons for the many delays in the two-decade long effort to build a museum documenting the city's deep links to the Nazi movement on the former site of the notorious Nazi Party headquarters, the Brown House. Moving to the north, Marc Buggeln and Inge Marszolek's "Concrete Memory: The Struggle over Air-Raid and Submarine Shelters in Bremen after 1945" investigates the ways in which a site of slave labor and death was subjected to postwar amnesia and evasion in the Hanseatic city. Their essay analyzes how National Socialist military installations have been incorporated into the built vernacular of Bremen's urban landscape. Finally, Annah Kellogg-Krieg's "Restored, Reassessed, Redeemed: The

SS Past at the Collegiate Church of St. Servatius in Quedlinburg" discusses how issues of aesthetics at the important medieval Church of St. Servatius were used in its postwar restoration to elide any serious investigation of the building's appropriation by Heinrich Himmler's SS. Both the church and the historic architecture of the town were promoted in the GDR and postunification period for their impressive forms, which were increasingly popular with tourists. Here, the medieval past could be mobilized to avoid the Nazi era's period appropriation of the church by claiming an authentic premodern world, a claim that was anything but accurate.

Part 4, "Jewish Sites: Commemorating the Holocaust," evaluates how certain German cities have tried to commemorate the Nazis' persecution of the Jews through the erection of memorials within the context of specific geographies of past oppression. Michael Meng's "The Politics of Antifascism: Historic Preservation, Jewish Sites, and the Rebuilding of Potsdam's Altstadt" explores how the ideological concerns of the East German government led to the demolition of Potsdam's only synagogue and expressed a deeper impulse toward evading the Nazi legacy. Shifting from East Germany back to West Germany, Natasha Goldman devotes "Marking Absence: Remembrance and Hamburg's Holocaust Memorials" to examining several important monuments documenting the wartime fate of the Jewish community. She argues that Hamburg has exhibited some serious shortcomings, if also some worthy achievements, in attempting to wrestle with the shameful legacy of genocide. Finally, Susanne Schönborn's "The New Börneplatz Memorial and the Nazi Past in Frankfurt am Main" argues that another city not usually regarded as possessing a major connection to Nazism has, in fact, dealt quite awkwardly with the challenge of documenting the fate of its Jewish community. In particular, she shows how attempts at commemoration in Frankfurt's public spaces have often conflicted with postwar efforts to project an image of exuberant modernity.

The Variability of Responses to the Nazi Past

Overall, the essays in *Beyond Berlin* reveal several notable trends. First, they highlight the ability of different areas of the built environment to both obscure and illuminate the past, to both hinder and promote remembrance. The field of historic preservation, for example, has just as frequently been implicated in efforts to evade the Nazi legacy—as is shown by the selective reconstruction of historic churches in Cologne, Dresden, Rostock, and Quedlinburg—as it has been able to promote the cause of public enlightenment by documenting the past at perpetrator sites, whether Nuremberg's Reich Party Rally Grounds or Bremen's submarine bunkers. Similarly, if modern architecture was easily mobilized in the attempt to distract attention from the past by creating a glittering facade of progressive modernity in such places as Wolfsburg and Essen, it could also serve the cause of directly confronting the legacy of the Third Reich, as in the case of the new synagogue in Dresden. Predictably perhaps, monuments have been equally ambiguous as indexes of memory. While some, such as those erected in Hamburg, Frankfurt, and Cologne, were praiseworthy in their forthrightness, others have suffered from serious shortcomings and have displayed an unmistakable ambivalence about their underlying commemorative mission. The same can be said about museums. While Cologne and Nuremberg's documentation centers have done a worthy job of confronting the historical reality of National Socialism head-on, Munich's plans for a museum have proved so divisive that they have thus far remained confined to paper. On the whole, these examples remind us not to privilege one area of the built environment over another in seeking to understand the workings of memory in German cities.

Second, the essays help us better periodize the broader evolution of urban *Vergangenheitsbewältigung* in postwar Germany. Many of the case studies—for example, those on Potsdam, Cologne, and Bremen—confirm that the early postwar years were largely defined by a desire to marginalize the Nazi past. While this may not be overly surprising and mostly confirms prevailing trends in the scholarly literature, the authors argue that we should interpret this era not as a period of complete amnesia, as is often assumed, but as one of highly selective memory. Building on this, the essays reveal that the 1980s—a decade typically perceived as a conservative one eager to relativize the significance of the Third Reich—were crucial for taking the cause of remembrance into the mainstream. The new interest in documenting the history of the Nazi years in the built environment was largely part of a dialectical reaction against prior efforts to hide it. The first notable example of this trend is one not discussed in this volume but of significance nonetheless—namely, the effort in the 1980s of left-liberal and self-proclaimed "antifascist" groups in West Berlin to create the Topography of Terror exhibition on the grounds of the former Gestapo headquarters on the Prinz-Albrecht-Strasse, whose sordid history had been blatantly ignored by conservative city officials eager to transform the area into a tourist-drawing museum district in the late 1970s.[33] Significantly, the same dialectical reaction emerged in many other German cities at this time, whether Frankfurt, Munich, Wolfsburg, or Bremen, all of which witnessed the emergence of popular initiatives to document the Nazi era in reaction to prior efforts to marginalize it. In this sense, Berlin's lead proved to be inspirational in other parts of West Germany. To be sure, East Germany was slower in advancing beyond its static cold war position, but the move of the government under the SED (Sozialistische Einheitspartei Deutschlands, the Socialist Unity Party) to renovate the Oranienburgerstrasse Synagogue in East Berlin around the time of the city's 750th anniversary in 1987 signaled a shift in commemoration strategies in that state as well. Coupled with the massive public debate about German national identity after the fall of the Berlin Wall in 1989, the decade of the 1980s formed a crucial break with the reigning strategies of dealing with the Nazi past. In short, a close relationship existed between the national and the local, between the center and the periphery, in shaping the evolution of urban *Vergangenheitsbewältigung* in that era.

Third, while Berlin's influence on other German cities may have been substantial, the essays also reveal that the perceived success of the Topography of Terror exhibition has by no means been reproduced in other localities across the nation. Indeed, German cities have pursued the task of urban *Vergangenheitsbewältigung* with profoundly varying degrees of success. One notable trend is that German cities have typically confronted the Nazi past in direct proportion to the level of responsibility their inhabitants have felt after 1945 for the regime's unprecedented crimes. It goes without saying that while no German cities were entirely innocent during the years of the Nazi dictatorship, some were more closely tied to the Nazi movement than others. Munich, Nuremberg, and Hamburg, for example, were three of the five cities that Hitler grandly proclaimed to be *Führerstädte* in 1937, and they enjoyed major ideological significance throughout the years of the Hitler State. Wolfsburg was a city entirely created by the Nazi regime as the Stadt des KdF-Wagens (City of the KdF Car) and possessed singular importance within the Nazi labor organization, the Deutsche Arbeitsfront (German Labor Front). Potsdam was long regarded as a bastion of Prussian militarism and thus ranked as a significant point of reference for the Nazi movement. Quedlinburg had the honor of being embraced by Heinrich Himmler as a cultic center for the SS due to the presence of the tomb of the Ottonian emperor Heinrich I. Dresden who had a reputation as a bastion of pro-Nazi political sentiment even before Hitler's seizure of power. By contrast, such cities as Bremen, Rostock, Frankfurt, Cologne, and Essen were not as associated with the Nazi regime, largely because their economic and social character—whether maritime, commercial, or industrial—kept them from becoming breeding grounds of the Nazi movement during the Weimar period and fervent supporters of the dictatorship after 1933.

How these cities proceeded to deal with their past behavior during the Third Reich after 1945—how they tried to admit to or evade their varying degrees of responsibility for assorted crimes or misdeeds—is a complicated story. Those cities that had major legacies to live down after 1945 could have been expected to have exhibited more difficulties in doing so than those whose ties to the Nazi regime were more minor. Yet the diverging experiences of German cities during the years 1933–45 did not, in fact, deterministically shape how well or poorly they dealt with the Nazi past during the postwar period. An interesting case in point is provided by the three former *Führerstädte* of Munich, Nuremberg, and Hamburg. For its part, Munich is the most predictable example of a city whose deep ties to the Third Reich (as the "capital of the movement") made its postwar task of facing the past especially difficult and, perhaps understandably, prone to failure. By contrast, Nuremberg (the "City of the Reich Party rallies") faced an equally major historical legacy but exhibited, in recent decades, a far greater readiness to engage in moral reckoning, if not always for the purest of political motives. Meanwhile, the *Führerstadt* of Hamburg (the "City of German Shipping") occupies a more ambiguous place, for while it has exhibited a desire to atone for the Holocaust through a series of ambitious memorials, they have all displayed serious shortcomings. The other cities with major links to Nazism—Dresden, Potsdam, and Quedlinburg—all evaded responsibility for their pasts by embracing a victimized form of identity with the aid of East German antifascism.

Significantly, less burdened cities have exhibited problems in coming to terms with the Nazi era as well. Having never been saddled with the reputation of being bastions of Nazism and never facing the kind of pressure experienced by other urban centers, these cities could easily slip under the radar of public attention after 1945 and live up to the low expectations of them by neglecting to undertake any major efforts at reckoning with the past. A good example of this trend is Rostock, a city that, not particularly Nazified during the Third Reich, had many of its architectural remnants from the past effaced by the postwar SED city government. Similarly, the industrial and working-class city of Essen was never a center of Nazi agitation and essentially used this identity as cover after 1945 in an attempt to refashion a site of Nazi industry into a symbol of democratic idealism. Frankfurt, Cologne, and Bremen all exploited their distinguished histories as venerable cities of trade and culture after 1945 to evade some of their responsibilities in dealing with the Nazi era.

The different levels of success attained by German cities in confronting the Nazi heritage since 1945 reveals the problematic nature of viewing Berlin's recent public endeavors in memorializing and commemorating the past as representative of broader national trends. For this reason, Brian Ladd's epilogue, "The View from Berlin," at the end of this volume, is crucial for understanding regional variations in Germany's overall urban landscape. In the end, while many cases in this book confirm the general pattern established by Berlin, others diverge considerably. We have attempted to lay out in this introduction some of those important points. Nevertheless, the best cases are made by the contributors themselves. These essays ask us to be more attuned to the relative power of place, plan, and the instrumentalization of form when analyzing the memory of the National Socialist past in postwar German cities. Collectively, they have taken the challenge of getting beyond Berlin and have opened up new comparative possibilities for the study of urban *Vergangenheitsbewältigung* as a means of better understanding Germany's ongoing efforts to come to grips with the legacy of Nazism.

NOTES

1. The vast literature on *Vergangenheitsbewältigung* includes the following works: Aleida Assmann and Ute Frevert, *Geschichtsvergessenheit, Geschichtsversessenheit: Vom Umgang mit deutschen Vergangenheiten nach 1945* (Stuttgart, 1999); Ulrich Brochhagen, *Nach Nürnberg: Vergangenheitsbewältigung und Westintegration in der Ära Adenauer* (Hamburg, 1994); Helmut Dubiel, *Niemand ist frei von der Geschichte* (Munich, 1999); Norbert Frei and Sybille Steinbacher, eds., *Beschweigen und Bekennen: Die deutsche Nachkriegsgesellschaft und der Holocaust* (Göttingen, 2001); Peter Reichel, *Vergangenheitsbewältigung in Deutschland* (Munich, 2001); Jeffrey Herf, *Divided Memory: The Nazi Past in the Two Germanys* (Cambridge, MA, 1997); Peter Graf Kielmansegg, *Lange Schatten: Vom Umgang der Deutschen mit der nationalsozialistischen Vergangenheit* (Berlin, 1989); Manfred Kittel, *Die Legende von der zweiten Schuld: Vergangenheitsbewältigung in der Ära Adenauer* (Berlin, 1993); Charles Maier, *The Unmasterable Past: History, Holocaust, and German National Identity* (Cambridge, MA, 1988).

2. Jennifer A. Jordan, *Structures of Memory: Understanding Urban Change in*

Berlin and Beyond (Stanford, 2006); Brian Ladd, *The Ghosts of Berlin: Confronting German History in the Urban Landscape* (Chicago, 1998); Elizabeth A. Strom, *Building the New Berlin: The Politics of Urban Development in Germany's Capital City* (Lanham, MD, 2001); Karen Till, *The New Berlin: Memory, Politics, Place* (Minneapolis, 2005); Michael Z. Wise, *Capital Dilemma: Germany's Search for a New Architecture of Democracy* (Princeton, 1998). More broadly, see Kathleen James-Chakraborty, *German Architecture for a Mass Audience* (London, 2000); James E. Young, *At Memory's Edge: After-Images of the Holocaust in Contemporary Art and Architecture* (New Haven, 2000).

3. Johann Wolfgang von Goethe, "Of German Architecture," trans. Geoffrey Grigson, reprinted in *Art History and Its Methods,* ed. Eric Fernie (London, 1995), 80–84.

4. Mitchell Schwarzer, "Origins of the Art History Survey Text," *Art Journal* 54, no. 3 (Fall 1995): 24–29.

5. Thomas DaCosta Kaufmann, *Toward a Geography of Art* (Chicago, 2004), 43–104; Bruce Lincoln, *Theorizing Myth: Narrative, Ideology, and Scholarship* (Chicago, 1999).

6. Barbara Miller Lane, *Architecture and Politics in Germany, 1918–1945* (Cambridge, MA, 1968); James-Chakraborty, *German Architecture for a Mass Audience;* Eric Michaud, *The Cult of Art in Nazi Germany* (Stanford, 2004); Frederic Spotts, *Hitler and the Power of Aesthetics* (New York, 2004).

7. Scholars have increasingly begun to refer to a "memory boom" and a "memory industry." See, for example, Charles Maier, "A Surfeit of Memory? Reflections on History, Melancholy, and Denial," *History & Memory,* Fall–Winter 1993, 143; Andreas Huyssen, *Twilight Memories: Marking Time in a Culture of Amnesia* (New York, 1995), 8; Kerwin Lee Klein, "On the Emergence of Memory in Historical Discourse," *Representations* (Winter 2000): 127–50; Jay Winter, *Remembering War: The Great War between Memory and History in the Twentieth Century* (New Haven, 2006).

8. See, for example, Alon Confino, "Traveling as a Culture of Remembrance: Traces of National Socialism in West Germany," *History & Memory,* Fall–Winter 2000, 92–121; Elizabeth Heineman, "Gender, Sexuality, and Coming to Terms with the Nazi Past," *Central European History,* no. 1 (2005): 41–74; S. Jonathan Wiesen, *West German Industry and the Challenge of the Nazi Past, 1945–1955* (Chapel Hill, NC, 2001); Andrei Markovits and Simon Reich, *The German Predicament: Memory and Power in the New Europe* (Ithaca, NY, 2001).

9. The practice of using the term *site* in expanded fashion was popularized by Pierre Nora's edited volume *Realms of Memory: Rethinking the French Past,* vols. 1–3 (New York, 1996–98), which investigated French memory in many nonspatial sites.

10. Huyssen, *Twilight Memories;* Lisa Saltzman, *Anselm Kiefer and Art after Auschwitz* (Cambridge, 1999). See also the representative essays in the following works: Benjamin H. D. Buchloh, *Neo-Avantgarde and Culture Industry: Essays on European and American Art from 1955 to 1975* (Cambridge, MA, 2000); Eckhart Gillen, ed., *German Art from Beckmann to Richter* (Cologne, 1997).

11. Maurice Halbwachs, *The Collective Memory* (New York, 1980), 140.

12. Kenneth Foote, *Shadowed Ground: America's Landscapes of Violence and Tragedy* (Austin, TX, 1997); David Lowenthal, *The Past Is a Foreign Country* (Cambridge, 2005).

13. Dolores Hayden, *The Power of Place* (Cambridge, MA, 1995); M. Christine Boyer, *The City of Collective Memory: Its Historical Imagery and Architectural Entertainments* (Cambridge, MA, 1994).

14. Aldo Rossi, *The Architecture of the City* (Cambridge, MA, 1982); Robert Venturi, Denise Scott Brown, and Steven Izenour, *Learning from Las Vegas* (Cambridge, MA, 1977).

15. John Czaplicka and Blair Ruble, eds., *Composing Urban History and the Constitution of Civic Identities* (Washington, DC, 2003); Daniel J. Walkowitz and Lisa Maya Knauer, eds., *Memory and the Impact of Political Transformation in Public Space* (Durham, NC, 2004).

16. Thomas Nipperdey, "Nationalidee und Nationaldenkmal in Deutschland im 19. Jahrhundert," *Historische Zeitschrift* 206 (1968): 529–85. See also Pierre Nora, "Between Memory and History: Les Lieux de Mémoire," *Representations* (Spring 1989): 7–25.

17. Rudy Koshar, *From Monuments to Traces* (Berkeley, 2000); *Germany's Transient Pasts* (Chapel Hill, NC, 1998). For Berlin, see note 2 to this introduction. See also Koshar's important study *German Travel Culture* (Oxford, 2000).

18. Klaus Herding and Hans-Ernst Mittig, *Kunst und Alltag im NS-System: Albert Speers Straßenlaternen* (Giessen, 1975); Werner Durth, *Deutsche Architekten: Biographische Verflechtungen 1900–1970* (Brunswick, 1987); Werner Durth and Niels Gutschow, *Träume in Trümmern: Planungen zum Wiederaufbau zerstörster Städte im Westen Deutschlands 1940–1950* (Brunswick, 1988); Winfried Nerdinger, ed., *Bauhaus-Moderne im Nationalsozialismus: Zwischen Anbiederung und Verfolgung* (Munich, 1993).

19. James E. Young, *The Texture of Memory: Holocaust Memorials and Meaning* (New Haven, 1993); Peter Reichel, *Politik mit der Erinnerung: Gedächtnisorte im Streit um die nationalsozialistische Vergangenheit* (Munich 1995).

20. Harold Marcuse, *Legacies of Dachau: The Uses and Abuses of a Concentration Camp, 1933–2001* (Cambridge, 2001).

21. See, for example, Anthony Vidler, "Building in Empty Spaces: Daniel Libeskind and the Postspatial Void," in *Warped Space* (Cambridge, MA, 2001), 235–42. For a different model, see Tim Cole, *Selling the Holocaust: From Auschwitz to Schindler; How History Is Bought, Packaged, and Sold* (New York, 1999).

22. Peter Reichel, ed., *Das Gedächtnis der Stadt: Hamburg im Umgang mit seiner nationalsozialisticher Vergangenheit* (Hamburg, 1998); Gavriel D. Rosenfeld, *Munich and Memory: Architecture, Monuments, and the Legacy of the Third Reich* (Berkeley, 2000). See also the case studies in Klaus Neumann, *Shifting Memories: The Nazi Past in the New Germany* (Ann Arbor, 2000).

23. One of the better efforts to draft a model for coming to terms with difficult pasts is Martha Minow's *Between Vengeance and Forgiveness: Facing History after Genocide and Mass Violence* (Boston, 1999).

24. Gavriel D. Rosenfeld, "The Architects' Debate: Architectural Discourse and the Memory of Nazism in the Federal Republic of Germany, 1977–1997," in "Passing into History: Nazism and the Holocaust beyond Memory," ed. Geulie Ne'eman, special issue, *History & Memory*, Fall 1997, 189–225.

25. Jeffry M. Diefendorf, *In the Wake of War: The Reconstruction of German Cities after World War II* (Oxford, 1994), 71–72 (Goethe House); Reinhard Rürup, ed., *Topographie des Terrors: Gestapo, SS und Reichssicherheitshauptamt auf dem 'Prinz-Albrecht-Gelände,' Eine Dokumentation* (Berlin, 1991); Young, *The Texture of Memory*, 28–37 (the Hamburg monument).

26. That said, its efforts toward commemorating the Jewish community in East Berlin were an increasingly important part of local cold war politics. See Herf, *Divided Memory*, 334–72.

27. This is not to say that the impulse toward normalization entirely disappeared. Helmut Kohl's decision to refashion the Neue Wache memorial in Berlin testified to the endurance of a cold war tendency to elide the differences between Nazism and Communism.

28. See, for example, Bill Niven, *Facing the Nazi Past: United Germany and the Legacy of the Third Reich* (London, 2002); Jeffrey K. Olick, "What Does It Mean to Normalize the Past? Official Memory in German Politics since 1989," *Social Science History*, Winter 1998, 547–71. Already in 1981, Peter Steinbach described the Germans' postwar relationship to the Nazi era as a "radical confrontation with the past, singular in human history" (*Nationalsozialistische Gewaltverbrechen: Die Diskussion in der deutschen Öffentlichkeit nach 1945* [Berlin, 1981], 8).

29. Robert Moeller, "Germans as Victims? Thoughts on a Post–Cold War History of World War II's Legacies," *History & Memory*, Spring–Summer 2005, 147–93.

30. W. G. Sebald, *Luftkrieg und Literatur* (Munich, 1999); Jörg Friedrich, *Der Brand: Deutschland im Bombenkrieg* (Berlin, 2002); Günter Grass, *Im Krebsgang* (Göttingen, 2002); Anonymous, *Eine Frau in Berlin* (Munich, 2005).

31. Hermann Kurthen, Werner Bergmann, and Rainer Erb, eds., *Antisemitism and Xenophobia in Germany after Unification* (Oxford, 1997).

32. Till, *The New Berlin*, 22.

33. Ladd, *Ghosts of Berlin*, especially 148–67.

PART I

Sites of Reconstruction:
Between Reclaiming and Evading the Past

The Politics of New Beginnings
The Continued Exclusion of the Nazi Past in Dresden's Cityscape

Susanne Vees-Gulani

Victor Klemperer was one of just a few dozen Jews left in Dresden when the city was heavily bombed on February 13 and 14, 1945. The ensuing firestorm, which destroyed fifteen square kilometers of the inner city, including such well-known sites as the Zwinger (with its art galleries), the Frauenkirche, the castle, the opera building, and the art academy, ironically saved his life.[1] By removing the star from his clothes and blending in with other refugees, he escaped from pending deportation. Nevertheless, Klemperer mourned the destruction of Dresden as a "catastrophe."[2] Despite his daily experiences of Nazi terror, Klemperer saw the city's architectural splendor as emblematic of the Germany he cherished. Almost until the end, he identified more strongly with this image than with his Jewish heritage, which he believed the National Socialists had forced back on him. Only when the last sign of his idealized notion of Germany had fallen into literal ruins did Klemperer's vision become clearer. While he lamented Dresden's downfall, he could not help but feel some satisfaction: "every time I think of the pile of rubble at Zeughaus Street 1 and 3, I thought and think, I had and have the atavistic feeling: Jehovah! This is where they burnt down the synagogue in Dresden."[3]

Yet this connection between Nazi persecution and the firestorm has not inscribed itself deeply into the city's remembrance of the past. Since the war, Dresden's local government and inhabitants have repeatedly negotiated their city's urban identity in an interplay of destruction, construction, and reconstruction that has almost entirely excluded the memory of the Holocaust. This was just as true during the years of the German Democratic Republic, when the city pursued an ambitious urban planning program inspired by Socialist ideals, as in the years since reunification, which have been defined by the demolition of buildings from the Communist era and the effort to restore the city's prewar form. Regardless of political context, discussions about Dresden's self-definition have consistently been defined by an insistence on the population's victimization during World War II. This discourse of victimhood is a direct continuation of National Socialist propaganda about the city's destruction, which was portrayed as a senseless act of Allied violence against a place of culture. Even the East German government readily embraced these assumptions to distance itself from the West. This attitude in Dresden has changed little with reunification. Even though increased sensitivity has been displayed toward the Nazi past, residents today still perceive the city's National Socialist history mainly through the bombing experience.

One of the most representative structures that has been involved in this discourse is the city's well-known icon, the Frauenkirche. Nearly entirely destroyed in 1945, its role in the discourse of victimization becomes particularly poignant when contrasted with the rhetoric surrounding the Dresden synagogue, which was burnt down several years earlier during the Nazi pogrom of Kristallnacht on November 9, 1938. Even though these two sites and their seemingly disparate histories are not usually evaluated together, precisely the interplay between the two events they are associated with—the firebombing on February 13, 1945, and the destruction of the synagogue—reveals a consistent pattern of remembrance in Dresden. During the years of the East German regime, the ruins of the church were showcased as a place of commemoration, while the site of the synagogue (like the Holocaust in general) was ignored. Even today, public discussion of the synagogue's destruction is continuously tied to the Frauenkirche. In addition, much attention is now focused on the East German past, as Dresden sees itself as a victim of the GDR's building policies. Due to this strong ongoing quest for victim status, the perpetrator component of the National Socialist past has been continuously excluded both from Dresden's cityscape and from its residents' memories.

Dresden and National Socialism

When Georg Bähr built the famous Frauenkirche from 1726 to 1743, there was no Jewish community to speak of in Dresden, as trade, living, and religious restrictions as well as extreme financial burdens made it almost impossible for Jews to settle there.[4] By the end of the eighteenth century, other German states had started to establish laws that offered some possi-

Fig. 1. The Dresden synagogue built according to the design of Gottfried Semper in 1838–40. Lithograph after photograph by L. Thumling, ca. 1860. (Photo: Heinrich, 1954. Institut für Denkmalpflege, Dresden. SLUB/Deutsche Fotothek.)

bilities of social and cultural integration to Jews, but anti-Semitic prejudice widely prevailed in Saxony.[5] Only in the 1830s were laws passed encouraging the integration of Jews into the community, albeit on a very limited scale.[6] It then became possible for Dresden's Jews to form a congregation and construct their own house of worship.[7] After purchasing a plot of land on the Elbe, near the Brühlsche Terrasse in the northeastern part of the historic city center, the Jewish community hired the well-known architect Gottfried Semper, whose resulting design combined an imposing neo-Romanesque exterior with a lavishly appointed Moorish interior.[8] Completed in 1840, the building was immediately hailed as a masterpiece of synagogue architecture (fig. 1).[9]

Despite registering this notable milestone, however, the Jewish community continued to be viewed with suspicion by many Dresden residents. By the end of the nineteenth century, Dresden had become a stronghold of anti-Semitic political agitation and repeatedly sent anti-Semitic representatives to the Reichstag.[10] During the Weimar Republic, moreover, anti-Jewish sentiment persisted, despite the promulgation of federal laws concerning freedom of religion.[11] With Hitler's rise to power in 1933, Dresden came to be considered a political stronghold of Nazi Germany.[12] Before long, Dresden's Jews began to suffer anti-Semitic persecution and were gradually purged from the urban environment. Beginning in 1937, Nazi city officials terminated the leases of Jewish apartment dwellers and began to evict them from their dwellings.[13] In October 1938, Dresden deported 724 Polish Jews (90 percent of the Polish Jewish population of the city) to Poland.[14] Finally, on November 9, 1938, members of the Sturmabteilung (SA) and other Nazi groups plundered the synagogue and set it on fire. Three days later, on November 12, 1938, its ruins were demolished by city authorities and were eventually used as landfill.[15] Less than a century after being constructed, the synagogue had vanished from the cityscape, leaving nothing but an empty space in the city center.

Despite the political significance of the event, as well as the cultural loss of Semper's architectural masterpiece, November 9, 1938, has not etched itself deeply into the postwar memory of most Dresden residents. According to popular opinion, the destruction of Dresden's architectural treasures only truly began several years later, on February 13 and 14, 1945, when the city was firebombed by British and American forces. The destruction of the synagogue has thus been overshadowed by the 1945 raids, which, in turn, play a significant role in the way that Dresden's inhabitants view themselves and their city. While the experience on the ground was clearly horrific, the Nazi propaganda machine found ways to heighten the horror. The bombings were described as "terror attacks" that exemplified the barbarism of the Allied enemies against defenseless victims. It was through such propaganda that the myth of Dresden as the city of culture without military or industrial significance was born.[16] While it is understandable that the bombings' severity made it difficult to reflect properly on the Nazi past, Dresden's location in the Soviet sector and then in the newly founded GDR significantly contributed to the lack of attention toward the Nazi crimes against the city's Jews.

Building for the Future: Dresden from 1945 to 1989/90

Immediately after the war, attempts were made to evaluate the role of Dresden's residents and the city government in the persecution of the Jews. Nora Goldenbogen, a historian and chairwoman of the local Jewish community, reports discussions in the city council as early as September

1946 about developing a park and erecting a monument commemorating the destruction of the synagogue at its location at the Zeughausplatz.[17] However, while a small park was indeed established near the site, no monument—not even a plaque—was installed for several decades.[18] This course of action corresponds to other changes that took place in the realm of urban planning policies and in postwar parameters of East Germany's self-definition. With Dresden in complete ruins, its government was initially preoccupied with rebuilding the many architectural treasures that had been destroyed in the war and restoring the city's old baroque silhouette. In so doing, they could count on large support by the public, which, in its desolate situation, yearned to normalize the present by reconnecting to prewar conditions.

In 1950, however, the East German government developed official planning guidelines, with some already strongly emphasizing Soviet building ideas, as they were implemented all over the Eastern bloc. The city centers were to become gathering spots for the citizenry and serve as the site of festivities between monumental central buildings.[19] While these guidelines took many years to be implemented in other East German cities, planners in Dresden decided early on that the rebuilding efforts should no longer focus on complete historical rebuilding but should instead aim for a Socialist construction style.[20] Previously known for its splendor, nobility, and the strong presence of bourgeois values, Dresden was now supposed to be revamped by this new design to signal a better political system. This strategy was followed particularly aggressively in the 1950s and 1960s, but as early as 1946, Dresden became the site of the radical clearing of whole streets of salvageable historical ruins, leaving behind immense amounts of empty space.[21] The city government also changed street names and planned the installation of a large number of monuments, memorials, sculptures, and wall paintings depicting Socialist themes.[22]

While some limited restoration occurred with the rebuilding of the Zwinger and the Hofkirche, the emphasis was placed on the enlargement of city squares and the creation of wide marching avenues, which did not correspond to Dresden's historical proportions. The Altmarkt was increased threefold into an immense demonstration square, and the streets connecting the city's east and west sides were widened up to three and a half times, to sixty-five to seventy meters, to form a major throughway in accordance with Soviet examples.[23] The north-south axis known as the Prager Strasse, previously some fourteen to eighteen meters wide, was expanded to sixty-eight to eighty-five meters, and a large cultural center, the Kulturpalast, was placed in the city center as a new focal point.[24] The message associated with this urban planning was clearly one of political and cultural change. Instead of a city of the eighteenth and nineteenth centuries, Dresden was supposed to become a city of the Socialist future.

Yet it was impossible to negate completely Dresden's former historical architectural splendor. Most of the population and the city's office for historic preservation were immensely critical of the new direction envisioned by city and state politicians. It became clear that to unite the population behind the Socialist plan, there had to be found a new relationship to the past that allowed a connection of people's memories with the official vision of the future in the new state and a way of distinctly defining themselves in opposition to the Western NATO alliance. At the same time, this new approach had to serve as a justification for the new urban structures symbolizing the establishment of Socialism.

The theme that offered itself for this endeavor in Dresden was the bombing war against Germany. A large part of the population had experienced its horror, its effects were still shaping the landscape, and the Soviet forces had played no role in it. The destruction of German cities during the war thus became an important tool in the foundation myth of the GDR. Thomas Widera suggests in his study about postwar Dresden: "In the totality of the destruction lay the singular chance to present the utopia of the new time in contrast to a past that had been completely wiped out and to define in their entirety the memory structures [of this event]. . . . From then on, the aerial bombardment of Dresden was portrayed as a senseless 'terror attack' by the Western Allies."[25] By describing the bombings in this manner for propaganda purposes, the East German government continued both in rhetoric and intent the course of the National Socialist exploitation of the bombings in their effort to stir up strong emotions against the Allied forces.

For many, the Frauenkirche represented the center of Dresden's cultural reputation and the city's true soul. Its destruction in February 1945 was seen as embodying the barbarism of the events and their unnecessary cruelty. The Frauenkirche could serve convincingly as a concrete site of remembrance in Dresden and also form a symbolic point of reference. Consequently, the city government decided neither to clear nor to rebuild the Frauenkirche on the Neumarkt but to preserve the ruins the way they were. The destroyed Frauenkirche became a powerful monument that could be used to revise the past safely as well as to comment on the present and the future in the cold war atmosphere (fig. 2).

Fig. 2. Post-1945 ruins of the Dresden Frauenkirche built according to design of Georg Bähr in 1743. (Photo: Möbius, 1957. SLUB/Deutsche Fotothek.)

With the formation of the GDR, the bombings came to be seen as a symbol of the German people's wartime suffering, marginalizing immediate postwar approaches that had connected the destruction of German cities to the question of German guilt, the rise of National Socialism, and the beginning of the war.[26] The question of guilt was now projected solely onto the Western Allies, a position with which many East Germans could easily identify. A plaque installed at the site of the Frauenkirche ruins read: "To the tens of thousands of dead, and an inspiration to the living in their struggle against imperialist barbarism and for the peace and happiness of man."[27] Depending on the relationship between the Soviet Union and the United States, the anniversaries of the destruction were differently nuanced in their message and commemorated with varying degrees of vigor in front of the Frauenkirche; never, however, was the fundamental premise of the bombing as a terror attack against defenseless civilians and a place of exquisite cultural value questioned. Particularly during the height of the cold war, the anniversaries served as a welcome occasion for official demonstrations against the West—the imperialist fascist enemy of

Socialism—or as reminders of the horrors of war.[28] East Germany ultimately equated the destruction of Dresden with the crimes committed under National Socialism by portraying the Western allies as fascist powers and the bombing of Dresden as a fascist act.[29] East Germany thus prioritized a victim discourse that excluded questions about its own responsibility during the Nazi era.[30]

In this climate, the Nazis' persecution of the Jews could no longer play a central role in the official East German memory discourse, since this discussion would have addressed perpetrator questions. While East Germany did not deny Jewish persecution, its gruesome results were simply folded into the larger victim discourse. In his study on East Germany and the Holocaust, Thomas C. Fox has pointed to this phenomenon at GDR concentration camp memorials. While the exhibits did not deny Jewish suffering in the camps, they often downplayed the numbers of victims and emphasized Communist suffering.[31] Fox also points out the role of these memorials in transmitting to visitors the antifascist struggle East Germany claimed for itself.[32] The Ehrenhain memorial park at the Dresden Heidefriedhof cemetery, where most of the victims of the Dresden bombings were buried in mass graves, exemplifies similar sweeping generalizations and shifts in emphasis to support the political message of the GDR.[33] It was partially established in 1948 and completed in the 1960s. Behind an obelisk with the sign of the International Federation of Resistance Fighters (FIR), fourteen columns, each listing a place-name, stand in a large circle: six columns are inscribed with the locations of concentration camps, seven list places that were sites of World War II atrocities committed by Germany or that were bombed by the German Luftwaffe, and one column is inscribed with the name "Dresden." In addition, the Ehrenhain concludes with a wall memorial for the victims of the Dresden raids. This combination of places not only elevates the Dresden bombings to a war crime and equates German victims of these attacks with those of German atrocities but also portrays concentration camps simply as part of a general structure of terror in war.

The GDR viewed antifascism as a key foundational principle. However, since the bombings of (East) German cities were portrayed as fascist acts by the Western Allies against antifascist victims, the strong racial element of National Socialism, its widespread support by the population, and the unparalleled severity of Jewish persecution had to be negated. Coming to terms with the Nazi past in the GDR simply required residents to "smash capitalism," which was seen as lying at the core of National Socialism.³⁴ There was no acknowledgment of any particular responsibility or obligation toward the Jewish population and their suffering.³⁵ The consequence of this view was not only a redefinition of history but a hindering of any discussion of anti-Semitism in the GDR—a hindering that influenced the debate after reunification.³⁶ There is also strong evidence that anti-Semitic prejudice existed within the East German government.³⁷ Given this political climate, the general trend in the GDR was to ignore or downplay November 9, 1938.

It is thus not surprising that the original plans in Dresden for a memorial at the site of the former synagogue were quickly abandoned. Dresden had become a key player in the cold war discourse about the population's victimization by the capitalist West. A memorial that identified only one particular group as victims of Nazism and alluded to the culpability of Dresden residents could have severely undermined this official portrayal of German suffering. For several decades, Dresden's political climate allowed room for only the Frauenkirche memorial or the synagogue, and the Frauenkirche was clearly favored. While its ruins served as a backdrop for official remembering, the site of the synagogue was subjected to Dresden's rebuilding and modernization effort. The whole area had been changed significantly, with a new bridge, the widening of roads, streetcar tracks, and the enlargement of the Rathenauplatz, as well as new buildings on the other side of the square.³⁸

In the 1970s, the GDR began to have a slightly more visible engagement with the Holocaust and the November 1938 pogroms. However, much of the official remembrance followed already established patterns. In 1975, the site of the former synagogue finally received the memorial that had been discussed right after the war. Yet, contrary to the inscription's claim, it was put up not where the synagogue was originally located but closer to the Brühlsche Terrasse, in an area with some greenery. At this memorial, which is designed in the shape of a menorah with six arms (to represent the six million Jews killed in the Holocaust), the victims are more clearly identified. Yet the inscription still refers to them as part of a larger victim group, and the responsibility for the building's destruction is simply attributed to "fascists."³⁹

From 1978 on, there was a significant increase in the official remembrance of November 9, 1938, partially in response to similar events in the West. Since the GDR was now trying to gain more international recognition, the memory of the bombings ceased to be a centrally organized propaganda event.⁴⁰ In accordance with this view, remembering November 9,

1938, entailed emphasizing the time after the war, especially the successful overcoming of inequality, prejudice, and fascism in East Germany. In addition, the Jewish victims were again incorporated into a larger victim group by portraying them as martyrs in their fight against Hitlerian fascism.[41] The emphasis was only on the victims, without exploring the perpetrators' role in their suffering. In this way, the discourse on Dresden's bombing victims could be preserved without creating opposing memories. A postcard printed in 1985 by VEB-Foto-Verlag Erlbach in the Vogtland exemplifies the continued polarization and falsification of history in East Germany. It shows a picture of the Semper synagogue before its destruction in 1938, with the caption "Dresden Synagogue, 1838–40, Gottfried Semper. Before its destruction by Anglo-American bombing units on February 13, 1945."[42]

The Future in the Past: Dresden after Reunification

In *The Collective Silence,* psychotherapist Barbara Heimannsberg reminds us: "We tend to play . . . pride off against . . . historical responsibility. The parts of the past that detract from a sense of pride are toned down and ignored."[43] She finds that such behavior is particularly strong after significant political changes and names the return to nationalist trends after German reunification as an example.[44] After the GDR ceased to exist, Dresden residents quickly tried to reassert themselves. However, rather than striving to take part in a larger national identity, Dresden's self-worth was bound up with local developments. Dresden residents saw their city as exceptional, with a transnational flair—an assessment based largely on its architectural reputation. Reconstruction debates thus quickly arose in Dresden yet again. The city's inhabitants were afraid of what they called its "third destruction." After the first destruction caused by the Allied firebombing and the second caused by Socialist East German reconstruction projects, they now feared the fervor of Western investors who were interested in redeveloping the many empty lots in the city's center with the help of contemporary architecture.[45] The wide use of the phrase "third destruction" gives an understanding of the immense unpopularity of the East German approach to rebuilding in Dresden and reveals the disdain most Dresden residents had for any modern forms of architectural expression. The goal quickly became to re-create Dresden in its historic prewar condition.

Fig. 3. Post-1945 architectural ensemble along the Prager Strasse in Dresden. View from the northwest. (Photo: Würker, 1974. SLUB/Deutsche Fotothek.)

Despite much protest by artists and architects, Dresden residents have undertaken popular initiatives to ensure the rebuilding of almost all parts of the historic city center the way they looked before the firebombing in 1945, even if this means the destruction of buildings erected during East German times. The Prager Strasse, for instance, which many view as a key example for "one of the most spectacular and successful" architectural ensembles in the Socialist style (fig. 3), was soon scaled down at several spots by buildings placed onto the wide pedestrian zone.[46] According to city plans, this trend will continue in order to reach the original width of eighteen meters and will also include tearing down several buildings.[47] In addition, streets that had not been reconstructed according to their original pattern will be restored in the new layout of the area.[48]

The Neumarkt has received particular attention from the reconstruction supporters. It was originally surrounded by a large number of burgher houses and had witnessed no major new construction aside from the modern large annex to the eighteenth-century police headquarters that was erected in the years 1979 to 1983. This annex was torn down in 2005. Particularly through the pressure of a citizen's action committee, the new buildings surrounding the Neumarkt are being constructed according to the ground layout from before the destruction of 1945, with the buildings' historical facades, roofs, and heights. They are intended to serve as commercial space.[49]

The prime example of this reconstruction effort, however, has been the highly symbolic Frauenkirche in the middle of the Neumarkt, which was recently completed as an exact copy of the church destroyed during the bombing raids in 1945 (fig. 4).[50] Despite the general view among preservation experts and architects that the church "constitutes a new building, which follows the forms of the original Dresden Frauenkirche," its supporters, embracing the term "archeological reconstruction," describe its completion as returning one of the most important monuments to the world community.[51] The incredible number of donations that financed the church's reconstruction suggests that the population widely shares this view. For its consecration alone, on October 30, 2005, over sixty thousand people came to the Dresden Neumarkt.[52] For many Dresden residents, the resurrected Frauenkirche offers the opportunity to reconnect to a prewar and pre-GDR past that excludes the years 1933–1989/90. City officials as well as private preservation groups would like to re-create Dresden as a place that appears to be solely defined by culture and beauty. Such a nostalgic view of an idealized and altered past can serve the present needs of the population.[53] The residents' close identification with their architectural surroundings lets them indirectly claim a similar status for themselves. At the same time, these restorations are financially attractive, since the city government hopes that a major part of Dresden's future will be defined by tourism.

Postreunification Dresden thus aims to establish a distinct countermovement to the previous political situation, with most inhabitants seeing their future in the pre–National Socialist past. As the planned changes in the city's appearance suggest, the urban developments of the GDR era are particularly hated by the population and by many city representatives, and attempts are being made to erase them as thoroughly as possible.[54] However, while the rebuilding decisions emphasize the exclusion of most of the twentieth-century developments in Dresden and Germany as a whole, the movement's underlying belief structures are actually a continuation of the East German postwar discourse. Most obviously, such rebuilding is meant to heal the wounds inflicted by the war upon the city and, by association, upon its inhabitants.[55] Dresden residents and city officials have tried to signal a new direction, stressing that a painful chapter has now been closed with reunification and that the city is off to a fresh start. The emphasis on

Fig. 4. Reconstruction of the Dresden Frauenkirche. (Photo: Bregulla, 2004. SLUB/Deutsche Fotothek.)

the present, which suppresses the immediate past almost completely, closely parallels the rhetoric of the GDR in regard to Nazi Germany. The only difference is where these new beginnings are located. In the GDR, both the society and environment were supposed to be designed according to Socialist principles shared by the other countries that belonged to the Soviet bloc, while Dresden residents now define their city and themselves through the "archeological reconstruction" of a cultural site possessing world class status. Through the re-creation of such key buildings as the Frauenkirche, which is portrayed as an international cultural icon, Dresden emphasizes its importance as a UNESCO World Heritage Site. Cultural heritage is here "lauded as the legacy of all mankind," which ultimately raises Dresden above national boundaries.[56] In this sense, Dresden residents can now claim that their city was not merely a part of Nazi Germany or East Germany but belongs to the world at large.

While the Frauenkirche project was under way immediately after the collapse of East Germany, a discussion about building the synagogue arose much more slowly. By the end of the GDR, the Jewish community of Dresden had become extremely small and consisted mainly of older members. With the opening of the Eastern bloc, however, the Jewish community experienced a significant revitalization through immigration. There was consequently a lot of interest in building a new synagogue that would be able to house all its members. Yet while euphoria surrounded the Frauenkirche plans, there was less excitement about the synagogue. As Siegfried Reimann, a strong supporter of the synagogue building project, recounts, while there were repeated discussions in the early 1990s, silence and stagnation had taken over by 1995.[57] In a letter to the mayor in that year, Reimann reminded the city of the responsibilities connected with the rebuilding of the Frauenkirche: "Considering the reconstruction of the Dresden Frauenkirche, it appears to me and also to the Jews of our city as increasingly oppressive that there is no public discussion of their house of worship, which had been taken from them through criminal pillage. I know that the city is talking about some plans to rebuild a synagogue. However, in contrast to the significant time and effort invested in the rebuilding of the Frauenkirche, these plans represent a point zero."[58]

The synagogue project eventually gained stronger support due to political developments. Right-wing neo-Nazi groups have always understood the raids on Dresden as a central defining event for their worldview and their historical revisionism. Since reunification opened up the possibility to travel freely to the city, Dresden has become a central location for repeated national neo-Nazi activities. This focus on the city and its destruction became widely apparent when five thousand neo-Nazis from all over Germany marched through Dresden on the sixtieth anniversary of the bombings in 2005, in the country's largest right-extremist demonstration since the end of the war. In Saxony itself, right-wing politics have also been on the rise since reunification. The extremist NPD (Nationaldemokratische Partei Deutschlands, the National Democratic Party) has become increasingly popular and can now count on a stable base among Saxons. In 2004, the NPD managed to gather 9.2 percent of the vote for the Saxony state parliament. This national reputation as a right-wing stronghold runs counter to the image of the innocent place of culture that most of the Dresden population and many city officials favor. It is thus also important for the city government and many of its residents not to have their remembrance of the bombing identified with this movement. The strong interest in attracting tourism to the city undoubtedly also plays a significant role in this desire. In the course of these developments, renewed memorialization of the destruction of the synagogue has taken place. Interestingly, while the Frauenkirche and synagogue had functioned mainly as exclusive symbols until reunification, they now are often paired.

Since initiatives emerged to build a new synagogue, the image of the burning Semper synagogue was increasingly evoked in speeches and commemorative events that involved the Frauenkirche, particularly to counteract any suggestion of right-wing historical revisionism. The Frauenkirche became a site for the collection of donations for the new synagogue. A message given out to the population by then Dresden mayor Herbert Wagner concerning the remembrance activities of February 13, 2001, is a representative example for this continuous endeavor. He reminded the Dresden inhabitants that they should not let other groups take over the memory of the bombings and should unite "when forces try, try again and again, to disturb our day, our commemoration, and our mourning . . . of the destruction of the city, . . . for the dead of the war and in [a] will to achieve reconciliation."[59] He later distinctly referred to the synagogue, emphasizing that there is a relationship between its destruction in 1938 and the destruction of the Frauenkirche in 1945. He concluded, "In the same manner, the building of the synagogue and the reconstruction of the Frauenkirche are now closely connected."[60]

Even though donations were significantly smaller for the synagogue than for the Frauenkirche and the project experienced funding problems, construction was completed in 2001. While using part of the site where the original Semper synagogue had stood, the Jewish community decided not to try to rebuild it but instead agreed on a contemporary design by the architectural office Wandel, Höfer, Lorch, and Hirsch. With their plans, the architects specifically wanted to counteract such historical reconstructions as the Frauenkirche, with which "not only a political, but also a spatial caesura is blocked," since they suggest an uninterrupted "continuity between past and present" states.[61] For the synagogue, with its distinct history, such continuity appeared questionable. The Jewish community also emphasized the need not to reconstruct the temple or rebuild it in some historicized form. After the Holocaust, they agreed, one should not connect to the past as if nothing had happened.[62] The New Synagogue consists of two separate structures: the larger one, closer to the Elbe, serves for worship, while the other, toward Dresden's Old Town, houses a community center. The two blocks are connected by a courtyard. Here, parts of the original layout of the Semper synagogue are made visible on the courtyard's floor, so that this space between temple and community center creates a "gap" in which the memory of the destruction of the former synagogue can unfold.[63] Since the terrain did not allow the traditional alignment of the New Synagogue toward the east, the allocated design contains a "twist": while the blocks are arranged in straight lines, cantilevered bricks at each corner literally orient the structure eastward (fig. 5).[64]

With the contemporary design of the New Synagogue and the reconstructed Frauenkirche both in its city center, Dresden now displays an interesting symbiosis of old and new, remembrance and forgetting, in its urban structure. Even though the emphasis is clearly on reconstruction, one might think that a workable relationship of Dresden to the Nazi past could develop through these two buildings and the rhetorical association that has been established between them. However, a look at the way February 13, 1945, is generally perceived and at the reception of the two buildings by Dresden residents show that the facing of the Nazi past is only possible under certain premises, which reflect well-established belief structures.

Despite the frequently evoked connection of the bombings and the destruction of the synagogue, there has been little change in the actual view of the raids. The traditional discourse about Dresden being the victim of a unique act of senseless violence, a discourse first established during the Nazi era, still continues into the present. This belief has become strongly ingrained in the collective memory of the city's inhabitants and was fur-

Fig. 5. The new Dresden synagogue built according to the design of Wandel, Hoefer, Lorch, and Hirsch in 1998–2001. View from the northwest. (Photo: Bregulla, 2004. SLUB/Deutsche Fotothek.)

ther confirmed by East Germany's continuous "self-staging as an antifascist state."[65] The power of these convictions becomes particularly visible when analyzing responses to any critical discussion of the accepted history of the February raids. Most recently, the historian Helmut Schnatz faced fierce opposition for his critical analysis of the Dresden firebombing. Schnatz analyzed the claims that during the daytime raids, which were flown by American bomber pilots, people on the streets were targeted with machine-gun fire by low-flying aircraft. These stories of deadly American attacks against completely defenseless civilians have widely served as a basis for the innocent victim rhetoric in Dresden since February 1945 and are repeatedly referenced to show the cruelty of the attacks. However, in his detailed study, Schnatz concluded that while such strafing incidents had taken place in other cities, none had taken place in Dresden. For his work, Schnatz has been accused by Dresden residents to be an "evil historical revisionist" who engages in "mocking the victims."[66]

In other aspects, the victim discourse from 1945 has been changed to accommodate the political situation of the times. As has been shown already, the GDR identified the perpetrators as fascists, so that Dresden residents came to be viewed as victims of both Western forces and National Socialism. After reunification, the definition of victim was made even more inclusive, since now the GDR was also seen as a victimizer. The current relationship between rhetoric and remembering the bombings demonstrates these shifts. Frequently, the rhetoric and views of East Germany are kept alive in the evaluation of the events—for example, by referring to the bombings as "acts of terror."[67] Yet in other regards, the GDR has also been absorbed into the canon of the victimizers, as the establishment of the Frauenkirche as a place of remembrance of the bombing victims demonstrates. Its symbolic meaning carried over from the GDR, but it is now defiantly restored to its original appearance, something widely supported in Dresden but never allowed during East German times. This identification of East Germany as victimizer, even as part of an expanded perpetrator group, can become so overpowering that attempts to pay proper attention to the Nazi past in Dresden are quickly drowned out by the dominant concerns with the GDR past.

The population's reaction to the rebuilding of the synagogue is a strong indication that rhetorical support for its construction does not necessarily include a revisiting of the Dresden residents' own role in Nazi Germany and Jewish persecution. When the Jewish community purposefully selected a contemporary design, an outcry of anger went through the population. This resentment was widely expressed at model exhibitions following the architectural design competition, in guest books that contained numerous comments about "vain, career-driven architects" and the disfiguring of Dresden.[68] In the *Sächsische Zeitung,* a reader expressed her hope that such "creative attacks of God-like creators (also called architects) . . . will in the future immediately end up in the shredder."[69] While Dresden residents have been continuously critical of contemporary architecture, the decision not to rebuild the synagogue according to Semper's design caused particular outrage. It appears that it is based on two regrets: that a modern structure is part of the city's Elbe panorama and that there exists now a widely visible memorial to the events of 1938 that contrasts strongly with the local historical environment.

Most telling, however, are the opinions that express doubt that such a design can achieve the "tolerance and togetherness in harmony" that Dresden residents want.[70] When such opinions are taken together with the most often evoked term concerning both the rebuilding of the

Frauenkirche and the construction of the New Synagogue—"reconciliation"—the old underlying belief structures about Dresden and its destiny become visible. There is still the distinct feeling of shared victimhood. This continuous victim discourse has not lost its power. First a part of National Socialist propaganda, where Dresden residents were innocent victims of the enemy's inhumane aggression, the discourse continued into the GDR, which portrayed its citizens as victims of a cruel fascism performed by former National Socialists and Western capitalists. After reunification, the self-identification of victims of Socialism was added to this idea of all-encompassing victimhood. Consequently, Dresden residents, as "fellow victims," thus feel justified in suggesting and requesting signs of "reconciliation" and "harmony" from the Jewish community. Yet since this discourse is solely focused on peace and reconciliation for the present and future and not on the past events, it continues to avoid an honest confrontation with history and a reevaluation of the involvement in National Socialist crimes.

The historical rebuilding of such structures as the Frauenkirche, which has almost absolute support from the Dresden population, is thus also still a sign of defiance against various powers by which Dresden residents see themselves as victimized: the Nazi dictatorship, which ultimately led to Dresden's first destruction; Britain and America, which executed the bombings; the East German regime, which further destroyed Dresden's cityscape; and Western investors who now try to ruin the city through modern designs. While the New Synagogue prevents Dresden from having the same Elbe panorama as before 1938, its residents still have to decide whether they will engage in the new offer of possible confrontation with the past that its urban space now provides. So far, however, such confrontation has been rare. Instead, most Dresden residents have made the decision to include the New Synagogue in their rhetoric of shared victimhood but to exclude the building as much as possible from the way the city portrays itself to the outside. Dresden's central cityscape now restricts itself to an area further west, particularly around the Frauenkirche at the Neumarkt, which is built up as a true tourist attraction. When a tourist would like to leave the historic city center and view other aspects of Dresden history, such as the synagogue, it might prove an almost impossible endeavor. There is no sign pointing the way to the New Synagogue or the memorial from 1975, and the large stylized maps put up in the city center, which houses such important buildings as the Frauenkirche, the Schloss, or the Hofkirche, do not include the synagogue, even though it is located only a few hundred meters further east. The souvenir shops do not carry postcards of the temple, and city walking tours ignore it as well. One is left hoping that when the historical rebuilding has been finished and the hype has ebbed, Dresden might be able to address the past with methods that do not simply pose a continuation and expansion of already established patterns but, rather, engage in new ways of introspection. Opening up the definition of Dresden to include not only its historical but also its East German and contemporary buildings could be a first step toward remembering both victims and perpetrators.

NOTES

1. F. Reichert, "The Destruction of Dresden," in *The Revival of Dresden*, ed. W. Jäger and C. A. Brebbia, Advances in Architecture Series (Southampton, 2000), 10–12.

2. Victor Klemperer, *Tagebücher: 1945*, ed. Walter Nowojski (1995; repr., Berlin, 1999), 31.

3. Ibid., 45. German sources have been translated by the author.

4. For a description of the situation in Dresden, see Emil Lehmann, "Der polnische Resident Berend Lehmann, der Stammvater der israelitischen Religionsgemeinde zu Dresden" (1885), in *Gesammelte Schriften* (Dresden, 1899), 116–53.

5. Simone Lässig, "Vom Mittelalter in die Moderne? Anfänge der Emanzipation der Juden in Sachsen," *Dresdner Hefte* 45 (2000): 11.

6. Adolf Diamant, *Chronik der Juden in Dresden: Von den ersten Juden bis zur Blüte der Gemeinde und deren Ausrottung* (Darmstadt, 1973), 30–31.

7. Ingrid Kirsch, "Das Ringen um die rechtliche Gleichstellung der Dresdner Juden und ihrer Religionsgemeinde von 1830 bis 1871," *Dresdner Hefte* 22 (2000): 19–26.

8. Emil Lehmann, *Ein Halbjahrhundert in der israelitischen Religionsgemeinschaft zu Dresden: Erlebtes und Erlesenes* (Dresden, 1890), http://www.diss-duisburg.de/Internetbibliothek/Artikel/kirche_und_synagoge.htm.

9. Harold Hammer-Schenk, *Synagogen in Deutschland* (Hamburg: Hans Christians Verlag, 1981), 130; Hannelore Künzl, *Islamische Stilelemente im Synagogenbau des 19. und frühen 20. Jahrhunderts*, ed. Johann Maier (Frankfurt am Main, 1984), 182–83.

10. Gerald Kolditz, "Zur Entwicklung des Antisemitismus in Dresden während des Kaiserreichs," *Dresdner Hefte* 45 (1996): 40.

11. Ingrid Kirsch, "Die Israelistische Religionsgemeinschaft zu Dresden während der Zeit der Weimarer Republik," in *Einst und jetzt: Zur Geschichte der Dresdner Synagoge und ihrer Gemeinde* (Dresden, 2001), 80–81.

12. Frederick Taylor, *Dresden: Tuesday, February 13, 1945* (London, 2003), 54.

13. Marcus Gryglewski, "Zur Geschichte der nationalsozialistischen Judenverfolgung in Dresden 1933–1945," *Die Erinnerung hat ein Gesicht. Fotografien*

und Dokumente zur Nationalsozialistischen Judenverfolgung in Dresden 1933–1945, ed. Norbert Haase, Stefi Jersch-Wenzel, and Hermann Simon (Leipzig, 1988), 110.

14. Nora Goldenbogen, "Nationalsozialistische Judenverfolgung in Dresden seit 1938—ein Überblick," *Dresdner Hefte* 45 (2000): 77; Gryglewski, *Erinnerung*, 113.

15. Nora Goldenbogen, *Die Dresdner Synagoge: Geschichte und Geschichten* (Teetz, 2004), 37.

16. Matthias Neutzner, "Vom Alltäglichen zum Exemplarischen: Dresden als Chiffre für den Luftkrieg der Alliierten," in *Das rote Leuchten: Dresden und der Bombenkrieg*, ed. Oliver Reinhard, Matthias Neutzner, and Wolfgang Hesse (Dresden, 2005), 111.

17. Goldenbogen, *Synagoge*, 38.

18. Ibid., 41–44.

19. Printed in Klaus von Beyme et al., eds., *Neue Städte aus Ruinen: Deutscher Städtebau der Nachkriegszeit* (Munich, 1992), 30–31.

20. Jürgen Paul, "Dresden: Suche nach der verlorenen Mitte," in Beyme et al., *Neue Städte aus Ruinen*, 323.

21. Ibid., 316.

22. Norbert Göller, "Der Weg der Roten Fahne—Denkmale des sozialistischen Menschen in Dresden," *Dresdner Hefte* 57 (1999): 67.

23. Paul, "Dresden," 324.

24. Ibid., 325, 332.

25. Thomas Widera, *Dresden 1945–1948: Politik und Gesellschaft unter sowjetischer Besatzungsherrschaft* (Göttingen, 2004), 416.

26. Gilad Margalit, "Der Luftangriff auf Dresden: Seine Bedeutung für die Erinnerungspolitik der DDR und die Herauskristallisierung einer historischen Kriegserinerung im Westen," in *Narrative der Shoah: Repräsentationen der Vergangenheit in Historiographie, Kunst und Politik*, ed. Susanne Düwell and Matthias Schmidt (Paderborn, 2002), 190.

27. Quoted in Ian Buruma, *The Wages of Guilt: Memories of War in Germany and Japan* (New York, 1994), 300.

28. For a classification of the phases of the remembrance of the bombing, see Matthias Neutzner, "Vom Anklagen zum Erinnern: Die Erzählung vom 13. Februar," in Reinhard, Neutzer, and Hesse, *Das rote Leuchten*, 128–63.

29. For the instrumentalization of the bombings in Dresden, see Gilad Margalit, "Der Luftangriff auf Dresden."

30. For a distinctly East German description of the bombings, see such books as Max Seydewitz's *Die unbesiegbare Stadt* (Leipzig, 1955) or Walter Weidauer's *Inferno Dresden* (Berlin, 1966).

31. Thomas C. Fox, *Stated Memory: East Germany and the Holocaust* (Rochester, 1999), 43, 54.

32. Ibid., 40.

33. For a detailed discussion of this monument, see Christiane Hertel, "Dis/Continuities in Dresden's Dances of Death," *Art Bulletin* 82, no. 1 (2000): 83–116.

34. Jeffrey Herf, *Divided Memory: The Nazi Past in the Two Germanys* (Cambridge 1997), 111.
35. Harald Schmid, *Antifaschismus und Judenverfolgung: Die "Reichskristallnacht" als politischer Gedenktag in der DDR* (Göttingen, 2004), 17.
36. Ibid., 19; Mario Kessler, "Verdrängung der Geschichte: Antisemitismus in der SED 1952/53," in *Zwischen Politik und Kultur: Juden in der DDR*, ed. Moshe Zuckermann (Göttingen, 2002), 34–35.
37. Herf, *Divided Memory*, 133.
38. Goldenbogen, *Synagoge*, 53.
39. The inscription reads: "As a constant reminder of the victims of fascism: Here stood the Synagogue of the Israelite religious community of Dresden, built 1838–1840 by Gottfried Semper, consecrated by chief rabbi Dr. Zacharias Frankel and destroyed on 9 November 1938 by the fascists."
40. Matthias Neutzner, "Vom Anklagen zum Erinnern," 157.
41. Schmid, *Antifaschismus*, 91.
42. Annegret Nippa and Peter Herbstreuth, *Eine kleine Geschichte der Synagoge aus dreizehn Städten* (Hamburg, 1999), 311.
43. Barbara Heimannsberg, "The Work of Remembering: A Psychodynamic View of the Nazi Past as It Exists in Germany Today," in *The Collective Silence: German Identity and the Legacy of Shame*, ed. Barbara Heimannsberg and Christoph J. Schmidt (San Francisco, 1993), 163.
44. Ibid., 163–64.
45. Norbert Göller, "Droht die 'dritte' Zerstörung Dresdens?" *Sächsische Zeitung*, August 23, 1997, http://www.sz-online.de/archiv.
46. Joachim Fischer, "Prager Straße in Dresden: Zur Architektur-Soziologie eines utopischen Stadtensembles," *Ausdruck und Gebrauch* 5 (2004): 13.
47. Examples are the Centrum Warenhaus and the Restaurant International.
48. "Begründung zum Bebauungsplan Nr. 155 Dresden-Altstadt I Nr. 28, Prager Straße/Nord-West Einkaufszentrum" (Dresden), 6, http://www.dresden.de (accessed September 2005).
49. Bettina Klemm, "Willkommen an der Wand," *Sächsische Zeitung*, August 9, 2005, http://www.sz-online.de/archiv.
50. For a more detailed discussion, see Susanne Vees-Gulani, "From Frankfurt's Goethehaus to Dresden's Frauenkirche: Architecture, German Identity, and Historical Memory after 1945," *Germanic Review* 80, no. 2 (2005): 143–63.
51. Jürgen Trimborn, "Das 'Wunder von Dresden': Der Wiederaufbau der Frauenkirche; Ein kritischer Blick auf das größte Rekonstruktionsprojekt des Jahrhunderts," *Die Alte Stadt* 97 (1997): 141; E. Burger, "The Reconstruction of the Frauenkirche in Dresden," in Jäger and Brebbia, *Revival of Dresden*, 141.
52. Vera Kämper, "Dresdens Herz schlägt wieder," *Spiegel Online*, October 30, 2005, http://www.spiegel.de.
53. David Lowenthal, *The Past Is a Foreign Country* (Cambridge, 1985), 348.
54. Jörn Düwel and Niels Gutschow, *Städtebau im 20. Jahrhundert* (Stuttgart, 2005), 270.
55. A booklet about the rebuilding of the Frauenkirche states: "We are allowed, yes we must heal wounds, if we can. The reconstruction of the

Frauenkirche is not a way of avoiding history. The new Dresden Frauenkirche... will be again a monument to history: not only for the baroque Dresden, but also for the courage to rebuild out of destruction, for the moral will of the present to heal, to start anew and to devise the future" (Jürgen Paul, Thomas Kantschew, and Uwe Kröger, *Der Wiederaufbau der Frauenkirche zu Dresden,* 3rd ed [Dresden, 1997], 20).

56. David Lowenthal, *The Heritage Crusade and the Spoils of History* (London, 1996), 229.

57. Siegfried Reimann, "Der 'Förderverein Bau der Synagoge Dresden e. V.'— Seine Entstehung und seine Ziele," *Dresdner Hefte* 45 (2000): 86–87.

58. Ibid., 87.

59. Quoted in "Es ist der Tag der Dresdner," *Sächsische Zeitung,* February 13, 2001, http://www.sz-online.de/archiv.

60. Ibid.

61. Wandel et al., "Zur Architektur der Neuen Synagoge in Dresden," *Dresdner Hefte* 45 (2000): 90.

62. Birgit Hilbig, "Moderne Synagoge mit einer Drehung gen Osten," *Sächsische Zeitung,* August 23, 1997, http://www.sz-online.de/archiv.

63. Wandel et al., "Zur Architektur der Neuen Synagoge," 90.

64. Roland Halbe, "Star of Dresden," *Building* 266 (December 14, 2001): 19.

65. Fox, *Stated Memory,* 7.

66. Jens Schneider, "Der Schrecken des Tschi-tschi-tschi," *Süddeutsche Zeitung,* April 22, 2000, (accessed through Lexis Nexis Academic, November 30, 2005).

67. Herbert Goldhammer and Karin Jeschke, *Dresdner Gedenkorte für die Opfer des NS-Regimes* (Dresden, 2000), 20.

68. Göller,"Droht die 'dritte' Zerstörung."

69. Julia Tews, "Ideen für den Reißwolf," *Sächsische Zeitung,* May 14, 1999, http://www.sz-online.de/archiv.

70. "Entwürfe umstritten," *Sächsische Zeitung,* July 15, 1997, http://www.sz-online.de/archiv.

Reconciling Competing Pasts in Postwar Cologne

Jeffry M. Diefendorf

The most famous literary figure in postwar Cologne was the novelist Heinrich Böll, and much of his work centers on the complicated legacies of National Socialism. Böll was deeply rooted in his home city, acutely aware of just how problematic it was for Cologne and its inhabitants to confront what had happened between 1933 and 1945. Böll knew that such a city was a complex mixture of people, spaces, buildings, and traditions. It was a mixture of things old and new, the physical, the material, the spiritual, and the cultural. In 1961, he published one of his most important novels, *Billiards at Half-Past Nine,* a story of the Fähmels, a family of three generations of architects whose lives revolved around the creation, destruction, and rebuilding of a neo-Romanesque abbey. Heinrich Fähmel built the abbey in 1908. As a demolitions specialist, Heinrich's son Robert followed orders to destroy it late in World War II. In 1958, when the events in the novel take place, Robert's son Joseph has the commission to rebuild the abbey. Although Cologne was not specified as the setting, German readers would immediately recognize references to that city. The actions and thinking of the main characters resonate with the actual discussions and decisions that took place in Cologne as it was rebuilt.[1] Like his fellow Cologners, Böll wrestled with how best to remember the evils of the past and reconcile the memories of the Nazi years with the needs of the present. Böll, like other Cologners, chose a path marked by ambivalence and avoidance of direct confrontation.

In *Billiards at Half-Past Nine,* the Fähmels are, at least among themselves, highly critical of what they see as the root of the evils in both the past and the new Germany: a ruthless militarism, an acceptance of violence, and a willingness to sacrifice innocent people for political ends, all sanctioned and celebrated by politicians, by industry, and, perhaps worst of all, by the Catholic Church.[2] Militarism (not Nazism) and Hindenburg (not Hitler) symbolize this evil, and the Fähmels are bitter that militarism has apparently risen again in the rearmament of the new Germany, bringing with it the rise of men who had prospered during the Third Reich. When the abbot of Saint Anthony invites Robert and his father to come to the opening of the rebuilt abbey, where the chancellor and cabinet members will speak, he says: "My official speech will be made not in the spirit of indictment but of reconciliation; of reconciliation also with those powers who, in their blind passion, destroyed our home. But not, of course, reconciliation with those destructive powers [meaning Communism and the Soviet block] which once again are threatening our culture."[3] Both Robert and his father politely accept, while to themselves they mentally decline because neither is reconciled to the deaths of the innocent or the fact that Robert's brother had died a Nazi.[4] Both realize the absurdity of dwelling on the destruction and rebuilding of a cultural artifact, especially one that was neo-Romanesque and hence an essentially false re-creation of a medieval Christian ethos undercut by the church's collaboration with the very forces that had led to Germany's destruction. They are not really reconciled with past evils, but they find ways to live in the present.

The Fähmels clearly represent the views of Böll, but they are also characteristic of the real ambivalence with which Cologne sought to balance judgments about the past and the concerns of the present. Cologne was one of the German cities most badly damaged in the war. It was the subject of repeated air raids. By the war's end, perhaps 90 percent of the buildings in the Altstadt, the area inside the Ring boulevard, had been destroyed, and the city was covered by twenty-four million cubic meters of rubble. Most of the population had either fled or been evacuated. Of a prewar population of 770,000, 40,000 emerged from bunkers and cellars to witness the arrival of American troops. By the end of 1945, however, they were joined by another 400,000, who returned to start rebuilding their city.

The return of these Cologners to the ruined city reflected the deep affection with which its citizens held this two-thousand-year-old stronghold of German Catholicism. They were fiercely proud of its historic buildings, its distinctive dialect, and its traditions, such as its raucous Lenten carnival celebrations. Cologne had been a free imperial city-state from the Middle Ages until the arrival of the armies of the French Revolution, and although it ended up belonging to Prussia after 1815, it never abandoned the pretense of enjoying a special place in Germany—independent and more in touch with Western Europe and France than with Eastern Europe and Prussia.

It is not surprising, therefore, that Cologne conceptualized its physical and cultural reconstruction in terms of reestablishing visible links to what it saw as a venerable and honorable history, a history perhaps tainted by the years of National Socialism but by no means characterized by them. Individual memories of the Third Reich were bound to lose in a contest with collective memories of the more distant past. As was evident in the pageantry staged in 1950 for the 1900th anniversary of the city's founding, most Cologners did not so much want to forget or conceal what happened under Hitler as to push it aside, to relegate the Nazi years to a relatively small place in the city's long history. As Böll suggested in his novel, the destruction of the city, the suffering of its inhabitants, and the evils of the Third Reich could be seen as having roots in Prussian militarism and brutal, Prussian-style politics and values.[5] Rhenish Cologne was not Berlin, Konrad Adenauer was not Hindenburg, and the nearby presence of the seat of West German government and its political parties was welcome. Cologne's citizens concentrated on rebuilding their own very local identities as they rebuilt their city.

City officials and civic leaders took the position that Cologne had never been a stronghold of Nazism. During imperial and Weimar Germany, it had been a bastion of the Catholic Center Party, and Konrad Adenauer, the leading Center politician and the city's mayor during the Weimar years, was more a Rhinelander than a German patriot. When Hitler came to Cologne on February 18–19, 1933, to speak at a huge rally at the fairgrounds in Cologne-Deutz, a part of the city lying just across the Rhine, Adenauer refused to allow the Nazis to decorate city buildings, and swastika flags hung from the Rhine bridge were removed. Hitler's speech, in turn, was an attack on the Center Party and Adenauer. Cologne's Nazi newspaper, the *Westdeutscher Beobachter,* claimed that one hundred thousand people lined the streets to cheer Hitler and the fifteen thousand SA and police units who marched in his honor.[6] The Nazis subsequently won the most votes (33 percent) cast in Cologne in the March 5, 1933, Reichstag election.[7] The Nazis never won a majority in the city council, but in the communal election of March 12, 1933, they did get the most votes and thirty-nine of ninety-five seats—not enough to take over the city government without first insisting that Communist delegates not be seated and then winning over the delegates of the German National People's Party.

This maneuver cleared the way for the Nazis to oust Adenauer and other officials. The dominant postwar memory was thus of a city seized by the Nazis, not a city truly enthusiastic about Nazism.

The Nazis' physical imprint on Cologne was not as great as on other cities, but it was not insignificant. To be sure, it would have been enormous had Nazi-era plans for transforming the city been realized. Already in 1935, two years before Hitler's formal program for the redesign of more than thirty German cities was promulgated, the Cologne architect Clemens Klotz won a competition to design a "Haus der Arbeit" as centerpiece for a Gauforum—an ensemble of monumental buildings and a vast parade ground.[8] To be built on the lands of the fairgrounds in Deutz, Klotz proposed an enormous neoclassical structure that would have rivaled the city's famed cathedral. It is important for Cologne's understanding of its relationship to Nazism that the Haus der Arbeit and other monumental buildings were not erected. The city planning office, however, developed plans that called for demolishing much of the old city in favor of large new buildings along new east-west and north-south axes that would bisect historic Cologne (fig.1). Demolition began for the east-west axis, though it was halted by the onset of the war. The years before the war also saw the "renewal" of an area around the Romanesque Church of Gross St. Martin under the auspices of the city conservator. "Asocial" residents were removed, substandard buildings gutted, and new or renovated structures erected imitating historic styles but with updated interiors. Over one thousand buildings were constructed in the city during the Nazi era, but the vast majority were unremarkable apartment or office buildings entirely in keeping with their surroundings.[9] They were not seen then, nor are those still remaining seen now, as characterizing Nazi aesthetics or values.

The Nazis, of course, put their mark on the city. The old university building was converted into the party Gauhaus. Squares and streets were renamed to honor party leaders. Ominously, in December 1935, a building nearing completion on Appellhofplatz for the businessman Leopold Dahmen (and hence labeled the EL-DE-Haus) was confiscated by the Gestapo for use as its local headquarters. Cellar rooms were converted into cells used to torture and hold prisoners. Starting in May 1940, part of the fairgrounds was used as a holding area for Gypsies rounded up for deportation, and that area later became an actual small concentration camp—a satellite camp for Buchenwald. Prisoners of various kinds, including some prominent local politicians, were held there. Some of the prisoners were

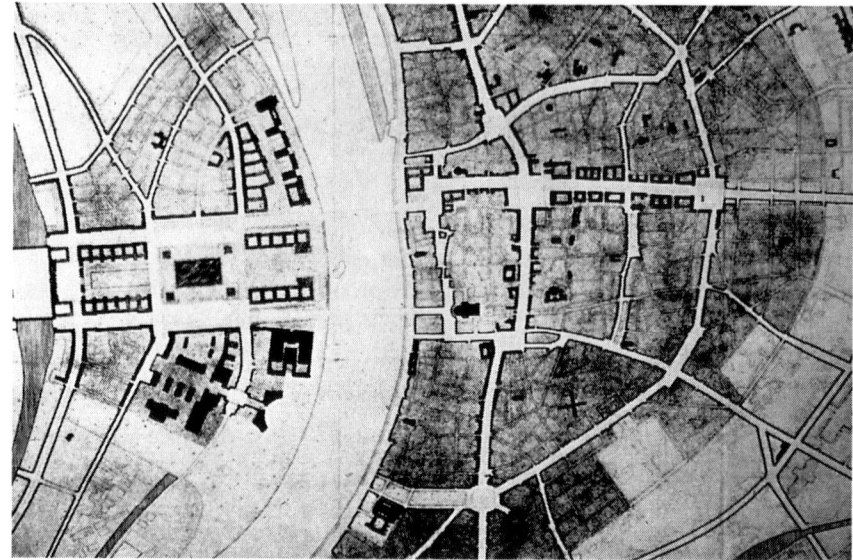

Fig. 1. Plan for transformation of central Cologne, 1939. (Photo: Historisches Archiv der Stadt Köln. Reproduced with permission.)

used as laborers to clear the rubble or work on bunkers. Since they were trucked from the camp into the city center, residents had to observe their presence.[10] Between 1942 and 1945, there was also a large camp to hold a contingent of forced foreign laborers on the grounds of the Ford Motor Company's factory in the northern suburb of Niehl.[11]

All of this suggests that Cologne could hardly claim innocence when it came to the crimes of National Socialism. Naturally Cologne's substantial and largely assimilated Jewish community, some sixteen thousand strong, suffered in the same way as Jews elsewhere in Germany. They were victims of the boycott of April 1933. Jewish books were burned at the university. Jewish professionals were deprived of their livelihoods, and Jewish firms were Aryanized. By 1938, 60 to 70 percent of all Jewish firms were no longer in Jewish hands, and more than half of all Jewish workers were unemployed. In the pogrom of November 9, 1938, all of the city's synagogues were burned, Jewish stores were looted, and Jews were beaten by Nazi thugs while the city's inhabitants looked on. Many Jewish families emigrated in the face of this persecution, but others could not or chose to stay. By late 1941, when the Nazis began to deport German Jews to camps in the east, only sixty-two hundred Jews remained in Cologne. Jewish property was sold and household goods were auctioned off. Once the bombing began, the Nazis distributed furniture and household goods confiscated from Jews in other countries to Germans whose homes were destroyed.[12]

None of this, however, was in the forefront in the minds of Cologne's authorities and citizens when they faced the enormous task of rebuilding their lives and their city after the war.[13] During the immediate postwar years, the people of Cologne gave little special attention to surviving buildings that were either built or used by the Nazis. Instead, memory work concentrated on recalling the historic city that had been reduced to rubble and memorializing its citizens who had died or suffered.

One of the first attempts at public remembrance was an exhibition of the photographs of Hermann Claasen. A Cologne native, Claasen had illegally photographed wartime air raids and cleanup as well as immediate postwar Cologne, leaving a brilliant record of the destruction. He never filmed the dying or the dead, feeling that this violated the human integrity of the victims. Instead, he made pictures of the bomb damage and the efforts of dazed survivors to hold their world together. In 1947, he published a book containing his photographs.[14] Some two hundred of his pictures were then exhibited in a November 1947 exhibition entitled The Tragedy of a City. Mounted in the Eigelsteintorburg, which served as a temporary city art museum while the main museum buildings were in ruins, the exhibition and its solemn opening ceremony, featuring an address by Lord Mayor Pünder, sought to memorialize the city's fifty thousand human war victims, both civilian and military, even though the pictures did not portray them. The exhibition was also supposed to encourage the population to rebuild their ruined city.

The photographs remain hauntingly beautiful to this day. As documents of human suffering and a city destroyed in the bombing, they both memorialize the destruction of buildings and constitute part of the record of reconstruction. Later on, exhibitions of photos showing the prewar condition, war damage, and reconstruction would be permanently mounted in some of the city's churches.

Cologne took other steps to remember those who died in the war. In February 1947, the city council's executive committee commissioned the expressionist sculptor Gerhard Marcks to create a statue for the courtyard next to the Romanesque basilica of St. Maria im Capitol. When the statue, entitled *Angel of Death* but with an inscription "To the Dead," was dedicated in November 1949, the church itself was still in ruins. This monument, in the form of an angel standing beside a Christian church, followed in the tradition of war monuments constructed after the Franco-Prussian War and World War I, except that after World War II, patriotic and nationalist references were omitted.[15] Newspaper photos of the dedication ceremony show a small crowd of some 150 persons gathered on a cold day to hear speeches by the Lord Mayor Robert Görlinger (a Social Democrat), city deacon Robert Grosche, and a representative of Cologne's remaining Jewish community, Moritz Goldschmidt. (According to the paper, it was All Saints' Day, and most citizens were making pilgrimages to the cemeteries. Presumably, city authorities failed to anticipate that people would prefer to visit a family grave site rather than a general monument.)

Görlinger sought to give the monument a meaning that would embrace all sorts of victims.[16] The monument, he said, honored not only the fallen soldiers but also "the women, mothers, and children who died a multitude of deaths in the ruins of our beloved city, the workers whom death visited in their places of work, those evacuated [from their homes] who died far away from their Heimat, and those persecuted for political, racial, or religious reasons who were victims of a criminal insanity." "The dead," Görlinger said, "were all members of the human community; they suffered and died through it and within it." He urged that one remembers the dead not just in consolation for loss but also to admonish the living and future generations to build "a peaceful social order" and thereby to avoid the catastrophe that those present and the dead had experienced.[17] Goldschmidt, in his turn to speak, mentioned the thousands of dead Cologne Jews, but then he added: "In this hour, however, no one should make accusations, because all people are equal in mourning and death."[18] He thus neither claimed a special place for the suffering of his fellow Jews nor used the occasion to condemn the Nazis who had caused that suffering. The day was about memory and mourning, reconciliation and reconstruction, not accusations.

Two years later, Lord Mayor Ernst Schwering, a Christian Demacrat, gave another speech before Marcks's statue that echoed that of Görlinger. Schwering mourned the fallen soldiers, those buried in the rubble of the city, prisoners of war who died suffering behind barbed wire, and the innocent victims who, because of "belief, race, or political conviction, fell victim to the base irrationalities [*Ungeiste*] of the past years." Schwering also observed that "death not only greedily seized people by the hundreds but destroyed Cologne, our beloved city, Cologne with all its buildings, churches and byways, monuments and intimate spaces." Like Görlinger, Schwering urged his audience to think about "the origins of the catastrophe" that so afflicted the city and its citizens and thereby to prevent any repetition of those events.[19]

In neither speech did Cologne's mayors mention the Nazis by name. Instead, both made general references to anonymous forces of persecution that brought on the great catastrophe. Those responsible were portrayed as insane or irrational criminals, not as neighbors. Implying the difference from militaristic Berlin, Schwering proclaimed that "the spirit of Cologne was always peaceful and it would remain so," thus denying complicity on the part of the city's citizens in what had happened. In its setting by a ruined church, the monument was clearly intended to help Cologne's citizens be inclusive in their remembrance of all kinds of victims, both human and inanimate; to reflect generally on the evil deeds of the recent past; and to minimize, if not forget, any actual complicity in those deeds.

A second monument to the dead echoed the statue by Marcks in several respects. In 1952, a recasting of a bronze sculpture of an "angel of death" by another expressionist sculptor, Ernst Barlach, was installed in the Antoniterkirche off the main pedestrian shopping street. This massive figure, suspended in the air from chains, had originally been made for the cathedral in Güstrow to honor the dead of World War I. Barlach's work was considered decadent by the Nazis, and his original statue was broken up in 1937 and melted down for armaments. Shortly before his death, Barlach made a new casting, which was hidden away during the war. In 1952, it was offered to Cologne's city museum, which in turn offered it for the memorial. The tablet in the Cologne church contained simply the dates of both wars, thereby blending together civilian and military dead with no mention of the causes of the deaths.[20]

Probably the most noteworthy attempt by Cologne to honor those who died in the war combined the ruins of the Gothic Church of St. Alban with those of an adjacent building, the Gothic-era Gürzenich meeting hall.[21] Both sets of ruins stood near the town hall, thereby giving the ensemble a prominent place in the civic life of the city. The Gürzenich (1441–47) was a late Gothic work that had served many purposes over the years, ranging from a festival hall to a place serving merchants. In the nineteenth century, it became a Festhaus, often used by the city's carnival societies. It was destroyed in an air raid in 1943. Discussions began in 1946 about restoration, with the carnival societies taking the lead and raising money. The new building was to serve many purposes, as a modern concert facility, a meeting hall for large and small congresses, a hall for carnival dinners and balls, a hall for festive city occasions, and so forth. This required a complicated technical apparatus and much design work, which meant that the process of reconstruction was very slow. (A provisional roof was put over the building to allow staging the opening ceremony for the 1950 celebration of the city's founding nineteen hundred years earlier.)

As was typical throughout Germany when important buildings were at issue, an architectural competition was announced. Limited to architects living in or having lived in Cologne, the competition produced two winning design entries: that of Rudolf Schwarz and Josef Bernard and that of Karl Band with Hans Schilling. (This result was controversial. Schwarz was the chief city planner, and Band also worked for the city. Both had labored on designs for the Gürzenich for a year or more prior to the competition, which gave them a major advantage over the other sixty-seven architects who submitted proposals.) Before any contract was let, the city acquired the property of the destroyed St. Alban's from the Catholic Church, which had decided not to rebuild because even before the war there were too few parishioners to support it. The city then asked Schwarz and Band to cooperate on a final design that would enlarge the Gürzenich by using the site of the church ruins.[22] The architects and contractors needed until October 1955 to complete their work, some six years after the competition was held.

The final design was what one journalist called "a phenomenal architectonic event" because it combined a "Totenhof," or courtyard honoring the dead, with a building designed for pleasure—concerts, wine tasting, drinking beer, celebrating carnival, and the like.[23] Some of the original facade of the medieval Gürzenich was retained, but new sections were added for the considerably enlarged building. Most important, Schwarz incorporated a remaining wall of the ruined church into the rebuilt Gürzenich. The shell of the church stands exposed to the elements, and it is visible both from outside and through the windows of the stairwell of the concert hall (fig. 2). Schwarz said that the ruins should "remain for all time," adding, "the ground would be covered with stones and not prettied up with forgiving grass; and this space would be dedicated to the statues of a kneeling couple by Käthe Kollwitz expressing meaningless suffering."[24] Like Ernst Barlach and Gerhard Marcks, Kollwitz was an expressionist artist whose work had been rejected by the Nazis.

It is significant that the original versions of the statues date from after

Fig. 2. Memorial courtyard designed by Rudolf Schwarz for the ruins of the Church of St. Alban, Cologne, 1955. Statues by Käthe Kollwitz. (Photo: Author.)

World War I and stand in a Belgian military cemetery, where Kollwitz's son lay buried. Once again, an ensemble of church ruins and statuary evokes the earlier tradition of monuments to fallen soldiers that combined patriotic and Christian themes, though here the figures are mourning parents rather than heroic soldiers. The dead of both world wars are linked, and there is no attempt to address the causes of the wars or explain why, in Schwarz's words, the suffering of the victims and their families was meaningless. This memorial, however, included an additional message: a screen just inside the memorial space contains a tablet saying, "Prisoners of war still await their return home." Some 130 newspapers printed stories (usually based on the press release of the city) on the opening of the Gürzenich, and about a fifth mentioned or had pictures of the St. Alban Totenhof. The dedication of the memorial was supposed to take place on March 2, 1956, the anniversary of the last great air raid on the city, thereby honoring the civilians who died in the raids, but the dedication was put off until May 1959.[25]

In time, the Gürzenich still proved too small, and today a new concert hall serves to host most major events.[26] Nevertheless, the ensemble by

Rudolf Schwarz and Karl Band remains a unique architectural monument of the reconstruction period. It is a document of the stylistic concerns of that time as well as a reminder of the kind of architecture that disappeared beneath the bombs of the war. In the words of Angela Pfotenhauer, it constitutes an "island of tradition" that helps Cologne's citizens understand and identify with their city's complex history.[27] Moreover, just as the original St. Alban's and Gürzenich were considered worthy of historic preservation, so the new ensemble is now the focus of a struggle between those who wish to preserve it as a leading example of reconstruction architecture and those who wish to further enlarge and modernize the Gürzenich hall to make it more functional.

The decade of the 1950s also saw the installation of the one memorial, a tablet on the Hansaring, that specifically honored victims of the Nazis and not German civilians or soldiers who died in the war. The inscription of 1951 says simply: "Here lie seven victims of the Gestapo. At this moment, think of Germany's most shameful period, 1933–1945." In 1958, the memorial was enlarged with the addition of a bronze statue of a mother and child by the Dutch sculptor Mari Andriessen. The original meaning of the memorial was thus modified to include civilians more generally, and at the dedication of the statue, Lord Mayor Theodor Burauen honored those who died for "freedom and equality," not just those who died at the hands of the Nazis.[28]

A few rather modest steps were taken to recognize and remember what had happened to the city's Jews. In April 1952, Else Falk, a prominent member of the prewar Jewish community, returned for a visit at the invitation of the city. She was the widow of the former city representative Bernard Falk. From 1920 to 1934, she had chaired the Stadtverband Kölner Frauenvereine. The Falks left Germany in 1939 for Belgium and then Brazil. In a ceremony attended by city leaders, a tablet was placed on a home for working women that Else Falk had founded in 1929 in the suburb of Zollstock. It simply said, "Else-Falk-Haus, erbaut 1929"—though in his speech, Lord Mayor Schwering observed that the event was an attempt "to make good" the wrong done to her. Chancellor Adenauer, who had been mayor at the time the Falks had been city leaders, spoke at a birthday celebration the next day. He rejected the idea of "collective guilt" but admitted "feeling nonetheless a certain guilt that we have toward you all," presumably meaning the Jews.[29] The year 1959 saw both the dedication of the rebuilt synagogue on the Roonstrasse—with a speech by Chancellor Adenauer—and the founding of the Germania Judaica, an archive and library collection devoted to the study of German Judaism. (On Christmas Eve, 1959, two young workers belonging to the right-radical Deutsche Reichspartei painted over the inscription on the memorial to the victims of the Gestapo on the Hansaring and wrote, "Juden raus" [Throw the Jews out], on the walls of the synagogue on the Roonstrasse. The workers were apprehended the next day, but their actions, which were promptly condemned by local officials and members of the leading parties, received national and international attention in the press. This event focused nationwide concern about the continued presence of anti-Semitism in Germany.)[30] In 1968, a plaque was placed on the opera house in memory of the pogrom of November 9, 1938, and the synagogue that had stood on that spot in the Glockengasse.[31] All of these events acknowledged that Jews had been victims, though nothing was said to identify explicitly the perpetrators.

It was not until the 1970s that the citizens of Cologne began to acknowledge the physical remains of the Third Reich. Crucial here was an exhibition at the city archive in 1974 on Cologne during the Nazi years. The exhibit called attention to the small concentration camp at the fairgrounds and the use of the EL-DE-Haus by the Gestapo. It turned out that the prison cells in the EL-DE-Haus, where prisoners had written on the walls, still existed and were being used for storage. Max Leo Schwering, the head of the city museum, and Hiltrud Kier, the city conservator, pushed to preserve the basement cells and wall writings. Finally in 1979, the city government adopted plans to create a documentation center and to preserve the cellar of the EL-DE-Haus. The cellar was opened to the public in December 1981, and the documentation center, devoted to the study of the Nazi era, opened in 1988. The first major publication of the center appeared in 1994 and was entitled *Versteckte Vergangenheit* (A Hidden Past), a provocative title demanding that Cologne's citizens acknowledge what had happened during the Third Reich.[32] A plaque on the outside of the building was added only after the owner of the building, the son of the original owner Leopold Dahmen, insisted that it say that the building had been confiscated by the Gestapo for use in the oppression of opponents of National Socialism, thereby distancing the family name from what had happened in the building. In 1981, a memorial plaque was installed at the fairgrounds noting the existence of the Buchenwald satellite camp. In 1993, a more prominent plaque augmented that information, stating that the Gestapo had held political prisoners there and that Jews and Gypsies had been deported to their deaths from that spot.[33]

Measures such as these are laudable attempts to remind the city's residents that Nazism had been present in Cologne and was a part of its history. There are still places where the connections between physical structures and National Socialism could be made more clear. Kier has observed that the city's public health office on Neumarkt is housed in a building acquired in 1938 when it was Aryanized, and several thousand forced sterilizations took place there. No plaque raises this awkward history. The suburban villa, where banker Kurt Schröder met with Hitler and Franz von Papen on January 4, 1933, to engineer Hitler's appointment as chancellor, stands under historic preservation as an outstanding example of villa architecture, not because of the ominous meeting that took place there.[34] Such buildings, however, were not responsible for the crimes of the Nazi regime. In traffic-choked Cologne, putting up plaques stating that the one broad east-west artery was begun during the Nazi era would probably not have the desired result of getting citizens to reflect on the evils of the past.

Neither the commemoration of loss, whether of human lives or the destruction of a city, nor meaningful memory of the horrors of National Socialism can depend on monuments or plaques noting significant sites. When such physical memory references as ruins and monuments become part of everyday life, they are no longer seen and experienced in such a way as to produce the kind of conscious reflection that was their purpose, especially when they are viewed by those who are too young to have shared the experiences of that period.[35] In 1983, when the photographer Hermann Claasen was asked what he thought his pictures of the destruction of Cologne mean to the younger generation, he replied: "Absolutely nothing. Whoever did not experience it cannot imagine it. One must have the smoke in one's eyes; one must have inhaled the smoke and the fear of everything. One cannot describe the atmosphere of that time."[36] The statue of the angel of death by Gerhard Marcks probably means little to the present generation. The basilica of St. Maria im Capitol is now completely restored. The statue just stands there in the courtyard beside it, without any inscription to indicate the name of the artist or the purpose of the work, and few people encounter it. The statue has become a piece of decorative art, except on those few occasions when someone lays a wreath. Ruins, architecture, and monuments become artistic objects inviting aesthetic judgment more than the contemplation of events past.[37] The statues by Käthe Kollwitz are seen as part of her artistic corpus. The designers of the Gürzenich/St. Alban's ensemble expected it always to have a prominent place in the collective consciousness of the city. Today, however, the daily life of the city no longer flows past the ensemble. This reduces its impact, although it is considered an example of good postwar architecture and design and thus worthy of preservation as a monument to the era of reconstruction. None of this is surprising. Cologne's current inhabitants live in a setting vastly different than that of both their parents and grandparents.

Ambivalence about how to reconcile the past with the present remains. Consider one of the odder monuments honoring Cologne's war dead, which is located in Hindenburg Park on the southern edge of the Neustadt, just outside the Ring and close to where Heinrich Böll lived. The local veterans' association erected this monument in 1927.[38] The park is part of an earlier defense belt around the city, and the monument consists of a brick tower with an enormous bronze eagle on top and a plaque with the words "Den Helden, von 1914–18" (fig. 3). On the upper part of the monument, a Latin inscription ("Numero oppressis menti invictis") notes that the soldiers of World War I succumbed to superior numbers but were never conquered in spirit. Sometime in the 1950s, the dates "1939–1945" were added, without any other commentary, in order to include the fallen soldiers of World War II (fig. 4).

Beginning in the late 1950s, after West Germany joined NATO and rearmed, veterans' ceremonies to honor the dead were held at this monument. In 1970, an early part of the "extraparliamentary opposition" demonstrated against this militaristic activity, and there was an unpleasant conflict between the veterans and leftist demonstrators. Subsequently, another alternative group decided to petition the city for permission to stage an event for children to play in Hindenburg Park. The city failed to notice that the appointed day was the same as the veterans' ceremony. When the veterans showed up and found the children there, they surrendered and moved their ceremony elsewhere. According to Martin Stankowski, a journalist who leads alternative city tours, local mountain climbers now use the vertical tower for practice and have even named and marked new routes. At some point, a climber painted the eagle red. Upon removing the paint, the city conservator discovered the eagle had deteriorated and had it removed for repair. Then, either while on the ground or once it was put back up, the eagle was tarred and feathered. Eventually it was cleaned up and reinstalled atop its pedestal, though the base is defaced by graffiti. This monument now stands mute and largely unknown by the city's citizens, a demonstration of the ambivalence still felt toward com-

Fig. 3. Veterans' monument in Hindenburg Park, Cologne, 1927. (Photo: Author.)

memoration of soldiers. For Heinrich Böll, Hindenburg symbolized militarism run amok. He must have been amused at the fate of the monument in Hindenburg Park.

For monuments to retain something of their original purpose, local citizens and authorities must be prepared to expend some energy to keep the collective memory behind these monuments alive, even if each new and younger viewer will experience the monuments in an individual, personal way. Monuments, after all, can have many functions, including providing consolation for loss, reconciliation between foes, and solidarity between those who died and those who survived.[39] Ceremony and ritual are needed, as are an active desire and commitment to remember and periodic discussions of just which memories should remain alive. Monuments con-

Fig. 4. New inscription on the veterans' monument in Hindenburg Park, Cologne, ca. 1950. (Photo: Author.)

stitute only one of the points of intersection between the public's conception of history and history as conceived by historians. An active partnership between the public, the builders and maintainers of monuments, and historians can help moderate the swing between attention and neglect, highly charged memory and oblivion. This has been the goal of the documentation center in the El-DE-Haus—to use publications and exhibitions to keep the memory of the horrors of the Third Reich alive. Nevertheless, the collective memory of the inhabitants of Cologne is more the memory of normal, everyday life set in a modern city still shaped by remnants of its two-thousand-year history. Both the terrors of the Nazi years and the struggle to rebuild afterward have become a small part of that history.

NOTES

1. Böll's copy of Hans Schmitt's *Der Neuaufbau der Stadt Köln* (Cologne, 1946) is filled with Böll's underlinings of Schmitt's argument that the character of the city was to be found in its narrow streets and its way of doing things, not just in its buildings.

2. Böll calls those who practice this evil "Büffel," or "buffaloes," and in a parody of Catholicism, he terms their worship of this evil the "sacrament of the buffalo."

3. *Billiards at Half-Past Nine* (New York, 1962), 227–28.

4. See J. H. Reid, *Heinrich Böll: A German for His Time* (Oxford, New York, and Hamburg, 1988), 126–30. Reid notes that Jean-Marie Straub's 1965 film based on the novel was titled *Nicht versöhnt* (Not Reconciled). See also Elizabeth Snyder Hook, "Awakening from War: History, Trauma, and Testimony in Heinrich Böll," in *The Work of Memory: New Directions in the Study of German Society and Culture,* ed. Alon Confino and Peter Fritzsche (Urbana and Chicago, 2002); Lawrence F. Glatz, *Heinrich Böll als Moralist: Die Funktion von Verbrechen und Gewalt in seinen Prosawerken* (New York, 1999), especially 166–80.

5. For good examples, see Jürgen Brügger, "Das Kölner Domjubiläum 1948: Vom Versuch, sich eine neue Vergangenheit zu geben," and Jeffry M. Diefendorf, "Das Stadtjubiläum 1950 und die Selbstdarstellung Kölns," both in *Köln in den 50er Jahren: Zwischen Tradition und Modernisierung,* ed. Jost Dülffer, Veröffentlichungen des Kölnischen Geschichtsvereins, vol. 44 (Cologne, 2001).

6. Various articles, *Westdeutscher Beobachter,* February 19, 1933, in Historisches Archiv der Stadt Köln, microfilm.

7. Carl Dietmar, *Die Chronik Kölns* (Cologne, 1991), 380–81.

8. For the following, see Wolfram Hagspiel, "Die nationalsozialistische Stadtplanung in und für Köln," *Geschichte in Köln,* no. 9 (1981); Ursula von Petz, *Stadtsanierung im Dritten Reich,* Dortmunder Beiträge zur Raumplanung, vol. 45 (Dortmund, 1987); Jeffry M. Diefendorf, "Städtebauliche Traditionen und der Wiederaufbau von Köln vornehmlich nach 1945," *Rheinische Vierteljahrsblätter* 55 (1991). For wartime reconstruction planning in Cologne and other German cities, see Jeffry M. Diefendorf, *In the Wake of War: The Reconstruction of German Cities after World War II* (New York and Oxford, 1993); Werner Durth and Niels Gutschow, *Träume in Trümmern: Planungen zum Ziederaufbau zerstörter Städte im Westen Deutschland 1940–1950,* 2 vols. (Braunschweig and Wiesbaden, 1988).

9. Hiltrud Kier, "Zur Vermittelbarkeit von Bauten aus der NS-Zeit als Objekte der Denkmalpflege," in *Architektur und Städtebau der 30er/40er Jahre,* ed. Werner Durth and Winfried Nerdinger, Schriftenreihe des Deutschen Nationalkomitees für Denkmalschütz, vol. 48 (Bonn, 1994).

10. Martin Stankowski, *Köln: Der andere Stadtführer,* 2 vols. (Cologne, 1988–89), 2:235.

11. Reinhold Billstein, Karola Fings, Anita Kugler, and Nicholas Levis, *Working for the Enemy: Ford, General Motors, and Forced Labor in Germany during the Second World War* (New York and Oxford, 2000).

12. Britta Bopf, "Zur 'Arisierung' und den Versuchen der 'Wiedergutmachung'

in Köln," in *Versteckte Vergangenheit: Über den Umgang mit der NS-Zeit in Köln,* ed. Horst Matzerath, Harald Buhlan, and Barbara Becker-Jákli, Schriften des Dokumentationszentrums der Stadt Köln, vol. 1 (Cologne, 1994); Barbara Becker-Jákli, *Ich habe Köln doch so geliebt: Lebensgeschichten jüdischer Kolnerinnen und Kölner* (Cologne, 1993).

13. Georg Mölich and Stefan Wunsch, eds., *Köln nach dem Krieg: Facetten der Stadtgeschichte,* Kölner Schriften zu Geschichte und Kultur, vol. 24 (Cologne, 1995); Jost Dülffer, ed., *"Wir haben schwere Zeiten hinter uns": Die Kölner Region zwischen Krieg und Nachkriegszeit,* Veröffentlichungen des Kölnischen Geschichtsvereins, vol. 40 (Cologne, 1996).

14. See Hermann Claasen, *Gesang im Feuerofen: Köln—Überreste einer alten deutschen Stadt* (Düsseldorf, 1947); *Das Ende: Kriegszerstörungen im Rheinland* (Cologne, 1983). Claasen's books anticipate Jörg Friedrich's *Der Brand: Deutschland im Bombenkrieg 1940–1945* (Munich, 2002) and suggest that the memory of wartime suffering in the bombed cities was not, as Friedrich argues, immediately suppressed.

15. George L. Mosse points out that, unlike the Americans, the Germans rejected building "memorial" halls and theaters, because these buildings were profane, rather than sacred (*Fallen Soldiers: Reshaping the Memory of the World Wars* [New York and Oxford, 1990], 100). Meinhold Lurz estimates that there are perhaps between thirty-five thousand and forty thousand war monuments in the twenty-five thousand communities of the Federal Republic alone (*Kriegerdenkmäler in Deutschland,* vol. 6, *Bundesrepublik* [Heidelberg, 1987], 9). Walter Grasskamp claims that Germany is unique in having memorials to the victims of Germans and not just to Germans who were the victims of others ("Die Behaglichkeit des Gedenkens," in *Die Zeit,* November 25, 1994, international edition, 13–14). Ulrike Puvogel's *Gedenkstätten für die Opfer des Nationalsozialismus: Eine Dokumentation* (Schriftenreihe der Bundeszentrale für politische Bildung, vol. 245 [Bonn, 1987]) contains approximately 750 pages of listings of monuments and memorials of various types that commemorate the victims of National Socialism. See also Peter Reichel, *Politik mit der Erinnerung: Gedächtnisorte im Streit um die nationalsozialistische Vergangenheit* (Munich and Vienna, 1995).

16. The subject of the Germans as victims has received much discussion since the publication of Friedrich's *Der Brand* and W. G. Sebald's *On the Natural History of Destruction* (New York, 2003). For excellent counterarguments, see Robert G. Moeller, "Germans as Victims: Thoughts on a Post–Cold War History of World War II's Legacies," in *History & Memory* Spring–Summer 2005; Mary Nolan, "Air Wars, Memory Wars," and Thomas Childers, "'*Facilis descensus averni est*': The Allied Bombing of Germany and the Issue of German Suffering," both in *Central European History,* no. 1 (2005).

17. Historisches Archiv der Stadt Köln/Abt. 2 Oberbürgermeister/628: Totenfeier 1949 und 1951, Enthüllung des "Todesengels" von G. Marcks, p. 18.

18. Quoted in Simone Derix, "Der Umgang mit dem Nationalsozialismus in Kölner Mahnmalen der fünfziger Jahre," in Dülffer, *Köln in den 50er Jahren,* 263.

19. Historisches Archiv der Stadt Köln/Abt. 2 Oberbürgermeister/628: Toten-

feier 1949 und 1951, Enthüllung des "Todesengels" von G. Marcks, speech by Schwering on November 1, 1951, 2–9.

20. Derix, "Der Umgang mit dem Nationalsozialismus," 264. See also Peter Paret, *German Encounters with Modernism, 1840–1945* (Cambridge, 2001), chaps. 7, 9.

21. Rudy Koshar argues that postwar Germans suffered from an "allergy to ruins" (*From Monuments to Traces: Artifacts of Germany Memory, 1870–1990* [Berkeley, 2000], 153). See also Koshar, *Germany's Transient Pasts: Preservation in National Memory in the Twentieth Century* (Chapel Hill, 1998), 219–20.

22. Ruins of one other Cologne church, St. Kolumba's, were preserved. A small new chapel was erected next to the ruins of the church tower.

23. Henry Blackmann, "Köln hat seinen Gürzenich wieder," *Westfalenpost*, October 4, 1955, clipping in Historisches Archiv der Stadt Köln/Acc. 148 Nachrichtenamt/171/Pressestimmen zum Wiederaufbau der Gürzenich, p. 36.

24. Historisches Archiv der Stadt Köln/Acc. 148 Nachrichtenamt/200, pp. 7–8.

25. Derix, "Der Umgang mit dem Nationalsozialismus," 268.

26. The new hall was built next to the cathedral.

27. See Angela Pfotenhauer, "Die Kölner Traditionsinseln: Eine Betrachtung der Altstadt unter besonderer Berücksichtigung der Traditionsinsel Gürzenich-Sankt Alban" (Ph.D. diss., University of Cologne, 1991).

28. Clipping from *Kölner Stadt-Anzeiger,* November 10, 1958, in Historisches Archiv der Stadt Köln/Acc. 2/2136/14; Derix, "Der Umgang mit dem Nationalsozialismus," 270–73.

29. Quoted in Jürgen Zieher, "Im Schatten von Antisemitismus und Wiedergutmachung: Jüdisches Leben in Köln in den fünfziger Jahren," in Dülffer, *Köln in den 50er Jahren,* 283.

30. Zieher, "Im Schatten von Antisemitsmus," 300–301.

31. Martin Stankowski, "Wem gehört die Erinnerung? Formen des Gedenkens und die Auseinandersetzung um Gedenktafeln in Köln," in Matzerath, Buhlan, and Becker-Jákli, *Versteckte Vergangenheit,* 311.

32. Matzerath, Buhlan, and Becker-Jákli, *Versteckte Vergangenheit.*

33. Ibid., 313–16; Kier, "Zur Vermittelbarkeit," 61. For Cologne's memorials, see Puvogel, *Gedenkstätten,* 557–75. Stankowski (*Köln: Der andere Stadtführer,* 2:235) is quite critical of the city's acknowledgment of its participation in Nazi crimes.

34. Kier, "Zur Vermittelbarkeit," 61.

35. Walter Grasskamp, "Die Behaglichkeit des Gedenkens," in *Die Zeit,* November 25, 1994, international edition, 13–14.

36. Claasen, *Gesang im Feuerofen,* 16.

37. James E. Young, *The Texture of Memory: Holocaust Memorials and Meaning* (New Haven and London, 1993), 12.

38. Martin Stankowski, "Von Böll ist nichts zu finden," in *Heinrich Böll und Köln,* ed. Viktor Böll (Cologne, 1994), 281–85.

39. John Bodnar, *Remaking America: Public Memory, Commemoration, and Patriotism in the Twentieth Century* (Princeton, 1992), 3–9.

Evading What the Nazis Left Behind
An Ethnographic and Phenomenological Examination of Historic Preservation in Postwar Rostock

Susan Mazur-Stommen

> In words worthy of Saki, Montaigne sang the praises of forgetfulness. Forgetting, he observed, is creative.
> —James Fentress and Chris Wickham, *Social Memory*

Everyday Mythmaking

This essay outlines how a medium-sized city in the far north of the former East Germany has (or has not) grappled with the traces of the National Socialist legacy in the built environment. In the case of Rostock, we can see a corpus of myths arising that subtly casts locals as the helpless victims of serial dictatorships and external acts of aggression. Rostock, in the state of Mecklenburg-Vorpommern, on the Baltic Sea, has confronted the legacy of National Socialism very differently from Berlin, whose own struggle has been so ably chronicled by Brian Ladd's important study *The Ghosts of Berlin*.[1] In reading his book before beginning my ethnographic fieldwork in Rostock at the turn of the millennium, I was impressed and inspired by Ladd's dissection of the processes and policies surrounding the contemporary archaeology that is Berlin dealing with its history. Despite the impressiveness of Ladd's study, I was convinced that Berlin remains singular, so I turned my back on that city, in search of the *Alltagskultur* of the new unified Germany.[2]

In Rostock, as opposed to Berlin, there has not been any real "struggle" over what to remember and how. There has been little public "debate" about buildings to save and buildings to demolish. Where there is public debate, it tends to focus on the pragmatic and the aesthetic rather than the historical. For example, the Rostock Denkmalschutzamt (Historic Preservation Bureau) had temporarily preserved a portion of the ruined Neptun Werft, a former shipyard overlooking the river Warnow near Lübecker Strasse, and though I found this industrial remnant evocative, most people who mentioned it thought that it was hideous and should be torn down. Any "remembrance" that takes place does so only in darkling parks and obscure corners of the university, as with the permanent exhibit—dedicated to the "Opfer deutscher Diktaturen" (victims of German dictatorships)—located in the basement of the history department of the University of Rostock.[3] There is no equivalent to Berlin's Topography of Terror exhibition.[4] No qualms seem to surface about reusing any buildings dating from the National Socialist period, even buildings built explicitly for aggressive use by the Nazis, such as the contemporary Marineamt barracks.[5] Hardly any public discussion takes place concerning the spaces and places affected by the events of the period and/or the roles of local citizenry. Instead, we have the genesis of a mythos that places the Nazis, the Allies, the KGB, Soviet soldiers, and officials of the Stasi (short for *Staatssicherheit,* or "State Security," i.e., the East German secret police) into a broader category of external enemies to Rostock.

This essay examines some of the new myths created by citizens of Rostock as they navigated a landscape studded with accidental reminders of the past. Due to a variety of factors—internal migrations at the end of World War II, the industrial needs of the German Democratic Republic, and German unification itself—many residents of modern Rostock have little organic connection to the history and experiences that marked the city they live in. As with the Nikolai Quarter in Berlin discussed by Ladd, aspects of contemporary historical reference are reminiscent of Eric Hobsbawm's idea of an "invented tradition"—that is, "a set of practices, normally governed by overtly or tacitly accepted rules and of a ritual or symbolic nature, which seek to inculcate certain values and norms of behaviour by repetition, which automatically implies continuity with the past ... [but whose] continuity ... is largely fictitious."[6] The links between emerging myths about Rostock's experiences during the twentieth century and the events that inspired them, though perhaps retaining a kernel of truth (the definition of legend), are by and large incomplete, reworked, fictitious, and recontextualized. As such, the entire corpus of mythic history in Rostock is an "invented tradition." This essay demonstrates how these partial histories and myths fit together with particular places and spaces to create what Merlin McDonald calls "external symbolic storage."[7] In particular, the denotation of certain bounded spaces as places of Nazi (or Allied, Stalinist, and Stasi) intervention allows residents to contain events of the past (and their ramifications) symbolically and get on with their lives. It reduces the enormity of the period to manageable symbolic sites, such as "the roof of the gymnasium" and "the basement of the barracks."

Methods

Because I am an anthropologist and not a historian, many of my methods are interpersonal, subjective, and embodied. Heidegger points out that a person cannot be separated from their "being in the world."[8] Similarly, the data I collected is phenomenologically empirical, in that it cannot be separated from the filter of who I am and how I engage with people, my sources, during fieldwork. This necessarily involves all aspects of my being, including personality and affect, age and gender, linguistic fluency, even physical mobility. This distinction is critical to understanding the potentialities and limitations of ethnographic research for unraveling historical processes. To understand agency, the researcher must engage with people as they are taking action. This type of data is qualitatively different from the type of data acquired through archival sources. Generally, archives do not house such inchoate material of everyday life and action. This is the raw process of people defining and constructing a narrative through which they experience history in their everyday landscape. The processual nature of such data is particularly important when discussing such topics as memory and forgetting. The editing and deletion of data that could make conducting one's daily life difficult is what I call "active forgetting." The researcher then hunts for the absence of memory by looking for omissions and distortions in the collective narrative.[9]

During my fieldwork in Rostock, I walked, photographed buildings and streetscapes, and collected various artifacts and documents (fig. 1). I was particularly interested in anything that showed the inhabitants' vision/imagining of their city: pictures, postcards, calendars, a map of the city printed onto a place mat. Following Kevin Lynch, I felt that such items reveal the cognitive processes shaping the memory of spaces, routes, and pathways that we create in our negotiation of cities.[10] These cognitive processes are tools put to use in "making" a city out of the layers of individual encounters and shared public experiences of these routes and pathways.[11] This essay also rests on personal observations and interviews made in 1999–2000. During that year, I worked as an unpaid intern in the Office

Fig. 1. Aerial view of downtown Rostock, looking eastward, 2000. (Photo: City of Rostock. Courtesy of Dr. Andreas Schubert.)

of City Marketing, as a liaison/translator with the European Union project Integrated Urban Planning and Management, and as a lecturer at the University of Rostock. My pool of informants was drawn primarily from urban planners employed by the city and from architects and planners with the Rostocker Gesellschaft für Stadterneuerung, Stadtentwicklung und Wohnungsbau GmbH (Rostock Society for Urban Renewal, Development and Housing; hereinafter RGS), a public-private entity with ownership shared between Hanseatic Rostock, its sister city Hanseatic Bremen, and private investors. I spent much of my time at the Bürgerhaus building on Budapester Strasse, where activists, politicians, and historians met and worked, particularly in the Café Waldemar and Margarete, owned and operated by a former archaeologist. The café was a venue for local taste and culture, where such figures as Markus Wolf talked to rooms packed with Ostalgic fans.[12] Further, as a university lecturer and Fulbright fellow, I connected with and interviewed current and former academics in the departments of sociology, history, and foreign languages. Many of these groups overlapped, with academics taking consultancies with the city or RGS and with RGS employees operating in various capacities on different projects scattered around the city.

The group of actors involved in the revitalization and historic preservation of Rostock was a prototypical anthropological face-to-face community with crisscrossing relationships. Not only did many of the same individuals work on multiple projects, but some people were in long-term romantic relationships, while others formed platonic domestic arrangements. The center of these was a weekly Wednesday-night dinner at the home of an RGS planner and another architect, where the crowd and conversation was heavily skewed in the direction of shoptalk.[13] Through classic "snowball" sampling, my set of acquaintances spiraled outward in a centrifugal pattern during the year. Ultimately, contacts and conversations occurred with people from almost every age-group, class membership, and neighborhood location, including bartenders, waitresses, church leaders, advocates for the homeless, army officers, church administrators, lawyers, police officers, university students, little children, elderly pensioners, visiting journalists, archivists, businessmen, senators, and numerous others. One method for validating ethnographic research is through triangulation, where one finds the same phenomenon or pattern of phenomena repeating. If the same trope or leitmotif can be found in casual conversation, formal interview settings, commemoration devices (e.g., plaques), and documents (both everyday and archival, public and private), I believe it is fair to consider the data robust.

In his article "A Way of Seeing People and Place: Phenomenology in Environment-Behavior Research," Kansas State University geographer David Seamon lays out a trenchant case for the use of a phenomenological orientation toward an analysis of the built environment. He writes that "provided the phenomenologist has access in her own experience to the phenomenon she plans to study, first-person research can offer clarity and insight grounded in one's own lifeworld."[14] For anthropologists, the observations Seamon makes will be familiar, but the application of the ethnographic perspective to environment and architecture is instructive. For example, he is using the term generally to describe a search for "underlying, essential qualities of human experience."[15] According to Seamon, almost any experience we can have is grounds for its own field of investigation, using the embodied researcher. This rings true with the methodology of ethnography, which continues to promote the advantages of using a lone researcher as the primary instrument for data collection, analysis, and interpretation. For Seamon, as for many anthropologists, the goal is "a rigorous description of human life as it is lived and reflected upon in all of its first-person concreteness, urgency, and ambiguity."[16]

In his article, Seamon resists the reductive quality of much contemporary ethnography, with its "case study" format and refusal to engage in building big theories. Seamon wants us to use phenomenology to seek out "underlying commonalities," or what I would call "regularities." If, following Seamon, we are to see phenomenological inquiry as "radical empiricism," it is because it involves "the researcher's direct contact with the phenomenon." Through the classically anthropological research methods of immersion and participant observation, we can experience firsthand the phenomena of living in and shaping a city. According to Seamon, one can judge the trustworthiness of the results of such methods via "four qualities [citing Polkenhorne]: vividness, accuracy, richness, and elegance." In these terms, issues of subjectivity, which otherwise dog first-person accounts, are trumped by the "power to convince." In other words, when dealing with people's memories and interpretations of history, we need not prove an argument at the level of that chimera of "scientific certainty"; we need only present an account that "engages" and speaks "to the realm of human experience in general."[17]

In short, the present essay reflects the experience of encountering National Socialist artifacts within a modern, often locally unmarked context. It also reflects as accurately as possible the expression of the opinions and thoughts of residents who live with and among such reminders. Data produced through fieldwork comes from sources that may have agendas, faulty memories, or ulterior motives. Like most anthropologists, I have a deep attachment to "my people" and "my fieldwork site," and, of course, most Rostockers are perfectly nice, pleasant people. On an interpersonal level, one can understand that the huge effort behind unification leaves little energy for making grand gestures about the past. A city is constantly evolving through the actions of its inhabitants; even the choice by one individual to pursue any given route can have a subtle yet detectable impact on the shape of the city. Over time, such choices change the form of a city profoundly. It is understandable that individuals residing in a city will not want to shoulder a past that does not feel as if it belongs to them. Yet, at the same time, the collective choice to forget has had a corollary in which the ideals and actions of the Nazi past remain endemic to the region as neo-Nazism. What I believe to be interesting about the opinions cited in this essay is that, in each case, they were unsolicited. I was not doing research on the National Socialist period—I was interested in the transition to post-Socialism. But despite this fact, the topic emerged organically. I believe this is due to the local presence of a virulent form of modern neo-Nazism, which was seen most infamously in a 1992 attack on a refugee asylum in an outlying suburb called Lichtenhagen.[18] The repercussions were still being felt as I did my fieldwork eight years later. Estimates at the time were that some 30 percent of the state's youth harbored "extreme right sympathies."[19] Structurally, Rostock, a "polycentric" city (as one of my informants termed it), can be framed anthropologically as a "moiety" with leftists in the core and with the periphery belonging to right-wing elements.[20] Left-identified individuals comprised the group I was interacting with, and they were enormously disturbed by this situation.

In a survey I conducted among a class of students studying English at the university, three out of seventeen mentioned "neo-Nazis" when asked what they did not like about Rostock, while another three mentioned either "pigheaded people" or "narrow-minded people." An additional mention was made of "pit bulls," a phrase I believe was linked, particularly in the summer of 2000, with neo-Nazis. Further, not only was the problem of neo-Nazis on people's minds, but there was much graffiti distributed around the city inscribed with the word *Nazi*—ironically mostly by Antifa (antifascist) youth—for example, "Nazis Raus" (Nazis out) and other similar slogans (fig. 2).[21] Overall, this could give the impression of a city obsessed with Nazis, which was true, but the obsession was with the Republikaner movement, the modern nationalist conservatives, not with the original perpetrators whose outline they are attempting to fill.

Can we call Rostock a "Nazi City"?

One of the parameters structuring the myths of Rostock is that from 1933 to 1945 there was a historical caesura—an interruption in the flow of history. This phenomenon becomes visible in the context of locally produced documents. Reading many of these sources, one gains the impression that for a period ranging from ten to twelve years, time was suspended and most municipal and political life stopped. So, what actually went on in Rostock during this period? Was it "less Nazi" than any other German city? Defining Rostock as Nazi or not is more difficult than it may appear. To some degree, the region appears to have escaped attention. The two biggest employers were the Arado and Heinkel companies, both of which were active in the armaments industries.[22] However, even though Rostock sat (and still sits) on a major transportation line to Sweden and Denmark via the ferries, no major death marches or deportations seem to have taken place in or through the area—at least according to the maps on the Web

Fig. 2. Antifa graffiti on an Altstadt building undergoing conversion to luxury condominiums, Rostock, 2000. (Photo: Author.)

site of the United States Holocaust Memorial Museum.[23] The nearest concentration camps were Neuengamme in Hamburg and Ravensbrück in Brandenburg. However, in both Mecklenburg and Brandenburg, there were *Aussenlager* (subcamps) that were subordinated to Ravensbrück and Sachsenhausen.[24]

What can we discern about the city's intangible aspects, such as its worldview, during this period? Trying to assess ideological commitment from voting patterns, another approach, is difficult in an environment that was about to suspend democracy indefinitely, but looking at the results for the November 1932 Reichstag election, we see that for the general region (Gebietseinheit Mecklenburg-Schwerin), 37 percent of votes were cast for the Nationalsozialistische Deutsche Arbeiterpartei (NSDAP), or National Socialist German Worker's Party, with the Sozialdemokratische Partei

Deutschlands (SPD; the German Socialist Party) coming in second (29 percent) and the conservative Deutschnationale Volkspartei (DVNP; the German National People's Party) (17 percent) and left-wing Kommunistische Partei Deutschlands (KPD; the German Communist Party) (12 percent) following the Socialists. In the area immediately surrounding Rostock, the relative percentages remain constant, although the NSDAP gained in its share, with 40 percent of the vote. The pattern reverses in the city proper, with the SPD gaining 34 percent, the NSDAP in second place with 27 percent, and the DNVP (20 percent) and KPD (10 percent) again bringing up the rear. So we see the region around Rostock as being slightly more inclined to vote NSDAP than the average for the entire region, while the percentage of NSDAP voters drops significantly within the boundaries of the city proper. By looking at voting patterns as right-wing, centrist, and left-wing clusters, we can more clearly see a rightward direction for AMT Rostock, while opinions in *Stadt* Rostock (the city of Rostock's boundaries) are nearly split in half, with 49 percent of voters casting their ballots for the right-wing NSDAP, DNVP, or Deutsche Volkspartei (DVP; the German People's Party) and 46 percent voting for the liberal or left-wing Deutsche Demokratische Partei (DDP; the German Democratic Party), SPD, KPD, or Wirtschafts Partei (or, more correctly but less colloquially, Wirtschaftspartei des Deutschen Mittelstandes [WP; the Economic Party of the German Middle Classes]).[25] This pattern is similar to the one we see in Rostock today, with a "Red-Red" coalition dominating Rostock municipal politics in the 1990s and with many inner-city residents expressing leftist opinions, while the most infamous right-wing violence takes place in suburbs just outside the city limits (in Rostock AMT), such as Lichtenhagen (1992) and Toitenwinkel (2000). The spatial distribution that links the historic NSDAP and today's neo-Nazis is clear and persistent.

It is also important to keep the population shifts affecting Rostock in mind when thinking about present-day responses to that time period.[26] The population of the city was approaching 60,000 people prior to World War I and continued to grow during the Great Depression.[27] In fact, it could be argued that Rostock flourished under the Nazis—it certainly grew. In 1919, there were about 75,000 inhabitants of Rostock. By 1939, that number swelled to 120,000. It is also estimated that approximately 10,000 Rostock residents were actually *Zwangsarbeiter/Innen* (forced laborers)—of both sexes—from Poland and the Soviet Union.[28] By some estimates, there were as many as 200,000 inhabitants in Rostock by the end of the war, many of whom were refugees fleeing from Prussia and Königsberg.

Whole populations were on the move internally over a period of approximately the next forty years. At the end of World War II, Danzig went to Poland and became Gdansk, transforming Rostock into East Germany's only deepwater seaport. With the partitioning of Europe into Allied and Soviet spheres of influence, millions of people headed to the west. Simultaneously, many southern Germans headed north (particularly from Saxony), where there were shipbuilding and fishing jobs. In time, Rostock's population rose to the 250,000 it registered in 1989 when the Berlin Wall fell. The turnover in population, as well as the changing form of the city due to new residents in new neighborhoods, has meant that many people living in Rostock currently have little or no connection to local culture and history. With multiple infusions of residents from elsewhere in the former Reich and, later, a special status within the GDR, Rostock became more cosmopolitan than it was before, and ties between residents and their neighborhood histories were loosened. Of my various informants, roughly one-third had deeper roots in the region; another third were Western transplants, particularly among the professions; and a final third came from other parts of the GDR, mostly the area around Dresden. They were concentrated especially in the *Plattenbau* (high-rise) neighborhood of Schmarl, a redoubt for many former middle-class professionals of the GDR and their families. Even today, the vast majority of out-migration from Rostock proper is channeled toward the new suburbs surrounding the city. As has happened elsewhere, older, more central neighborhoods, such as the Kröpeliner Tor Vorstadt, have become home to a miniscule (3 percent) but rising number of foreign-born immigrants, a further dissolution of connective tissue between locality, history, and narrative.

The Marineamt

One example of the dissolution mentioned in the preceding section of this essay came out in my interview with the press officer, Captain Lieerts, at the Marineamt military installation, which is well ensconced within the city limits but lies just outside the core area, in a neighborhood known as the Hansaviertel. This branch of the military could be best described as a cross between a coast guard and a navy, with light weaponizing of vessels used in search-and-rescue operations. The buildings and grounds now occupied by the Marineamt take up about four square city blocks in the

Hansaviertel neighborhood (across Kopernikus Strasse from the former Neptun Schwimmhalle and the Ostsee Stadion) and were laid out and constructed for the German Army in 1936. Currently, they are being used for its academy of four hundred students, with fifteen full-time residents. Approximately 30 percent of those serving their *Wehrpflicht* (compulsory military duty) are drawn from the local region. During our interview, Captain Lieerts (originally from Wilhelmshaven in Ostfriesland) repeatedly referenced the GDR era with regard to changes that have been made to the physical plant since unification, but he never brought up the National Socialists. One of the aspects that the captain saw as symbolic was the 1998 replacement of a masonry wall surrounding the barracks with one of metal posts and wire. He saw this as representative of a greater "openness" in relations between the military institutions of unified Germany and the citizens of Rostock. Clearly, he could see one historic period symbolically and could explicitly relate it to the built environment he inhabited. Just as clearly, he chose not to apply the same perspective to another relevant period. The fact that he, as a West German, had emotional distance from the GDR may not have protected him from the National Socialist period. Perhaps "actively forgetting" that the barracks we were sitting in were built to house the men who fueled the Nazi war machine allowed Captain Lieerts to come to work there every day from his home in the suburbs between Rostock and Bad Doberan.

The Gymnasium am Goetheplatz

Of all the sites mentioned in this essay, informants explicitly described only the Gymnasium am Goetheplatz as the site of a Nazi intervention (fig. 3). The local story holds that the original building was of a modern design, with a flat roof. When the Nazis came to power, they did not like the roof, and they ordered a more traditional, peaked roof to replace it. The roof was never restored to its original design. One respondent explained this fact with a shrug: "It is better for our climate. A flat roof, with the snow . . ." According to the Landesamt für Denkmalpflege in Mecklenburg-Vorpommern, the state-level agency for historic preservation, the story is slightly more complicated, though the gist has withstood the test of time. The history of the Gymnasium is found in some detail in their series *Denkmalschutz und Denkmalpflege in Mecklenburg-Vorpommern.* Conceived and built to a plan by Rostock architect and *Stadtbaudirektor* (city official in charge of

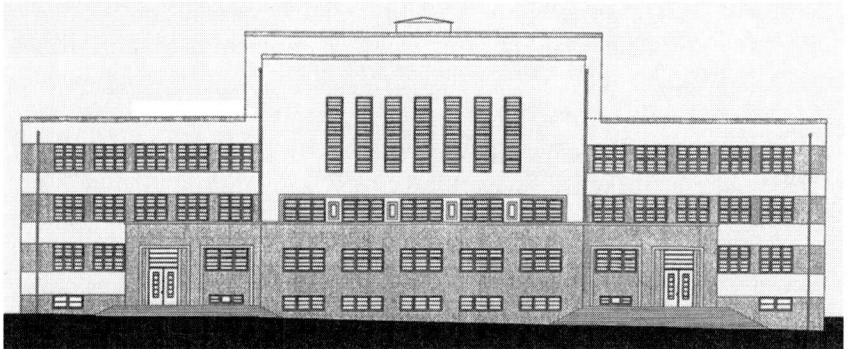

Fig. 3. Reconstruction drawing for the Gymnasium am Goetheplatz built according to the design of Gustav Berringer in 1927–30, Rostock. (Drawing: Leo Dainat. Courtesy of Leo Dainat, Rostocker Gesellschaft für Stadterneuerung, Stadtentwicklung und Wohnungsbau GmbH.)

municipal building projects) Gustav Wilhelm Berringer between 1927 and 1930, the original building contained a four-story main portion with attached three-story wings.[29] The central building housed the *Turnhalle* (Gymnasium). The site was conceived with flat roofs, and the roof over the *Turnhalle* was specifically envisioned for holding classes outdoors and exercising in the fresh air. Berringer intended the entire layout of the school to incorporate modernist ideals, such as increasing the availability of sunlight into every classroom; as such, the school was perceived to be "one of the most modern school buildings of the time" during the late 1920s.[30]

However, already at the time of the building's completion in 1930, there were signs of local discontent—newspaper articles referred to it as "Bolshevistic" and "the cigar box." It is little surprise, then, that by 1937, "the roofs were leaking" and needed to be replaced swiftly, despite "a lack of funds in the city coffers."[31] By 1938, the *Turnhalle* had received a *Walmdach,* a roof with steep pitches on all four faces. This type of roof, rooted in the vernacular style of architecture found across Germany, possessed National Socialist overtones and was utilized in several instances during this period instead of the *Flachdach* (probably a conscious override of architect Berringer's aesthetic, as he had deliberately edited a *Walmdach* out of plans for the *Kurhaus* in Warnemünde, citing as his reason "the altered contemporary conception of architecture").[32] It almost appears that the use of the *Walmdach* in the 1930s can be seen as a fingerprint for Nazi interference.

In this case, popular memory today appears to have disregarded official and functional explanations and cut straight to the heart of the intent underlying the change. The Landesamt's story makes clear that interest in replacing the pitched roof with a flat roof truer to the building's original modernist design grew in the late 1980s, particularly among the institution's students and teachers. Interestingly, this period coincides with the loosening of cultural restrictions and the expansion of interest in the city's history and built environment prior to the GDR.[33] But this new enthusiasm for Bauhaus-style modernism had its limits; while it led some of the participants to go so far as to request the recasting of metal doorknobs from original molds and the repainting of classrooms in historically accurate color schemes, "no restoration of the roof was foreseeable at that time."[34] It was not until 2002, when a proposed restoration once more brought attention to the roof, that its historic importance as "one of the few witnesses to modernism in Mecklenburg-Vorpommern" was recognized.[35]

The problem for the historic preservationist becomes a thorny one—does one restore the intent of the architect and thus enable the experience of a particular aesthetic and Zeitgeist? Alternatively, in recognition that the act of replacing the roof was significant for the time period, does that justify leaving it intact? I must stress that this discussion does not reach the level of public debate, or at least it had not during the period of my fieldwork. It seems that the issue may be decided pragmatically, with preliminary investigations indicating that the entire *Walmdach* must be removed due to long-term structural damage (notably after seventy years, not seven as with the original repair). If that happens, it seems unlikely that it will be replaced. As of this writing, while a restoration project is under way, one informant reports that no change to the roof is visible from the outside. Leo Dainat, from the RGS, provided me with the drawing in figure 3 and informed me in a recent personal communication that if renovation funding being sought on the city's behalf is forthcoming, the flat roof will be restored.

The exceptional nature of the roof of the Gymnasium am Goetheplatz and its overt local association with the National Socialist period contrast with the wealth of Rostock stories from the GDR period. Spaces affected by "external" actors receive the most attention in local narrative. Those associated with any of the external enemies outlined earlier in this essay are bulldozed or given new functions without a second thought.[36] If we follow Michael Lambek's instruction "to understand memory . . . as a form of moral practice," the lack of attention paid to the history of architectural sites and forms in Rostock is troubling.[37] It also has real-world repercussions in the form of enabling current expressions of the same ideology to take root in the region.

Celebrated Wounds

In contrast to the silence surrounding places in Rostock that were built or renovated during the National Socialist period, such as the Marineamt and the Gymnasium am Goetheplatz, some places are mentioned repeatedly and are even celebrated as evidence that, as residents might say, "We suffered too!" The level of suffering endured by residents who remember the period or whose roots are in Rostock appears commensurate with emotions ranging from offhanded awkwardness to open pride.[38] Counterbalancing sites of probable Nazi origin/intervention, such as the Gymnasium am Goetheplatz, are three sites of World War II "victimhood" claimed to some degree by Rostockers: the former Jewish cemetery at Lindenpark, various *Bombenlücken* (bombed sites) in the inner city, and the Petrikirche Turm (Tower of St. Peter's).

Lindenpark is the most unintentionally mournful spot I have ever visited and, in my opinion, is stunningly unsuited to its new role as a park, though municipal literature enthusiastically promotes it for nature lovers. This park, containing both the Old City cemetery and the former Jewish cemetery, demonstrates the results of halfhearted *Vergangenheitsbewältigung* (coming to terms with the past). There is very little in the way of an explication of the history of the park, other than a small plaque denoting the "Ehemaliger Jüdischer Friedhof" (former Jewish cemetery).[39] Nowhere in Rostock did I find any sort of public display, commemoration, or explanation as to what happened to make the graveyard a "former" one. Worse, many of the gravestones, some of which are replacements, are cracked in places from having been toppled in the recent neo-Nazi actions that have plagued the region since unification.

The many spatial voids in town known as *Bombenlücken*, or "bomb holes," are handled in an even more casual manner than the unfortunate Lindenpark. These are empty spaces left behind after Allied bombing runs destroyed the structures that had previously stood there. Many remain unfilled sixty years later. One, right behind the *Fussgängerzone* (pedestrian zone) of Kröpeliner Strasse, had ripped a hole in the city fabric that was left untouched. These voids were worn lightly, pointed out to the visiting American with an air of sangfroid that said, "Look what you guys did—we were hit too!"[40] The site is surrounded by buildings of all eras and functions, many of which had been renovated for retail and university occupancy in the years since the *Wende* (reunification). So why were these spaces left empty in what was the most expensive commercial district in

Rostock, if not the entire state of Mecklenburg-Vorpommern? Rostock is a city filled with local, state, federal, and extranational agencies and actors dedicated to the complete revitalization of the city, bursting with funds, and bristling with cranes. Why else would such expensively located voids be allowed to remain if they were not testimonials to something Rostockers chose to remember? Like the Kaiser Wilhelm Gedächtniskirche (Kaiser Wilhelm Memorial Church) in Berlin, the *Bombenlücken* become symbolic storage spaces, reminding both Rostockers and visitors of the cost of war. Michael Rowlands has argued that "in contexts where objects are destroyed . . . such objects become a memory in their absence, and therefore the essence of what has to be remembered."[41] Rowlands, following Bradley, sees such formal remembrance as part of a long set of cycles stretching back to European prehistory, where "cycles of preservation and curation of monumental built form" interweave with "the deliberate destruction of property."[42] Since aspects of the city are missing, the significance of their absence is, according to Rowlands, in their instruction "towards the future."

One of the difficulties in writing about such memorial spaces is that one is perforce reading significance into absence. According to Rowlands, the force behind the pedagogical nature of such memorials lies within a traditional conception of a linear cultural memory that is "basic to many Western senses of personal and group integrity and coherence." Nevertheless, what if this linearity, this straight connection to the past, is exactly what endangers a contemporary sense of cultural coherence? How can a culture that places a high value on tradition and longevity of custom and situation incorporate periods that may be repugnant to their sense of self? Employing negation (as represented by the empty spaces), rather than preservation or restoration, is one way to solve this problem. As with the Jewish cemetery, a caesura in the linear flow of cultural transmission and memory is resolved through an "unconscious failure to remember."

A case in point is offered by the many stories surrounding the "blowing up" of the bell tower of the Petrikirche. The framing of the facts suits a narrative of victimhood that can leave an outside observer uneasy. The Petrikirche is the beating heart of the Altstadt. The whitewashed, simple interior is a pristine example of northern Lutheran architecture and design. Hanging above the altar is a ship's model, reminding us of the relationship between St. Peter and the area's inhabitants. The streets around the church still are named after their humble occupations: fishermen, tanners, weavers, and thieves.

Soaring into the sky (fig. 4), the recently restored tower causes one to lean back—it is nearly impossible to capture in a camera frame from anywhere nearby. The local narrative is that this tower replaces the one blown off by the Allies during bombing raids from April 24 to 27, 1942. The tower was rebuilt despite the best efforts of GDR authorities to block or slow the permit and fund-raising processes. It was left roofless until 1960, when the church congregation was allowed to erect a rudimentary roof. The tower and a historically authentic roof had to wait until after the *Wende* for completion, which occurred in 1994. This is a heroic narrative of opposition to both Allied and GDR authorities' actions, except for the fact that the Petrikirche Turm seems to be uniquely liable to being burned down, blown off, or otherwise toppled by lightning strikes regularly across the centuries.[43] One can even surmise, by looking at etchings of the city done at various times, that the Petrikirche has spent at least as much time without its tower as with it. Of course, the Petrikirche does double mythopoeic duty—it is a reminder that locals suffered at the hands of both the Allies and the GDR.

Conclusions

Contrasting Rostock with Berlin is striking. In Rostock, the focus is on the GDR period, not World War II. The mythopoeic treatment of the Stasi fits well into an established pattern—it was an external enemy, not one composed of coworkers, employers, neighbors, friends, and even family. As such, stories about the agency have much of the same emotional texture as the stories about the KGB or the Allies. I lack space to go further into the complicated emotional world of the former GDR. There were obvious power inequities within that society, as in others. Winners during that time period may be losers in the current era. Several informants and contacts of mine had seen the wheel of fortune upend their lives. One sociologist who had been briefly jailed for suggesting that people "needed incentives to work" ended his career as chair of his academic department. In another instance, an archaeologist whose father was so highly placed that his family was permitted to live in the United States ended his career in disgrace, running a failing café with his wife's income. Despite variation in personal outcome, clearly such a monumental and ongoing denial of the past and one's role in it can become problematic. In such a climate, the problems with neo-Nazi youth mentioned earlier in this essay are a pre-

Fig. 4. Modern Petrikirche bell tower above roofs of the Altstadt, Rostock, 2000. (Photo: City of Rostock. Courtesy of Dr. Andreas Schubert.)

dictable outcome, even where people would be horrified to think that their thoughts and actions could be linked in any way to such a result. The same denial of the past of spaces and places and their sometimes overly casual reuse are symptoms of the same phenomena. In Rostock, because the period of 1933–90 offered no respite from totalitarian organization, too many people are complicit for finger-pointing to work out well as a larger social strategy. Unfortunately, any acknowledgment, even one as specious and anodyne as "mistakes were made," can swiftly lead to such exchanges of accusation and forcible scab removal. This makes claims for ownership and purpose and ideological intent and representation complex and confrontational. Thus, it is easier to forget, leave unmarked, deny, or focus on external actors, such as the Allies. This strategy, however, allows local history to be lost from memory.

Whatever the objective facts represented in such stories may be, I, as an anthropologist, am interested in the contemporary and mythopoeic aspects of such tales. I have argued that this type of story suggests and reinforces the victimhood of locals in the face of external oppression. Here the word *mythopoeic* denotes the process that I believe is going on in such tales, that Rostockers are inventing a set of myths for their new society and its spaces and places. The myths that Rostockers tell outsiders consistently cast Rostockers themselves as victims, oppressed by outside forces beyond their control. Where they do not have stories, there is active negation or forgetting. Thus, a narrative landscape is shaped and framed by ruptures within an otherwise linear structure. What is interesting about this mythopoeic landscape is that it shows how the urbanity of Rostockers may be of a qualitatively different sort than that of Berliners who seem to see themselves as actors at the crossroads of history.

NOTES

1. Brian Ladd, *The Ghosts of Berlin: Confronting German History in the Urban Landscape* (Chicago, 1998).
2. I followed the genealogy of Edmund Husserl through Roland Barthes, Michel de Certeau, Henri Lefebvre, and Pierre Bourdieu, to name a few of the phenomenologically oriented writers and thinkers who have influenced theory and method in cultural anthropology.
3. http://www.uni-rostock.de/fakult/philfak/fbg/doku/hro/dokuauf.htm.
4. http://www.topographie.de.
5. The Marineamt is comparable to a coast guard but more heavily armed.
6. Eric Hobsbawm and Terence Ranger, eds., "Introduction: Inventing Tradition," in *The Invention of Tradition* (Cambridge, 1983), 1ff. Ladd (*Ghosts,* 46) notes, "The Nikolai Quarter . . . contributed to the German Democratic Republic's rediscovery of history during the 1980s."
7. Quoted in Colin Renfrew and Chris Scarre, eds., *Cognition and Material Culture: The Archaeology of Symbolic Storage* (Cambridge, 1998).
8. Quoted in David Seamon, "A Way of Seeing People and Place: Phenomenology in Environment-Behavior Research," in *Theoretical Perspectives in Environment-Behavior Research,* ed. Seymour Wapner (New York, 2000), 157–78.
9. Gina Kolata's *Flu: The Story of the Great Influenza Pandemic of 1918 and the Search for the Virus that Caused It* (New York, 2001) documents just such a deletion.
10. Kevin Lynch, *The Image of the City* (Cambridge, MA, 1960).
11. Michel de Certeau, *The Practice of Everyday Life* (Berkeley, 1986).
12. Rostocker Gesellschaft für Stadterneuerung, Stadtentwicklung und Woh-

nungsbau GmbH, *The Community Initiative URBAN: From Brussels into the Kröpeliner Tor Suburb to Rostock* (Rostock, 2001). Wolf was spymaster and head of the Hauptverwaltung Aufklärung (HVA), East Germany's counterpart to the CIA.

13. The home was in the row of houses designed by Walther Butzek on Kosegarten Strasse (see n. 35).

14. Seamon, "A Way of Seeing People and Place," 165.

15. Ibid., 158.

16. Howard R. Pollio, Tracy B. Henley, and Craig B. Thompson, *The Phenomenology of Everyday Life* (Cambridge, 1997), 5, as cited in Seamon, "A Way of Seeing People and Place."

17. Seamon, "A Way of Seeing People and Place," 171.

18. Susan Mazur-Stommen, *Engines of Ideology: Urban Renewal in Rostock, 1990–2000*, vol. 1 (Berlin, 2005).

19. Ibid., 103.

20. A moiety is a society cleaved into two complementary subsets—neither subordinate to the other—that have ritual and political significance and are often marked out spatially.

21. A similar phenomenon was noted by Uli Linke in "Fantasizing Violence," *City and Society,* Annual Review (Arlington), 1998, 135.

22. Rostocker Gesellschaft für Stadterneuerung, *The Community Initiative URBAN.*

23. http://www.ushmm.org.

24. http://www.stiftung-bg.de/Aussenlager.

25. Statistisches Reichsamt, ed., *Die Wahlen zum Reichstag am 31. Juli 1932 und am 6. November 1932 und am 5. März 1933 (Sechste bis achte Wahlperiode),* Statistik des Deutschen Reiches, vol. 434 (Berlin, 1935), http://www.gonschior.de.

26. In 1945, residents experienced severe privation when "48 percent of the flats, 42 percent of the industrial area, and 20 percent of the public facilities were destroyed [by the Allies]."

27. Population figures are drawn from several sources, including Johann Gerdes's *Sozialatlas Rostock* (www.soziologie.uni-rostock.de/sozialatlas/sozialatlas.html), Rostock Kurs 2010 (city document for internal use), and personal communication with sociologist Peter Voigt of the University of Rostock.

28. Kathrin Valtin, "Spurensuche: ENTSCHÄDIGUNG 'Für die Zwangsarbeit in Mecklenburg-Vorpommern will niemand Verantwortung übernehmen,'" *Freitag: Die Ost-West-Wochenzeitung,* December 17, 1999, http://www.freitag.de/1999/51/99510401.htm.

29. Landesamt für Denkmalpflege Mecklenburg-Vorpommern, *Denkmalschutz und Denkmalpflege in Mecklenburg-Vorpommern,* vol. 9 (Schwerin, 2002), 4. See also Elke Onnen, "Das Kurhaus in Warnemünde: Nutzungsanforderungen verändern ein Baudenkmal . . . ," in Landesamt für Denkmalpflege Mecklenburg-Vorpommern, *Denkmalschutz und Denkmalpflege in Mecklenburg-Vorpommern,* vol. 8 (Schwerin, 2001), 1–9.

30. Landesamt für Denkmalpflege Mecklenburg-Vorpommern, *Denkmalschutz und Denkmalpflege in Mecklenburg-Vorpommern,* 9:4.

31. Ibid.

32. Onnen, "Das Kurhaus in Warnemünde," 3.

33. Ladd (*Ghosts,* 46) refers to "the German Democratic Republic's rediscovery of history during the 1980s."

34. Landesamt für Denkmalpflege Mecklenburg-Vorpommern, *Denkmalschutz und Denkmalpflege,* 9:4–5.

35. See Onnen, "Das Kurhaus in Warnemünde," 3–6. Berringer was one of three architects working in the new style in Rostock at this time. His colleague and collaborator on the Kurhaus was Walther Butzek, who also designed a row of houses on Kosegarten Strasse in Rostock—one of which was the venue for the Wednesday-night dinners mentioned earlier in the present essay. The third architect was Walter Baresel, who worked into the GDR period.

36. Alternatively, old functions are sometimes given new buildings. During my fieldwork, there was a push to build a new *Stadthalle* to replace the relatively recent and structurally intact building from the GDR.

37. Michael Lambek, "The Past Imperfect: Remembering as Moral Practice," in *Tense Past: Cultural Essays in Trauma and Memory,* ed. P. Antze and M. Lambek (New York, 1996), 235–56.

38. University of Rostock sociologist Peter Voigt estimated in a conversation with me that approximately 30 percent of present-day residents are originally from elsewhere—primarily Saxony and Thuringia (personal communication, October 1999).

39. This may have changed since 2000.

40. Hannes Heer, co-originator of the infamous *Wehrmachtausstellung* that toured Germany in the early to mid-1990s, has written a book titled *Vom Verschwinden der Täter: Der Vernichtungskrieg fand statt, aber keiner war dabei* (Berlin, 2004). One reviewer writes: "In Germany today, Heer argues, the memory of the Third Reich coalesces more and more around the idea of Germans as victims, particularly of the Allied bombings, rather than Germans as the agents of genocide" (Kristen Semmens, "Murder without the Murderers," *H-German,* March 2006, http://www.h-net.msu.edu/reviews/showrev.cgi?path_280941147364074).

41. Michael Rowlands, "The Role of Memory in the Transmission of Culture," *World Archaeology* 25, no. 2 (1993): 146. All quotations from Rowlands in this paragraph and the next are on p. 146 of this source.

42. Richard Bradley, *The Passage of Arms: An Archaeological Analysis of Prehistoric Hoards and Votive Deposits* (Cambridge, 1990), cited in Rowlands, "The Role of Memory," 149.

43. For the definitive discussion of the heroic narrative, see Joseph Campbell, *The Hero with a Thousand Faces* (Princeton, 1972).

PART 2

Sites of New Construction: Industrial Cities and the Embrace of Modernism

Memento Machinae
Engineering the Past in Wolfsburg
Jan Otakar Fischer

When the Wolfsburg city hall was inaugurated in 1958, local politicians praised their building as a symbol of renewal and commitment to democratic principles. At the ceremony, the Wolfsburg city fathers emphasized the openness, transparency, rational planning, and modesty that characterized their new Rathaus. As visitors mounted the steps, they saw six bronze entrance doors covered with a long sans serif text, cast in relief. Still legible today, though corroded, it begins:

> The city of Wolfsburg thanks its existence to the founding of the Volkswagen factory in a favorable location in the center of Germany / In the valley of the Aller / along the Mittelland Canal / on the Berlin–Ruhrgebiet train line / near the Autobahn between Harz and Altmark / where an urban accent was lacking / construction was planned and started on farmland in 1938 . . .

The rest of the text tells a story of slow but steady postwar regeneration and ends with a list of the era's Wolfsburg notables, including the city hall architect Dr. Titus Taeschner and the planning director Peter Koller, "whose plans provided the basis for the town's development in 1938." What is most interesting is what is left out, namely, any indication of the genesis of Wolfsburg as a uniquely National Socialist project. The doors of city hall testify to an impulse common to towns throughout Germany in this period and especially strong in Wolfsburg: the suppression of uncomfortable truths in an effort to establish a new identity in a forbidding postwar landscape.

For Wolfsburg—the headquarters of the Volkswagen automobile company; the source of the famous Beetle; the representative site of the postwar economic miracle, or *Wirtschaftswunder*—was one of only two cities in Germany conceived and founded by the Nazis.[1] Unlike other German cities, where elements of Nazi planning were imposed on an existing, often ancient, urban fabric, Wolfsburg was essentially a tabula rasa before the first bulldozer arrived in 1938. Most of Wolfsburg's original traces date to the Nazi period and register its intentions. They do not intermingle with or overlay the historic substance; they *are* the historic substance. How have these traces come to be understood by Wolfsburgers today, busy as ever with their forward-looking *Pionierarbeit* (pioneering work)? What could be written on the doors of a city hall built today, besides the word *Volkswagen*?

The way Wolfsburg at first evaded and then slowly recovered its own past is certainly reflective of a national tendency in postwar Germany—a consensual disregard finally roused out of its complacency by the initiatives of *Vergangenheitsbewältigung* (coming to terms with the past) in the early 1980s. But Wolfsburg's narrative of remembrance is unusual, not because it eventually emerged as written, conventionally documented history, but because it was clearly, if subtly, manifested even earlier in the postwar architecture of the city.

Autoreligion: Stadt des KDF-Wagens

The first true "people's car" was Henry Ford's Model T, which began rolling off the assembly line in Dearborn, Michigan, in 1914.[2] Not until 1932 did Ferdinand Porsche, an engineering genius based in Stuttgart, begin obsessing over his own vision of a "Volkswagen," an automobile every German family could afford. Two weeks after the Nazis came to power on January 30, 1933, Hitler called for a radical *Volksmotorisierung* of the entire population.

Supplying the populace with a Volkswagen and giving them the means to use it would allow the Nazis more control over both work and leisure time. The development of the Volkswagen fell to the Deutsche Arbeitsfront (German Labor Front; hereinafter DAF), headed by Robert Ley. The DAF was the Nazi replacement for the traditional labor unions that were liquidated in 1933. A special subdivision of the DAF, named Kraft durch Freude (Strength through Joy; hereinafter KdF), offered a range of carefully vetted touristic and cultural activities that claimed to reinvigorate the workforce while helping form a more cohesive *Volksgemeinschaft* (people's community).[3] Ley committed himself to making the auto a key element of Hitler's social *Gleichschaltung* (bringing into line), and Porsche designed a prototype. In May 1937, Ley founded the Gesellschaft zur Vorbereitung des deutschen Volkswagens mbH (Company for the Preparation of the German Volkswagen, Ltd.), or Gezuvor. The company name was simplified a year later to Volkswagenwerk GmbH, with Porsche as chief managing director. A robust propaganda campaign began to promote the new car. All that was needed was a factory and a city to service it.

A young deputy of Robert Ley's, Dr. Bodo Lafferentz, the leader of the KdF "Travel, Hiking, and Relaxation" division, was named as one of Volkswagen's managing directors. Lafferentz found the ideal site for the enterprise: a sparsely populated rural corner of Lower Saxony that was nonetheless a few kilometers northeast of Braunschweig and crossed by a major train line, an autobahn, and the Mittelland Canal. The only notable existing building in the neighborhood was a compact stone castle called Schloss Wolfsburg, dating back to the fourteenth century. Albert Speer, the Inspector General for Building in Berlin, approved the location.[4] Lafferentz then asked four of the top industrial architects of the day—Emil Mewes, Fritz Schupp, Martin Kremmer, and Karl Kohlbecker—to submit proposals for the new Volkswagen plant. When the results proved largely uniform, Hitler ordered in December 1937 that the architects collaborate on a single design.

A planner was then sought to create a vision for a town that not only could support a dedicated workforce but would do so in conformance with Nazi social-utopian principles. Peter Koller, a young architect recommended to Lafferentz by Speer, was chosen, and from that moment on, the future town of Wolfsburg had its *spiritus rector*. Koller, an Austrian who came to Berlin in 1928 to finish his architecture diploma at the Technische Hochschule, studied under Heinrich Tessenow when Speer was the prominent Berlin architect's assistant.[5] Lafferentz was looking for an enterprising planner and offered him a chance at the Volkswagen job. His plan was endorsed by Hitler on March 31, 1938, and Koller, only thirty years old, was given a free hand to build his ideal town under Nazi patronage. When the foundation stone for the Volkswagen factory was laid during a ceremony on May 26, 1938 (fig. 1), Hitler predicted that the new town would be both "a demonstrative site [*Lehrstätte*] for the art of both urban and residential planning" and "a model German worker's city."[6] The Führer baptized the new car the KdF-Wagen, and the town thus became, economically, the Stadt des KdF-Wagens.

Koller was told he should plan for a city of ninety thousand inhabi-

Fig. 1. Adolf Hitler and Ferdinand Porsche admire a KdF-Wagen prototype at the Volkswagen factory founding ceremony, May 26, 1938. (Photo: Fritz Heidrich. Stadtarchiv Wolfsburg.)

tants, considered necessary for a labor force working three shifts. The factory dominated the northern side of the canal, with room to expand further in that direction. Koller therefore set the town to the south, on the other side of the canal between the factory and a wooded promontory known as the Klieversberg. His vision was a masterful synthesis of personal initiative, inherited modern theory, and prescribed political doctrine (fig. 2).

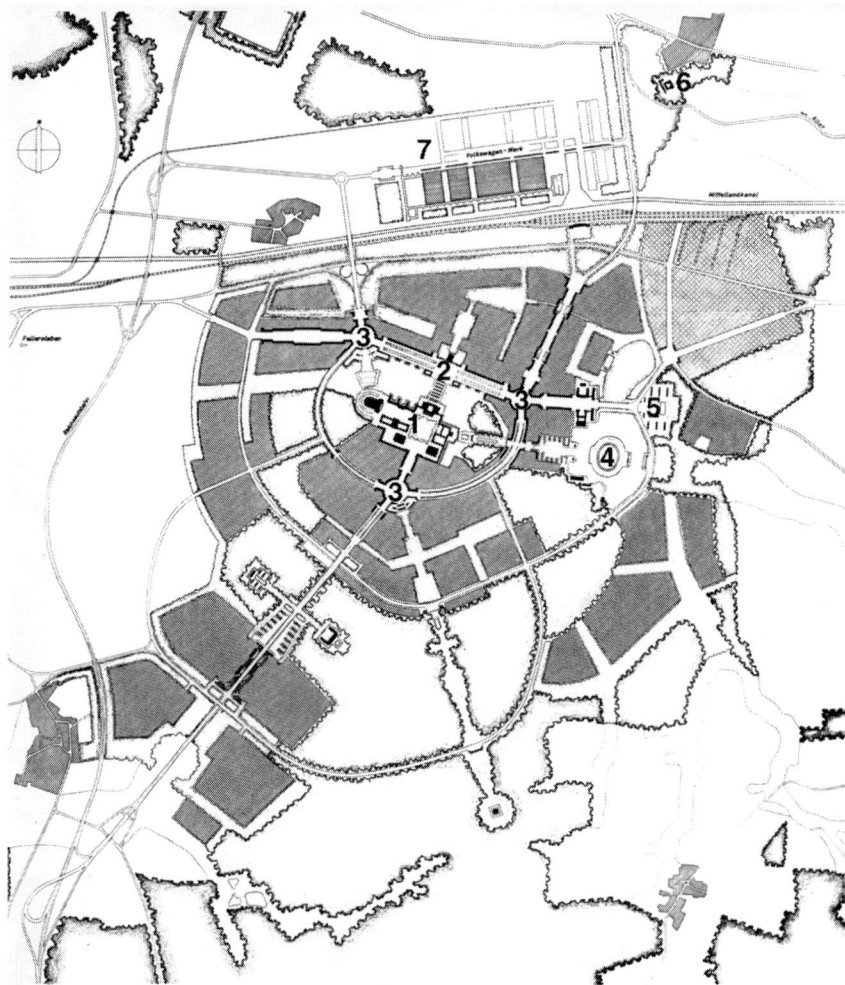

Fig. 2. Peter Koller's plan for the Stadt des KdF-Wagens (1 = *Stadtkrone,* 2 = main avenue with Rathaus, 3 = roundabouts, 4 = sporting arena, 5 = DAF complex, 6 = Schloss Wolfsburg, 7 = Volkswagen factory). (Photo: Stadtarchiv Wolfsburg. Originally published in "Die Stadt des KdF-Wagens" in *Die Kunst im Dritten Reich,* special publication [Munich], April 1939.

Koller accepted the view made explicit by the early twentieth-century garden city movement—that areas of work and habitation should be kept distinct and that housing blocks should be discrete, flexible elements in landscaped green zones. He disliked the congestion and overscale of big cities and instinctively understood natural topography. He was interested in traffic patterns and the functional dynamics of city life much more than in aesthetic exercises or conventional pattern languages. He found the pure formalism of Albert Speer (or Hitler) unsuited for reality.[7] So the Koller plan for the Stadt des KdF-Wagens evolved first as a sensitive response to the natural surroundings, in which forested housing estates (*Siedlungen*) were linked by a network of connecting roads expanding radially from a center point determined by the Klieversberg. These roads intersected at roundabouts and, at the edges of town, fed into highways directing traffic to the autobahn or the factory. The plan showed a remarkable consciousness of the growing role the automobile played in urban life.

Yet Koller, working for Ley and Speer, also understood that certain architectural elements were required by the Nazi hierarchy.[8] With Speer as his occasional watchdog, he integrated familiar items of the Nazi urban gestalt, widening several of his main streets, increasing the massing of buildings at intersections near a defined downtown, and making sure important institutions terminated major sight lines. Nazi officials, especially Ley, insisted on a sort of party acropolis atop the Klieversberg at the center and highest point of the city. The *Stadtkrone* (city crown) would have dwarfed the city hall at its feet and competed in scale and authority with the factory itself.[9] It appeared in the final plan, but Koller never elaborated the design. In fact, he successfully ignored it, preferring to concentrate on housing and infrastructure.

The Volkswagen factory, a wall of brick four stories high and nearly 1.5 kilometers long, with shed roofs and a heavily buttressed power plant, went up in haste. Wooden encampments arose to house the construction workers, both German and Italian. The first housing estate, Steimker Berg, and a large section of the town center, the Mitte, took form by the start of 1939. These two districts remain today the most fully realized remnants of Koller's Nazi-era planning in Wolfsburg.

On September 1, 1939, war broke out. Though Porsche and Koller had not anticipated war, Porsche had demonstrated that his automobile could be converted into a military vehicle simply by switching the chassis, and Koller's Steimker Berg homes were provided with reinforced basements for safety during air raids.[10] Not a single KdF-Wagen had yet been manufactured for public consumption. The factory was ordered to convert entirely to the war effort. Porsche transformed the KdF-Wagen, as promised, into an all-terrain transporter nicknamed the Kübelwagen (bucket wagon), which came into production after 1940 and served the Germans in much the way the jeep did the Americans. More than sixty-six thousand Kübelwagens were manufactured by the end of the war.[11] But Porsche's state-of-the-art facility quickly mutated into what Hans Mommsen, the principal chronicler of Volkswagen's wartime history, has called "eine Art Lumpensammler der Industrie"—an all-purpose, low-tech shop room for repairing airplane wings and assembling fuel tanks and other parts.[12] Perhaps the most specialized product to emerge from the Volkswagen plant during the war was the Fi 103, or V1, flying bomb, over twenty thousand of which were fabricated by 1944.

The factory was extensively damaged by Allied bombers toward the end of the war, although the town and its sea of barracks—which eventually housed an estimated eighteen thousand workers, two-thirds of them forced laborers—were mostly spared. Urban construction had continued fitfully until 1942, when it ceased for lack of material and funding. Koller, ignoring his seven children and good connections, volunteered for military service and was sent to the Eastern Front, where he was taken prisoner by the Soviets. Porsche stayed on the job until January 1945, when he retreated to his family estate at Zell am See in Austria. He was eventually arrested by the French and spent twenty months in prison for his role in the German war effort. Despite the chaos of the final months, a few Kübelwagens continued to roll off the assembly line until April 10, 1945. One day later, the American army occupied the Stadt des KdF-Wagens.

Frontier Miracles: Wolfsburg

On May 25, 1945, the town was officially renamed Wolfsburg, after the lonely castle that still hovered in view slightly north of the factory. Lower Saxony came under the British zone of occupation after the armistice. Aware of their own shortage of vehicles and realizing that the factory was easily reparable, the British, under the leadership of Major Ivan Hirst, decided to get Volkswagen up and running again immediately, this time producing the cars Porsche had intended all along. Rather than being dismantled, as were many other German armaments industries, Volkswagen found itself an Allied priority project, with financial backing and access to raw materials otherwise rare in postwar Germany. Within the year, Volkswagen had a jump on all other German automobile manufacturers.

The Kdf-Wagen needed a new name for the postwar era. In June 1938, an article in the *New York Times* had referred to Porsche's car as "a shiny little beetle," and the nickname *Käfer* somehow found approval in

Germany.[13] When the Federal Republic of Germany was founded in 1949 and Volkswagen was handed over to German state control, the Beetle was already being exported to the United States and the company was under the firm direction of Heinrich "General" Nordhoff, who would spend the next twenty years realizing Porsche's original ambition. Every second automobile in Germany was a Käfer by 1954, and the millionth model rolled out of Wolfsburg a year later. In 1962, every second car exported from Germany was a Volkswagen. With startling ease, the lowly Beetle became a pop icon, a totem of innocent hippie freedom, and the premier symbol of the German postwar *Wirtschaftswunder.* In 1972, it finally surpassed the Ford Model T as the best-selling automobile in history.

Koller had survived the war and returned to his family in Wolfsburg. As a former Nazi Party member, he was not allowed to participate in municipal planning. Yet by 1955, he had maneuvered himself back into local politics enough to be named Wolfsburg's city planning commissioner (*Stadtbaurat*) and was once again responsible for the town's development. Koller largely expanded the vision of his prewar plan—with several significant adjustments. Under his supervision (which lasted five short, but critical, years) and that of his successors, Wolfsburg became a sprawling conglomerate of independent suburban enclaves, strung together on curving roadways. The roundabouts were discarded. The strong axes were eliminated except for the long avenue (later named the Porschestrasse) that visually linked the Klieversberg with the Schloss Wolfsburg. The Klieversberg itself, freed from the burden of an ill-defined *Stadtkrone,* was left a wooded park. All the elements of the plan that had reflected the representative desires of the higher Nazi authorities were therefore excised.

The old garden city idea was modified to fit a new urban paradigm, dubbed *die gegliederte und aufgelockerte Stadt* (the articulated and dispersed city), in which isolated, multistoried apartment blocks would be distributed along ring roads, set deep into green zones, and provided with extensive parking. Koller and his team unhesitatingly embraced a rehabilitated rationalist idiom—in this case, perhaps more Scandinavian than Bauhaus—that led to prefabricated concrete buildings with flat roofs, projecting balconies, extensive glazing, and no ornament.[14] Wolfsburg expanded, as Koller had anticipated in 1938, well to the south and the west of the Mitte. In 1972, twenty scattered communities radiating out from the core of Wolfsburg were officially amalgamated, raising the city's population (by 40,000) to 130,000 and the land area from thirty to two hundred square kilometers overnight.

Fig. 3. Postcard view from above the Klieversberg, 1953 (Volkswagen factory in distance, beyond Peter Koller's Mitte housing). (Photo: Schöning Verlag, Lübeck. Stadtarchiv Wolfsburg.)

Throughout this early period, the town devoted itself resolutely to transforming a tide of displaced, often demoralized persons into Wolfsburgers. A severe labor shortage was eventually countered by a massive influx of new German refugees streaming into Wolfsburg from former eastern German territories. The barracks continued to be occupied for a time, and some were even expanded.[15] After 1950, Volkswagen was able to start building permanent housing for its workforce once again (fig. 3).

The effort to create a new community mirrored the larger effort to create a new postwar German society. It also, ironically, revived the original idea to forge a model community of workers bonded by the task of producing a single product. Identity was promised through a brand that had survived to become the symbol of a nation reborn and, even more unexpectedly, a symbol of an emerging global culture. In retrospect, the former KdF-Wagen was, as Erhard Schütz has succinctly put it, "the collective symbol of remembrance of how Germans after 1945 sought to return to their self-conception as normal, unprepossessing, useful members of society." The redemptive transition was not straightforward, however: "Out of a racist, militarily mobilized, predatory community

[*Beutegemeinschaft*], a civil, individualized, mobile consumer society would gradually be born—but with the price that at first both the racist framework and the criminal goals of the past would be denied and repressed."[16]

Memory Work: The *Lehrstätte*

The myth of the *Stunde Null* (zero hour), the caesura of May 1945 after which Germans expected to experience a new historical beginning, was particularly easy for the first Wolfsburgers to accept as an article of faith. What did Wolfsburg have to offer in the way of history anyway? There was the huge factory, swiftly and expertly rebuilt without alteration, viewed no longer as an instrument in the machinery of war but as a providential source of livelihood. The worker barracks were either dismantled or prudently refitted to absorb refugees. The great wooden Tullio-Cianetti-Halle (named after the president of the fascist Italian Industrial Workers Association, the model for the DAF), the sole cultural facility of the Stadt des KdF-Wagens, was also gone, a victim of a fire in 1945. Beyond the barracks were Koller's partially finished row houses, in great demand even as fragments of a Mitte that was yet to be. Finally, tucked somewhere off in a forest nearby stood the Steimker Berg housing estate, untouched by war and still occupied by the managerial elite of Volkswagen. In the first years after the capitulation, all these structures could only have been considered purely utilitarian, detached from history. The one significant exception was the largely Renaissance Schloss Wolfsburg, the modest stone bastion that became the single historical reference point for city and factory officials. Koller had aimed one of his major avenues, later named the Porschestrasse, directly at the Schloss, to connect it visually with the center of town and the Klieversberg and establish it in the consciousness of each citizen. Every subsequent planner has considered this axis more or less sacrosanct.

For the majority of inhabitants, there remained no local impediment to a concentrated focus on the future, no inclination to reflect on how Volkswagen and Wolfsburg were formed in the same wartime crucible, no distractions from the *Stunde Null*. But the central, long-evaded facts concerning Volkswagen's activity during World War II were these: production proved impossible without the use of forced labor; and those responsible for production did not hesitate to exploit forced labor, regardless of its source. As Hans Mommsen has pointed out, the Volkswagen factory employed forced labor to an unusual extent, because it had had no time to establish a workforce of its own before the war started.[17] During the nearly six years that the factory was in service between 1939 and 1945, several distinct groups of forced laborers were conscripted. First came Polish women and military prisoners, followed in 1941 by Soviet prisoners of war (despite official qualms about employing "racially inferior" peoples) and, later, forced laborers from France and Holland (fig. 4). In 1944, a special concentration camp (*Konzentrationslager,* or KZ) was built, the KZ-Laagberg, and its inmates were put to work building the V1. By 1943, forced laborers comprised two-thirds of the workforce—a percentage among the highest in the German war industry.[18] In 1944, there were about eighteen thousand workers in the factory, of which twelve thousand were forced laborers. Jews were among the last to arrive. Hard as the work was, many Jews who survived the war after working at Volkswagen later described their period in the factory as an unexpected reprieve from the practice of *Vernichtung durch Arbeit* (extermination through work) that they had experienced at Auschwitz.[19] Still, it is estimated that about five thousand concentration camp prisoners were forced to work at Volkswagen, and many hundred died as the result of hardship, disease, or hunger, despite the fact that it was in Volkswagen's interest to keep them alive. There is no evidence that the Volkswagen administrators objected to the use of forced labor in their factory—indeed, they did what they could to encourage it, with Porsche repeatedly seeking Reichsführer SS Heinrich Himmler's help in obtaining additional workers.[20]

In 1975, it was still possible for one chronicler to publish a book on the city in which slave labor within the wartime Volkswagen factory was not discussed and the word *Zwangsarbeiter* (forced laborer) did not once appear.[21] It was not until the start of the mid-1980s that a handful of academics began an exhaustive examination of Wolfsburg's early history. A prime catalyst was the Bundestag speech given by President Richard von Weizsäcker on May 8, 1985—the fortieth anniversary of the German capitulation at the end of the war—in which he called on Germans actively to accept moral responsibility for the crimes of the Nazi period. In that year, a Wolfsburg citizens' initiative supported by the local Green Party and the Social Democrats forced a rededication of the *Ausländerfriedhof* (foreigners cemetery), where, during the war, the bodies of Volkswagen's forced laborers, war prisoners, and concentration camp inmates who died were unceremoniously deposited in a mass grave next to the city garbage

Fig. 4. Soviet prisoner assembling a Kübelwagen on Volkswagen factory assembly line, 1942. (Photo: Stadtarchiv Wolfsburg.)

dump.[22] The site was officially renamed the Memorial to the Victims of National Socialist Tyranny. A year later, Klaus-Jörg Siegfried, head of the Wolfsburg Stadtarchiv (city archive), published a book entitled *Armaments Production and Forced Labor in the Volkswagen Factory, 1939–1945,* the first analysis of its kind. The book provided such an awkward jolt to Volkswagen's public relations that the corporation commissioned Hans Mommsen, one of West Germany's most distinguished historians of the Third Reich, to write his own book on the subject, offering him unlimited access to all company documents. In 1987, a simple memorial was erected at the site of the KZ-Laagberg (of which no trace remained), at the request of French former prisoners. The next year, a series of debates erupted about the wartime role of Porsche, prompted by preparations for the fiftieth anniversary of Wolfsburg, which had been planned without reference to the Nazi past. Siegfried then published his follow-up survey, entitled *Life for Forced Laborers in the Volkswagen Factory, 1939–1945.*[23] The genie was truly sprung.

An exhibition designed by Siegfried called Documentation about the Victims of National Socialist Tyranny was installed permanently at the

Stadtmuseum Schloss Wolfsburg (City Museum at Castle Wolfsburg) in 1990 and enhanced in 1999. The largest impact was felt following the long-awaited publication, in 1996, of Mommsen's study—written and researched with the historian Manfred Grieger—entitled *The Volkswagen Factory and Its Workers in the Third Reich*.[24] This massive work confirmed and elaborated the earlier revelations by Siegfried and marked a watershed in the investigation of the complicity of German industry in Nazi war crimes. "At this time, no other company had ever consented to such a comprehensive scholarly examination of its history during the Nazi era," the Volkswagen administration was pained to admit, intelligently turning what could have been very bad publicity indeed into an expiatory exercise.[25]

Underneath Hall 1 on the west end of the factory was an underground bunker where forced laborers had sought shelter during Allied air raids. In 1999, Grieger, who had since been named "Head of Corporate History" for the Group Communications division of Volkswagen, opened a permanent memorial exhibition, the Place of Remembrance of Forced Labor in the Volkswagen Factory, in the bunker.[26] The memorial displays prisoner letters, company protocols, personnel files, postwar interviews, construction drawings, and parts of VI flying bombs. In a parallel initiative, Volkswagen created a one-time twelve-million-dollar indemnification fund that has targeted and paid over two thousand former forced laborers, living in twenty-two different countries—most in Eastern Europe.[27]

Birgit Schneider-Bönninger, who replaced Klaus-Jörg Siegfried in 2005 as director of the Wolfsburg Stadtarchiv, asserts that "the critical exposure of Wolfsburg's early history up until 1945 has been accomplished and has now passed into the consciousness of the town's population." Researchers have moved on to examine less understood periods, such as the town's immediate postwar efforts at denazification, democratization, and the founding of political parties.[28] In Wolfsburg, at least, the new millennium did indeed appear to draw the previous two decades' official focus on revelation—what is referred to as the "critical reappraisal phase" (*Aufarbeitungs-Konjunktur*)—to a close.

Shifting Utopias: The *Musterstadt*

The architectural decisions made in Wolfsburg since the war, in certain key instances, can be understood as reactions to the town's Nazi legacy, an urban commentary alternatively conscious and unconscious, endorsing and renunciatory. The assignment of key postwar building projects to such architects as Alvar Aalto and Hans Scharoun by the Wolfsburg city planning office in the late 1950s and 1960s revealed a special determination the city felt to construct institutions—cultural, educational, religious—that would galvanize communal feeling within a social model, or *Leitbild,* profoundly unlike the one imposed by the Nazis or implied by the "monoculture" of assembly-line production. This effort, set in motion by a series of fortuitous decisions, amounted to nothing less than an early critique of the Nazi past made before this critique could be ventured in words—a repudiation of the DAF model of control over both work and leisure activity, of "Strength through Joy" propaganda, of pompous monumentalism in architecture, of the systematic degradation of the concentration camps, of subjugation to the machine. Progressive architects stepped in where historians were yet to tread, their political sponsors showing a fascinating early willingness to confront the past by imagining its opposite. In order to understand that process, it is necessary to reject the problematically imprecise category called "Nazi architecture" and look more closely at the constituent elements of each specific building enterprise.

The Nazis were unable to develop a consistent prescriptive doctrine for German architecture and, more often than not, allowed different building types to adopt radically different stylistic treatments.[29] The case of Wolfsburg is illustrative. The Nazis planned three building types for the Stadt des KdF-Wagens: the industrial, the residential, and the institutional. Only the industrial and remnants of the residential were actually constructed. Although the factory has been extended over the decades, its original facade still dominates the town. All the pre-1942 housing together, however, accounts for only 5 percent of the total housing in Wolfsburg today. The institutional type, the *Stadtkrone,* exists only as a sketch. It would have been the building type most readily associated with Nazism. Since there was not enough time and since Koller was not inclined to build it, Wolfsburgers were spared the monumental structure, "half Walhalla, half *Reichsparteitagsbau* [Reich Party rally building]."[30]

The housing at Steimker Berg is a tacit acknowledgment of the Nazi-propagated *Heimatschutzstil* ("heritage conservation," or folk style), an impulse to return to the basic agrarian values and traditional "German" dwelling forms favorably contrasted to those of the much-maligned *Großstadt* (metropolis). One strain of the racist *Blut und Boden* (blood and soil) ideology implied that German families would better preserve their identities when living closer to the plaster and thatched-roof realities of their forefathers. Yet Steimker Berg was far from a pastoral idyll. It was conceived as a preserve for the captains of Volkswagen, and even though it rejected the Weimar-era rationalism of flat roofs and strip windows, Steimker Berg was designed with automobile transport, central heating, and a communal wash service in mind, not the peasant hearth. The denser urban neighborhoods of Wellekamp and Schillerteich in the center of Wolfsburg—designed for another class of inhabitants, the factory workers—are a step further from the *Heimatschutzstil* ideal. If anything, they are closer in spirit to the courtyard-based row house configurations of the Prussian eighteenth century but also (paradoxically) to the calculated setbacks of interwar modernism. Although intended for modest living, these multistory apartments came equipped with innovative domestic features, and if they had lost their pitched roofs and punched windows (as new housing promptly did after the war), they would have been accused of little more than figurative nostalgia by architects of the *Neues Bauen*. In the sphere of housing, the Stadt des KdF-Wagens no more spurned the *Großstadt* than it embraced *Blut und Boden*, despite a background of Nazi propaganda urging the contrary. No stigma is attached to the original housing stock in Wolfsburg today—all of it enjoys landmark protection and full occupancy.[31] Hitler was clearly not interested in vernacular housing—for him a lowly order of architecture—and there is no evidence that he ever had anything more to say about the Stadt des KdF-Wagens after founding day.[32]

The Volkswagen factory, by contrast, is the most sophisticated representative of the three categories of building planned by the Nazis in Wolfsburg (fig. 5). Neither the steroidal neoclassicism of the unrealized *Stadtkrone* nor the *Heimatschutzstil* of the rustic idyll were legitimate for technology-related structures, which for the most part continued to be built as rationalized sheds, in line with Bauhaus ideas of standardization. The modern spirit seemed to persevere in industrial architecture, and as late as 1938, in a speech honoring several innovators, including Ferdinand Porsche and Willy Messerschmidt, Joseph Goebbels proclaimed that "technology is also artistry."[33] After all, Nazism was as dependent on the dynamism of mass production and progress as it was on the myth of a restored ur-German patrimony—the symbolism of both was an integral part of its propaganda and its promise. The open display of reinforced concrete, glass skylights, strip windows, metal superstructure, unadorned facades, and machined materials—items unthinkable for a chancellery or a *Siedlung*—was permitted for industrial buildings as a matter of course. This kind of architecture, associated with a modernism that predated the

Fig. 5. The Volkswagen factory along the Mittelland Canal, designed by Emil Mewes, Fritz Schupp, Martin Kremmer, and Karl Kohlbecker, early 1950s (power plant in foreground; halls with bastions to left). (Photo: Stadtarchiv Wolfsburg.)

Nazis, emerged morally unblemished after the war and provided a convenient postwar cover for architects who had profited from Nazi industrial commissions.

For Wolfsburgers, the factory, the largest automobile plant in Europe, has never ceased to be a source of pride—their city is unthinkable without it. It is not a reminder of the dictatorship that brought the whole spectacle into being. Yet the traces are there. Nothing is hidden. The factory was designed with function in mind but also as a manifestation of the power mobilized by National Socialism. On the inside, it offered a neutral container for the needs of modern production, but on the outside, it showed all the monumental aggrandizement explicit in institutional landmarks across the Third Reich. The great southern facade, the public face of Volkswagen then and now, is outfitted like a fortress, complete with parapets, bulwarks, redoubts, and a moat (the Mittelland Canal). The sense of intimidation and awe is enhanced by a typical device of the period: a repetition of identical, outsized elements extending beyond the bounds of perception. In this case, it is the nineteen serial, bastionlike entry stairwells arranged in a "comb" formation (*Kammstruktur*) that conveys the monotonic, even martial, rhythm of worker and party solidarity—the "front" of the *Arbeitsfront* writ in brick, a parable of *Gleichschaltung*.[34] The absolute regularity of the facade is broken only on its terminals by the sober administration block and the compact, buttressed form of the power plant, whose expressive presence was magnified by the addition of four smokestacks in the early 1960s. The primary material is brick, humbler than the stone of Speer's *Hofstil* (imperial court style) but deployed with a similar blanket uniformity. The windows are vertically punched in the old-fashioned manner of pre–World War I factories (not horizontally stripped in the modern mode), and the entire facade deceptively screens the real internal workings of the four mammoth halls directly behind it.

The facade is a mask and a manifesto at once, and its sense of drama is subtly augmented by the inclusion of thirty-two carved travertine reliefs alongside the stairway portals, each depicting laborers from the various administrative districts (*Gaue*) of the Reich in heroic, godlike poses. Porsche wanted a high-tech factory; Ley dreamt of a "great Olympia of labor"—both were rewarded.[35] The special propaganda value of the Volkswagen complex, the representational gestalt grafted onto a functionalist core, and, above all, the complicity of the architects in advancing Nazi aims fully invalidates the idea (embraced by postwar practitioners) that industrial architecture was a moral haven for designers of the period.

The construction of the Rathaus in 1958 was a declaration of independence for the city without a soul or a center—the necessary grounding of a third pole relative to the Volkswagen factory and the ghost of the unbuilt Nazi *Stadtkrone*. As an attempt to create a communal focus and an open public forum, the city hall was a careful essay in purpose-built astringency. The design jury had rejected brick projects to avoid competition—or association—with the factory, in the end favoring Taeschner's proposal for crisp white travertine facades. The assembly block was divided from the administration office tower, and the whole ensemble was set back to provide a broad market square adjacent to the Porschestrasse. The Rathaus was a modest and popular start to the process of self-definition in Wolfsburg—the circumscribed text on the bronze doors notwithstanding. It was a standard-bearer of mainstream modernism: ordered, efficient, untainted.

But another version of modernism was already on its way. Just three months after the opening of the Rathaus, the city commissioners considered the proposals of two architects invited to design a new cultural center for the town, on a site alongside the Rathaus to the south. The building had a complicated program, for it was meant to unite a variety of functions in one structure: a city library, a youth club with a canteen, classrooms for a continuing education center, multifunction rooms, art studios and galleries, offices, and a string of shops. The design submitted by Alvar Aalto was promptly chosen, and his Kulturzentrum, completed in 1962, can be understood as the first salvo in a sustained local critique not only of totalitarian planning but also of a contemporary modernism no less guilty of losing sight of the individual human subject.

The Kulturzentrum sits relatively low to the ground, deferring to the Rathaus and preserving views along the Porschestrasse to the Klieversberg (fig. 6). It ingeniously wraps its functions around an open, rooftop terrace—an internal piazza—varying the sizes, shapes, and orientations of the different components to suit the contained activities. Five lecture halls of increasing size fan out and up toward the Rathaus plaza, their abstract marble-clad facades hovering over a forest of slender columns. There are surprises everywhere: the adult library has a sunken reading area, the children's library an outdoor reading garden, the youth center a retractable roof over a barbecue grill, the art atelier an enormous ceiling-high window. Skylights transmit sunlight into nearly every room, and in true Aalto fashion, the entire building is precisely detailed with natural materials as a *Gesamtkunstwerk,* down to the furniture, lamps, wall surfaces, and paving.

The Kulturzentrum was the antithesis of the old Cianetti Hall, an undifferentiated space where only orchestrated mass events took place. All Wolfsburgers were meant to meet and interact in the Kulturzentrum, and as Wilfried Wang has pointed out, the layout of the various program elements subtly reflects the stages of life itself: infancy, adolescence, adulthood, and old age find their corresponding venues in an integrated balance.[36] At the building dedication in 1962, Aalto spoke of his vision of a "human rationalism" and his "effort to bring the world of materials into harmony with the lives of people." He warned: "Mechanized work and industrial life bring with them the danger of monotony through the lack of variation. The new building shall provide a counterweight."[37] Aalto's redefined agora, with its intimate, decentralized, organic articulation, offered a new cultural antidote for a society that had thrown in its lot with a mechanized order that could produce automobiles and a *Wirtschaftswunder* but also the means of genocide and "total war."

Aalto also built two remarkable churches in Wolfsburg and was invited to join the competition, held in 1965, for another major cultural edifice urgently desired by planners in Wolfsburg: a city theater. Among Aalto's prominent competitors were Hans Scharoun, the designer of the

Fig. 6. The Wolfsburg Rathaus (*left,* designed by Titus Taeschner) and the Kulturzentrum (*right,* designed by Alvar Aalto), 1982 (Porschestrasse and Nazi-era housing of the Mitte in foreground). (Photo: Holger Floss. Stadtarchiv Wolfsburg.)

Berlin Philharmonic, and Jørn Utzon, famous for his Sydney Opera. Together, these three architects represented the cream of postwar organicism—the "other" path of modern design that did not accept the dogmatism of orthogonal box-making and reveled in the idiosyncratic and the synthetic. Scharoun won the competition, with a complex that would both acknowledge its natural setting and serve as an anchoring catchment for Wolfsburg's principal urban axis. Scharoun shared a predilection for asymmetry and abstraction with Aalto, but the jagged, prismatic exuberance of the theater (the only one he ever built) betrays his roots in Weimar-era German expressionism.

Wolfsburg built more than its share of banal, standardized architecture after the war, but the central works by Aalto and Scharoun, made more conspicuous by contrast to the norm, showed that another direction was possible.[38] The *Musterstadt* (model city) received a new paradigm, one whose qualities continue to influence the relationship between the city and its employer. A dynamic rivalry between the forces of corporate identity and

Fig. 7. The Autostadt, designed by Gunter Henn (Schloss Wolfsburg in center background), 2000. (Photo: Klaus Gottschick. Stadtarchiv Wolfsburg.)

those of municipal pride has been most recently, iconographically enshrined in the new Volkswagen Autostadt and the Phæno Science Center.

In the year 2000, Volkswagen opened the Autostadt, a sixty-two-acre customer center on its grounds (fig. 7). The Autostadt was conceived in 1996 as a theme park for Volkswagen interests, a "world of experience" (*Erlebniswelt*) that would pitch the product to an invited public. It was meant to allow people to explore the idea of "automobility" and "participate in Volkswagen's global vision," either as tourists or as customers arriving in Wolfsburg specifically to pick up their new cars.[39] Greeted in a colossal glazed orientation building, visitors may enjoy a number of activities at the site, including dining, visiting the eight highly eccentric pavilions that offer a presentation of each of the auto divisions of the Volkswagen group, dropping the children off at a miniature racing circuit, or the ultimate experience of watching one's own chosen automobile being plucked for personal delivery out of a twenty-story glass display tower. The nearly six-hundred-million-dollar *Erlebnis* has proven popular: around two million Germans visit the Autostadt every year, and close to six hundred site-manufactured Volkswagens are picked up daily.

The Autostadt forwards a model of consumerism that celebrates customer fidelity with ceremonies that uncannily reinvent the sacralizations of Robert Ley. In the modern era, the notion emerged that a new cult of production would replace previously held belief systems. Henry Ford himself endorsed this idea when he remarked: "The man who builds a factory builds a temple. The man who works there, worships there."[40] In these days of economic insecurity, however, the customer's devotion is worth much more than the worker's. The brand is now cult. The Autostadt "opens a world of diversity in branding, and brand philosophies," and each pavilion does its part by providing "the staged world of the brand shrine."[41] In this context, picking up a new car is transformed into a pseudoreligious event, consecrated in a special ritual after a voluntary pilgrimage to Wolfsburg.

The Autostadt is intended for a wide audience, but one that is still sold the dream of *Volksmotorisierung,* still meant to equate personal mobility with freedom and a product with a way of life, and still encouraged to come to the source, stay in a hotel, share in the myth, and take away the prize. This fixed marketing of the future, of course, does not permit the intrusion of any past beyond that which enhances the authenticity of the brand. Except for a multimedia narrative of the product—presented not in anything as archaic as a museum but, rather, in the "Zeithaus"—the Autostadt does not encourage remembering. No visitor to the Autostadt is informed about the existence of the bunker memorial beneath the factory floor or about the KZ-"Arbeitsdorf" that once incarcerated prisoners a stone's throw from the glitzy customer center. War and forced labor are not tendered subjects. The hulking "KonzernForum" and the two glass display towers cut off the once inviolable view of the Schloss from Wolfsburg down the Porschestrasse. "History," said Henry Ford, "is more or less bunk."[42]

In November 2005, Wolfsburg unveiled what it hoped would be an appropriate response to the Autostadt: a building so unusual it would simply be known as the Phæno (a play on the word *phenomenon*). The southern end of the Porschestrasse had been defined by the Klieversberg and Scharoun's city theater since the mid-1970s, but the northern end was unresolved for decades, a problem zone wedged between the canal, the train station, and several busy avenues. As Volkswagen began to develop its Autostadt site, also on Koller's famous axis, the city decided it was time to provide its own urban accent, directly opposite. The Wolfsburg councillor of city culture at the time, Wolfgang Guthardt, proposed to build an interactive science center based on San Francisco's popular Exploratorium, a flexible space where young people could conduct simple experiments designed to illustrate the laws of physics, chemistry, and biology. The Phæno concept openly shared the Autostadt's fixation with the future, but the program brief for the architectural competition held in 2000 specifically recalled the precedents of Aalto and Scharoun. It called for a "continuation of the 'other' modernism," not the classic modernism of Mies van der Rohe or Walter Gropius, but an architecture that was "free from prescribed formal requirements like 'regularized' geometries or traditional motifs."[43] The decisive winner was the Iraq-born, London-based Zaha Hadid, who for much of her career was considered an "unbuildable" architect, so distorted and gravity-defying were her designs.

The building that emerged is a great triangular wedge of incised concrete supported on ten irregular, truncated cones ("craters") that expand up through the entire structure (fig. 8). The cones are hollow and contain various essential services—entries, stairwells, elevators, restaurants, conference rooms—not immediately visible from the exterior. City traffic, mainly pedestrian, is meant to eddy and flow around the cones at ground level. At the side facing the train station, an earthen ramp rises to feed visitors into the wedge itself. Inside, a vast space unfolds, enclosed by an open steel frame roof but hardly any interior walls. The "experimental landscape" inside the Phæno has no columns, joints, or right angles. It is a free-flowing space that can be organized and reorganized to suit each of the 250 experimental stations distributed across it. The exterior of the Phæno is even more exuberantly plastic. The whole building seems cast from one piece of molded concrete and warps the normal expectations of perspective and scale.

While the Phæno's programming may no longer be novel (since the San Francisco Exploratorium opened in 1969, the concept has been exported worldwide), the building is unquestionably a challenge to the status quo and to the sterile artificiality of the Autostadt, where innovation is also propagandized but is only integrated (with luck) into the product. The architecture critic of the *New York Times* called the Phæno "the kind of building that utterly transforms our vision of the future," adding that Hadid "sees modernity as a project that was left incomplete, not a lost cause, so her buildings set out to resurrect a forgotten dream."[44] An element of this dream, once shared by Aalto and Scharoun, is that architecture can and should act as a vehicle for individual empowerment, even atonement.

Fig. 8. The Phæno Science Center, designed by Zaha Hadid, 2005. (Photo: Klemens Ortmeyer.)

Before the historians got busy and debate became public, Wolfsburg employed architects to challenge and interpret its Nazi origins, perhaps only half-consciously. The city was a pioneer in this respect. Now there are new challenges. Staking the future on a single brand is a gamble for any one-company town. Economic crises, poor sales, and rising costs have buffeted Volkswagen since the 1990s. In 2005, a series of bribery and sex scandals led to the dismissal of several top managers. In the same year, the Porsche motor company, the most profitable in the world, decided to take a controlling share of Volkswagen. David was stepping in to rescue Goliath, and the Porsche name was firmly reassociated with Wolfsburg.[45] The city is trying to diversify while facing down its globalizing corporate foes. In the meantime, all of the buildings by Aalto and Scharoun, now aged a half century, badly need renovation.

Wolfsburgers once imagined they could optimistically contemplate the future without the burden of memory. Now that their history is exposed and secured, they may feel it has been of no real benefit, for the future has again become uncertain. For many, it remains debatable whether knowing where we have been helps us determine where we are going.

A stroll up the Klieversberg is a useful reminder to those who still believe that the past gains no purchase on a brave new world. Just behind the stately, crystalline mass of Scharoun's city theater, a forest of beech trees rises. A path through the woods passes tree trunks on which Soviet prisoners, freed or about to be free, carved their names. At the top of the hill stands a small, overgrown wooden hut, the "Porschehütte," Ferdinand Porsche's former private workshop. A few paces to the west, an imposing stone stela rises, one of the ubiquitous "war memorials" (*Kriegerdenkmäler*) built after World War II in many German cities. The oval terrace around the stela is usually deserted. On a stone wall to the rear of the memorial, the names and shields of regions that used to belong to the Reich (East Prussia, Danzig, Galicia, Silesia, Sudetenland, etc.) are proudly displayed, along with a bronze plaque dedicated in 1953 honoring the many German exiled refugees who eventually became Wolfsburgers. Wedged into the ground in front of the terrace, like a giant cracked golf ball, a wartime concrete pillbox slowly sinks into the earth. Beyond this relic, to the north, a wide swath of grass opens toward Wolfsburg, and it is possible to take in the whole city at a glance. It is probably the same view Hitler enjoyed when he toured the site with Ley and Lafferentz and Koller, admired the construction site in the distance, and imagined a *Stadtkrone* beneath his feet. Now there is much more to see, but still dominating everything is the factory and its chimneys and its bright circle of light, beaming the two familiar letters of the Volkswagen emblem across the land.

NOTES

The author would like to thank Dr. Birgit Schneider-Bönninger, Dr. Manfred Grieger, Odert von Rutenberg, Katja Steiner, and Jane O'Reilly for their generous assistance.

1. Salzgitter, whose original name was Die Stadt des Hermann-Göring-Werke (City of the Hermann Göring Works), was also founded by Nazi planners.

2. *Volkswagen Chronicle,* Historical Notes, vol. 7 (Wolfsburg, 2003), 2. In 1930, there were only a half million registered cars in Germany, compared to twenty-six million in the United States. See *Die Geschichte der Region, des Schlosses und der Stadt Wolfsburg,* exhibition catalog (Wolfsburg, 2000), 53.

3. See Erhard Schütz, "Der Volkswagen," in *Deutsche Errinerungsorte: Eine Auswahl,* ed. Etienne François and Hagen Schulze (Munich, 2005), 351–68. For a general history of the KdF, see Shelley Baranowski's *Strength through Joy: Consumerism and Mass Tourism in the Third Reich* (Cambridge, 2004).

4. Dietrich Kautt, *Wolfsburg im Wandel Stätebaulicher Leitbilder* (Braunschweig, 1989), 18–26.

5. Sigurd Trommer, "Peter Koller, Erbauer der Stadt des KDF-Wagens, Stadtbaurat von Wolfsburg," in *Aufbau West—Aufbau Ost: Die Planstädte Wolfsburg und Eisenhüttenstadt in der Nachkriegszeit,* ed. Rosmarie Beier, exhibition catalog (Ostfildern-Ruit, 1997), 75.

6. *Wortprotokoll der Übertragung der Grundsteinlegung des Volkswagen Werkes bei Fallersleben am 26. Mai 1938,* compiled by Rolf Linnemann, March 1987 (Stadtsarchiv Wolfsburg), 6.

7. See Trommer, "Peter Koller"; Kautt, *Wolfsburg.*

8. Trommer, "Peter Koller," 76. The degree to which Koller was forced to insert more demonstrative elements of party architecture cannot be fully determined, because of the dearth of recorded commentary by either Koller or his colleagues.

9. The word *Stadtkrone* was first employed by the German expressionist architect Bruno Taut in 1919, to describe a paradigmatic, utopian city on a mountaintop, symbolizing social regeneration.

10. Hans-Ernst Mittig, "Industriearchitektur des NS-Regimes: das Volkswagenwerk," in Beier, *Aufbau West—Aufbau Ost,* 52.

11. This quantity is fairly negligible, considering that Porsche had expected to produce half a million KdF-Wagens each year (see Schütz, "Der Volkswagen," 360).

12. Quoted in Schütz, "Der Volkswagen," 361.

13. *Käfer ade: Das Buch von Volkswagen zum Bandablauf des letzten Käfer in Mexiko* (Wolfsburg, 2003), 5.

14. For a close analysis of the evolution of Wolfsburg's residential and cultural infrastructure, see Ortwin Reichold, ed., *. . . erleben, wie eine Stadt entsteht. Städtebau, Architektur und Wohnen in Wolfsburg 1938–1998* (Braunschweig, 1998).

15. Several of the barracks were still in use for housing as late as 1962.

16. Schütz, "Der Volkswagen," 353.

17. Hans Mommsen, introduction to *Place of Remembrance of Forced Labor in the Volkswagen Factory,* catalog of the Volkswagen factory bunker memorial and documentation center (Wolfsburg, 1999), 3–9.

18. The average deployment of forced labor in German armaments factories during the war was 30 percent (Mommsen, introduction to *Place of Remembrance,* 3).

19. See *Surviving in Fear: Four Jews Describe Their Time at the Volkswagen Factory from 1943 to 1945,* Historical Notes, vol. 3 (Wolfsburg, 2005).

20. Klaus-Jörg Siegfried, *Rüstungsproduktion und Zwangsarbeit im Volkswagenwerk 1939–1945: Forschungsergebnisse 1986–1996* (Wolfsburg, 2005), 16–17; *Place of Remembrance,* 84, 121.

21. Dr. Adolf Köhler, *Wolfsburg: Eine Chronik, 1938–1948* (Wolfsburg, 1975), 76.

22. The site was later estimated to contain at least 476 bodies, 131 of them children. See the essays by Manfred Grieger and Birgit Schneider-Bönninger in *Topographie der Erinnerung: Gedenkstätten für die Opfer des Nationalsozialismus im Gebiet der Braunschweigischen Landschaft* (Braunschweig, 2004).

23. Klaus-Jörg Siegfried, *Rüstungsproduktion und Zwangsarbeit im Volkswa-*

genwerk 1939–1945 (Frankfurt am Main, 1986); *Das Leben der Zwangsarbeiter im Volkswagenwerk 1939–1945* (Frankfurt am Main, 1988).

24. Hans Mommsen with Manfred Grieger, *Das Volkswagenwerk und seine Arbeiter im Dritten Reich* (Düsseldorf, 1996).

25. Quoted in Klaus Kocks and Hans-Jürgen Uhl, *Learning from History*, Historical Notes, vol. 1 (Wolfsburg, 1999), 15.

26. See *Place of Remembrance*. The idea for a Volkswagen memorial exhibition was in large part initiated by Wolfsburg students who had been involved in Volkswagen-sponsored Auschwitz concentration camp excursions during the mid-1990s. According to Manfred Grieger, the exhibition is still the only one in Germany installed by a company on its grounds to document its own Nazi-era history.

27. This fund, which has provided about six thousand dollars per individual, has been carefully referred to as a *humanitäre Leistung* (humanitarian obligation/gesture) rather than an *Entschädigung* (compensation), for legal reasons—no doubt to hinder future lawsuits.

28. Interview with Birgit Schneider-Bönninger, November 17, 2005. The Nazi Party enjoyed early and substantial support in the region where the Stadt des KdF-Wagens came to be located (over 68 percent in 1932), and in the 1948 elections, the same percentage of Wolfsburg's population voted for the extreme right (the result was annulled). See Grieger's essay in *Topographie der Erinnerung*, 159–60.

29. For a detailed analysis of the contradictions within Nazi building doctrine, see Barbara Miller Lane, *Architecture and Politics in Germany, 1918–1945* (Cambridge, MA, 1968).

30. Kautt, *Wolfsburg*, 44.

31. Steimker Berg received landmark status in 1980 after a citizens' initiative.

32. Curiously, Albert Speer never once mentions the Stadt des KdF-Wagens, Volkswagen, or Koller in his memoir *Inside the Third Reich* (New York, 1970).

33. Joseph Goebbels, "Auch Technik ist Künstlertum," quoted in Andreas Nentwich, "Monumenta Germaniae," in *du—Zeitschrift für Kultur*, "Architektur und Macht. Eine monumentale Verführung," no. 755 (April 2005): 38.

34. Many of the largest Nazi-sponsored buildings (institutional and industrial) employ the *Kammstruktur* layout. Berlin's Tempelhof Airport and the KdF resort of Prora on the island of Rügen are notable examples.

35. See Mittig, "Industriearchitektur." Mittig's is one of the few detailed—and convincing—architectural analyses of the Volkswagen factory.

36. Wilfried Wang, *Stadt werden—Mensch sein: Alvar Aalto's Kulturhaus und Hans Scharoun's Theater in Wolfsburg als Leitbilder der Heutigen Architektur* (Wolfsburg, 2000), 22–23.

37. Klaus-Jörg Siegfried, "Die 'Autostadt': Zur Selbstdarstellung Wolfsburgs in der Nordhoff-Ära," in Beier, *Aufbau West—Aufbau Ost*, 243.

38. It was, intriguingly, Peter Koller's son, Peter Thomas Koller, who recommended that Aalto be invited to submit a design for the Kulturzentrum. Peter Koller took over Hans Scharoun's professorship at the Berlin Technische Universität in 1960.

39. Autostadt GmbH, promotional brochure, April 2005.

40. Quoted in Robert Hughes, *American Visions: The Epic History of Art in America* (New York, 1997), 385.

41. Autostadt GmbH, memorandum of February 2000, Škoda Auto Pavilion brochure.

42. Quoted in Philip Roth, Postscript to *The Plot Against America* (New York, 2004), 378.

43. Wettbewerbsprogramm [official competition program] für des Science Center Wolfsburg, Stadt Wolfsburg, October 1999, 12.

44. Nicolai Ouroussoff, "Science Center Celebrates an Industrial Cityscape," *New York Times,* November 28, 2005.

45. In 1997, Wolfsburg city officials decided not to change the name of the street, the stadium, or the school named after Ferdinand Porsche, the "father of the city"—the aura of the genius inventor was too great—but agreed to add a mildly accusatory text to the memorial bust that was placed in front of the city hall in 1978. The Porsche family has retained its links to Wolfsburg. The CEO of Volkswagen from 1993 until 2002 was Ferdinand Piëch, the grandson of Ferdinand Porsche. He is still the most important player on the Volkswagen board.

Inventing Industrial Culture in Essen
Kathleen James-Chakraborty

Discussions of memory in relation to the German cityscape typically focus on buildings with obvious connections either to the Nazis or to their victims.[1] Limiting our consideration of memory to such sites, however, ignores the multiplicity of ways in which the Third Reich permeated daily life and in which amnesia about the past continues to color German urban planning and preservation decisions. Since World War II, political, economic, and intellectual elites in Germany have embraced modern architecture and design, which they have equated with industrial modernity, as a means of distancing themselves from the Third Reich.[2] The recent elevation of the pithead of a defunct coal mine in the industrial city of Essen into the surrounding region's leading symbol of industrial culture exposes the inherent tensions between this idealization of form and the realities of its original production.[3] How did the Zeche Zollverein Pithead XII (fig. 1)—designed and built during the Weimar Republic but embraced after 1933 as a model for both the artistry and the modernity of National Socialist industrial architecture—come to be the centerpiece of the Ruhrgebiet's ongoing effort to reinterpret its industrial heritage as politically and socially progressive art? The answers tell us a great deal about who manufactures memory and why in Germany today.

The story of the official commemoration of the Third Reich in Essen in the years after 1945 offers few surprises. The changing fate of the city's enormous synagogue, dedicated in 1913 and located on the edge of Essen's medieval core, has served as a barometer of public willingness to memorialize a once vibrant Jewish community.[4] In Essen, as in other German cities, the focus during the 1950s was on repairing the city's physical fabric and acknowledging the suffering of ordinary Germans. By the 1980s, this trend had given way to the efforts of local activists to ensure that neither

Fig. 1. Zeche Zollverein Pithead XII, designed by Fritz Schupp and Martin Kremmer, Essen, 1932. (Photo: Gerdy Troost, ed., *Das Bauen im neuen Reich*, vol. 2 [Bayreuth, 1943], 109.)

the Nazis' crimes nor their victims would be forgotten.[5] Torched on Kristallnacht in 1938, the synagogue was abandoned for more than two decades before its shell was converted into a hall for industrial design exhibitions and then the German poster museum. Following a second fire in 1979, it was reconstructed as a museum honoring the city's Jewish community and documenting the Nazi terror. By 1991, a series of historical markers throughout the city drew further attention to sites associated with the deportation of Jews, political and religious resistance, and slave labor.[6] In the 1990s, however, the task of rehabilitating the region's industrial heritage eventually began to overshadow remembering the horrors of the Third Reich. Hopes for a more prosperous future pushed aside a full accounting of the past.

Official memory in Essen always had clear limits. The particular form it has taken has often been specific to the Ruhrgebiet, where opinion makers have preferred to remember the radical politics of its workers rather than the tacit support that many industrialists offered the Third Reich. Alfried Krupp von Bohlen und Halbach, the heir to the steelworks that sparked Essen's transformation from a modest eighteenth-century town into a bustling industrial center, was sentenced at the Nuremberg Trials in 1948 to prison for twelve years for his firm's use of slave labor, but he served only three years before being pardoned.[7] No markers mention him or stand in front of the factories and mining installations that were central to rearmament and the Nazi war effort.

Instead, the city's industrial relics—most prominently the Zeche Zollverein—have been interpreted as symbols of technological and cultural innovation. Reinvented as high art, the Zeche Zollverein pithead tower was a prominent component of Essen's successful entry for becoming the cultural capital of Europe for the year 2010.[8] On December 15, 2001, the inhabitants of the Ruhrgebeit, western Germany's rust belt, awoke to find the front page of the local newspaper announcing proudly that this imposing structure had been placed on the UNESCO World Heritage List. The headlines equated the "Eiffel Tower of the Ruhr" with some of the most famous structures already on the list, the Pyramids of Egypt.[9] Throughout the 1990s, geographers, city planners, architects, and arts administrators, working closely with the political and business community, made this mining structure, abandoned in 1986 after just over fifty years of operation, the emblem of their efforts to revitalize the former heartland of continental Europe's coal and steel industry. Their particular focus was the industrial districts to the north of the major urban centers. The steel latticework of Pithead XII's tower graces almost every recent publication on the region.[10]

This ubiquitous publicity seldom failed to tie the elegant industrial installation, designed by the local firm of Fritz Schupp and Martin Kremmer, to the most enduring architectural symbol of progressive Weimar ideals, the Dessau Bauhaus, designed by Walter Gropius and completed in 1926 (fig. 2).[11] An early draft of the UNESCO nomination equated "the strongly Cubist form of the individual buildings" with the "architectural ideals of the Bauhaus."[12] Misattributing Louis Sullivan's dictum "Form follows function" to the Bauhaus, the author, Udo Mainzer, the chief of conservation for the Rhineland, went on to imply that the dedication of Pithead XII ("the most modern and beautiful mine in the world") in the year "that the closing of the Bauhaus began" represented the continuation of the controversial school's precepts in the face of Nazi persecution.[13] After admitting that the mechanization and rationalization of Pithead XII

Fig. 2. The Bauhaus, designed by Walter Gropius, Dessau, 1926. (Photo: Gustav Adolf Platz, *Die Baukunst der neuesten Zeit* [Berlin, 1927], 415.)

contributed to the unemployment that helped bring the Nazis to power, the report noted, "The completion of the mine installation coincides . . . with the end of the German reparations payments to the Allies."[14] This interpretation discounted miners' memories of Pithead XII as ruthlessly rational.[15] Miners' accounts of visits by high-level Nazi officials were also purged from a history that equated architectural modernism with liberal democracy as well as economic development.[16]

The Zeche Zollverein is an emphatically modern building, but it was the product of a different aesthetic and political position from that of the Bauhaus, which was almost certainly anathema to both its architects and their nominal client, the man for whom it was named, Albert Vögler, the head of Vereinigte Stahlwerke AG, at the time Europe's largest steel company. The strong sense of order and stability displayed in the choice of a masonry cladding, the steel grid that framed that cladding, and the imposition of axial symmetry as much as possible on the disposition of groups of buildings are at complete odds with cubism's rejection of Euclidean geometry as embodied in the Bauhaus's pinwheel plan and with Gropius's choice of cantilevered stucco and glass planes that appeared to float as if suspended above the ground. Pithead XII was an important template for Nazi industrial architecture, which was as much a showpiece for the regime as the more often cited neoclassical ensembles built or projected for Munich, Nuremberg, and Berlin.

Two generations of historians have reiterated that neither German nationalism in general nor National Socialism in particular were antimodern.[17] This enormous and sophisticated corpus of scholarship, much of it specifically grounded in architectural examples, has had little impact, however, on the way in which many Germans continue to portray modern architecture as inherently antifascist. The conviction that the cultural values of urban planning, architecture, and design offer concrete solutions to political and economic problems was common across the German political spectrum throughout the twentieth century.[18] The overwhelming postwar identification with institutionalized modernism has sheltered German elites from either admitting the role that modernism played within the Third Reich or accepting the degree to which their supposedly oppositional cultural positions have often served to legitimize the political and economic status quo.

In the debate over the reconstruction of the center of Berlin in the 1990s, the equation of architectural transparency with democratic politics generated by this modernist myth clashed with two different architectural strategies for addressing memory. The first was the revival of neoclassical forms that embodied nostalgia for civic order independent of capitalist real estate values, the second the invention of deliberately destabilizing forms intended to ensure continued consciousness of the Nazi annihilation of European Jewry.[19] What was viewed elsewhere as an outdated allegiance to modernism was challenged by two conflicting positions within the contemporary international architectural debate: postmodern neoclassicism and deconstruction.

Planners in the Ruhrgebiet, where tastes throughout the twentieth century have often diverged substantially from the German mainstream, relied instead on technological modernity recast as avant-garde art to expunge heavy industry's nationalist and antidemocratic past. For them, the preservation of the region's outmoded industrial infrastructure demonstrated a historical commitment to state-of-the-art technology and created the cultural resources that might attract new, future-oriented investment. Although no economic resurgence materialized, this provincial approach to rust belt landscapes helped catapult neomodernism into the mainstream of international architectural culture.

The case of the Zeche Zollverein is particularly interesting because there is no reason whatsoever to believe that those who reinvented Pithead

XII's past to serve their own present had any sympathy whatsoever for the conservative nationalist politics it originally represented. On the contrary, their ability to ensure its preservation depended in large part on their strong ties to city and state governments led by the Social Democratic Party.[20] Despite these left-of-center political affiliations, their efforts implied that artistic form trumps political action as an expression of political dissent. This demeaned in particular the local working class, who throughout the twentieth century voted in large numbers for Roman Catholic, Socialist, and Communist parties without ever expressing much enthusiasm for modern architecture and design.[21] The willful distortion of history in the official memories manufactured for Pithead XII calls into question the degree to which other prominent examples of German "remembering" are shared by the society as a whole. To what degree, for instance, did the restoration of the Old Synagogue in Essen and the erection of commemorative plaques represent the sentiments of the entire community?

Modernism and Modernity in the Interwar Ruhrgebiet

No architectural form inherently represents a particular political or social position. The relationship between a building and a political stance must be established through the examination of the creation and reception of each individual structure. Furthermore, the associations attached to particular architectural styles and ways of organizing space change over time. The "reactionary modernism" of the Zeche Zollverein Pithead XII, although firmly tied to the political and economic point of view espoused by Vögler, was also emblematic of the reluctance that patrons of all classes and political positions from the Ruhrgebiet displayed throughout the years of the Weimar Republic toward adopting new architectural ideas from Berlin and the Bauhaus.[22] There are, for instance, no dazzlingly cubistic workers' housing settlements in the region. Instead, despite increasingly rigorous attention to cost, which curtailed the use of superfluous ornament, garden city nostalgia for premodern village life prevailed.[23]

The Zeche Zollverein mine was established in 1847 in what is now the northern Essen neighborhood of Katernberg. It was named after the customs union that, at the close of the twentieth century, was described by those who advocated the mine's preservation as a crucial first step toward German democracy. They also implied that the Zollverein was an important precedent for the establishment of the European Union, which helped finance the mine's restoration.[24] In 1928, two years after Vereinigte Stahlwerke took over the mine, the local director Friedrich Wilhelm Schulze Buxloh commissioned Pithead XII. It opened four years later, replacing two earlier shafts.[25] The new pithead buildings were universally recognized to be the acme of industrial efficiency. Not only was the complex technologically up to date; it was also self-consciously beautiful.

Since the first decade of the twentieth century, German industry had turned to artist-architects to give their factories, the products produced in them, and the advertising for those products a gloss of culture. The intent was to make them more marketable, as well as to redeem modern industrial society by ensuring the preservation of strictly cultural values. The first phase of this effort climaxed in Peter Behrens's work for the Allegemeine Elektrizitäts-Gesellschaft (AEG) and in the founding in 1907 of the Deutsche Werkbund, an alliance of industrialists, politicians, critics, and designers. Simmering tensions within that organization—between those inclined to see the design of the environment as a way of creating a public art tied to personal and potentially class liberation and those focused on the economic welfare of industry and the state—boiled over at the annual meeting in the summer of 1914 (fig. 3).[26]

The experiences of World War I temporarily soured the excitement that many young German architects had had about an architecture of demonstrable economic and industrial utility.[27] When their enthusiasm returned with the stabilization of the German economy at the end of 1923, Walter Gropius, Ernst May, and Erich Mendelsohn were among those who romanticized mass production as a path to greater social equality, adopting industrial forms to critique not only nineteenth-century historicism but also the Wilhelmine penchant for monumentality. Those who condemned this rejection of vernacular precedent as unpatriotic, even Bolshevist, resisted their efforts.[28] A middle group, to which Schupp and Kremmer belonged, were content to use new materials in the creation of buildings closely associated with modernity. Although this group increasingly eschewed ornament, they continued to favor materials and compositions that created a reassuring aura of stability and permanence at a time of enormous social, economic, and political uncertainty.

Fritz Schupp would have been startled if, as he was in the process of supervising Pithead XII's construction, he had heard it equated with the Bauhaus. In a 1930 interview, he mockingly dismissed many of the architectural features associated with the school—including flat roofs, corner

Fig. 3. The model factory designed by Walter Gropius and Adolf Meyer for the Werkbund Exhibition of 1914 in Cologne. (Photo: Platz, *Die Baukunst der neuesten Zeit,* 369.)

windows, and steel furniture—as "literary" and "romantic." Describing an encounter with a society lady who regarded him as an architect who could hang a rotating house from a mast, he noted, "So Eva tempted the poor architects with the apple, and thus also are designed the projects that smell of printing ink."[29] Instead of following what he dismissed in highly gendered terms as a fashion for novelty, he preferred to strike a balance between old and new (envisioning a modern church in which one could place a Riemenschneider altar, for example, or a living room filled with Persian rugs): "We must try to win an absolute standard that finds the good in the old as well as in the new and rejects the rest."[30] Schupp clearly associated good taste not only with respect for the past but also with luxury, which was to be reserved for those who could afford it.

Schupp and Kremmer had studied with Paul Schmitthenner, whose deep respect for architectural tradition put him at complete odds with Gropius, who after the war had him sacked from his professorship in Stuttgart.[31] Although they appear to have had nothing whatsoever to do with the Bauhaus, Schupp and Kremmer did number among Germany's leading interwar industrial architects. Schupp continued to be an important industrial architect after his partner's death in Berlin in 1945 at the hands of the Russian invaders. Both men were deeply indebted to the Werkbund's goals of integrating industry and culture. Although in the 1920s, many of the group's members embraced the more radical aesthetic epitomized by the Bauhaus, the organization's original dedication to the ennoblement of industrial and graphic design, as well as of the architecture of both production and consumption, retained its appeal to most cultured Germans.

Vögler, for whom Pithead XII was originally named, was typical of the emphatically modern Germans who espoused this position without allying themselves with political liberalism or avant-garde design. As the leader of the Vereinigte Stahlwerke, founded in 1926, he was one of Germany's leading businessmen. Although he never joined the Nazi Party, his politics were consistently antidemocratic. Vögler's decision in 1931 to close entire factories, leaving sixty-nine hundred workers jobless, contributed to the political instability of the Weimar Republic's final years. Although his influence waned during the Third Reich, he committed suicide upon its defeat.[32]

Vögler's intellectual outlook was similarly conservative. He was friendly with Oswald Spengler and, during World War II, worked closely with Albert Speer. He was also a leading supporter of new, psychologically based management techniques intended to ease the antagonism that politically engaged workers felt for their employers.[33] Above all, Vögler, whose name was originally emblazoned on Pithead XII in a Gothic script that represented the political as well as artistic antithesis of the sans serif associated with the Bauhaus, was committed to the rational organization of German industry. He envisioned a situation in which competition, whether between capitalists or between workers and management, would no longer impinge on economic efficiency.[34]

The ubiquitous equation of modernity with a specific strand of architectural modernism epitomized by the Bauhaus has hindered our understanding of the way in which interwar Germany's most technologically advanced industrial installations could be designed in a style that was at once entirely new and yet divergent from the avant-garde's representation of mass production. Modernity generated multiple modernisms, among them the fusion of high-tech with evocations of order and stability displayed in Pithead XII. The inhabitants of the Ruhrgebiet—who, during the Weimar Republic, uniformly preferred evocations of a premodern past to modernist architecture and design—may have welcomed this transposition of neighboring Münsterland's wood-framed, vernacular agricultural buildings with brick infill into modern materials. Certainly, throughout the twenties, they displayed very little interest in the Bauhaus or the work of the other members of the Ring, the group of architects formed to lobby Berlin officials to approve their controversial designs for modern buildings.[35]

Gropius and the other members of the Ring insisted that their designs embodied modernity. New materials, themselves the products of new technologies, generated new spaces and forms, they argued, indivisible from the experience of mass production, and, in the eyes of some, progressive social ideals.[36] In fact, despite their apparent rejection of nineteenth-century historicism's reliance on association, this architecture was equally and profoundly symbolic. In consequence, it seldom flourished in places—whether New York, London, Paris, or the Ruhrgebiet—whose modernity was obvious.[37] From the beginning, modernist buildings were prized for their ability to communicate with particular conviction the presence of a potentially fictitious modernity. During the Weimar Republic, popular infatuation with mass production and mass culture was as much an emotional response to the country's debilitating defeat in World War I and to continued economic and political instability as a reflection of Germany's impressive degree of industrialization.[38]

Modernism's denial of its own symbolic character has complicated recognition of the range of responses to interwar modernity in Germany. The New Building (the term used by the German supporters of this modern architecture of the Bauhaus and the Ring) was heralded by many of its proponents and condemned by its detractors as the exclusive property of the Left. That modernity had no intrinsic relationship to progressive politics is demonstrated by the Nazis' mastery of many of its manifestations, including film, radio, and high-speed automobile and airplane travel.[39] Technological innovation could and did spawn environments diametrically at odds with the aesthetics associated with the Bauhaus.

The Zeche Zollverein and the Third Reich

The Zeche Zollverein Pithead XII was not a Nazi building. Nor, because the number of people who worked on the site was so small, was it an important site of slave labor.[40] Pithead XII has, nonetheless, been repeatedly, if mistakenly, published as a factory of the Third Reich era. This confusion dates to 1938, when Gerdy Troost, the widow of Hitler's favorite architect, included Schupp and Kremmer's building in her definitive survey of architecture in the Third Reich (figs. 1 and 4).[41] This suggests that Pithead XII looked to party loyalists as if it had been built as part of

Fig. 4. Powerhouse of Zeche Zollverein Pithead XII. (Photo: Troost, *Das Bauen im neuen Reich*, 2:108.)

Hitler's massive rearmament effort. Troost's assumption that it was built after 1933 also demonstrates the degree of enthusiasm the Nazis had for industrial aesthetics in what was understood to be their proper setting—actual factory architecture. Also crucial was that because of their solidity and symmetry, Nazi factories, like Pithead XII, bore no resemblance to the cubist-constructivist architecture the Nazis and other conservative cultural critics had long termed "Bolshevist."

The misinterpretation of Pithead XII as a Nazi-era building demonstrates the degree to which the study of twentieth-century architecture is dependent on the examination of the published, rather than the built, record. It is unlikely that any of the authors involved had seen Pithead XII for themselves, as they all have reproduced the same photograph of the powerhouse (fig. 4), which they describe as "a factory in Westphalia."[42] Troost used Pithead XII to illustrate her description of factories built since 1933 as "buildings of weight and order, effective through economic and clear lines, symbols of the precise clean work that is performed in them."[43] This mystification would continue well past the Nazi era. In the 1990s, while the preservation of Pithead XII was well under way, but before the related publicity campaign had kicked into high gear, two important German accounts of the degree to which the architectural profession had collaborated with the Nazis republished Pithead XII as evidence of how "Bauhaus" aesthetics remained permissible after 1933.[44]

From a more critical perspective, workers' accounts from the time of Pithead XII's creation and that of its preservation stress the connection between industrial efficiency and nationalist politics. In the days after the factory opened, an article in a local newspaper decried that it would leave twelve hundred workers and employees to starve, before noting the degree to which heavy industry was working with Hitler.[45] Dismissals resulting from its opening pushed the total number of Esseners looking for work to 78,951.[46] In 1992, Albert Bock, who worked at Pithead XII from the beginning, recalled the visits of Hermann Goering and other Nazi dignitaries, as well as the installation's importance to Hitler's rearmament policies.[47]

Throughout the thirties, Pithead XII continued to be published as a model industrial installation in journals devoted to architecture and to industrial engineering.[48] Furthermore, in the Third Reich, industrial architecture remained an outpost of frankly modernist architecture. Like the Zeche Zollverein, new factories conformed to the new regime's coupling of technology and order (fig. 5). After the war, architects involved in this effort would defend themselves by pointing to the style in which they had worked, implying that they had in subtle ways resisted Hitler, who preferred bombastic neoclassicism. As Winfried Nerdinger pointed out, however, the fact that industry was central to the regime's campaign of terror makes it difficult to accept this claim.[49] Pithead XII was one of a number of industrial installations throughout the Ruhrgebiet, many of them designed by Schupp and Kremmer, that established the key precedent for Nazi industrial architecture.

Manufacturing Amnesia

The transformation of the Zeche Zollverein from a relatively obscure outmoded mine into a widely recognized symbol of the region was largely the result of the International Building Exhibition (IBA) Emscher Park, for which it served as a centerpiece.[50] This decade-long effort concluded in 1999. Its goals included the conversion of the region's industrial heritage into cultural landmarks that would serve as nodes for tourism and demon-

Fig. 5. The Staatliche Deutsche Versuchanstalt für Luftfahrt, designed by Hermann Brenner and Werner Deutschmann, Berlin-Adlershof, begun in 1936. (Photo: Troost, *Das Bauen im neuen Reich,* 2:103.)

strate to potential investors the region's long heritage of technical innovation.[51]

Before the IBA and its development of a "Route of Industrial Culture," for which Pithead XII served as the linchpin, no particular attention had been paid to the Zeche Zollverein, either in guidebooks to the region or in histories of German architecture. Walter Buschmann, the author of an early scholarly account, was an expert on the history of German industrial architecture. Seeking to defend the importance of his subject, he tied it to the mainstream of the modern movement in two ways. First, he described it as a descendent of Gropius's relatively conservative Wilhelmine writings about industrial architecture. Second, he pointed to the similarity between the framing system Schupp and Kremmer used at Schacht XII and that employed less than a decade later by Mies van der Rohe, the third and final director of the Bauhaus, for his buildings on the campus of the Illinois Institute of Technology in Chicago.[52] Both were legitimate claims; by suggesting Mies's awareness of mainstream German architectural practice during the 1930s, the second placed Buschmann in the forefront of establishing the architect's ties to the middle ground of the modern movement.[53]

Meanwhile, by the 1970s, the precipitous decline of the Ruhrgebiet's coal and steel industries was beginning to awaken admiration bordering on nostalgia for an environment that had earlier been more often denounced for the extraordinary degree to which it had been shaped solely by capital. Artists already steeped in modernism's industrial aesthetic were the first to effect this transformation. The photographs of Bernd and Hilla Becher encouraged appreciation of the rapidly vanishing industrial landscape. The Bechers' coolly rational work, which included an important series of depictions of pitheads from Britain, France, and Belgium, as well as the Ruhrgebiet, focused on typological similarities. For the Bechers, industrial architecture was in most cases vernacular design, which acquired artistic status largely through their carefully positioned lenses. Their photographs of the Zeche Zollverein, taken in 1973, emphasized its resemblance to other pitheads in the region, many of which had already been demolished (fig. 6).

The Bechers began photographing such structures in 1957, with Bernd switching from painting and graphic arts to photography, his wife's medium, in order to capture more objectively the standardization of the original artifacts, as well as the state of decay that already surrounded many of them. The onset of what would become their life's work thus coincided with the codification in the Federal Republic of the association of an industrial aesthetic with liberal democracy. In particular, the Bauhaus came to be viewed during the fifties and sixties as the ultimate symbol of liberal Weimar democracy.[54] This equation of industry and democracy was not entirely credible. The Bechers' documentation of the machine hall of the Zeche Zollern in Dortmund lingered on a series of compressors installed in the building in 1940.[55] And the Zeche Germania, which immediately follows Pithead XII in their series on pitheads, was a Nazi-era building realized, according to their own documentation, between 1939 and 1944.[56]

By 1989, when the IBA Emscher Park was launched, the Bechers numbered among Germany's most respected artists. The IBA converted the Bechers' detached perspective toward an apparently impotent past into public policy designed not only to preserve but also to rehabilitate. Its achievements included the conversions of brownfield sites into internationally renowned public parks that preserved the traces of former industrial activity. By turning rust belt relics into local landmarks that doubled

Fig. 6. Zeche Zollverein, Essen, 1973. (Photo: Bernd and Hilla Becher. Reproduced with permission.)

as showpieces for avant-garde cultural activities, the organizers hoped to manufacture the high culture the region had historically lacked. The intent was to rejuvenate a flagging economy by making the region attractive to high-tech and service industries.[57] These businesses employed people, the preservationists implied, for whom cultural resources matter more than they had for miners and factory workers.

The IBA organizers were well aware of the Zeche Zollverein's problematic political history.[58] At the same time that they began to describe Pithead XII as a Bauhaus building, their own enthusiasm for it stemmed largely from its deviance from canonical modernism. This deviance made it appear especially interesting at a time when orthodox modernism was obviously outmoded. Just as Schupp and Kremmer established a middle ground between the cubist-inflected Bauhaus and Speer's bombastic neo-classicism, the rehabilitated Zeche Zollverein bridged the rationalism of Aldo Rossi, Rob Krier, and O. M. Ungers, on the one hand, and, on the other, the high-tech style of Norman Foster, which by the turn of the millennium placed industrial imagery and symbolism once more at the forefront of international architectural culture.

By 1989, the year in which the IBA Emscher Park began, integrating an appreciation of history into the design of new German environments was no longer a radical act. Postmodernism's attention to precedent dovetailed in Germany with the creation of a new landscape of commemoration. The IBA participated in these developments in a somewhat paradoxical fashion. It used a lingering attachment to technology to erase the environmental and social damage wrought by industrial processes, while preserving the traces of those processes, which were now perceived as beautiful. This was quite distinct from harnessing postmodernism's obsession with the palimpsest to uncover previously ignored layers of potentially disturbing meaning.

Finding appropriate uses for Pithead XII worthy of the grandiose claims now being made on its behalf proved difficult. From the beginning, the emphasis that IBA planners placed on its outstanding design encouraged consideration of art-related uses, but the relatively obscure locale made it difficult to attract tenants of suitable standing. The region's most prestigious museum, the Folkwang, had little interest in moving from its site in prosperous south Essen—only minutes by foot from downtown, the main train station, and the opera house—to a remote and somewhat dingy neighborhood.[59] Because design so effectively symbolized the transition the region had to make to a service economy, a series of design-related institutions were eventually installed at Pithead XII.

As in the Third Reich, art offered a state-sanctioned means of sanctifying capital. Although Karl Ganser, the head of the IBA, ensured that the actual physical restoration gave jobs and training to people who had long been unemployed, the complex's working-class neighbors, many of Turkish origin, comprised only a marginal component of the audience for the direction taken by the IBA.[60] As its attention gradually shifted from attracting high-tech industry to creating cultural programming, the IBA's efforts were increasingly targeted at those with larger disposable incomes and more obviously marketable talents.

Emblematic was the choice of Foster for the conversion of the powerhouse into the Red Dot Design Museum (fig. 7). Foster was one of the star architects who reinvigorated modernism by refocusing attention on technology and on energy efficiency. The design center for the state of North Rhine-Westphalia opened in the former powerhouse, shorn of its former smokestack, in 1996.[61] Peter Zec, its director, lamented the constrictions

Fig. 7. Interior of the Red Dot Design Museum, designed by Norman Foster, Essen, 1996. (Photo: Simon Bierwald. Reproduced with permission.)

that the building's status as a cultural monument placed on the use of the space, but the museum continued to trumpet familiar clichés about modern design.[62] One exhibit began by contrasting giant photographs of Gropius's office at the Weimar Bauhaus with Mussolini's pompously traditional headquarters in Rome.[63]

Today, although the site continues to be underutilized, grand plans are gaining momentum. The Dutch Office of Metropolitan Architecture, headed by Pritzker Prize winner Rem Koolhaas, has prepared a master plan.[64] A new EU-subsidized school of management and design moved in 2006 to premises designed by the internationally celebrated Japanese partners Kazuyo Sejima and Ryue Nishizawa. The school's novel fusion of Master of Fine Arts and Master of Business Administration degrees testifies to continued faith in the Werkbund's original ideals.[65] The region's most prominent local history museum, the Ruhrlandmuseum, is scheduled to move from its present quarters, which it shares with the Folkwang, to the Zeche Zollverein colliery. Some preservationists are angry, however, that the colliery's original fittings have been partially dismantled to accommodate the new tenant.[66]

The story of the reinvention of the Zeche Zollverein as a monument to the progressive political as well as artistic values popularly associated with the Weimar Republic and the Bauhaus demonstrates the durability of comfortable, if not particularly credible, conclusions about the relationship between modern technology and enlightened public policy. By the time the last coal was sorted in Pithead XII, modernist architecture's triumphal narratives appeared as exhausted as the heavy industry from whose vernacular they had drawn so much inspiration. The fall of the Berlin Wall precipitated the "Critical Reconstruction" of the old heart of Berlin by architects and planners committed to the preservation of the city's neoclassical heritage. If the IBA failed to generate economic revitalization within the Ruhrgebiet, it proved prescient of early twenty-first-century aesthetic trends. Peter Latz's Landschaft Park in northern Duisburg and Thomas Sieverts's Westpark in Bochum have become international models of landscape architecture.[67] Pithead XII may yet become as celebrated an attraction as the Tate Modern, a former London power plant converted into a modern art museum by the Swiss firm of Herzog and De Meuron. Their adaptive reuse of the Küppersmühle into a museum of modern art, also an IBA project, opened in Duisburg's Inner Harbor in 1999.[68]

Fame is not likely to promote a more complete understanding, however, of the site's history. Interpreting Pithead XII as an example of Bauhaus architecture helped sanitize the crucial contribution that heavy industry made to the rearmament of Germany and to the war effort. Offering design as a substitute for economic planning diverted resources from unemployed workers—already denigrated for their unwillingness to patronize the inevitably more expensive modernist objects that mistakenly symbolize opposition to fascism—to the offices of international architectural stars. It also enhanced the status of those locals for whom the project bought access to such celebrities. Although launched by Socialist governments, the IBA is the most recent chapter in a century-long effort on the part of German intellectuals to harness art to the service of economics, in part in order to ensure their own continued relevance.

Many of the particulars of this story, including Weimar-era resistance to avant-garde modernism and the more recent disdain for postmodern historicism, are resolutely local. The chasm throughout the twentieth century between tastes in the Ruhrgebeit and in Berlin highlights the continued importance of regionalism in German cultural experience. Yet, attaching demonstrably untruthful narratives about the past to particular physical sites in order to enhance the position of ruling elites is neither new nor, as David Lowenthal has demonstrated, uniquely German.[69] Indeed, the particular myth that industry, industrial modernism, and enlightened political positions, whether Socialist or democratic, are inextricably intertwined is one of the most salient examples of the obliteration of memory, not only in Germany, but also in many other countries, including the United States. Modernism's break with historicism encouraged formalist readings of the Zeitgeist divorced from rigorous archival research.[70] Celebrating the Zeche Zollverein as an example of "Bauhaus" architecture entailed a deliberate erasure of the fact that interwar Germany's extreme politicization of architecture did not spare any style or architectural technique from being harnessed to nationalist political and economic goals. Because remembering this fact compromises not only those who embraced modernism in order to rehabilitate themselves but also many of those who continue to base their claim to cultural authority on "enlightened" taste, forgetting remained easier.

NOTES

My research was funded by the Deutscher Akademischer Austausch Dienst (DAAD), the Deutsche Forschungsgemeinschaft (DFG), and both the Center for German and European Studies and the Committee on Research at the University of California, Berkeley. I thank Klaus Tenfelde, my host at the Stiftung Bibliothek des Ruhrgebiets, Bochum, and my research assistants Noga Wizansky and Anja Ziebarth. Jonathan Wiesen and Ulrike Laufer generously read the manuscript and made many useful suggestions.

1. Examples are Gavriel Rosenfeld's *Munich and Memory: Architecture, Monuments, and the Legacy of the Third Reich* (Berkeley, 2000) and James Young's *At Memory's Edge: After-Images of the Holocaust in Contemporary Art and Architecture* (New Haven, 2000) and *The Texture of Memory: Holocaust Memorials and Meaning* (New Haven, 1993).

2. Gwendolyn Wright, *The Politics of Design in French Colonial Urbanism* (Chicago, 1991), 10–11; Sarah Williams Goldhagen, "Something to Talk About: Modernism, Discourse, Style," *Journal of the Society of Architectural Historians* 64 (2005): 144–67.

3. A pithead is the top of a mine shaft, through which the products extracted are brought to the surface.

4. *Stationen jüdischen Lebens: Von der Emanzipation bis zur Gegenwart* (Essen, 1990).

5. *Essen: Aus Trümmern und Schutt wächst eine neue Stadt, 10 Jahre Planung und Aufbau der Metropole an der Ruhr* (Essen, 1956).
6. Ernst Schmidt, ed., *Essen Erinnert: Orte der Stadtgeschichte im 20. Jahrhundert* (Essen, 1991).
7. Jonathan Wiesen, *West German Industry and the Challenges of the Nazi Past, 1945–1955* (Chapel Hill, 2001).
8. The tower was highlighted at http://www.kulturhauptstadt-europas.de/start.php (accessed December 22, 2005). By October 26, 2006, all mention of it was cut from the site. For the Zeche Zollverein, see Walter Buschmann, ed., *Zechen und Kokereien im rheinischen Steinkohlenbergbau: Aachener Revier und westliches Ruhrgebiet* (Berlin, 1998), 414–85.
9. "Zollverein—bedeutend wie die Pyramiden," *Westdeutsche Allgemeine Zeitung,* December 15, 2001.
10. Roland Günter, *Im Tal der Könige: Ein Handbuch für Reisen zu Emscher, Rhein und Ruhr* (Essen, 2000); Roy Kift, *Tour the Ruhr: The English Language Guide* (Essen, 2003).
11. See Kift, *Tour the Ruhr,* 93; almost any citation of the building in the *Westdeutsche Allgemeine Zeitung;* http:://www.unesco.de/unesco-heute/202/zollverein.htm, whose text, written by Birgitta Ringbeck, includes the heading "Vom Bauhaus beeinflusste Industriearchitektur"; http:/www.essen.de/module/meldungen/m_detail.asp?MNR=1281; and http://www.bkkvorort.de/magazin/wellness-und-freizeit/zeche-zollverein-in/essen. These Web sites were accessed on June 7, 2005. More recently, the Zollverein Web site—http://www.zollverein.de/index.php?f_categoryId=85&f_menu3=85 (accessed October 26, 2006)—has retreated from this position.
12. Udo Mainzer, "Die große Geschichte," Die Zollverein-Zeche in Essen/Schacht XII/Eine Denkmal-Landschaft von Weltrang im Herzen Europas/ Eine Denkschrift zur Begründung des Antrags zur Aufnahme in die UNESCO-Liste des Welt-Kulturerbes (Entwurf, Stand: April 1997), 6, in Akten 223, IBA Emscher Park Archiv, Stiftung Bibliothek des Ruhrgebiets, Bochum, Germany (hereafter cited as IBA Akten).
13. Ibid., 6.
14. Ibid., 8.
15. "Die Forderungen der christlichen Bergarbeiter," *Allgemeine Wattenscheide Zeitung,* February 2, 1932.
16. Dirk Hautkapp, "Wenn dem Buxloch 'was nicht gefiel," *NRZ Essen,* February 1, 1992. Complaints from 1961 about the installation's toxic emissions are documented in Ulrich Borsdorf, ed., *Essen: Geschichte einer Stadt* (Essen, 2002), 514.
17. See Jeffrey Herf, *Reactionary Modernism: Technology, Culture, and Politics in Weimar and the Third Reich* (Cambridge, 1984); Michael Prinz and Rainer Zitelmann, *Nationalsozialismus und Modernisierung* (Darmstadt, 1991); Geoff Eley, *Reshaping the German Right: Radical Nationalism and Political Change after Bismark* (New Haven, 1980); Geoff Eley, ed., *Society, Culture, and the State in Germany, 1870–1930* (Ann Arbor, 1996). From art history, see Barbara Miller Lane, *Architecture and Politics in Germany, 1918–1945* (Cambridge, 1968); Werner Durth,

Deutsche Architekten: Biographische Verflechtungen, 1900–1970 (Brunswick, 1987); Winfried Nerdinger, ed., *Bauhaus-Moderne im Natinoalsozialismus: Zwischen Anbiederung und Verfolgung* (Munich, 1993); Paul Betts, *The Authority of Everyday Objects* (Berkeley, 2004).

18. See Kathleen James-Chakraborty, *German Architecture for a Mass Audience* (London, 2000). For a recent summary on aesthetics in the Third Reich, see Richard Etlin, ed., *Art, Culture, and Media under the Third Reich* (Chicago, 2002).

19. Brian Ladd, *The Ghosts of Berlin* (Chicago, 1997); Deborah Ascher Barnstone, *The Transparent State: Architecture and Politics in Postwar Germany* (London, 2005); James Young, *At Memory's Edge*.

20. Funding for the project came from the city of Essen, the state of North Rhine-Westphalia, and the European Union.

21. See Betts, *Authority of Everyday Objects*. For Essen election results, see Borsdorf, *Essen*, 568–78.

22. The term comes from Herf, *Reactionary Modernism*.

23. ALLBAU Allgeminer Bauverein Essen AG, ed., *Wohnen und Markt: Gemeinnützigkeit wieder modern* (Essen, 1994); Marion Gondau, "Vom guten und schlechten Geschmack: Arbeiter- und Intellektuellenästhetik am Beispiel Wohnen," in *Arbeiterwohnen: Ideal und Wirklichkeit; Zur Geschichte der Möbilierung von Arbeiterwohnungen 1850–1950*, ed. Museum für Kunt und Kulturgeschichte der Stadt Dortmund (Dortmund, n.d.), 87–102.

24. Abschlussbericht der Projektgruppe Zollverein, Aufsichtsrat/Zollverein/19. Sitzung/3.9.92, IBA Akten 47, 14–19.

25. http:/www.zollverein.de/englisch/start.php (accessed June 8, 2005).

26. John Maciuika, *Before the Bauhaus: Architecture, Politics, and the German State, 1890–1920* (Cambridge, 2005); Frederic J. Schwartz, *The Werkbund: Design Theory and Mass Culture before the First World War* (New Haven, 1996).

27. Marcel Franciscono, *Walter Gropius and the Creation of the Bauhaus in Weimar: The Ideals and Artistic Training of Its Founding Years* (Urbana, 1971); Iain Boyd Whyte, *Bruno Taut and the Architecture of Activism* (Cambridge, 1982); Wolfgang Pehnt, *Die Architektur des Expressionismus* (Ostfildern-Ruit, 1998).

28. Lane, *Architecture and Politics*. See also Christian Otto and Richard Pommer, *Weissenhof 1927 and the Modern Movement in Architecture* (Chicago, 1991).

29. "Industriebauten der Architekten Schupp & Kremmer, Berlin-Essen," *Baukunst* 4 (1930): 104.

30. Ibid., 107.

31. See Wilhelm Busch and Thorsten Scheer, eds., *Symmetrie und Symbol: Die Industriearchitektur von Fritz Schupp und Martin Kremmer* (Cologne, 2002), especially Ulrike Laufer, "Die Architekten: Fritz Schupp und Martin Kremmer" (15–30); Wolfgang Voigt and Hartmut Frank, *Paul Schmitthenner, 1884–1972* (Tübingen, 2003).

32. Manfred Rasch, "Über Albert Vögler und sein Verhältnis zur Politik," *Mitteilungsblatt des Instituts für Soziale Bewegung: Forschungen und Forschungsberichte* 28 (2003): 127–56. See also Wiesen, *West German Industry*, 151–55; Gerald Feldman, *Hugo Stinnes: Biographie eines Industriellen, 1870–1924*, trans. Karl Heinz Siber (Munich, 1998).

33. Rasch, "Über Albert Vögler."

34. Buschmann, *Zechen und Kokereien,* 450. I thank Hans Hanke for reminding me of the Gothic script's political dimension.

35. Kathleen James, *Erich Mendelsohn and the Architecture of German Modernism* (Cambridge, 1997), 115. Mendelsohn was one of the few members of the group to actually build in the region.

36. Their destabilized compositions were also inspired by modern physics. See Ulrich Müller, *Raum, Bewegung und Zeit im Werk von Walter Gropius und Ludwig Mies van der Rohe* (Berlin, 2004).

37. Two helpful studies of taste are Kenneth E. Silver's *Esprit de Corps: The Art of the Parisian Avant-garde and the First World War, 1914–1925* (New Haven, 1989) and Katherine Solomonson's *The Chicago Tribune Tower Competition: Skyscraper Design and Cultural Change in the 1920s* (Cambridge, 2001).

38. Wolfgang Schivelbusch, *The Culture of Defeat: On National Trauma, Mourning, and Recovery,* trans. Jefferson Chase (New York, 2003), 214–30.

39. Herf, *Reactionary Modernism.*

40. There were certainly slave laborers at the Zeche Zollverein. See Klaus Tenfelde and Hans-Christoph Seidel, eds., *Zwangsarbeit im Bergwerk: Der Arbeiteinsatz im Kohlenbergbau des Deutschen Reiches und der besetzten Gebiete im Ersten und Zweiten Weltkrieg* (Essen, 2005), 624.

41. Gerdy Troost, *Das Bauen im neuen Reich,* vol. 1 (Munich, 1938), 73.

42. Troost, *Das Bauen im neuen Reich;* vol. 1; Durth, *Deutsche Architekten,* 139; Nerdinger, *Bauhaus-Moderne,* 173.

43. Troost, *Das Bauen im neuen Reich,* 1:73.

44. Durth, *Deutsche Architekten,* 139; Nerdinger, *Bauhaus-Moderne,* 173. The photograph published by Troost and in these two later works originally appeared in Fritz Bauer's "Zeche 'Zollverein' in Essen-Karternberg" (*Zentralblatt der Bauverwaltung vereinigt mit Zeitschrift für Bauwesen* 54 [1934]: 101), where no date was given for Pithead XII's construction.

45. "Die Forderungen der christlichen Bergarbeiter," *Allgemeine Wattenscheide Zeitung,* February 2, 1932.

46. "Weitere Zunahme der Arbeitslosigkeit," *Generalanzeiger für Dortmund und das gesamte rheinisch-westfälische Industriegebiet,* February 9, 1932.

47. Hautkapp, "Wenn dem Buxloch 'was nicht gefiel."

48. For the entire bibliography, see Buschmann, *Zechen und Kokereien,* 414–15.

49. Nerdinger, *Bauhaus-Moderne,* 173–75.

50. Examples of IBA-generated publicity are "Route: Industriekultur: Endeckerpass 2003," published by the Kommunalverband Ruhrgebiet, and *Internationale Bauausstellung Emscher Park, Katalog der Projekte,* (IBA, 1999), 333–38.

51. Ilse Brusis, "Vorwort," in *Internationale Bauausstellung Emscher Park, Katalog;* anonymous editorial, in *Internationale Bauausstellung Emscher Park, Katalog,* 8–14; Günter, *Im Tal der Könige,* 397–516.

52. Walter Buschmann, "Zeche Zollverein in Essen," *Rheinische Kunststätten* 219 (1987): 9, as consulted in Zollverein/im Spiegel der Presse/Teil III/Januar 1992–April 1992, IBA Akten 222. Buschmann's conclusions are repeatedly echoed in the IBA files. See Ammerkungen zur Zecheanlage Zollverein Schacht XII, 3,

Zollverein XII/AR, 1. Sitzung/12. Febr. 1990, IBA Akten 46; Wilhelm Busch, F. Schupp, M. Kremmer: Bergbauarchitektur, *1919–1974*, Landeskonservator Rheinland, Working paper 13 (Cologne, 1980).

53. Fritz Neumeyer, *The Artless Word: Mies van der Rohe on the Building Art*, trans. Mark Jarzombek (Cambridge, 1991). For Neumeyer, writing at postmodernism's height, this tied Mies to neoclassicism, but Mies's support for Rudolf Schwartz (Mies wrote the introduction to the English translation of Schwartz's *The Church Incarnate: The Sacred Function of Christian Architecture* [New York, 1958]) suggests a broader sympathy for less radical modernism.

54. In addition to Betts's *Authority of Everyday Objects,* see Walter Gropius's *Apollo in der Demokratie* (Mainz, 1967).

55. Bernd Becher, Hilla Becher, Hans Günther Conrad, and Eberhard G. Neumann, *Zeche Zollern 2: Aufbruch zur modernen Industriearchitektur und Technik* (Munich, 1977), plates 67, 69, 73–74, 76. The publication of this series was explicitly tied to attempts to preserve the building.

56. Bernd Becher and Hilla Becher, *Mineheads* (Essen, 1985), 16, 168.

57. Cover letter to the Abschlussbericht der Projektgruppe Zeche Zollverein Schacht XII, July 29, 1992, 14–18, Aufsichtsrat/Zollverein/19. Sitzung/3.9.92, IBA Akten 47.

58. In addition to Busch's dissertation on Schupp and Kremmer, they had access to the critical perspective displayed in "Abschlussbericht der Projektgruppe Zollverein," 19, Aufsichtsrat/Zollverein/19. Sitzung/3.9.92, IBA Akten 47, and "Einige Überlegungen zur Umnutzung stillgelegter Schachtanlagen der Zeche Zollverein im Nordosten Essens," Eine Studie der Planergruppe Oberhausen GmbH (undated, probably 1988), 12, IBA Akten 222.

59. For a report on the plan to move the museum, see Mko, "FDP will mehr Geld für Kultur," *Westdeutsche Allgemeine Zeitung,* Febuar 28, 1992, Zollverein/im Spiegel der Presse/Teil III/Januar 1992–April 1992, IBA Akten 222. A clipping from the *Unicum Essen,* headlined "Folkwang-Designhochschule Essen" (37/Sitzung [Feb. 7, 1995], IBA Akten 111), includes comments that the Folkwang's music school should not move, for reasons of location.

60. Borsdorf (*Essen,* 533) notes that this part of northern Essen had the city's highest concentration of Turks.

61. See Buschmann, *Zechen und Kokereien,* 447, for two photographs from 1932 and 1995 showing the powerhouse flanked by the machine workshop and the electric workshop, the first showing the smokestack, the second taken after its demolition.

62. Zec quoted in *Office Design,* March 1997, 60; clipping in 55. Sitzung [November 7, 1997], IBA Akten 113.

63. I saw this exhibit in visits to the site in the summers of 2002 and 2003.

64. http://www.oma.nl (accessed December 14, 2005).

65. http:://www.zollverein-school.de (accessed October 26, 2005).

66. Irmgard Bernreider, Die UNESCO droht der Essener Zeche Zollverein mit der Roten Liste, Source: *Rheinischer Merkur,* Grubenarchäologische Gesellschaft, http://www.unterlage.com/cms/content/view/103/83 (accessed June 7, 2005).

67. Peter Reed, *Groundswell: Constructing the Contemporary Landscape* (New York, 2005).

68. Gerhard Mack, *Herzog and De Meuron, 1992–1996* (Basel, 2000), 90–113, 212–21.

69. See David Lowenthal's *The Heritage Crusade and the Spoils of History* (Cambridge, 1998), which builds on his *The Past Is a Foreign Country* (Cambridge, 1985).

70. Siegfried Giedion, *Space, Time, and Architecture* (Cambridge, 1941).

PART 3

Perpetrator Sites: Representing Nazi Criminality

The Reich Party Rally Grounds Revisited
The Nazi Past in Postwar Nuremberg
Paul B. Jaskot

Few topics loom as large in the recent literature on German architecture and urban planning as the impact of the National Socialist past on postwar design practice. While most scholarship has concentrated on Berlin, the ongoing presence of perpetrators in the postwar era, the use of prominent Nazi sites, and the memorialization of specific past events have also influenced regional architectural debates. Nuremberg has been no exception. With its late medieval walls, large castle, and prominent Gothic churches, the city has long attracted the interest of art historians and tourists. Yet, because of its selection as the site of the Nazi Party rallies, Nuremberg's more recent and notorious history has come to the fore in the last few decades as a focus of local debate and tourist fascination. As succinctly summarized by the sardonic local catchphrase used to describe visitors' interest in the city—"from Dürer to Führer"—the geographies and events of Nuremberg's National Socialist past now match the prominence and ideological importance of its late medieval history (including its most famous native son, the painter Albrecht Dürer) almost to the exclusion of all other periods.[1] Scholars interested in the city's Nazi buildings have most often questioned how architectural and urban remnants embody in their forms and associations abstract concepts of public memory. In the process, though, they have at Nuremberg and elsewhere generalized the relationship between architecture and audience, form and politics, ideology and memory. Academic debate has avoided a more sober analysis of the ways that specific monuments function dynamically for particular patrons and differentiated audiences. The question of aesthetic form trumps the analysis of instrumental use.

What happens when we remove our investigation from the symbolic and overheated interpretations of memorial sites to the seemingly more banal politics of use? If scholarship on Berlin embodies the former position, does a focus on more regional locales, such as Nuremberg, tell us something different about the latter? What is the relationship, in this case, between center and periphery in terms of attempts by architects to preserve, historicize, and make use of remnants of the Nazi past? How do these geographies of memory mutually clarify each other? Nuremberg obviously lacks the high-level politics of Berlin or even the Bavarian capital of Munich. Yet Nuremberg does have the largest single relatively intact building site of National Socialist monumental architecture, the Reich Party Rally Grounds (fig. 1). How city officials, architects, and citizens have dealt with the postwar history of the site indicates the variable interests at stake. An analysis of the postwar function of the rally grounds thus helps connect more explicitly the political and social instrumentalization of the Nazi past to the developing conditions of architectural production and reception.

A clear and more materially grounded account of how Nuremberg's Nazi past became useful to various individuals and groups utilizes art historical questions about the built environment as well as established historical scholarship on a differentiated understanding of *Vergangenheitsbewältigung* (coming to terms with the past).[2] In Nuremberg, a public and political debate emerged that was surprisingly different from more famous cases, such as Peter Eisenman's recently completed Holocaust memorial in Berlin. Whereas Eisenman's design and its construction were a flash point of conflict, the postwar history of the rally grounds shows an unexpected degree of local political consensus during the same period. Both the conservative Christian Social Union (CSU) and the liberal Social Democratic Party (SPD) approached the problem of the Nazi monument with pragmatism, particularly through the 1990s, as the city council (Stadtrat) worked to prepare Nuremberg for its role as one of several German host cities for the 2006 World Cup soccer championship. Of course, different politicians and party position papers still emphasized different opinions, interpretations, and policies. What is most striking, however, is the consensus politics of the Nuremberg Stadtrat, especially in contrast to the case of such high-profile centers as Berlin.[3] Ironically, the monumental scale of the site, a fundamental formal characteristic favored by Speer and Hitler, helped subsume the plurality of views within a unified politics of use.

More broadly, a different concept of *Vergangenheitsbewältigung* is at stake in this analysis. The work of Jeffrey Herf, Norbert Frei, and others convincingly shows that we can no longer generalize about the reception

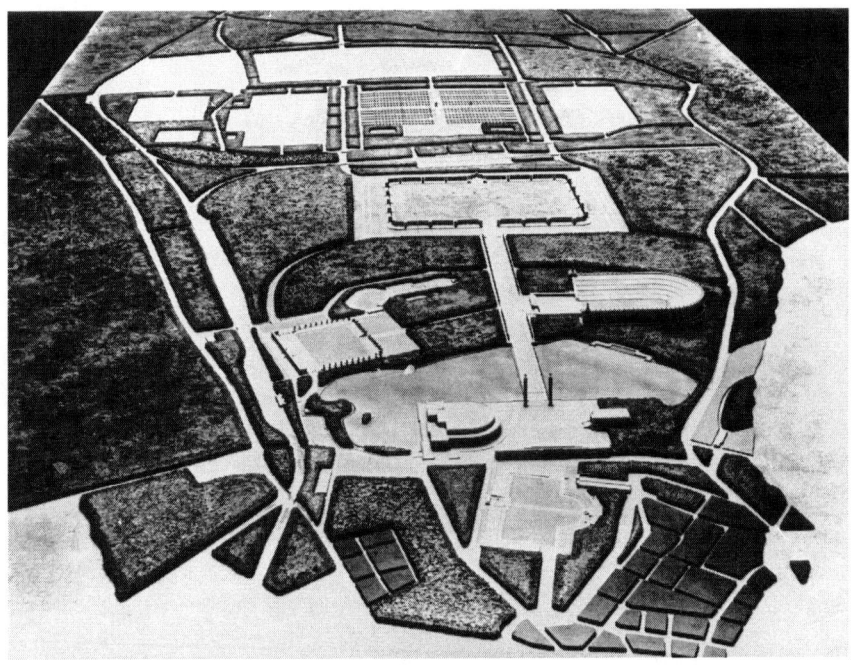

Fig. 1. Model for the Reich Party Rally Grounds, designed by Albert Speer, Nuremberg, 1937. The model shows, from top to bottom, the March Field, the German Stadium (to the right), Zeppelin Field (to the left), Congress Hall, and the Luitpoldhain. The Grosse Strasse runs down the center of the model. (Photo: Gerdy Troost, ed., *Das Bauen im neuen Reich* [Bayreuth, 1938].)

of the Jewish genocide in postwar Germany, as the event and the very term *Holocaust* were understood in various ways at different times. Similarly, we need to analyze critically the function of the concept of *Vergangenheitsbewältigung*. Scholars have used the term to indicate that the postwar relation to the Nazi past has involved a struggle that is consistently present, if based on greater or lesser degrees of repressed memory. Further, intellectual debates take as a given that *Vergangenheitsbewältigung* is a primary fulcrum around which decisions are made about memorialization, preservation, and the remnants of the built environment. But an attempt to argue that the Nazi past produced sustained conflict between specific groups related to that history cannot be maintained. *Vergangenheitsbewältigung* as a descriptive term, like the definition of the Holocaust, depends on geographic and historical factors that give it a periodicity and make it most appropriate for only certain kinds of memorializations or specific eras in the development of commemoration. We might think, for example, of how the initial moment of German defeat produced commemoration driven by the local occupying authorities, such as the Soviet monument in Berlin on Unter den Linden. Such interests became national and ideologically significant sites of struggle only over time, culminating in the quick expansion in the 1980s of memorials and explosive debates relating to specific Nazi locations. As this period of primary and intense struggle over the past fades away, we need to question the appropriateness of the term *Vergangenheitsbewältigung* and, if necessary, reject the historical dynamic it is meant to describe, in favor of a more analytic account.

I am not arguing that local constituencies at Nuremberg have actually succeeded in coming to terms with the past because of consensus politics nor that they now ignore all influence of National Socialist history on their decisions. Rather, social and political groups have rejected *Vergangenheitsbewältigung* as the determining concept in dealing with the past, embracing instead what we might characterize as a laissez-faire historicism that foregrounds other political economic concerns and allows for relative agreement on the preservation of the site. This approach is based on many, often conflicting factors, such as the dying out of the wartime generation, the ability of conservatives to incorporate commemoration of the Nazi past into their politics, the interest of liberal politicians in getting beyond the generational politics of the 1960s, the acceptance of National Socialist architecture as part of the preservation landscape, and the increase in tourist interest in Nazi sites. Not surprisingly, a laissez-faire historicism that allows these perspectives to be incorporated occurs most likely in a location where the ideological and symbolic debates are less loaded than in Berlin—the periphery distinctly leads the center.[4] As a result, an interrogation of the postwar use of the rally grounds at Nuremberg highlights a new regional variability to the political instrumentalization of the Nazi past and a need to confront critically the tendency of cultural studies to generalize terms of analysis.

The Reich Party Rally Grounds from the Wilhelmine Era through the Cold War

The site of the future Reich Party Rally Grounds along the waters of the Dutzendteich had great significance to the people and city of Nuremberg well before the Nazi era. In the early nineteenth century, citizens used the area around the water as the major park of the city, and boating, ice-skating, or promenading kept the location well populated. With the Bavarian Jubilee Exhibition of 1906, the city more formally organized the lands and established the landscaped area of the Luitpoldhain. The exhibition proved to be a huge success, with over 2.5 million visitors celebrating the strength of Nuremberg as the largest industrial city in Bavaria. In 1930, the local government dedicated a war memorial (designed by Fritz Mayer) in the Luitpoldhain to commemorate the World War I dead. Even before Hitler came to power, the function of the site for economic, recreational, and memorializing purposes was firmly established.[5]

As is well known, construction on the site during the Nazi period was dramatic after Hitler chose Nuremberg as the permanent location for the Reich Party Rally Grounds. Between 1934 and 1937, Albert Speer completed the comprehensive plan as well as the design of all of the new buildings with the exception of Ludwig and Franz Ruff's Kongresshalle (Congress Hall). The program followed the basic formal layout and ideological projection favored by Hitler in all of the major state- and party-sponsored projects. In terms of planning, the buildings were unified through the consistency of materials (in this case, stone), a shared monumental scale, symmetry, and a stripped-down modified neoclassicism, all arranged along the central axis of the Grosse Strasse (fig. 2). Ideologically, the buildings combined elements of various classical architectural traditions, which could be used to support both racial claims of the supposed Aryan connection of Germans to ancient Greeks as well as interpretations of Germany as the new Roman Empire. The buildings served as the backdrop for the announcement of key National Socialist policies, such as the Nuremberg Racial Laws in 1935 and the Four-Year Plan in 1936. Combined with Hitler's keen interest in architecture, the development of the rally grounds formed a continuum with the political and ideological goals of the state. As such, local and national administrators privileged its construction well into the war. By 1942, however, the stone collection and work on various buildings on the site predominantly stopped.[6]

In the postwar period, the most prominent building associated with Nuremberg became the courthouse that in 1945 hosted the Nuremberg Tribunals for the major war criminals, an event that would play a key role in inextricably linking the city to international human rights proceedings.[7] But in relation to the monumental architecture of the former rally grounds, the occupying forces of the U.S. Army most strongly influenced

Fig. 2. Zeppelin Field, designed by Albert Speer, Nuremberg, 1936.
(Photo: Werner Rittich, *Architektur und Bauplastik der Gegenwart* [Berlin, 1938].)

the development and use of the area. Beyond blowing up the swastika on top of the Zeppelinfeld (Zeppelin Field), the army changed little of the architectural remnants other than their use. For example, the Märzfeld (March Field) and its eleven completed towers remained but became depots for munitions and fuel for the American military. Soldiers used the field itself (like the Zeppelinfeld) either as a recreational site or for military exercises. That said, the cold war context of the U.S. presence in Nuremberg did not preclude the continuity of multiple interests expressing their desire to use the area. Nuremberg citizens enjoyed the Dutzendteich and park areas as sites for recreation, and the Zeppelinfeld served as a grandstand for concerts and other events. Meanwhile, on the large camping grounds south of the Märzfeld train station (where, during the war, Bavarian Jews had been deported to their deaths), U.S. forces first set up in 1946 an internment camp for captured Waffen-SS members as well as a site to house displaced persons. Beginning in 1948, the city constructed a series of permanent housing estates in this area (called Langwasser) for German refugees from the east and foreign guest workers. Langwasser has continued to serve this function until the present day. By 1967, after many years of delay by the U.S. authorities, the towers of the Märzfeld were blown up, and occupying officials gave the rest of the site over to the city for expansion of the housing settlement.[8] No attempt was made to commemorate or consider the site's historical significance.

What is notable in this period of the postwar *Wirtschaftswunder* (economic miracle) is the total lack of interest in the architecture's historical and ideological significance. While avant-garde artist Alexander Kluge could choose the stands of the Zeppelinfeld as the location for his exploration of fascism in his film *Brutalität in Stein* (1960), city officials and the U.S. Army treated the site as little more than a convenient set of bleachers. Further, the city designated the former foundation of the Deutsches Stadion (German Stadium) as a dumping ground that produced a lake (the Silbersee) of poisoned runoff full of chemicals. The lack of attention necessitated the removal in 1967 of the colonnade atop the Zeppelinfeld due to its imminent structural collapse. The historical significance of the architecture was not as yet socially or politically useful on a local or national level. It was thus with some annoyance that city officials took on the problem of maintaining and restoring key parts of the site (in particular, the remains of the Zeppelinfeld and the Kongresshalle) after the entire rally grounds were classified as a historical monument in the 1973 revision of the Bavarian Denkmalschutzgesetz (Historic Preservation Law).[9] Still, in the same year, a large parcel of land was cut out of the southern quadrant around the area of the Deutsches Stadion with no consideration of its historical significance. The city council turned over the area to the new trade center, a modular structure built for expanding the private development of Nuremberg as an economic hub for conventions and trade shows. The convention center's bland modernist architecture literally and figuratively turned its back on the rest of the area with the exception of the Grosse Strasse, which, due to its vast scale, could be conveniently used for overflow parking.[10] The conservative trade fair's use of steel and glass as a stylistic rejection of Speer's classicism, symmetry, and monumentality would be the first of many architectural gestures attempting to counteract the past.

Thus, by the time the Bavarian state began to recognize the architecture as a significant object of historical interest, the commercial, recreational, and military expediencies had already asserted themselves. With initiatives of the city and the U.S. Army, as well as the return of the land as a leisure ground for the local population, the multiple interests of use limited any monolithic interpretation or preservation of its historical import. This pattern remained firmly entrenched, even after the site became a locus of ideological confrontation in the 1980s as a result of the increasing German interest in commemorating the events leading up to the fortieth anniversary of the end of World War II. Throughout this era (the high point of *Vergangenheitsbewältigung*), Speer and Hitler's preference for monumental scale significantly contributed to the site's ability to absorb an unfocused plurality of uses, even after its designation as a historical monument.

Return of the Repressed? The Reich Party Rally Grounds through Reunification

While the economic interests of the trade center, the open-air events at the Zeppelinfeld, and the general recreational use of the site indicate a variety of interests at stake in the postwar development of the rally grounds, concerns about architectural significance did not begin to influence the land's use in any major way until the 1980s. In this sense, the development of the historical plans for the grounds paralleled other efforts in Germany, particularly the spate of commemorative monuments and countermonuments that increased dramatically after the rise of Helmut Kohl to power in 1982. Kohl and his Christian Democratic Union (CDU) government became quickly embroiled in the ideological debates of commemoration politics because of the multiple plans to mark the fortieth anniversary of World War II. The SPD opposition at the national level excoriated Kohl for his bungled attempts to use various sites for conservative advantage and cold war politics, most famously at the 1985 ceremonies with Reagan at Bitburg cemetery. SPD criticism paralleled the unprecedented organization of independent left-liberal citizen initiatives at the local level that confronted the attempts of the CDU to bracket the Nazi period—such sites as Berlin's Topography of Terror exhibition. Control and debate over the architectural and urban remains of the Nazi past became one of many areas around which the political confrontation between Kohl's conservative agenda and the varied opposition positions crystallized.[11]

These national debates were not lost at the local level, but their politicization was significantly different. In Nuremberg, the SPD had dominated the Stadtrat for over thirty years. As in other Bavarian cities, such as Munich, the entrenched power of the SPD at the municipal level countered the equally strong control of the CSU at the state level. Such a splintering limited the ability of preservationists to garner needed state and local funds for major commemorative interests, as each dominant party wanted the other to pay for specific plans. This situation left the door open for a variety of attempts to use private industry to develop the rally grounds—in particular, the fantastically bungled idea, put forth in 1987, to turn the Kongresshalle into a multipurpose site encompassing a senior center, penthouse condominiums, and a shopping mall.[12] But the political split related to funding also meant that when specific attempts at historicization did succeed in moving forward, the will had to come from independent initiatives outside of public institutions.

The work of independent groups in Berlin and elsewhere and the commemorations of World War II spurred on Nuremberg citizens interested in memorializing the Nazi past. For example, an initial attempt in 1983 by the city's *Kulturreferent* (cultural director) Hermann Glaser to create an exhibition in conjunction with the fiftieth anniversary of Hitler coming to power failed, although it did show that at least some bureaucrats were interested in focusing on the Nazi past. More effectively, in the same year, local historians consolidated a plan for an educational exhibition about the importance of the Nazi rallies and grounds. By 1985, this left-liberal group had successfully lobbied for the use of the unheated mosaic hall within the Zeppelinfeld for its installation of the exhibit *Faszination und Gewalt* (Fascination and Terror). The exhibition featured rough wooden boards covered in text that documented the rally grounds, an aesthetic choice meant to counteract the monumentality and prestigious masonry materials of the site. The pressure of the group as well as the popularity of the exhibition pushed the SPD and the minority party of the CSU in the Stadtrat to agree that the site should be commemorated; but they equally agreed that the National Socialist past was a national heritage and thus had to be funded at the national level. The local SPD-Green coalition received no such support from Kohl's national government.[13]

The political struggle inherent in the funding situation changed dramatically in the 1990s. At the national level (above all, in Berlin), Kohl reversed his cold war resistance to expanding commemoration sites by proposing a centralized location for mourning the victims of fascism, Communism, and war at Schinkel's Neue Wache and embracing plans for Eisenman's memorial. As both the victim and perpetrator generations were fading away, Kohl could promote these abstract sites as generally positive signs that his government took the past seriously but also as a way of marking the past as distinct from postreunification institutions. The architectural sites were becoming increasingly ideologically useful as the continuity between wartime and postwar generations seemed more and more ruptured.[14]

While Nuremberg was naturally affected by these broader trends, the shift in national policy paralleled an institutional change that played out very differently at the regional level, particularly around the political consensus of the parties in the Stadtrat. In 1994, the city appointed Franz Sonnenberger to head all of the local museums and set him the task of creating a unified plan for the nine relatively disparate collections. By this time, the exhibition Fascination and Terror had also become the responsibility of the city museums, and Sonnenberger proposed the creation of a more permanent facility on the site for this installation. He pushed for a contemporary building that would recall the lighthouse removed by the Nazi government in 1933, a form that aesthetically and conceptually was meant to break with the monumental neoclassicism of Speer's architecture as well as to signal, literally, the "enlightenment" of the postwar years. His idea would become the basis for the creation of the Documentation Center of the Reich Party Rally Grounds (Dokumentationszentrum Reichsparteitagsgelände).[15]

But to achieve such plans, Sonnenberger still faced the challenge of funding, which was complicated by the CDU/CSU resistance to the local SPD government. Such resistance could only be overcome after the surprising CSU victory in the communal vote of 1996, displacing the forty-year SPD dominance of the Rathaus. Under the new mayor, Ludwig Scholz, Nuremberg achieved an almost unique position in commemorating the Nazi past: political and local consensus. Relatively quickly, leaders of the two dominant political parties agreed to Sonnenberger's suggestions and began to support the idea of a permanent exhibition pavilion. Certainly Scholz, like other conservative regional politicians, always downplayed the question of any real local postwar connection to the Nazi past by emphasizing that the history of the site was not specific to Nuremberg but remained a national heritage. Furthermore, he denied that the new building was part of a plan to take advantage of the increased popularity of tourists fascinated by fascism—that is, of having a conservative economic motive for promoting a new museum. Nevertheless, despite Scholz aligning himself with obvious CSU positions, the various parties involved (including the independent citizens groups) came together to approve the new Dokumentationszentrum.[16] This decision would be the first serious attempt by city politicians to prioritize the history of the Nazi past above other interests in the site. Notably, however, politicians did not achieve consensus on how to historicize the rally grounds as a whole, only on how to use one part of the site for the (now national) memorialization agenda. The use of the site pedagogically and historically would be incorporated into the dominant tendency of earlier local governments to promote pragmatic solutions rather than any systematic attempt to grapple with the National Socialist heritage.

In 1998, an architectural competition was held for the Dokumentationszentrum. The Austrian Günther Domenig won with a plan for a museum that slashed through one corner of the Kongresshalle. His design, while rejecting Sonnenberger's lighthouse proposal, remained true to the original suggestion by emphasizing the disparity between the fragmented steel and glass museum and Ruff's monumental stone Kongresshalle. Reporters and politicians widely commented on the new structure's asymmetrical cut into the side of the Kongresshalle as a symbolic rejection of the Nazi past by a democratic present (fig. 3). In this sense, the Dokumentationszentrum continued the pattern established by the self-reflective Fascination and Terror exhibition and the modernism of the convention center. Here, too, officials proclaimed that the aesthetic choices antithetical to the monumental masonry and axial plans at the site were transparent to historical critique. The federal government initially dismissed the plans (citing the need to channel any cultural funds to the new states in the East), but by 1999, it had agreed to help fund the project.[17]

The city building administration under Walter Anderle used the consensus surrounding the development of the Dokumentationszentrum as a reason to promote the first postwar comprehensive plan to integrate the functional and historical uses of the rally grounds site as a whole. The stated impetus for the plan was that the multiplication of uses had resulted in a cacophony of architectural forms and alterations to the landscape that demanded a unified planning approach as well as a clearer presentation of historical information in line with the Dokumentationszentrum. For example, the trade fair facility continued to lobby for more use of the land regardless of its historical import, while local citizens expanded the recreational activities with a variety of new functions. Anderle emphasized that such random development of uses could not be sustained. The city needed to have a comprehensive strategy that respected the various interests (economic, social, historical) but somehow made sense of the monumental scale and history of the site. While ultimately limited in architectural

Fig. 3. Documentation Center of the Reich Party Rally Grounds, designed by Günther Domenig, Nuremberg, begun in 1998. (Photo: Author.)

scope, his plan, like that of the Dokumentationszentrum, found consensus in the fragile coalition of the CSU Rathaus, and the Stadtrat approved an international architectural competition of ideas in May 2000.[18]

The competition took place in 2001. The task of the participants was a difficult one, as it involved integrating the varied uses of the site without significantly changing the architectural remnants under historical protection. Preservation, however, was hardly the number one goal in all aspects of the program, as the convention center's plans to expand its parking facilities demonstrated; this new structure (approved before the competition) was on the site of Speer's Deutsches Stadion and required the removal of the one historically significant remnant of that building, the cornerstone laid by Hitler in 1937. While consensus had been achieved around the need for a comprehensive plan, the variety of interests at stake led to multiple contradictions and limitations for the participating architects. In particular, the competition revealed—to a much greater degree than the Dokumentationszentrum—the emphasis on the site's instrumental use for goals other than historical or historicist ones.[19] Given the massive scale of the site, such multiplying uses and interests could push for control over bits and pieces of the grounds without seeming to damage the unity of the whole. In the process, however, the ability to achieve consensus between all of the diverse stakeholders became increasingly remote.

The results of the competition confirmed that any unified historical or architectural plan would be sacrificed to the multiple interests at stake. More specifically, the jury members' competing ideas about how to subsume National Socialist history within the demands of variable recreational and economic uses strongly influenced the results. The jury—made up half of architects, planners, and historians; half of city representatives—did not reach a consensus for a first prize. Rather, it split between those who favored doing as little as possible to change the grounds or mark their historical significance and those who wanted a more aggressive architectural solution. As a result, it awarded two second-prize winners. The proposal of Erik Meinertz and Harms Wulf (fig. 4) won one of these prizes because of its minimal changes to the site. Despite the fact that this plan seemed to emphasize Speer's original intention by adding a structure across from the Kongresshalle and another in front of the trade fair buildings that exaggerated the symmetry and hence the monumentality of the grounds, it became a focal point for both those disgusted with any acknowledgment of the architectural merit of the site and those who wanted its historical resonance to fade into the background. In addition, preservationists argued that it did the least damage to the historical fabric. Those jury members that favored a dramatic architectural solution awarded the other second prize to the plans of Martina Erbs and Martin Stadtler (fig. 5), who proposed a series of incisions and ruptures that cut across and partially fractured the unity of the whole (Daniel Libeskind's Jewish Museum design seems influential in this regard, as was Domenig's Dokumentationszentrum, under construction at the time). The intersecting axes visually linked the important components of Speer's plan but also emphasized the historical rupture of fascism. Erbs and Stadtler planned for specific points that disrupted the unity of the whole, particularly evident in the interruption, for example, of the Grosse Strasse as that axis crosses the Dutzendteich. This solution extended and exaggerated the more public and apparently critical aesthetic engagements with the land that had produced such exhibition spaces as Fascination and Terror.

Yet, while the aesthetic rejection of Speer's monumentality may have been fine for one corner of the Kongresshalle for city representatives of many political stripes, the nonarchitectural representatives on the jury

Fig. 4. Entry by Erik Meinertz (architect) and Harms Wulf (landscape architect) for the Competition of Ideas for the Former Reich Party Rally Grounds, Nuremberg, 2001. (Photo: Author. Reproduced with permission of Harms Wulf.)

found the strategy too disruptive of the many interests at stake, both historical and pragmatic. Thus, despite the original political consensus around the need for a comprehensive plan, the diverse jury could not get beyond the contradictions inherent in the call for participants that had been approved by the fragile CSU coalition in the city council. They could not agree on a formal or historical solution, only on a fragmentary response that allowed for the most flexible of pragmatic uses.[20] As a counterweight to such lack of consensus, the Dokumentationszentrum was opened to great fanfare on November 4, 2001, with an exhibition that aimed for a popular audience and, as Sonnenberger has stated, specifically related to the conceptual and museological strategies of the U.S. Holocaust Memorial Museum.[21]

The competition's results, which implicitly sacrificed any attempt to create a coherent historical experience in favor of pragmatic pluralism,

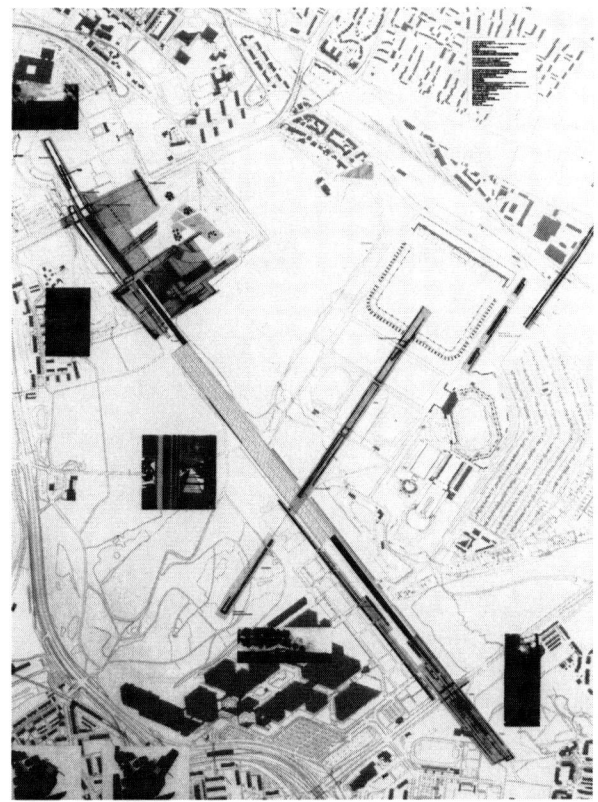

Fig. 5. Entry by Martina Erbs and Martin Stadtler for the Competition of Ideas for the Former Reich Party Rally Grounds, Nuremberg, 2001. (Photo: Author. Reproduced with permission of Martina Erbs.)

were ironically a more accurate expression of the reigning political and social (if not aesthetic) consensus. This was explicitly articulated after the communal vote of 2002, when the SPD won back the mayor's office and the city council, with Ulrich Maly as mayor. In a February 2003 letter directed to a wide range of local constituents, Maly rejected the original intention of the competition, with its attempt to achieve a total architectural solution for the site. Indeed, by this point, the competition had become, in administrative memos, a prominent symbol of what to avoid. Instead, his cultural department came up with a position paper that proposed a series of discussions, to be held over time, that allowed the functional use of the land to develop organically as befits a "democratic pluralistic" society. In essence, the new plan was to have no plan, or at least no fixed plan, and Maly explicitly rejected a single architectural solution to the site. While the intent was to provide flexibility and an ongoing debate with the historical significance of the area, in practice, this plan avoided any serious critical reckoning with the grounds beyond the central facility of the Dokumentationszentrum. As a result, however, it also avoided the local contradictions that surfaced when architectural and historical solutions faced off against the narrow protection of variable uses that had doomed the 2001 competition. The one architectural gesture that Maly's new plan made to deal with this past was the proposed development of some kind of small-scale system of information panels. Scattered around the grounds, these panels expanded the historical message beyond the Dokumentationszentrum in time for the 2006 soccer championships, for which the city hosted qualifying matches.[22]

If Nuremberg were Berlin or even Munich, one would perhaps have expected that, with a shift from CSU to SPD as well as the stakes of the World Cup, more explicit ideological allegiances would have been formed as the various perspectives clashed over the proper way to emphasize the city's historical Nazi burden. Intensification of struggle is a key component of *Vergangenheitsbewältitung,* after all. But such was not the case. Rather, after some initial debates in the 1980s, when emphasizing the National Socialist past became a national project, Nuremberg entered a phase of political consensus, in which each side could find what it needed in the site. For the left-liberal independent initiatives, that meant an institutionalization of the grassroots effort to confront the Nazi past through tours and through the historical displays in the Dokumentationszentrum. For the liberal SPD, that meant emphasizing the pluralistic uses of the site, particularly as this favored its own position on guest workers, youth, and other groups within its policy interests who used the area recreationally. For the CSU, the site was not going to be overly documented, the economic engine of the convention center was to be undisturbed, and the state and federal government were to acknowledge through funding that, after all, the need was not to particularize a local history but, rather, to generalize a national history. Given these conditions, it is no wonder that the 2001 competition was the exception that proved the rule. Its failure to propose a comprehensive solution indicated the necessity of a consensus solution that allowed for multiple responses that could colonize and make use of bits and pieces of the massive Nazi site to match a larger matrix of competing interests and concerns.

The Stadtrat unanimously approved Maly's position on May 19, 2004. This vote incorporated multiple interests because the historical significance of the site and its scale—the latter, a distinctive contribution of Speer's original plan—could be easily subsumed into a variety of uses. Hence, each stakeholder could rest assured that his or her vision of the site would be actualized to some degree.²³

This overview of the contemporary use of the Nuremberg Reich Party Rally Grounds leads to several conclusions. First and foremost is the point that, although the development of the site began to follow the national trends of ideological conflict over the past between the Left and the Right in the 1980s, the debates about its use achieved an exceptional state of consensus in the late 1990s, at least in terms of the general goals for the land. Such consensus rested on a complicated series of factors involving the regional and national interests and local coalition politics. But the consensus itself managed to avoid, surprisingly, the particularly contentious debates in Berlin that centered on the questions of whether the Nazi past should be commemorated at a particular site and who should control that ritualization of historical memory. Clearly, a variety of interests was and still is at stake in how the architecture and land are used. Still, the smaller scale of regional politics as well as the centralized authority of the city administration in the development process (and the key role of consensus builders, such as museum director Sonnenberger) in many ways forced the dominant parties to push through a series of initiatives that would not be possible in the higher stakes national centers of Berlin or Munich.

While the city's latest proposal makes clear that the local consensus of the last decade is as subject to change as any other, it nevertheless indicates that the supposed burden of the past is much more variably handled than historians of architecture have previously assumed. In this sense, the struggles and debates characterized by *Vergangenheitsbewältigung* may suffice to describe the situation of Nuremberg a few decades ago but are insufficient to account for the last decade of policy concerning the rally grounds. The ideologically driven debates about the importance of the Nazi past have been subsumed by a functional pragmatism where specific interests dominate symbolic considerations, a trend that is increasingly visible elsewhere. At the rally grounds, the variable postwar political uses of Nazi architecture could not be more concretely demonstrated. Through consensus and pragmatic interests, local constituencies have relegated questions of symbolic import and the ideological signification of the National Socialist past to a secondary concern best characterized as laissez-faire historicism. Hitler's aesthetic interest in monumentally scaled sites allows this attitude to play itself out particularly well in Nuremberg.

The variable interests that came together at Nuremberg challenge the fundamental abstraction of current debates about architecture and memory in much of the historical and art historical literature on Berlin and the built environment. Far from a generalized notion of mourning and melancholia in which architectural patrons put forward solutions that result in some kind of vague collective reception, the instrumentalization of former sites of perpetrators and victims requires a closer look at the agency of individuals and institutions that lead to results that are in turn understood and reinstrumentalized by local constituencies. Such instrumentalization is, of course, much more often about contemporary conditions than about any coherent "politics of memory." The complexity and contradictions of these conditions are critical factors for explaining the functional significance of the built environment. Revisiting the Reich Party Rally Grounds at Nuremberg allows for a more sober and less hyperbolic understanding of the political function of architecture and clarifies the continued resonance and utilization of National Socialist cultural production in postwar German cities.

NOTES

Thanks to Robert Buerglener and Barbara McCloskey for their critical comments on this essay. Special thanks are due to the excellent editorial advice of Gavriel Rosenfeld.

1. Not surprisingly, National Socialist propagandists themselves understood the value of connecting Dürer to their movement. See Anonymous, "Die Albrecht Dürer-Feier," *Völkischer Beobachter,* April 12, 1928, 1–2.

2. Jeffrey Herf, *Divided Memory: The Nazi Past in the Two Germanys* (Cambridge, 1997). For the built environment, see Jeffry Diefendorf, *In the Wake of War: The Reconstruction of German Cities after World War II* (Oxford, 1993).

3. Peter Reichel, *Politik mit der Erinnerung* (Munich, 1995), 209–17.

4. Sociologist Edward Shils first articulated the center/periphery theory in 1961, although it became more influential once taken up by Immanuel Wallerstein in his discussions of colonization. While scholars used its earlier form to argue that the core always influences outlying areas, more recent historians have used the concept to describe the interaction between centers of power and contingent peripheral areas. See Amy Turner Bushnell and Jack P. Greene, "Peripheries, Centers, and the Construction of Early Modern American Empires: An Introduction," in *Negotiated Empires: Centers and Peripheries in the Americas, 1500–1820,* ed. Christine Daniels and Michael V. Kennedy (New York, 2002), 1–14.

5. Eckart Dietzfelbinger and Gerhard Liedtke, *Nürnberg—Ort der Massen* (Berlin, 2004), 11–22.

6. Paul B. Jaskot, *The Architecture of Oppression* (London, 2000), 47–79; Alex Scobie, *Hitler's State Architecture* (University Park, PA: 1990), 69–92. See also the

indispensable overview in Siegfried Zelnhefer, *Die Reichsparteitage der NSDAP* (Nuremberg, 1991). It should be noted that much of the German scholarship on the site is regionally produced.

7. For a sweeping text that includes a strong chapter on the postwar cultural means by which Nuremberg was represented to the world, see Stephen Brockmann, *Nuremberg: The Imaginary Capital* (Rochester, 2006).

8. Geschichte für Alle, eds., *Langwasser: Heimisch werden in Nürnbergs jüngsten Stadtteil* (Nuremberg, 2001), 6–20; Eckart Dietzfelbinger, *Fascination and Terror: The Nazi Party Rally Grounds in Nuremberg* (Nuremberg, 1996), 49–52; Dietzfelbinger and Liedtke, *Nürnberg,* 93–112.

9. Dietzfelbinger, *Fascination and Terror,* 49–50.

10. Stadt Nürnberg, *Auslobungstext: Städtebaulicher Ideenwettbewerb für das ehemaligge Reichsparteitagsgelände* (Nuremberg, 2001), 30. See also documents for the planning of the convention center in Archivbestand Baureferat, C 75, no. 831 (1968–70), Stadtarchiv Nürnberg.

11. Geoffrey H. Hartman, ed., *Bitburg in Moral and Political Perspective* (Bloomington, 1986); Brian Ladd, *The Ghosts of Berlin: Confronting German History in the Urban Landscape* (Chicago, 1997), 217–35.

12. Dietzfelbinger and Liedtke, *Nürnberg,* 112–13; cf. Peter Reichel, *Politik mit der Erinnerung,* 35–42.

13. Dietzfelbinger and Liedtke, *Nürnberg,* 120–23; Volker Probst, "Was bleibt vom Gedenken?" *Plärrer* 7 (July 1995): n.p.; Peter Schmitt, "Hitlers Aufmarschplatz als Dokumentationszentrum," *Süddeutsche Zeitung,* February 17, 1998, n.p. All newspaper citations are taken from the "Presseberichte, Dokumentationszentrum Reichsparteitagsgelände" (Collection of Museen der Stadt Nürnberg) unless otherwise noted. My thanks to Franz Sonnenberger for providing me with this collection.

14. See the numerous publications on this subject by Peter Reichel.

15. Annekathrin Fries, "Aus der Geschichte lernen," *Nürnberg Heute,* December 1996, n.p.

16. Raimond Kirch, "Wir haben nur etwas die Phantasien beflügelt," *Nürnberger Zeitung,* July 16, 1997, 3.

17. Anonymous, "Bund zahlt für Doku-Zentrum," *Abendzeitung,* December 17, 1999, n.p. See also the overview of the competition in Dietzfelbinger and Liedtke, *Nürnberg,* 123–28. For architecture as a countermonument to Nazi monumental building, see, for example, Deborah Ascher Barnstone, *The Transparent State: Architecture and Politics in Postwar Germany* (London, 2005).

18. Stadt Nürnberg, *Dokumentation: Städtebaulicher Ideenwettbewerb für das ehemalige Reichsparteitagsgelände* (Nuremberg, 2001), 4; Siegfried Zelnhefer, "Ludwig Scholz nimmt Bund und Land in die Pflicht," *Nürnberger Nachrichten,* July 16, 1997, 13.

19. Stadt Nürnberg, *Auslobungstext,* 30–31; Protokoll des Kolloquiums zum Wettbewerb ehemaliges Reichsparteitagsgelände am 19.03.2001 (Ingo Schlick, Baureferat, Stadt Nürnberg [author's collection]). In the interest of full disclosure, it should be noted that I participated in this process as a nonvoting historical advisor to the jury.

20. Stadt Nürnberg, *Dokumentation*, 6–9; Siegfried Zelnhefer, "Ideen für NS-Areal," *Nürnberger Nachrichten*, August 2, 2001, 1, 11.

21. André Fischer, "Finanzierung muß schnell geklärt werden," *Nürnberger Zeitung*, June 14–15, 1997, n.p.; Verlag Hans Müller, *Nürnberger Facetten* (Nuremberg, 2001), 256–59. Sharon Macdonald is currently completing a sociological analysis of postwar Nuremberg, including how the rally grounds are understood by local constituents.

22. Stadt Nürnberg, "Ein Diskussionsbeitrag über den Umgang mit dem ehemaligen Reichsparteitagsgelände in Nürnberg," February 2003 (author's collection). A digital version can also be found at http://www.kubiss.de/kulturreferat/reichsparteitagsgelaende/downloads/omb-rpg.pdf (accessed April 2006).

23. "Beschluss des Stadtrates vom 19.05.2004: Nutzung des ehemaligen Reichsparteitagsgeländes," http://www.kubiss.de/kulturreferat/reichsparteitagsgelaende/downloads/Beschluss.pdf (accessed April 2006).

Memory and the Museum
Munich's Struggle to Create a Documentation Center for the History of National Socialism
Gavriel D. Rosenfeld

Among all German cities, Munich has arguably had the most difficulty during the postwar period in coming to terms with the legacy of the Third Reich. From the moment World War II ended in 1945, the citizens of the former Nazi "capital of the movement" (*Hauptstadt der Bewegung*) had to live down the ignominious fact that their city was the birthplace of the political party that had brought death and destruction to Europe on an unprecedented scale. It is no wonder, then, that in attempting to reconstruct their war-devastated city in the years after 1945, the people of Munich largely chose to evade its shameful historical legacy. As I argued in my book *Munich and Memory: Architecture, Monuments, and the Legacy of the Third Reich,* the conservative postwar restoration of the city's damaged historic architecture, the embrace of traditional (rather than modern) architecture for new postwar construction projects, the normalized reuse of Nazi buildings, and the hesitant erection of monuments documenting Nazi crimes all attested to a desire to play down, if not deny, local responsibility for the Third Reich.[1]

This evasive tendency, to be sure, has not stood unopposed during the postwar period. In the decades since 1945, a countervailing inclination to confront the past has slowly gained support among citizens committed to directing public attention to the city's historic links to National Socialism. Especially since the late 1980s, the impulse to acknowledge the city's Nazi past has steadily gained strength in direct proportion to the enduring local effort to marginalize it. This growing tendency to face the Nazi legacy head-on suggests that Munich has begun to turn away from its prior postwar tradition of evasion.

Yet even as many people in Munich have expressed a growing desire to confront the past, others continue to exhibit serious difficulties in doing so. This difficulty is best illustrated by the long controversy over the creation of a Documentation Center for the History of National Socialism (NS-Dokumentationszentrum). In the middle of 2002, after many years of discussion, Munich municipal officials, together with Bavarian state authorities, announced a historic agreement to create a Documentation Center in the vicinity of one of Munich's most famous squares, the Königsplatz. By January 2003, however, the project had collapsed amid bitter recriminations that led the local media to describe the city as the "laughingstock of Germany's memorial landscape."[2] Further controversies since then have added to the museum project's woes—so much so that it is doubtful whether it will be completed by the end of the decade.

What accounts for the ongoing difficulties in establishing a Documentation Center for the History of National Socialism in Munich? What does the failure to create such an institution reveal about the city's evolving relationship to its Nazi past? What are its implications for the course of urban *Vergangenheitsbewältigung* within Germany at large? This essay attempts to answer these and other questions by chronicling the saga of the twenty-year struggle in Munich to build a museum for memory.

The origins of the documentation center project reflect the dialectical relationship between forgetting and remembrance that has defined broader attitudes toward the Nazi past in postwar Munich. The proposal to create a documentation center emerged in the late 1980s as part of a reaction against increasing efforts to expunge from the local cityscape prominent buildings built by or associated with the Nazi regime. Important milestones in this larger destructive trend were the demolition of the city's historic beer hall and infamous Nazi Party rally site, the Bürgerbräukeller, in 1979; the vocal calls a decade later to demolish the notorious Nazi art museum, the Haus der Deutschen Kunst (designed by Paul Ludwig Troost, 1933–37); the partial demolition in 1990 of the Kongressaal of the Deutsches Museum (designed by German Bestelmeyer, 1933–35); and the 1994 partial demolition of the Riem airport complex (designed by Ernst Sagebiel, 1937–39).[3]

This trend manifested itself most dramatically, however, at the Königsplatz in 1987–88. Located just to the northwest of Munich's Altstadt, the Königsplatz was created as a broad neoclassical forum in the early nineteenth century by King Ludwig I, who commissioned the construction of three prominent edifices that, taken together, comprised one of the city's grandest squares (fig. 1).[4] After the Nazis' rise to power in

Fig. 1. The Königsplatz before the war, Munich, ca. 1925. At lower right is the Propyläen. Immediately above it is the Kunstausstellungsgebäude. To its left is the Glyptothek. At the upper left is the Frauenkirche. (Photo: Stadtarchiv

1933, Hitler appropriated the Königsplatz and transformed it to suit his own ideological purposes. In 1935, he replaced the square's lush green lawn with twenty-five thousand square meters of granite slabs (soon dubbed the Plattensee, "flagstone sea") in order to create a spot for mass assemblies. Two years later, in 1937, Hitler commissioned the erection of two new monumental party buildings on the square: the Führerbau and the Verwaltungsbau der NSDAP. That same year, finally, he arranged for the construction of the Ehrentempel, two central "temples of honor" to house the sixteen "martyrs" of the failed Beer Hall Putsch of 1923 (fig. 2). With the original party headquarters, the Brown House, directly next door (fig. 3) and with some sixty-eight other Nazi party buildings in the vicinity, the Königsplatz was the most Nazified spot in Munich's urban landscape.[5]

After 1945, local officials did their best to erase the Third Reich's presence from the Königsplatz. After the Ehrentempel were demolished in

Fig. 2. The Königsplatz during the Third Reich, Munich, ca. 1937. The square was paved over with granite slabs. The two monumental buildings near the top are the Führerbau, at left, and the Verwaltungsbau der NSDAP, at right. Between these two buildings are the Ehrentempel. Above them at the left is the Brown House. At the top is the circular Karolinenplatz. (Photo: Stadtarchiv München.)

1947, the remaining six-foot-high foundations were planted with bushes and shrubs and gradually disappeared from public view. The Führerbau and the Verwaltungsbau der NSDAP, meanwhile, were given new postwar functions and slowly became accepted as normalized buildings in the local cityscape.[6] The marching grounds of the Plattensee, by contrast, experienced a different fate. Having become degraded into a parking lot by the 1960s, the grounds gradually turned into an eyesore that the Bavarian state was eager to be rid of. As a result, plans for what came to be known as the "regreening" of the Königsplatz gathered momentum in the early 1980s, and in 1988, city and state officials finally completed the controversial plan, removing the Nazi Plattensee and restoring the square's original grassy appearance. With this event, an important portion of the Königsplatz's Nazi past was physically removed from view and essentially unmade. At the same time, in 1987, Bavarian state officials announced additional plans to demolish the remaining foundations of the Ehrentempel and replace them with a pair of new art museums. Against the back-

Fig. 3. The Brown House before the war, Munich, 1932. (Photo: Stadtarchiv München.)

drop of the demolition of the Bürgerbräukeller and the Plattensee, this new proposal seemed to confirm the accelerating elimination of the Nazi past from Munich's built environment.

The looming disappearance of the city's Nazi architectural heritage, however, soon helped to spark an unprecedented local effort to preserve and document it. Among the many initiatives that emerged at the time, the most notable was Free Democratic Party (FDP) city councilman Hildebrecht Braun's 1987 proposal for a Haus der Zeitgeschichte (House of Contemporary History) at the empty site of Hitler's Brown House just off the Königsplatz (fig. 4). Arguing that "Munich has always closed its eyes before the memory of the terror that emanated from [the]...buildings [on the Königsplatz]," Braun insisted that a museum erected on the historically sensitive site would help the Munich citizenry "own up to ... [its] history and abandon . . . [the] belief . . . that remembering the horrors of Nazism should take place in [the] neighboring town [of Dachau]."[7] One year later, in 1988, the city council drafted a bill based on Braun's initiative—the first expression of local city officials' support for what would later be called a Documentation Center for the History of National Social-

Fig. 4. Site of the former Brown House (and of the future NS-Dokumentationszentrum), Munich, current condition. To the left is the former Führerbau, which currently houses the Hochschule für Musik. (Photo: Birgit Woldt.)

ism. Bavarian state authorities, however, quickly declared their unwillingness to consider the plan and instead proceeded to hold its planned architectural competition for the pair of envisioned art museums at the site.[8] The ensuing competition brought in a large number of submissions. But, in a notable twist, the state's effort to use the competition to expunge the vestiges of the Nazi period from the site ended up backfiring. Many of the architectural designs drew explicit attention to the Königsplatz's unsavory history (e.g., by intentionally preserving the twin Ehrentempel foundations) and, in the process of doing so, undermined the state's unstated goal of eliminating the past from view. As criticism of the project began to intensify among local intellectuals and journalists, the state quietly dropped the project in 1991.[9]

The idea of building a museum at the Königsplatz dedicated to exploring the history of the Third Reich in Munich did not die as easily. Public interest in the Königsplatz's Nazi past grew dramatically after the early 1990s. One important factor behind this trend was the general surge in attention toward the Third Reich expressed in the countless commemorative ceremonies held throughout Germany in the years leading up to the fiftieth anniversary of the end of World War II. At this same time, interest in Munich's own Nazi past was stimulated by two exhibitions at the Stadtmuseum (city museum) in 1993-94: München—Hauptstadt der Bewegung, which focused on the city's links to the Nazi movement, and Bauen im Nationalsozialismus: Bayern, 1933-1945, about the history of Nazi architecture in Bavaria.[10] Finally, Berlin's success in developing the Topography of Terror exhibition at the site of the former Gestapo headquarters on the former Prinz-Albrecht-Strasse established a precedent that many activists in Munich believed could be duplicated at the Königsplatz.[11] Against the backdrop of these trends, the Königsplatz increasingly became the site of active commemorative efforts. In 1993-94, a series of provocative (albeit temporary) art installations set up on the site of the twin Ehrentempel foundations explicitly drew attention to the square's unseemly history. This trend intensified in 1995 with the organization of a major exhibition—Bürokratie und Kult, sponsored by the Technical University of Munich—that meticulously examined the Königsplatz's fate during the Nazi years. Finally, public attention to the site's past peaked later in 1995, when two local architecture students won city permission to erect a provisional plaque next to the eastern Ehrentempel foundation, explaining the structure's historical origins.[12]

For all of the progress registered by these installations, exhibitions, and memorials, however, their temporary nature meant that the city still lacked a permanent, institutionally based site for confronting its Nazi past. As a result, local political organizations began to take a more active role after the middle of the 1990s in pursuing the museum project at the Königsplatz. One of the project's most important supporters was the district committee of the Maxvorstadt neighborhood (Bezirksausschuss-Maxvorstadt), where the Königsplatz was actually located. Under the leadership of Klaus Bäumler, an activist politician devoted to unearthing the Nazi past of the Maxvorstadt, the district committee submitted a bill to the city council in mid-September 1996 calling for a renewed effort to create a documentation center in the vicinity of the Königsplatz along the lines of the highly successful Topography of Terror exhibition in Berlin.[13] For the next six years, however, no action was taken on the bill. Although the Munich city council continued to express its support for the project, Bavarian state authorities remained noncommittal, citing other construction plans in the vicinity as the putative reason for their inability to grant a go-ahead.[14] Eventually, though, intensifying lobbying by newly formed citizens' organizations, such as the Initiativkreis für ein NS-Dokumentationszentrum, and ongoing pressure from local political parties, such as the SPD and the Greens, eventually helped convince Bavarian state authorities to change their position.[15] Finally, on March 23, 2002, state authorities in the Bavarian Landtag approved a 2001 bill, sponsored by the SPD Landtag representative Hildegard Kronawitter, to "devise a scientifically grounded concept for the comprehensive representation of the National Socialist past of the capital city of Munich, especially its role as the 'capital of the movement' and as a site of resistance."[16] With this declaration of support (echoed several months later by a similar bill passed by the Munich city council), Bavarian officials had finally come around to the position long supported by Munich city authorities.

What explains the Bavarian state's decision to abandon its longstanding resistance to the creation of a Documentation Center for the History of National Socialism? It is difficult to answer this question given the fact that the state's opposition to the museum project was typically expressed in bureaucratic or logistical terms rather than historical or ideological ones. But one of the more important factors that likely contributed to the Bavarian government's new attitude was the growing sense that Munich had fallen behind other German cities in the task of publicly commemorating the Nazi era. Munich had been particularly outpaced by its longtime rival Berlin, which, around the turn of the millennium, had begun to earn considerable international attention and praise for pursuing high-profile commemorative projects, such as the Topography of Terror exhibition, the Jewish Museum, and the Memorial to the Murdered Jews of Europe. Munich had also been surpassed by other, more provincial cities in its own home state of Bavaria. In 1999, the Dokumentation Obersalzberg opened at Hitler's former alpine retreat in Berchtesgaden. Two years later, in 2001, the even more high-profile and architecturally ambitious Dokumentationszentrum Reichsparteitagsgelände opened in Nuremberg at the site of the infamous Reich Party Rally Grounds. The creation of both of these museums reflected a new commitment to problematizing, rather than normalizing, the surviving architectural heritage of the Third Reich in Bavaria and expressed a larger readiness within Germany in the 1990s to confront the actions of the perpetrators (as opposed to only the victims) of the Nazi regime. At the same time, of course, in abandoning the previous strategy of normalized silence at these sites, the cities of Berchtesgaden and Nuremberg raised the bar for confronting the

Nazi past in Bavaria and exposed Munich's general postwar approach as wanting.

The belief that Munich's response to its past was inadequate found increasing expression within the local, national, and even international media at this time. Repeated articles in Munich's main daily newspaper, the *Süddeutsche Zeitung,* drummed home the point made in late 2001 by Technical University architectural historian Winfried Nerdinger that Munich was "the capital of repression" and that "neither [its] citizens . . . nor tourists learn anything in the city's public space about Munich's role in the Nazi era."[17] Media coverage of several symposia on the future prospects of a documentation center, sponsored by local citizens' groups, further bolstered the growing conviction that Munich had serious "difficulties with remembrance."[18] Outside of Germany, the Swiss newspaper the *Neue Zürcher Zeitung* ran a large story on "Munich's trouble with the Nazi era," concluding, "the Bavarian capital is still quite uncomfortable with the brown legacy."[19]

Given this stream of negative publicity, it is probable that the decision of Bavarian authorities to finally approve plans for a documentation center in 2002 was intended to deflect criticism from the state's capital and restore its reputation. At a time in which Germans nationwide were starting to accept the history of the Third Reich as a key component of contemporary German identity, bringing Munich into sync with larger national trends was an indispensable part of the state government's broader public relations effort.[20] State officials, to be sure, made no explicit statements to this effect, but they could not have been unaware of the insistent comments of local political organizations, such as the Maxvorstadt district committee, which, in a 2000 bill, explicitly cited "the great resonance" achieved by the Berchtesgaden and Nuremberg documentation centers as proof that the time had finally come for the Bavarian state to abandon its "resistant stance toward pursuing the work of remembrance [*Erinnerungsarbeit*]" at the Königsplatz.[21]

It was not easy, of course, for the state to abandon its resistant stance, since it entailed abandoning the division of labor that had long existed in Bavaria for commemorating the Nazi era. For decades, state authorities had allowed Munich to avoid publicly documenting the Nazi past and had instead farmed the task out to the provinces—in the 1960s to Dachau, by the late 1990s to Berchtesgaden and Nuremberg. This division of labor had been part of a larger postwar effort to rehabilitate Munich's image (and no doubt stoke tourism) by promoting the city as a modern bastion of cosmopolitanism—the "metropolis with a heart" (*Weltstadt mit Herz*), as it was termed in the 1960s, or the "Olympic city" (*Olympiastadt*), as it was called for the 1972 summer Olympic games.[22] By the turn of the millennium, however, the shortcomings of this policy of promoting the city by ignoring its Nazi past had become glaringly obvious, and the increasingly unfavorable comparisons between Munich and its Bavarian neighbors were undoubtedly critical in leading Bavarian officials to abandon it. Whatever it was that ultimately led the Bavarian government to shift its stance, by the summer of 2002, there was much reason for optimism among the many supporters of a Documentation Center for the History of National Socialism in Munich. When city and state officials announced that a major public symposium would be held later in the year to discuss the concrete details of the museum's location, pedagogical content, and overall historical mission, therefore, it seemed that it was well on its way to being realized.

The hopes that many brought to this two-part symposium (held in December of 2002 and January 2003) were soon dashed, however, by new controversy. At the first meeting, two competing visions of the museum vied for approval. The first solution, which was advocated by most left-leaning politicians and citizens' groups, envisioned the creation of a centralized institution at the site of the former Nazi headquarters, the Brown House, in a new building whose design would be decided through a major international architectural competition. By contrast, the second solution, drafted by Institut für Zeitgeschichte historian Volker Dahm at the request of the Bavarian state's minister of culture, Monika Hohlmeier (CSU), recommended a more "decentralized" approach based on the idea of placing informational plaques adjacent to some thirty-six existing "perpetrator sites" throughout the city and integrating them into a kind of self-guided walking tour (*Besichtigungsstrecke*) of Munich's Nazi past.

When details of this latter proposal were first publicized at the December 2002 symposium, they sparked a wave of protests, especially when it became known that Minister Hohlmeier had already approved and forwarded the plan to the Bavarian Landtag for discussion without having first announced its particulars in a public hearing. For this reason, many of the plan's critics saw it as a clumsy attempt to avert an open discussion of the museum's fate and determine it from above by bureaucratic fiat.[23] But their suspicions of the state's motives deepened when the affidavit was finally released in full to the public in early 2003.

In many ways, the full content of the document reflected the continuing attempt of Bavarian authorities to relativize Munich's responsibility for the Third Reich. In the affidavit's first half, Dahm described at length the history of the Nazi Party in Munich, only to conclude that after 1933, the city had steadily lost political importance to Berlin and Obersalzberg, which became the places where "high-level policy...was formulated."[24] In light of what Dahm clearly implied was the minor "role that Munich played in National Socialism," a museum of "international stature" aiming for a national perspective on the Nazi era, he asserted, was "not urgently necessary."[25] Dahm's leading role in creating the Dokumentation Obersalzberg in Berchtesgaden may have led to his additional conclusion that a similar museum in Munich would duplicate its function (not to mention the function of the Nuremberg and Dachau documentation centers as well), but for good measure, he also added that another museum would be financially "indefensible in light of empty public coffers and high tax burdens."[26] Added to this, he observed, was a clear shortage of space and inadequate parking for an institution that he estimated would attract some four hundred thousand yearly visitors.[27] Such problems led Dahm to conclude that a scaled-down museum covering merely the local aspects of Nazism in Munich would "suffice in satisfying the needs for historical-political education in Bavaria."[28]

Following its release, however, Dahm's proposal met with a cascade of criticism from a wide range of journalists, scholars, citizens' groups, and ordinary Munich citizens. Some critics attacked the plan as a "shameful" attempt to confront the Nazi past on the cheap, one likening it to an "Aldi version of remembrance."[29] Others argued that the plan was intended to serve as a token, politically correct fig leaf to protect itself against attacks of insufficient commemorative piety.[30] Still others pointed out practical flaws in Dahm's *Besichtigungsstrecke* concept, noting the physical impossibility of visiting thirty-six buildings without essentially racing past them in a hasty kind of *Schautafelrennen* (plaque race).[31] Perhaps the most influential opposition to the state's plan, though, was voiced by Munich's own city council. In early 2003, the council, firmly committed to a centralized museum, commissioned Munich's city archive (the Stadtarchiv München) to produce an affidavit on the plan, which, when released later in the year, dismissed it as "conceptually one-dimensional," methodologically retrograde, and fatally marred by numerous errors of historical fact that ultimately resulted in a fundamental "misinterpretation of Munich's role in the Nazi power system."[32]

The Bavarian state's clumsy handling of the planning process for the documentation center reflected a variety of motives. At one level, financial considerations partly drove the state's support for a more limited museum. During a period of economic stagnation and tight budgets, Bavarian authorities were reluctant to assume the financial burdens of a major new museum project.[33] Yet, given the fact that Munich's city government also was suffering from serious budgetary problems but supported the large-scale version of the museum, it is clear that financial considerations were not the only reason.[34] Indeed, at the deeper level, the disagreement between the city and state over what kind of museum to create may have reflected politically rooted differences about how to deal with the Nazi past. In the decades since the beginning of the postwar era, the city of Munich and the state of Bavaria had rarely seen eye to eye politically, the former being largely ruled by the left-wing SPD and the latter solidly governed by the conservative CSU. Both parties, moreover, largely adhered to different historical memories of Munich's links to Nazism and the Third Reich. While the SPD could proudly look back to a history of persecution and resistance, the CSU had the more awkward task of explaining away the role of its own conservative political traditions in helping to give rise to and nurture the Nazi movement in the 1920s. It was no wonder, therefore, that many in the CSU-dominated Bavarian state government opposed a large-scale, centralized museum. As one journalist speculated, the embarrassing historical connections between the Nazi movement and Bavaria's traditional conservatism would inevitably be explored in much greater detail in a prominent museum than in a more superficial, self-guided walking tour past dozens of buildings associated with the Nazi years.[35] According to this line of reasoning, it was less the state's desire for fiscal restraint than its own selective historical vision and concern about its present-day image that determined its position on the museum project. Even though the Bavarian government had publicly and officially embraced the concept of a documentation center, it still wanted to control its broader historical narrative and tailor it to its own political needs.

The furor over the Bavarian state's attempt to bypass the city and create a fait accompli with respect to the museum, however, was hardly the end of the controversy. To break the deadlock caused by the disagreement over Dahm's affidavit, representatives of the city and state formed two new committees in early 2003 to revise plans for the museum project: one, a *Kuratorium* composed of politicians in charge of financing and development; the other, a scholarly committee composed of several prominent academics and museum officials from across Germany responsible for drafting a revised conceptual plan for the museum. Throughout the remainder of 2003, the latter committee deliberated at length, but by the early spring of 2004, it acrimoniously split apart into two competing factions, each of which ultimately offered contrary visions of the museum's future.

The larger faction—composed of the historian Norbert Frei, the program director of the Berlin Jewish Museum Cilly Kugelmann, and the director of the Buchenwald and Dora-Mittelbau memorial sites Volkhard Knigge—ambitiously envisioned the museum as an institution possessing national, if not international, significance, whose function would be to explore the "rise, history, and aftereffects of National Socialism in Munich in such a way as to serve as an exemplary case of coming to terms with this era of Germany's social history."[36] Of primary concern to this group was the museum's long-term ability to speak to future generations of German (as well as non-German) visitors—a goal that it aimed to ensure by utilizing state-of-the-art media technology, authentic "historical artifacts" (*Realien*) from the Nazi period, and biographical profiles of selected historical figures mostly from the 1933–45 "regime phase" of National Socialism. Significantly, this vision of the museum represented a direct challenge to the heretofore dominant vision of a "documentation center," which the trio of experts dismissed as outmoded in terms of its exhibition strategy and too narrowly focused on "regional-cultural" aspects, or the "particularities of Munich." For this reason, the members of this faction urged replacing the established title for the museum with the appellation "Haus der Geschichte des Nationalsozialismus in München" (House of the History of National Socialism in Munich).[37]

This vision of the museum was firmly rejected, however, by the committee's dissenting member, Technical University architectural historian Winfried Nerdinger. As one of the most long-standing and influential supporters of the documentation center project, Nerdinger disagreed fundamentally with the other members of the committee and, after withdrawing from it in late 2003, offered his own affidavit to the Munich city council in February of 2004. In this document, Nerdinger rejected the majority plan's broad vision for the museum as an institution possessing national significance, preferring a more particularistic focus on Munich's unique contributions to the origins and subsequent success of the Nazi movement in the years 1918–33. Further still, he objected to the majority faction's museological preference for a state-of-the-art museum over a documentation center, declaring that any attempt to make the Third Reich "exciting" or "entertaining" to the next generation by "exhibiting objects from the Nazi era" was to be "completely avoided" in favor of a sober presentation of "facts" through documents, photographs, and film excerpts.[38] Only by combining a strict focus on the historical particularities of Munich via a soberly objective selection of materials could the main historical question—"how could it happen?"—be answered.[39]

Several months after Nerdinger submitted his dissenting report, he was rewarded for his efforts with the Munich city council's decision on April 21, 2004, to approve his plan for the museum. This surprising decision (taken despite the support of the Munich city cultural affairs director, Lydia Hartl, for the majority faction) reflected a variety of specific considerations, but it largely expressed enduring insecurities within the Munich governing elite about how to view, portray, and generally deal with the Nazi experience.

The decision reflected the continuing fallout from another controversy that had erupted in 2002 over a city-sponsored exhibit at the Munich Stadtmuseum on the city's history during the Nazi period. The idea for such an exhibit had originated in the year 1997, when the Maxvorstadt district committee, having failed to gain any momentum for the documentation center project, succeeded in winning city council approval for a permanent exhibition entitled "Munich, 1933–1945."[40] Curated by Brigitte Schutz, who had organized a similar exhibition at the Stadtmuseum in 1993, the exhibit was supposed to open in August 2002 but was abruptly cancelled by an irate Mayor Christian Ude following a visit prior to the show's opening. Calling the exhibit an "uncritical collection of Nazi devotional objects," Ude was incensed by the fact that the artifacts on display—among other things, SA head Ernst Roehm's dagger, SA uniforms, and various examples of Nazi kitsch—largely lacked contextualized commentary and veered dangerously close to becoming a "folkloric SA Lederhosen show."[41] Similar comments appeared in the local Munich press, which noted that the exhibit perilously flirted with the "sacralization of the items [*Exponate*] and their elevation into cultic objects."[42] Ude's strong reaction to the show largely reflected his desire to protect the city's already damaged image. As he put it, if he had opened the exhibit in its current form, it would have "exposed the city to the heftiest criticism...along the lines of the Historians' Debate."[43] In the end, the reworked exhibit, entitled "National Socialism in Munich—Codes of Memory," finally opened in June 2003.[44] But the controversy had left clear lessons in the minds of

Munich city council representatives. First and foremost, the furor over the enduring auratic power of authentic Nazi artifacts and their ability to fascinate present-day Germans convinced the city council that Nerdinger's strictly documentary approach to exhibiting the Nazi era in a museum setting was the preferable choice.

The city council's decision in favor of the Nerdinger proposal further reflected concerns about increased neo-Nazi activity in Munich. Especially since April 25, 1995, when a right-wing fanatic, Reinhold Elstner, had burned himself to death in front of the Feldherrnhalle to promote his revisionist views of the Nazi era, awareness had grown that local sites associated with the Third Reich continued to exert an unhealthy fascination.[45] Several years later, in August 2002, a gathering of more than one hundred neo-Nazis at the Führerbau to celebrate Leni Riefenstahl's hundredth birthday provided further evidence of this reality.[46] These and other such episodes of right-wing attraction to Nazi sites proved to many in Munich that the rigorous demythologization of such sites was a crucial task for any future documentation center.[47] Furthermore, the increasingly vocal opposition of right-wing groups in Munich toward the very idea of a documentation center—opposition that was expressed in angry newspaper editorials and in a bill by the right-wing Republikaner city council faction in 2003—further convinced the museum's supporters of their mission's urgency.[48] Finally, the disturbing revelation in 2003 of a neo-Nazi terrorist plot to blow up the new Jewish synagogue, museum, and community center under construction on Munich's Jakobsplatz—an episode that made national headlines—drove the point home in dramatic fashion that the neo-Nazi movement was evolving in new and dangerous directions.[49] All of these worrisome trends, taken together, convinced the city council that a sober documentation center, located at the former national nerve center of the Nazi Party on the Königsplatz, would send a clear signal of the city's will to combat right-wing ideas.

Still, despite the growing sense of urgency about creating a documentation center, the project remained mired in partisan squabbling. Following the approval of Nerdinger's plan, the thorny question of the museum's location became a new stumbling block, as the Bavarian state remained reluctant to relinquish its ownership of the property desired by most supporters of the Nerdinger plan—the site of the former Brown House. Supporters of building the museum on this coveted spot were thus forced to expend valuable time and energy exploring alternate sites, none of which turned out to be viable.[50] An entire year passed, therefore, before city and state officials were able to agree on the formation of yet another steering committee to study the museum plans, this one headed by former federal finance minister Theo Waigel in April 2005.[51] In the meantime, the inability to settle on any final plans for the museum had assumed farcical proportions. As the *Süddeutsche Zeitung* opined, "compared with the tempo in which the Munich memory landscape is developing, the [notoriously stalled plans for a permanent museum housing the] Topography of Terror in Berlin appear to be making swift progress."[52]

A break in the deadlock finally emerged in November 2005, when Waigel's steering committee announced that the Bavarian state had finally given its permission to use the site of the Brown House for the new museum. In September 2006, the Bavarian state sweetened the pot by announcing that it was freeing up the site at no cost, without any expectation of financial reimbursement. In this budding climate of good feeling, city officials confidently announced that the symbolic cornerstone would be laid in 2008. Still, as the final go-ahead for the museum remained conditional on the willingness of the federal government to assume one-third of the project's estimated construction cost of thirty million Euros, uncertainty remained. At the time of this writing—August 2007—the federal government had still not stated its final position on financing the museum, so the overall fate of the museum still hangs in limbo at least to a degree.

Despite this lingering uncertainty, the prospects for a Documentation Center for History of National Socialism in Munich look better than ever before. Despite the many setbacks and years of delays, a museum will likely arise in the near future. Whenever the museum is finally completed, however, the question of what its creation saga reveals about Munich's relationship to its Nazi past will remain. At the most obvious level, one of the defining features of the eventual documentation center will be the enormous amount of time required to build it. Interpreting the significance of this fact, however, is complicated. Delays beset even uncontroversial large-scale architectural projects. It is all the more predictable that projects dealing with contentious subjects, such as the Nazi era, should suffer from delays even more. Other museums and memorials that today are celebrated as success stories in their approach to the Nazi past, for example, took many years to come into existence. It took seventeen years, after all, to plan, build, and dedicate the new Memorial to the Murdered Jews of Europe in Berlin; and it took sixteen years to do the same with the United States Holocaust Memorial Museum in Washington, DC. Berlin's Topography of Terror exhibition, moreover, still has not found a permanent exhibition space, some eighteen years after the call to create one was first voiced.[53] Compared to these examples, the documentation center project does not appear especially exceptional. Moreover, during the many years of planning and delay, these projects sparked healthy discussion and debate, all of which—if James Young's well-known claim is to be believed—may be as valuable as the actual final structures in preserving the memory of the Nazi years.[54] For Munich, the debate sparked by the proposal to build a Documentation Center for the History of National Socialsim has, indeed, been healthy. No matter how many delays have set back its prospects of realization, they have allowed the city's Nazi past to remain at the forefront of public consciousness and to be discussed with unprecedented intensity.

At the same time, however, the endless problems in planning the museum also suggest an enduring unwillingness to directly confront Munich's intimate connections to Nazism. This unwillingness, to be sure, should not be viewed in simplistic or monolithic terms as a widespread phenomenon broadly characterizing the city's population as a whole. As this essay has attempted to show, the enduring reluctance to fully face the past has partly been considerably rooted in the long-standing reservations of conservative Bavarian state officials about following the lead of more ambitious Munich citizens and municipal authorities in directly confronting the city's Nazi legacy. This division between state and city highlights a larger truth, namely, that Munich has long harbored multiple competing memories of the Third Reich. The relative influence of these memories, however, has shifted in recent years. While it is true that the dominant, state-supported memory has inclined to marginalize the past for much of the postwar period, the last decade and a half has witnessed the growing success of a vibrant countermemory advanced by those Munich citizens—at both the grassroots and official municipal level—committed to a more open and forthright process of historical reckoning. For this reason, at the same time that the Bavarian state's stubbornness needs to be held up to critical scrutiny, the tangible progress of local citizens' groups, academics, and city politicians in redirecting public attention toward Munich's Nazi legacy since the late 1980s needs to be credited.

Still, while the dominant memory in Munich has gradually accommodated the demands of countermemory, it has remained reluctant to entirely surrender its authoritative status within the city's memory landscape. Despite the fact that grassroots efforts to compel greater public remembrance of the Nazi past have registered important victories in recent years, they have remained limited by the enduring desire of political authorities at the state (and, at times, also the city) level to remain in control over the intensifying confrontation with the Nazi era in the urban landscape. To cite but two examples: in May 2003, Bavarian state officials prohibited the well-known Munich activist artist Wolfram Kastner from burning a black circle (or *Brandfleck*) into the lawn of the Königsplatz to commemorate the seventieth anniversary of the book burnings of 1933.[55] That same year, city authorities, led by Mayor Christian Ude, forbade Cologne artist Günter Demnig from embedding into city sidewalks several of his brass "stumbling stones" (*Stolpersteine*) bearing the names and addresses of Munich Jews killed in the Holocaust.[56] Given that Demnig by this point had already installed thirty-two hundred such stones in some twenty cities and towns across Germany, Munich's stubborn stance earned it the dubious distinction of "the only big German city without a single plaque."[57] Against the backdrop of such official resistance toward expanding the memory of the Nazi era in the urban landscape, it is clear that the city's relationship with the past remains far from normalized.

Munich's difficult relationship with its Nazi legacy is underscored, finally, by comparing it with that of other German cities. Berlin represents the most obvious foil to Munich by virtue of its intense pursuit of urban *Vergangenheitsbewältigung* since reunification. But other cities have also distinguished themselves by notable successes. Nuremberg earned considerable attention in the German and international media for its commemorative efforts at the Reich Party Rally Grounds and for its plans to open an exhibit at the site of the Nuremberg Trials, not to mention its general embrace of human rights.[58] Cologne has been praised for its own documentation center at the former Gestapo headquarters known as the EL-DE-Haus—a project that, significantly, was approved in 1979, a decade before Munich's own documentation center was even proposed.[59] Hamburg has been judged favorably by scholars for its ambitious monument construction program.[60] By contrast, Munich today remains perceived within Germany—and, increasingly, in the international media as well—as having "swept [the past] under the carpet."[61]

To be sure, progress has been made in recent years toward reversing this perception. Besides the intense public discussion about establishing a Documentation Center for the History of National Socialism, the city's decision to construct a new Jewish synagogue, community center, and museum complex on the Jakobsplatz testifies to the local willingness to make amends for the Nazi past within the urban environment.[62] A major

2006 exhibition on public sites associated with the Nazi era, Ort und Erinnerung—Nationalsozialismus in München, sponsored by the Architecture Museum of the Technical University, also demonstrates a local readiness to address the past.[63] Still, when all is said and done, Munich's reputation with relation to its handling of the Nazi past will ultimately rest—at least in the near future—on its ability to bring the long delayed documentation center project to completion. The longer plans for the museum drag on without tangible results, the longer Munich's reputation for evasiveness will persist. In the final analysis, it remains too early to offer conclusive judgments about the ultimate significance of the as yet unbuilt documentation center. But once it is completed, observers will need to recall its tortured origins. Only by doing so will it be possible to arrive at a comprehensive assessment of Munich's struggle to deal with its substantial Nazi legacy.

NOTES

I would like to thank Paul Jaskot for his excellent editorial suggestions and Bernd Landau at the Munich Cultural Affairs Office for forwarding me relevant archival materials.

1. Gavriel D. Rosenfeld, *Munich and Memory: Architecture, Monuments, and the Legacy of the Third Reich* (Berkeley, 2000).

2. Sonja Zekri, "Blamabler Plan," *Süddeutsche Zeitung* (hereinafter *SZ*), January 20, 2003.

3. Rosenfeld, *Munich and Memory*, 263–68.

4. On the north and west sides of the square stood two structures by Leo von Klenze: the Glyptothek, a museum of ancient Greek and Roman sculpture built from 1816 to 1830, and the Propyläen, a monumental stone gate built from 1843 to 1862 to commemorate the close relations between Bavaria and Wittelsbach-ruled Greece. Opposite the Glyptothek, on the south side of the square, stood Georg Friedrich Ziebland's Kunst- und Industrieausstellungs-Gebäude, an exhibition hall built from 1838 to 1845 and known as the Neue Staatsgalerie after 1919.

5. Rosenfeld, *Munich and Memory*, 86.

6. After 1947, the Führerbau served as the home of the "America House" and eventually became the home of the Hochschule für Musik; the Verwaltungsbau was eventually transformed into the Haus der Kulturinstitute, housing various cultural institutions, among them the Zentralinstitut für Kunstgeschichte (Rosenfeld, *Munich and Memory*, 92).

7. Rosenfeld, *Munich and Memory*, 273.

8. The city council plan was submitted on December 14, 1988, under the title "Building plan Nr. 1650." It was rejected by the Bavarian state on May 11, 1989.

9. Rosenfeld, *Munich and Memory*, 275.

10. Münchner Stadtmuseum, ed., *München—"Hauptstadt der Bewegung"* (Munich, 1993); Winfried Nerdinger, ed., *Bauen im Nationalsozialismus: Bayern, 1933–1945* (Munich, 1993).

11. Karen E. Till, *The New Berlin: Memory, Politics, Place* (Minneapolis, 2005), chap. 3.

12. Hans Lehmbruch, Ulrike Grammbitter, and Eva von Seckendorff in Iris Lauterbach et al., eds., *Bürokratie und Kult: Das Parteizentrum der NSDAP am Königsplatz in München, Geschichte und Rezeption* (Munich, 1995).

13. In a separate bill issued at the same time, the committee called on the Bavarian State Office of Historic Preservation to grant protected status to the twin Ehrentempel foundations. The bill was submitted on September 17, 1996. Although Bäumler himself was a member of the CSU, most of the Bezirksausschuss-Maxvorstadt was comprised of SPD members.

14. Bezirksausschuss Maxvorstadt, ed., *NS-Dokumentationszentrum am Königsplatz: Materialien zur Aktuellen Diskussion* (Munich, 2002), vii–viii.

15. Ibid., ix–x. The Green Party supported a documentation center in a September 2000 bill ("Ein neues Mahnmal für die NS-Opfer," *SZ*, September 9, 2000).

16. Text quoted at http://www.muenchen.info/ba/03/ba_info/Chronologie.htm.

17. Winfried Nerdinger, "München—Hauptstadt der Verdrängung," *SZ*, November 17, 2001. See also Eva-Maria Schnurr's article "Gedächtnis-Problem" (*SZ*, November 29, 2001), which declared, "Munich is a memory-hole." See also "Bräunlich," *SZ*, September 4, 2001.

18. "Beim Erinnern tut sich München schwer," *SZ*, July 14–15, 2001.

19. Quoted in Klaus Bäumler, ed., *NS-Dokumentationszentrum am Königsplatz: Materialien zur Aktuellen Diskussion* (Munich, 2002), vii.

20. This is the contention of Bill Niven's book *Facing the Nazi Past: United Germany and the Legacy of the Third Reich* (London, 2002).

21. Quoted in a bill submitted by the BA Maxvorstadt on December 12, 2000. Similarly, Munich mayor Christian Ude noted that Munich would do well to "learn from Nuremberg" (Sonja Zekri, "Von Nürnberg lernen," *SZ*, December 7–8, 2002).

22. Dachau, Berchtesgaden, and, to a lesser degree, Nuremberg, moreover, were more indelibly associated with the Nazi era in ways that Munich never was. As a result, Bavarian authorities may have thought the city could more readily evade its own substantial links to the Nazi era. I would like to thank Bernd Landau for raising some of these points with me in conversation.

23. Sonja Zekri, "Feigenblattgold: Eine Billigversion der Erinnerung?" *SZ*, December 9, 2002.

24. Volker Dahm, "Projekt eines NS-Dokumentationszentrums in München: Gutachten des Instituts für Zeitgeschichte, München—Berlin, erstattet im Auftrag der Bayerischen Landeszentrale für politische Bildungsarbeit, 4. November 2002," 18, 21.

25. Ibid., 24–25.

26. Ibid., 25. Dahm was the scholarly director (*fachlicher Leiter*) of the Berchtesgaden documentation center.

27. Ibid., 27–28.
28. Ibid., 25.
29. Aldi is a popular German discount store. Zekri, "Feigenblattgold." See also "So viel Anfang," *SZ,* January 23, 2003.
30. Zekri, "Blamabler Plan." See also Ira Mazzoni, "Hypotheken der Verdrängung," *die tageszeitung,* January 23, 2003.
31. This was Winfried Nerdinger's point, quoted in Zekri, "Blamabler Plan."
32. The document, "Stellungnahme zum 'Gutachten' des Instituts für Zeitgeschichte (Projekt eines NS-Dokumentationszentrums in München) vom 4.11.2002," was written by historian Andreas Heusler.
33. Roland Losch, "München erinnert sich an die 'Hauptstadt der Bewegung,'" *Associated Press Worldstream—German,* July 30, 2002.
34. Ibid.
35. One journalist pointed out, "it is impossible to criticize Hitler without criticizing conservatism" (Martin Fochler, "Auseinandersetzung um NS-Dokumentationszentrum," *Deutsch-Tschechischen Nachrichten,* December 2002, 11–12).
36. Landeshauptstadt München, ed., *Gutachterliche Empfehlungen an die Landeshauptstadt München für ein NS-Dokumentationszentrum* (Munich, 2004), 6.
37. "Haus der Geschichte des Nationalsozialismus in München," in Landeshauptstadt München, *Gutachterliche Empfehlungen,* 1–19.
38. For similar reasons, Nerdinger's supporters insisted on keeping the name for the museum "NS-Dokumentationszentrum," arguing that the alternative ran the risk of being misunderstood as a glorification of the Nazi era. See, for example, the stance taken by the Initiativkreis on the name, cited in "NS-Dokumentationszentrum," *Haidhauser Nachrichten,* May 13, 2004.
39. Winfried Nerdinger, "Gutachterliche Stellungnahme zur Errichtung eines NS-Dokumentationszentrums in München," in Landeshauptstadt München, *Gutachterliche Empfehlungen,* 1–10.
40. Bäumler, *NS-Dokumentationszentrum am Königsplatz,* viii.
41. "Ude kippt Nazi-Ausstellung," *SZ,* August 5, 2002.
42. Sonja Zekri, "Unter der SA-Lederhose wird gejodelt," *SZ,* August 9, 2002.
43. "Ude kippt Nazi-Ausstellung."
44. For a review, see Egbert Tholl, "Sitz, Porzellanhund!" *SZ,* July 15, 2004.
45. For the Nazis' use of the Feldherrnhalle, see Rosenfeld, *Munich and Memory,* 110.
46. "Riefenstahl-Geburtstag: Neo-Nazis feiern in der Musikhochschule," *SZ,* August 27, 2002.
47. Lauterbach, *Bürokratie und Kult.*
48. Bruno Wetzel, "Vergangenheits-statt Zukunftsbewältigung," *National-Zeitung,* 2003, http://www.national-zeitung.de/Artikel_03/NZ03_4.html. The Republikaner Party issued a bill opposing the creation of a documentation center and demanding the creation instead of a museum chronicling the "suffering of all peoples in the Second World War." The bill was issued on January 20, 2003. See http://www.rep-muenchen.de/anfragen_antraege/200103.htm (accessed June 2003).
49. "Szenerie des Grauens," *Frankfurter Allgemeine Zeitung,* September 13, 2003.

50. Most of these other sites were in the immediate vicinity of the Königsplatz but were already committed to other functions.

51. "Neuer Anlauf für das NS-Dokumentationszentrum," *Die Welt,* April 3, 2005.

52. Sonja Zekri, "Streit um NS-Dokumentationszentrum," *SZ,* March 31, 2004.

53. Till, *The New Berlin,* chap. 3.

54. James Young, *The Texture of Memory: Holocaust Memorials and Meaning* (New Haven, 1993), 21.

55. Kastner performed his first famous *Brandfleck* installation in 1996, with city permission.

56. Christian Ude mobilized the tired excuse that the plaques' vulnerability to vandalism made them an "inappropriate" way to remember the victims.

57. Kirsten Grieshaber, "Plaques for Nazi Victims Offer a Personal Impact," *New York Times,* November 29, 2003, B23.

58. See Paul Jaskot's essay in this volume.

59. See Jeffry Diefendorf's contribution in this volume.

60. See the introduction of Peter Reichel's edited volume *Das Gedächtnis der Stadt: Hamburg im Umgang mit seiner nationalsozialiastischer Vergangenheit* (Hamburg, 1998).

61. Of late, criticism of Munich has reached an English-speaking audience. See Peter H. Koepf, "Swept Under the Carpet," *Atlantic Times,* November, 2005, 18. See also "A Shift in the Landscape," *Economist,* December 18–31, 2004, 81; Gavriel Rosenfeld, "Munich Evokes the Past in Future Museum," *Forward,* February 10, 2006.

62. Gavriel D. Rosenfeld, "Munich Redux," *Forward,* November 3, 2006.

63. http://www.architekturmuseum.de/ausstellungen/detail.php?which=68&show.

Concrete Memory
The Struggle over Air-Raid and Submarine Shelters in Bremen after 1945

Marc Buggeln and Inge Marszolek

Walking through the Bürgerpark behind Bremen's central train station, one sooner or later strolls past two massive concrete cubes lying close to one another. Visitors often stop for a moment to listen to jazz music emanating from somewhere deep inside one of the structures. Graffiti on one of them testifies to someone's self-hatred: "I hate myself and want to die" (Kurt Cobain). Most people are familiar with the protective function that these World War II shelters once had, but few realize that, at the end of the war, it was from inside these shelters in Bremen that the Nazi Party (NSDAP) leadership attempted to hold off the *Götterdämmerung* (twilight of the gods) and to drive their soldiers, militias, and general population into a final war of attrition.

To the north of Bremen lies an idyllic landscape of rivers and streams. Cycling through the green fields and forests that follow the Weser River northwards, one is suddenly confronted by a gigantic and seemingly endless wall of concrete: the south face of the submarine shelter Valentin, one of the biggest military ruins left behind by National Socialism (fig. 1). The structure is 426 meters long, up to 97 meters wide, and up to 33 meters high, a concrete colossus of monstrous dimensions, seemingly indestructible, and built as if to last for eternity. The history of the shelter is indecipherable to passing cyclists and boaters. Locals have never liked talking to outsiders about it. When questioned by their children about the shelter, they may have muttered a few words about the National Socialist era, the war, and how terrible things were back then. What they never talked about was just how and under what conditions the shelter was built. When locals happen to talk about the massive structure, they avoid the subject of the war and National Socialism. Instead, they focus their discussion on the shelter's current users: the Federal Armed Forces.

Fig. 1. The submarine shelter Valentin, built in Farge-Rekum (a suburb of Bremen) from 1943 to 1945. View from the village of Rekum today. (Photo: Barbara Milies and Harald Schwörer. Reproduced with permission.)

The submarine shelter Valentin and other structures like it represent Bremen's largest architectural question marks and stand as constant reminders of the era of National Socialism. The strategies of dealing with this legacy have undergone many changes since 1945. Closer examination shows that, as ruins left over from the war, these shelters have raised different questions and presented different answers at different times. Occasionally they were made virtually invisible and thus unable to provoke questions. Alongside other shelters featured in this essay, the submarine shelter Valentin has acted as the projection surface for the positive visions of many people, while others have seen it as a monstrosity of war and a site of endless suffering. The intention of this essay is to outline the practices of memory as exemplified by the different approaches adopted in Bremen with respect to its surviving submarine and air-raid shelters. In the following pages, we will show how the public relationship to these structures has changed over time, and we will explore the local tensions between politics, architecture, and memory.[1] Examining these shelters as "sites of memory" (*Gedächtnisorte*) not only adds depth to the space of memory of postwar Bremen but helps us better grasp how actual places constitute public memory in Germany.

One principle challenge in this discussion lies in the use of the term *Vergangenheitsbewältigung*, which describes the process of coming to terms with the past.[2] The significance of place in the construction of "cultural memory" has only been analyzed in its basic outlines. While Pierre Nora has proposed a map of places of memory, on which actual places could be mapped alongside other relics of cultural—and, in Nora's case, national—heritage, we are attempting to describe the topography of the bunkers within the place of memory of the city.[3] To this end, we focus on the practices through which the shelters have been made "visible"—that is, on the social, cultural, and economic practices of concretizing (or objectifying) the past. The various ways of using or referring to the shelters in different historical periods can both heighten and diminish the shelters' visibility in the public sphere. Their "visibility" and "concealment" in public memory enables varying forms of discussion and multilayered processes of remembering.[4] At the same time, we draw on Michel Foucault's idea of heterotopy and view the shelters as "sites of otherness": some of them are underground, others—though solid and visible—somehow resistant to public perception.[5] The stories of these shelters' construction and their wartime function are inscribed not only in their usage and management concepts but also in the projections that these relics stimulate. The wartime "bunker communities" (*Bunkergemeinschaften*) were the sites of diverse experiences, which after the war constituted both communities of memory and communities of denial.

Bremen and National Socialism

Due to Bremen's long-standing independent political status as a free Hanseatic city, its history differs from that of German cities that were administratively integrated within larger regional states. In Bremen, political and economic life had long been in the hands of the mercantile and commercial bourgeoisie, which, over time, constructed a cosmopolitan and liberal identity for the Hanseatic city.[6] In reality, of course, the city's self-image was not as liberal and cosmopolitan as it claimed to be. The nationalism of the German Empire made its presence felt in the city to a large degree.[7] Moreover, the bourgeoisie's control of Bremen was challenged by the electoral successes of the Social Democratic Party (SPD) during the Weimar Republic. Still, even if the city was not as liberal as it imagined itself to be, it was sufficiently able to resist the rise of the

NSDAP, which did not fare particularly well in local elections, polling lower in the city than in other parts of Germany.[8]

This fact notwithstanding, the years 1933 to 1945 in Bremen were characterized by the political rule of the Nazis, whose leadership consisted mainly of individuals from the petty bourgeoisie.[9] During the first months of Hitler's rule in 1933, Nazi persecution predominantly targeted the Social Democrats and Communists, particularly as the Jewish community in Bremen was relatively small, due to the city's restrictive and strongly anti-Semitic residency policy from the nineteenth century. However, as was true of other cities throughout the German Reich, Jews in Bremen were discriminated against, persecuted, deported, and finally murdered. Overall, the National Socialist senate and the city authorities cooperated smoothly in the racist regime of persecution, and they did so with the general approval (or at least tacit understanding) of the majority of Bremen's citizens.

The National Socialist senators proved to be less than competent in many areas of political administration, and they frequently depended on the expertise of the administrative organs. These were still the domains of the Bremen bourgeoisie, who retained their decision-making competency over the economic and architectural development of the city. Bremen's business concerns focused traditionally on international trade and were initially skeptical of the National Socialist drive toward autarky. As in Hamburg, business circles in Bremen swung around during the course of the 1930s to become unconditional supporters of the path to war. Close ties existed between local arms producers and business groups in Bremen, which benefited from the rising profits of the armaments industry. In addition, the occupation of Eastern Europe also offered commercial interests in Bremen the prospect of new colonial development projects.

In the realms of architecture and urban planning, Bremen had long adhered to tradition and largely spurned modernist trends. This tendency dovetailed nicely with the architectural philosophy of the Nazi regime, and during the Third Reich, the major architectural changes in Bremen included the construction of garrisons within the city zone, the expansion of armaments production facilities, and the annexation of nearby settlements in 1939, which made Bremen a city of 450,000. Significantly, the first large-scale, modern building project in Bremen was the construction of air-raid shelters, which were built along purely functional lines. Accordingly, the shelters manifest few regional characteristics and lack any references to local traditions.

The Construction of Air-Raid and Submarine Shelters in Bremen, 1940-45

At the outbreak of the war, the German Reich and the city of Bremen were almost completely unprepared for aerial attacks. It was not until October 10, 1940, that a Führer decree ordered the construction of air-raid shelters in sixty-one cities.[10] In 1941, this program was the main area of building activity in Germany, and by October 22, 1941, the program had utilized 3.4 million cubic meters of concrete. Because there were insufficient numbers of German laborers, the majority of those working on the shelters were foreign forced laborers.[11] In 1942, the program was scaled down, and in September 1942, drastic cuts were made in the program to facilitate the construction of the Siegfried Line.[12] Even after work on the Siegfried Line was ended following the Allied invasion in Normandy in June 1944, German building efforts were not redirected to the construction of shelters for the civilian population. Instead, most resources were devoted to protecting the armaments industry.[13]

The construction of shelters in Bremen paralleled a similar development throughout the German Reich. However, Bremen's relative proximity to England and the importance of its harbors and industrial facilities for the German war effort made it one of the most threatened cities in the country. Accordingly, an extensive program for the construction of shelters was planned for Bremen. In October 1940, the erection of between 200 and 400 bombproof air-raid shelters was discussed, and in December 1940, Oberbaurrat Kummer, a senior councillor for construction, spoke of as many as 450 shelters. Only 131 had been built by August 1944, however, most of them *Hochbunker* (aboveground shelters), constructed by foreign forced laborers.[14]

Construction of the shelters was not centrally planned. Instead, the management of the program was regional, and all towns built their shelters in a different manner. Authorities in Bremen abstained from camouflaging their shelters with paint, thus failing to take the opportunity to integrate the shelters within the cityscape. One exception to this is a shelter located at the Diakonissenhaus (the home of a Protestant Community of women who cared for sick or elderly people) on Bremen's Nord Strasse, which was decorated with fake neo-Gothic windows.[15] In the inner city, rudimentary and temporary shelters were the only protection available for forced laborers, who were made to build proper air-raid shelters but forbidden to use them. At the close of the war, the official capacities of the air-raid shelter were exceeded twice or even three times over: approximately two hundred thousand people took shelter in the bunkers, roughly two-thirds of the total population. This statistic also explains the relatively small number of people killed during the air war: the bombing raids over Bremen killed 3,850 people including forced laborers.[16]

In Bremen, as throughout the Reich, the protection of industrial facilities important to the war effort was given priority over constructing shelters for the civilian population. The central sites were two major shipbuilding yards: Krupp's Deschimag AG Weser shipyards in Bremen-Gröpelingen and the Thyssen-owned Bremer Vulkan AG in Bremen-Vegesack. In late 1942, the decision was made to build large bunkers in both shipyards for housing and constructing submarines. The Deschimag bunker, code-named Hornisse (Hornet) was to be built directly at the shipyards.[17] In the case of the Vulkan bunker, Valentin, the authorities decided to relocate the facility to the township of Farge, ten kilometers downstream on the Weser River (fig. 2).[18]

During its planning phase, the construction of the submarine shelter Valentin became one of the German Navy's most important high-tech projects. Inside a massive production hall measuring more than 426 meters in length and 97 meters wide and protected by a concrete ceiling 7 meters thick, submarines were to be constructed using modern assembly-line techniques for the first time ever. The aim of building the submarines section by section was to accelerate the production process and enable the yards to release a completed submarine from the site every fifty-six hours. However, there were almost no German laborers available to work on the enormous construction project, so here, too, forced laborers carried out the construction, under tremendous time pressure.[19] Work at the site was especially debilitating for the malnourished inmates of concentration camps (fig. 3), and the death rate here was one of the highest at any of Neuengamme's satellite camps.[20] As a result of these ruthlessly exploitative and murderous working conditions, 90 percent of the construction had been completed shortly before the end of the war. Two direct hits during bombing raids by Allied aircraft on March 27 and 30, 1945, penetrated the ceiling of the bunker and ended work at the site just weeks before the war ended.

"Everything was different in Bremen": The Legend of the Free Hanseatic City after 1945

During the American occupation after 1945, politics in Bremen continued where the Weimar Republic had left off, with a coalition between the SPD,

Fig. 2. View of the south side of the construction site for the submarine shelter Valentin, 1944. This photo is part of a larger series taken by local photographer Seubert. (Photo: Private Archive of Inge Marszolek.)

the Christian Democratic Union (CDU), and the Free Democratic Party (FDP) governing the city until 1955. Thereafter, the SPD governed the city-state alone for almost forty years, with the exception of several short coalitions. The SPD and CDU would not form a coalition together again until the 1990s, following the collapse of a coalition between the SPD, FDP, and Greens.

For most of this period, the commemoration of National Socialism, its buildings, and its crimes was not a major priority in Bremen. With the removal of swastikas from town buildings, National Socialism was considered to have been overcome. Traditionalist and modernist architects were in agreement, moreover, on the need to avoid overt political symbolism in architecture, which both viewed as the essence of National Socialist architectural design.[21]

The approach taken in the management of the two monuments erected by the National Socialists in Bremen is typical of this dehistoricization. In 1935, the head of the Bremen School of Arts, Professor Ernst Gorsemann, designed a monument for the soldiers who fell in World War I. The monument, the Kriegerdenkmal Altmannshöhe (the Altar of the

Fig. 3. Concentration camp prisoners at work on the north side of the construction site for the submarine shelter Valentin, 1944. The prisoners are guarded by a so-called *Kapo* (prisoner-foreman). This photo is part of a larger series taken by local photographer Seubert. (Photo: Private Archive of Inge Marszolek.)

Altmannshöhe), was erected on one of the few hills within the city, close to the old defensive embankments, behind the town's art gallery (fig. 4). Although planned prior to 1933, the monument was clearly embedded within National Socialism's aesthetic glorification of heroic death. A certain degree of controversy surrounded the monument, which also listed the names of twenty-four Freikorps soldiers who were killed fighting against the Soviet Republic of Bremen in February 1919. In the 1950s, the senate considered enlarging the monument to include those killed during World War II—a proposal that reflected a general derealization of the monument's past political significance.[22]

A second monument, entitled *Sterbende Jüngling* (Dying Youth), was created in 1936 by Herbert Kubicka and also commemorates the soldiers of the Gerstenberg Division and the Freikorps Caspari who died in fighting against the Soviet Republic of Bremen. This statue of a youth crowned with a laurel wreath first stood in the Liebfrauenkirche on the inner-city market square. During the war, the statue was placed in the city's art

Fig. 4. The Kriegerdenkmal Altmannshöhe, Bremen, today. The altar is covered in red ink from an antifascist action. Because of this, the area is fenced off. The building behind the wall is the art gallery. (Photo: Marc Buggeln.)

gallery. In 1955, it was moved to the Wall-Anlagen Park, but without the victor's laurels and the inscription commemorating the Freikorps soldiers (fig. 5). This decision, too, reflected a desire to establish distance between the Nazi past and the democratic present.[23]

In the aftermath of the denazification process, during which representatives of the labor movement had fought for the harsher punishment of incriminated citizens, political interest in National Socialism declined. There was a tacit understanding between the SPD and the bourgeois parties that it was more important to look forward. This sentiment was also expressed in the artistic decoration of new buildings. The vision of an intact and peaceful world risen from the ashes dominated the 1950s, allowing little room for a critical discussion of the past and propagating an ahistorical reconciliation of humankind.[24]

Especially dominant was the myth that National Socialism had never been able to establish itself in Bremen. The story that Hitler had visited Bremen just once and had not liked the city at all was commonly recited

Fig. 5. Herbert Kubicka's *Sterbende Jüngling* and Jürgen Waller's Lidice Memorial, Wall-Anlagen Park, Bremen, current condition. (Photo: Marc Buggeln.)

with much pride.[25] The spirit that prevailed in Bremen in the postwar years is captured well in the judgment passed in the denazification hearing of a senior director at the Bremen utilities company (Bremer Stadtwerke). The judge explained:

> The promise of National Socialism came from Bavaria. From there Hitlerism spread out across the country to arrive finally in northern Germany. Here he encountered a bastion of free-spirited citizens. . . . It is only natural that this "new doctrine" was rejected by such free-spirited citizens. In fact, their attitude to National Socialism was one of animosity. . . . As far as Bremen was concerned National Socialism was simply imported goods. And senior Nazis knew this too; that's why Hitler and his chums so often swore and cursed the fools in Bremen. . . . It is a notorious fact that National Socialism was forced upon the citizens of the Hanseatic city against their will.[26]

With the widespread support of local historians, this view prevailed in the city for almost forty years. This state of affairs paralleled events in Hamburg, where the first postwar mayor, businessman Rudolf Petersen, created a similar legend. Petersen emphasized that it was simply a "fact that Hamburg was not affected by the crimes and excesses of National Socialism to the same degree as most other parts of the German Reich."[27] In Hamburg, local historians upheld this myth for forty years, until criticism began to assert itself in the early 1980s. The only factual basis that these myths were able to draw on was the relative unimportance of the NSDAP in both cities prior to 1933. Otherwise, these legends rested solely on the construct of the cosmopolitan and liberal businessman.

The Submarine Shelters Valentin and Hornisse, 1945–80

In the immediate aftermath of the war, the management of the militarily significant submarine shelters lay in the hands of the U.S. military missions. The German engineers managing the project were particularly proud that an American commission, which inspected the Valentin shelter after the war, had been impressed by its construction. This did not stop the commission from demanding the demolition of the shelter, however. But calculations showed that a complete demolition of the building was impossible without seriously damaging the surrounding township. As a first step, the commission had the diving test basin and the exit lock destroyed and the production facilities dismantled. But the ultimate goal of complete destruction was soon forgotten. The debate over the shelter's destruction only began anew after a military commission inspected the shelter again in 1948 and found the building still generally intact.

By this time, political institutions existed again in Bremen and demanded to be involved in the discussion. The position taken by Bremen's politicians and public at the outset of this debate was ambivalent. The population of Farge, together with a part of Bremen's government, planned to bury the shelter under rubble and debris. Plans were also circulated to bury the shelter under a hill of sand and build a coffeehouse on the summit. The port director, Professor Agatz, opposed these plans, however, and successfully fought power to preserve "his" creation.[28]

In the meantime, the British and American air forces had begun testing the effectiveness of new rocket-propelled bombs on the shelter. The tests were met by increasingly angry complaints from the local population, which repeatedly petitioned against the growing strength of the explosions. Representatives of the senate spoke out repeatedly, but it was not until a conversation with the senatorial president in November that the U.S. high commissioner for Germany, John McCloy, agreed to end the bombing.[29] By this time, the management of the shelter had passed to the Oberfinanzpräsidenten (Treasury Department) in Bremen. From this time on, the city of Bremen was greatly interested in finding a financially worthwhile use for the shelter.

In this context, the shelter became the projection screen for almost every kind of fantasy that was driving the young and ambitious Federal Republic. Following the short period of stillness when most were in favor of tearing down the relics of National Socialism, the mood changed. Within a few years, people were ready to look ahead again, liberate the shelters and bunkers from their shadows, and enlist them in the service of new dreams. According to one popular saying, the shelter in Farge was the "eighth wonder of the world."[30] The centerpiece of these popular fantasies was the archetypal architectural and industrial icon of the 1950s—the atomic reactor. As early as 1952, the senator for economics stated that his department would investigate whether or not the shelter could accommodate several atomic reactors.[31] Despite the negative conclusion of a study conducted on this question, the plans remained in discussion until 1957.[32] At the same time, plans to store nuclear weapons in the shelter began to circulate.[33] So, too, did plans to convert the shelter into a marina, a grain silo, and a synthetic fertilizer container.

All these plans were scrapped in October 1960, when the Federal Armed Forces decided to establish a depot for naval materials in the shelter. The front section of the shelter was overhauled for approximately five million Deutsche Marks, and the shelter passed from the state to the federal treasury. In 1960, the Federal Armed Forces also hindered the publication of photos of the shelter by Radio Bremen. Just fifteen years after the end of the war, the shelter again became a military secret and was removed from maps and aerial photos. The shelter disappeared from broader public consciousness. This development suited the local population quite well, as they had never relinquished their hopes that the shelter might be torn down and banished from memory. Their hope that the shelter would disappear under a mountain of sand remained unfulfilled, but the armed forces made the shelter as inconspicuous as possible, shielding it with trees and removing it from public maps. They also made it possible for the locals to give the site a new name. The terrible story of the submarine shelter Valentin faded away and was masked by a new name that referred only to the shelter's current use: Marine Materials Depot.

The history of the submarine shelter Hornisse is similar. The Allies also planned to destroy this shelter but never did. It stood derelict for many years, while construction companies formerly involved in the project fought with the senate over the salvage rights to the shelter, which now lay within the jurisdiction of the state of Bremen.[34] The Port Building Authority was unable to release the shelter for use until 1968. The logistics company Lexzau, Scharbau & Co. then built its administration building on top of the shelter, inaugurating it in June 1969.[35] The local newspaper wrote of a "fortress that towers over the Weser" but failed to mention one word about the concentration camp inmates who laid the foundations of this "fortress."[36] The shelter appeared on the horizon of public perception just this once, without any historical reference, and then immediately disappeared again.

Air-Raid Shelters in Bremen, 1945–80

After the war, Allied disarmament experts trained their sights on German air-raid shelters. Directive No. 22 issued by the Allied Control Council required the demolition of all air-raid shelters. The housing shortage in the western zones was so high that the living space provided by the bunkers seemed indispensable. Lengthy negotiations between the municipal authorities and the Allies followed, resulting in the demolition of most military bunkers and the conversion of many civilian air-raid shelters. The conversion of shelters included their tactical neutralization by drilling holes through the walls and ceilings, making them ineffective against bombs.

Although the shelters in Bremen were not used to provide accommodation for refugees, Allied plans to demolish them as war relics still met with resistance. Their demolition would have added substantially to the amount of rubble in the city. Some of the shelters built aboveground stood in the immediate vicinity of residential buildings, which would have been endangered by demolitions. Such actions seemed highly inappropriate considering the housing shortage in the city. The senator for economics also argued that the shelters were needed to provide storage for goods. Eventually the Allied Military Government declared that it would only demolish those shelters for which no use could be found.[37] One shelter, the invisible underground bunker on the Cathedral Square, was used by the military government, first as a private prison by the military police and later as a detention center. After 1948, the shelter was subsequently converted into an underground parking garage.[38]

When the Disarmament Branch ended its activities on September 12, 1950, the federal authorities ordered an immediate stop to the demolition of shelters. Debate over their future quieted down. In Bremen, even the aboveground shelters in the Bürgerpark, which had been used by the leadership of the NSDAP and the government in the final months of the war, remained standing. In 1951, a letter published in a local newspaper suggested covering the bunkers with greenery. The idea was taken up by Director Tippel, who began inquiries at the Garden and Landscape Department.[39]

In 1951, the first steps were also taken to prepare civil defense structures for the cold war and the threat of nuclear conflict.[40] In 1957, German experts were permitted to observe American tests of shelters exposed to atomic explosions in the Nevada desert. German cities were then requested to report to the federal authorities on the state of their air defenses, and in May 1960, the federal government issued its guidelines for the maintenance of shelters. According to the guidelines, existing shelters were to be retrofitted and their walls reinforced to a width of three meters. Due to the scarcity of funds, the program made slow progress, and in 1975, its overall goals were scaled down. The project was finally mothballed in 1992. Since then, funding for civil defense has only been made available for the general maintenance of existing shelters.

Hostels and Hotels in Shelters

In 1942, the Nazi mayor of Bremen suggested opening cheap hotels inside the shelters after the war.[41] In August 1945, this possibility was raised again, but without the added luxury of installing bathrooms. With the permission of the Reichsbahn management, the senator for health and social services made the eastern section of a shelter located below the forecourt of the central train station available to a humanitarian organization, the Innere Mission, which used the shelter to provide sleeping accommodation for refugees and travelers who filled the station's waiting rooms and halls.[42] Together with an aboveground bunker in an outlying suburb, the underground shelter below the central station forecourt was used to provide accommodation for homeless men until 1976. In 1960 alone, 70,248 men slept in the shelter below the central station.[43] Before long, however, the shelter's long-term use by the Innere Mission sparked controversy. In the late 1960s and early 1970s, several newspaper articles in *Die Zeit* harshly criticized the living conditions in the shelter.[44] Sanitation was next to nonexistent. New arrivals, picked up drunk by the police, were brought to the shelter in dog wagons. The men slept on the floor on newspapers. With neither daylight nor an infirmary, the shelter was the last station for alcoholics, disabled people, and the ill.

Supported by senate authorities, the Innere Mission began to look for a site for a new men's home. Local residents who took legal action against the project regularly thwarted their plans. Despite the assurances of the Innere Mission and the senate that most of the men were employed, nobody wanted the two hundred men from the shelter at the central station in their neighborhood. The Innere Mission's new home was finally opened in 1976. However, even today, the home is located outside of residential suburbs. But that is not the last story about the use of air-raid shelters in Bremen as emergency accommodation. In 1991, refugees arrived in Germany in large numbers, and many headed for the allegedly liberal city of Bremen. Three air-raid shelters were opened again to provide mass accommodation—this time for Africans and Kurds, as well as Sinti and Roma from Yugoslavia and Romania, all of whom filled the shelters in the Scharnhorststrasse, Zwinglistrasse, and Friedrich-Karl-Strasse.[45]

The 1980s: Bremen's Citizens Begin to Remember

The closing years of the 1970s saw the beginning of a paradigm shift within the field of historiography. Differing from the reigning tradition of structuralist social history, the new paradigm focused on the everyday lives and experiences of ordinary people. This new perspective was accompanied by a local historical movement, the history workshops, which were often closely tied to the "new social movements" of the time. In Bremen, the search for traces of the National Socialist era was also taken up, but with one important difference: from the outset, the workshops in Bremen had the support of the Social Democrats, who also dominated the city's administration. This fact may explain why the initial interest in the workshops in Bremen was stronger than in other industrial cities and was focused so strongly on the labor movement's resistance to the National Socialist regime.

In accordance with the Social Democratic policy of making educa-

Fig. 6. The air-raid shelter in the Admiralstrasse, Bremen, current condition. The painting is by Jürgen Waller. (Photo: Marc Buggeln.)

tion and the arts more accessible to a broader section of society, a program was conceived to place works of public art at buildings throughout the city. In the course of this program, many of the air-raid shelters were painted by Bremen artists, who used these war relics and their gray walls to make artistic statements about war and fascism.[46] One of five images painted on shelters by Jürgen Waller, on the air-raid shelter in the Admiralstrasse, was dedicated to the "opponents and victims of fascism" (fig. 6). Waller's work shows various forms of everyday resistance in a particularly plastic style of painting. The image is bordered by the names of resistance fighters in Bremen, mainly individuals from the labor movement and persons persecuted on account of their political beliefs or race. This painting illustrates the contemporary focus on the resistance movement, while the predominantly Jewish victims are marginalized. Other paintings on shelters concentrated more strongly on the message "Never again war!" The language of these paintings is more abstract and expressionistic, and as such they are often the targets of the bitter complaints by locals. Ironically, these shelters were also retrofitted as fallout shelters, and information evenings were regularly held by the Bundesverband für Selbstschutz (a nationwide civil defense association) in the shelter in the Admiralstrasse.

Today, the images on the bunkers are fading away and becoming invisible. In the local councils, the question of whether they should be repainted or simply allowed to disappear is the subject of heated discussions. At the same time, the city has also sold several shelters, and the new owners have built houses on their roofs. This practice has often made the shelters more visible to passersby than they previously were. But this form of visibility is ambivalent. Its primary characteristic is the private appropriation of the shelters, not the memory of their history, which has largely been ignored. Most new owners have beautified the shelters and hidden them from view with ivy, transforming the actual objects into mere foundations (fig. 7).

During the 1980s, both of Bremen's Nazi monuments were also reembedded in their historical contexts and became the focus of controversial discussion. In 1986, a peace group, the Friedensinitiative Ostertor, invited artists to submit designs for the alteration of the Kriegerdenkmal Altmannshöhe behind the town art gallery. The young Bremen-based artist Silke Hennig submitted an award-winning design that included radically altering the monument by fragmenting its rotunda. However, the municipal administration rejected the design on the grounds that the alterations would infringe on Gorsemann's intellectual property rights. Although the Altmannshöhe is still occasionally used as a meeting place for right-wing groups, the monument remains unchanged and without any signs that could explain its history. It is as if the city had chosen to erase the monument from memory by surrounding it with silence.

The *Sterbende Jüngling* statue was treated differently: in 1989, a new memorial was built in its immediate vicinity in remembrance of the destruction of the village of Lidice and the murder of its inhabitants by the Nazis.[47] The barren language of Jürgen Waller's design for the Lidice Memorial presents a strong contrast to the National Socialist monument's glorification of heroic death. In the 1980s, another memorial was erected close to where the former synagogue once stood, in memory of the Reichspogromnacht in 1938. The deaths of the five Jewish citizens killed in Bre-

Fig. 7. Former air-raid shelter in the Berliner Strasse, Bremen, current condition. The shelter is hidden behind plants and has functionless windows. There is a residence on top. (Photo: Marc Buggeln.)

men during the pogrom are commemorated here each year on November 9. Plaques on buildings throughout the city commemorate the persecution and murder of Jewish citizens.

In this period, the submarine shelter Valentin also reentered public memory. In 1981, Radio Bremen broadcast a program on the use of forced labor at the site. In 1983, a memorial was inaugurated directly outside the Federal Army's barbed-wire perimeter. Former concentration camp prisoners from France attended the ceremony. The activity around the shelter has not quietened down again since then, as local initiatives have continually informed the public of their work and have also developed exchange programs with former forced laborers and inmates of concentration camps. Gradually the Federal Armed Forces began to rethink their position. While representatives of the local initiative were photographed in the

1980s by the military secret service (MAD), these same individuals were permitted to escort former forced laborers through the shelter in the 1990s. It was then even possible to hold readings with former prisoners in the undecorated section of the shelter. This development inspired the Bremen Theater to use the shelter. Since 1999, an antiwar piece by Karl Kraus, *The Last Days of Mankind,* has been performed in the shelter for six years running. Meanwhile, the Federal Armed Forces are contemplating the closure of their base at the shelter. This would reopen the discussion on the shelter's future and its possible uses as a site of memory. A local initiative has already placed stone blocks to mark the grounds where the camps for the forced laborers stood and has put up signs explaining the site's historical significance.

This diverse range of initiatives and activities has anchored the submarine shelter Valentin firmly within the public's awareness. In the meantime, thousands of Bremen's citizens have seen the building with their own eyes and will hardly be able to forget its massive—even violent—dimensions. The commemoration of the shelter's history has been such a public success that a local reporter once said that he simply could not write another article about the shelter, as so much had been written in the last years. But change in Farge itself is slow. Few locals attend the ceremonies held annually at the shelter by former prisoners. One woman from Farge says that she tells the other locals at her church about the meeting every year, although it only makes them angry. When students from Bremen University recently stopped in Farge to ask for directions to the shelter, the first four people they asked told them that there was no submarine shelter in Farge. The fifth person they stopped asked whether or not they meant the Marine Materials Depot and then showed the students the way.

The Hornisse shelter also entered into public awareness for a time in the 1980s. In 1982, employees at the Bremen steelworks began to concern themselves with the history of the satellite camp formerly located on the company grounds. Prisoners from this camp had been used to build the Hornisse shelter.[48] Since this time, former French prisoners have visited the site of their suffering annually as part of the pilgrimage of the Amicale de Neuengamme. The company management has shown little understanding, and the former prisoners are still forbidden to set foot on the grounds of Lexzau, Scharbau & Co. Lying as it does in an industrial zone and recognizable from the river only as the foundation of an office block, the shelter is invisible to most of the city's inhabitants.

Concrete Memories

On the occasion of the sixtieth anniversary of the end of World War II in 2005, a local history workshop held an exhibition about the air war in a shelter in a working-class suburb of Bremen. Although the exhibition (which was only open for one weekend) drew many visitors, the air-raid shelters still appear to have an ephemeral and diffuse location in the private topography of memory. In the minds of most Bremen residents, the shelters were a place of protection but also a place of uncertainty and danger. The idealized *Bunkergemeinschaft* (shelter community) of Nazi ideology figures in their memory as a place where everyone fought for themselves, for food and for space. Apparently, solidarity was seldom extended beyond one's own family. When it was, it was directed against the *Bunkerwart,* or shelter leader.[49] After the war, the people of Bremen were glad to leave these stone giants, and for the people on the ground, they became what they were always supposed to have been to the Allied bomber pilots: invisible. Although the shelters are still perceptible to the eye, the memories tied to them have faded with time and the passing of generations, until they have become invisible elements of memory.

People were also "concealed" and made invisible within the shelters—individuals who were excluded, who did not fit into the society of the economic miracle, with its facade of propriety, moralism, cleanliness, and industriousness.[50] This function of the shelters has continued the mechanisms of exclusion so characteristic of modernity, mechanisms initiated with the birth of the prison, psychiatric clinic, and workhouse, which not only were especially evident in Nazi racial-hygiene policies but led to the deaths of those excluded. The fact that such "concrete" mechanisms of exclusion continued well into the 1970s and even in the 1990s in a city that projected a particularly liberal image of itself sheds some light on both the ambivalence of modernity and the authoritarian side of liberalism.

Sites of memory evolve and are constantly remodeled. That is what the stories of the air-raid shelters and the submarine shelter Valentin show us. These concrete relics do not become places on the maps of memory of their own accord, however gigantic, monstrous, or conspicuous they might be. This topography cannot be read in itself; it takes the aid of the stories to make the topography legible. It is only when the inhabitants of a city begin to place these relics in their specific historical contexts and make them a part of public discourse that we can decode the inscriptions on their concrete skin. It appears that the myth of the cosmopolitan and liberal

Hanseatic city of Bremen, whose commercial and political elites kept their distance to the National Socialist regime, was able to establish itself relatively undisturbed, because National Socialism had left the architectural topography of the city more or less untouched—as also occurred in Hamburg. In both cases, the underlying cause may be that the most significant sites of National Socialist crimes to survive the regime—in Hamburg the Neuengamme concentration camp, in Bremen the submarine shelter Valentin—are situated far away from the inner city. In both cases, the granting of new uses to the sites meant that the stories of these historical places could be overwritten with new meanings and thus "made invisible." This would obviously have been a difficult path to take in such cities as Berlin, Munich, and Nuremberg, where large architectural relics from the National Socialist period remain.

What place do the shelters have in the configurations of cultural memory? The "disappearance" or "overwriting" of these concrete relics of the war corresponds with the often cited "derealization" of National Socialism in the public discourse of the postwar era: the architectural remains of National Socialism were consistently cloaked in silence, recoded, and thus made "invisible" to memory. But as we have shown, these concrete relics, by virtue of their powerful and very physical existence in the visual world, simultaneously provoke memory's resistance to the dragging tide of oblivion. As heterotopical places, they combine the experiences of war and extermination with a contemporary period and simultaneously point toward the future. It was the history workshop movement, emerging out of the democratic protest culture of the 1960s and 70s, that opened up the city to the remembrance of the National Socialist era. In Bremen, this applies especially to the reinscription of the history of the submarine shelter Valentin in the public mind. Yet the status of the shelter remains fragile, diffuse, and uncertain. An open-ended process of remembrance was initiated with the site's new reinscription(s) on the map of memories. This process is open to many differing associations, and the concrete relics continue to be sites where memory is fought over. The establishment of everyday ways of using and referring to "the shelter" as a place can also reinforce the externalization of uncomfortable or unwanted layers of memory. The "visibility" and relative utility of the shelters in public space remains ambivalent. Architects, designers, and artists have discovered shelters as aesthetic spaces, which can be renovated and used as apartments. The shelters are also used for alternative cultural activities and as practice rooms for music groups. The question remains, how can a critical culture of remembrance be created by appropriating and redesigning sites with the intention of exposing and preserving the visibility of the various layers of memory embedded within them? As we have shown through the varying historical approaches taken in the city of Bremen, the evolving figuration of the shelters in public memory always holds two possibilities: the potential to forget or, alternatively, the opportunity to inscribe the shelters on the memory maps of the city as persistent and permanent carriers of a many-layered process of relating to and coming to terms with the past.

As relics of the war and testaments of forced labor, the shelters remain places of the Other, and they may all too easily be utilized as such—as shown by the use of shelters in Bremen to accommodate asylum seekers. The Other is a threatening figure, and concrete in particular seems to offer protection from those people who are to be excluded. The myriad expropriations and contaminations are inscribed in the concrete walls—not only the bodies seized by the war and the minds captured by the stage performances of National Socialism, but also the stolen lives of those who built the shelters. The difference between the civilian population that sought protection here and the forced laborers who had to build the shelters but were forbidden entry remains an often-concealed text within the walls of the shelters. It is one that has occasionally been read and spoken of in recent years. This text speaks of a difference that cannot be smoothed over but that is often overlooked on passing the shelters' smooth concrete walls.

NOTES

1. On the concept of cities as spaces of memory, see Gavriel D. Rosenfeld, *Architektur und Gedächtnis: München und Nationalsozialismus—Strategien des Vergessens* (Munich and Hamburg, 2004), 27ff.

2. Peter Dudek, "'Vergangenheitsbewältigung': Zur Problematik eines umstrittenen Begriffs," *Aus Politik und Zeitgeschichte,* nos. 1–2 (1992): 44–53.

3. Pierre Nora, *Zwischen Geschichte und Gedächtnis* (Frankfurt am Main, 1998).

4. Our understanding of visibility is partly based on the urban semiotics of Roland Barthes. See his "Semiologie und Stadtplanung," in *Das semiologische Abenteuer* (Frankfurt am Main, 1988), 199–209.

5. Michel Foucault, "Andere Räume," in *AISTHESIS: Wahrnehmung heute oder Perspektiven einer anderen Ästhetik,* ed. Karlheinz Barck, Peter Gente, and Heidi Paris (Leipzig, 1990), 34–46.

6. Malte Ritter, *Die Bremer und ihr Vaterland: Deutscher Nationalismus in der*

Freien Hansestadt (1859–1913) (Berlin, 2004). Even today, the self-image of Bremen's citizenry as free, cosmopolitan citizens standing in a long tradition clearly predominates among the city's influential figures.

7. Matthias Wegner, *Hanseaten: Von stolzen Bürgern und schönen Legenden* (Berlin, 1999).

8. In the last three national elections, the Nazi Party got 30.8 percent of the vote (July 31, 1932), 21.2 percent of the vote (November 6, 1932), and 32.6 percent of the vote (March 5, 1933).

9. Inge Marszolek and Rene Ott, *Bremen im Dritten Reich: Anpassung—Widerstand—Verfolgung* (Bremen, 1986), 131.

10. Michael Foedrowitz, *Bunkerwelten: Luftschutzanlagen in Norddeutschland* (Eggolsheim, 2002), 10–11.

11. Ibid., 53.

12. Olaf Groehler, *Bombenkrieg gegen Deutschland* (Berlin, 1990), 244.

13. Marc Buggeln and Inge Marszolek, "Bunker," in *Orte der Moderne: Erfahrungswelten des 19. und 20. Jahrhunderts,* ed. Alexa Geisthövel and Habbo Knoch (Frankfurt am Main and New York, 2005), 281–89.

14. Aufstellung vom August 1944, in Staatsarchiv Bremen (hereinafter StaB), 4,29/1-962. See Stand des Arbeitseinsatzes im LS-Bau vom April 1942, in StaB 4,29/1-1240.

15. Herbert Schwarzwälder, *Bremen und Nordwestdeutschland am Kriegsende 1945,* vol. 1, *Die Vorbereitung auf den "Endkampf"* (Bremen, 1972), 91.

16. Ibid., 91–94.

17. On the subject of forced labor at the submarine shelter of the Deschimag AG, see Marc Buggeln, "KZ-Häftlinge als letzte Arbeitskraftreserve der Bremer Rüstungswirtschaft," in *Arbeiterbewegung und Sozialgeschichte* 12 (2003): 19–36.

18. Schreiben des Oberkommandos der Marine betr. U-Bootsbunkerprogramm in der Heimat vom 22. Januar 1943, in Bundesarchiv-Militärarchiv Freiburg, W 04/18163.

19. Marc Buggeln, "Das Außenlagersystem des KZ Neuengamme," in *Abgeschlossene Kapitel? Zur Geschichte der Konzentrationslager und der NS-Prozesse,* ed. Sabine Moller, Miriam Rürup, and Christel Trouvé (Tübingen, 2002), 15–27.

20. Heiko Kania, "Neue Erkenntnisse zu Opferzahlen und Lagern im Zusammenhang mit dem Bau des Bunkers Valentin," *Arbeiterbewegung und Sozialgeschichte* 10 (2002): 7–31.

21. Eberhard Kulenkampff, "Ein paar VorWorte," in *Flugdächer und Weserziegel: Architektur der 50er Jahre in Bremen,* ed. Franz-Peter Mau (Worpswede, 1990), 8.

22. Eva Missler, *Das Reise- und Lesebuch Bremen* (Bremen, n.d.), 162–63.

23. Ibid., 164–65.

24. Hans-Joachim Manske, "'Unschuldige Provinzialität': Die 'Kunst am Bau' in den 50er Jahren," in Mau, *Flugdächer,* 65–75.

25. This myth is not unique to Bremen. Versions of it appeared in almost every industrial city within the Reich and held sway long into the 1970s.

26. Urteilsbegründung im Entnazifizierungsverfahren Friedrich Hopf vom 18.

Juli 1949, in StaB 4,66-I Hopf. Our thanks to Marcus Meyer for informing us about the existence of this judgment.

27. From Petersen's sworn statement for Curt Tothenberger from June 11, 1947, in Staatsarchiv Hamburg, 622-1 Familie Petersen, O.40, vol. 5, Sci-Z.

28. Agatz was a leading architect of the firm Baubüros, Agatz, and Bock, who were responsible from 1943 to 1945 for the design of the submarine shelter Valentin. For more on Agatz, see the uncritical biographical notes by Karl Löbe in "Ein erfülltes Ingenieurleben. Arnold Agatz 85 Jahre," in *Jahrbuch der Wittheit zu Bremen* 20 (1976): 87–131; StaB 4,29/1-963.

29. StaB 4,29/1-963.

30. *Weser-Kurier,* October 13, 1955.

31. *Weser-Kurier,* June 15, 1952.

32. *Weser-Kurier,* April 11, 1957.

33. *Norddeutsche,* June 15, 1957.

34. StaB 4,29/1-962.

35. Eike Hemmer and Robert Milbradt, *Bunker "Hornisse": KZ-Häftlinge in Bremen und die U-Boot-Werft der "AG Weser" 1944/45* (Bremen, 2005), 125.

36. *Bremer Nachrichten,* June 24,1969.

37. StaB 4,29/1-962.

38. Niederschrift der Senatssitzung vom 13. Januar 1948, in StaB 4, 29/1-962.

39. Schreiben Tippels an das Gartenbauamt v. 16. April 1951, in StaB 4, 29/1-962.

40. Auszug aus dem Senatsprotokoll v. 18. Mai 1951, in StaB 4, 29/1-962.

41. Vermerk über einen Anruf des Reg. Bürgermeisters beim Sen. f. das Bauwesen v. 25. November 1942, in StaB 4, 29/1-962.

42. Schreiben d. Sen. f. Wohlfahrt an Sen. f. Wirtschaft, Häfen und Verkehr v. 22. August 1945, in StaB 4,124/1-184.

43. *Weser Kurier,* September 2, 1961.

44. *Die Zeit,* April 8, 1966; April 3, 1970.

45. *Weser Kurier,* June 20, 1991; *die tageszeitung,* July 8, 1991.

46. *Kunst gegen Krieg und Faschismus in Bremen,* ed. Sen. f. Bildung (Bremen, 1986). More than twenty shelters were painted in total, five of which referred to the theme of war.

47. The memorial was made by Jürgen Waller. Lidice is one of Bremen's sister cities, and a local initiative has had long and extensive contact with the town.

48. Kollegengruppe der Klöckner-Hütte Bremen, *Riespott—KZ an der Norddeutschen Hütte: Berichte, Dokumente und Erinnerungen über Zwangsarbeit 1935–1945* (Bremen, 1984).

49. Interviews conducted with witnesses by a group of students in my project seminar of 2005 confirm this.

50. In this sense, the shelters should be read as heterotopies characterized by both crisis and deviation; see Foucault, "Andere Räume."

Restored, Reassessed, Redeemed
The SS Past at the Collegiate Church of St. Servatius in Quedlinburg
Annah Kellogg-Krieg

Situated at the foothills of the Harz Mountains along the Bode River, the town of Quedlinburg appears as a medieval time capsule, as if it had sidestepped the last six or seven centuries of advancements in building technology and urban planning. Crooked door jambs, crumbling clay shingles, and modern shop windows are the only indicators of the passage of time. Narrow cobblestone alleys named after various guilds lead to a market square encircled by half-timbered houses and a Gothic town hall. From this vantage point, the castle hill is barely visible. The hill lies to the south of the town center, inconspicuously rising from the fairy-tale skyline of red roofs and chimneys. King Heinrich I established his favorite imperial residence on the hill during his consolidation of the first German Reich in the early tenth century. He obtained valuable relics for the palatine chapel, including one of St. Servatius, the namesake of the convent founded by Queen Mathilde on the castle hill after Heinrich's death in 936. Thus, Heinrich never stepped foot in the current church, the fourth sacred structure on the site, which was constructed in the years 1071–1129 after fire had destroyed the prior building.[1]

The charm of the Church of St. Servatius's stocky Romanesque silhouette and the half-timbered town draw thousands of tourists, mainly Germans, to Quedlinburg each year. However, recent times have not been the first to witness mass pilgrimage to the site. The chief of the SS, Heinrich Himmler, was the most infamous visitor to St. Servatius in the twentieth century, as he sought to capitalize on Quedlinburg's important role in early German history and its stunning architecture. King Heinrich and St. Servatius were not simply tools of propaganda for the leader of the SS however. Rather, Himmler developed a deeply personal link with Heinrich and his reign. Himmler considered himself the reincarnation of Heinrich I and, within the SS, was frequently called "König Heinrich."[2]

Himmler regarded the first German king as providing the historical underpinnings for his elitist SS ideology. He found Heinrich's ruthless eastern military campaigns against "inferior people" (*Untermenschen*) to be particularly inspiring. The acquisition of land in the east for the virtuous German farmer in the tenth century vindicated the reconquest of this territory in the twentieth century. Although the unification of the German *Volk* in the tenth century was radically different from the unified nation-state of the nineteenth century, Himmler and the SS capitalized on the notion of King Heinrich I as the original unifier of the Germans. However dubious their conclusions may have been, the connections between Heinrich and the current reunifiers of Germany, Hitler and Himmler, wedded the ideology of the Third Reich to a glorious German history.

Himmler instigated the transformation of Quedlinburg into an SS Camelot, with St. Servatius as the focal point for ceremonies and memorials dedicated to the first ruler who ostensibly unified the Germans, King Heinrich I. However, provincial Quedlinburg would never have become the center for one of the most powerful leaders of the Nazi regime had it not been for a fortuitous coincidence. In 1935, an SS official learned of the city government of Quedlinburg's plans to celebrate in 1936 the thousandth anniversary of Heinrich's death. A letter to Himmler from a certain Brigadenführer-SS Reischle, director of the Race Office, expressed the excitement within the SS about the promise of this event: "If Heinrich I must be emphasized by us as the first German king, then the propagandistic potential of the thousandth anniversary next year is virtually a gift from heaven."[3]

Thus the thousandth anniversary of the death of the primogenitor of the original German Reich at St. Servatius on July 2, 1936, became a spectacle of SS pomp and propaganda. The SS transformed St. Servatius into a medieval king's hall for the momentous occasion; the pews were removed, and royal blue velvet and the coats of arms from the regions of Heinrich's empire adorned the walls of the nave.[4] At the eastern end of the crossing, a long black cloth embellished with the SS insignia covered the fourteenth-century Gothic choir.[5] The short-term decorations and rearrangements for the 1936 and 1937 Heinrich celebrations provided a temporary backdrop for SS rituals, but Himmler could not continue to ignore the fact that, functionally and stylistically, the church did not completely adhere to SS notions of nation and history. Therefore, his SS minions and compatriots in the historic preservation offices physically altered the appearance of St. Servatius to suit the ideological aims of the SS. These reconstructions, most significantly the removal of all overtly Christian elements and the Gothic east choir, inscribed a new layer of meaning and memory into the stones of St. Servatius, which have only just begun to be reevaluated and reconsidered in the public realm.

The principal phase of postwar East German reconstruction, from 1945 to the early 1960s, forms the linchpin of this essay. A general repression of the SS's involvement at St. Servatius and a refusal to perceive any connection between what were seen as practical reconstructions, SS ideology, and the National Socialist regime mark this period. Bookended by the SS-led alterations of St. Servatius in the late 1930s and early 1940s and the recent postreunification events, this watershed point reveals many continuities in historic preservation practices before and after 1945. Labeled the "Hallerian Way" after 1945 because of its origins in Halle, this preservation practice favored a unified aesthetic over the conservation of surviving original building material. The inherently destructive treatment of historical material promoted by the Hallerian Way easily lent itself to a highly tendentious view of history sponsored by Himmler and SS elites. In the postwar era, this blatant erasure of certain historical styles and the striving toward a unified aesthetic that highlighted only certain periods reflected the larger post-1945 phenomenon of repressing recent history and pursuing a politically neutral collective national identity.

Through careful formal analysis of the first postwar wave of renovations and reconstructions of St. Servatius, we can better understand the varying manifestations of the relationship between *Vergangenheitsbewältigung,* architecture, and the urban landscape. An investigation of historic preservation practices in an East German small town removed from major metropolitan centers and the spotlight of national-level media and public discourse reveals not only a more complex, less hierarchical set of dynamics among local and regional officials but also the greater ease in sweeping the painful past of a particular site under the rug. Because of its original sacred function and its centuries-old history as both collegiate and parish church, St. Servatius is a more complicated example of the afterlife of SS-sponsored architectural projects. Not only did the congregation play a significant role alongside the local and federal governments, but the issue of resanctification after 1945 also presented an exceptional conundrum. Furthermore, the Janus-faced nature of St. Servatius as both a religious edifice and a national symbol of German medieval heritage in East Germany separates this case study from those buildings constructed under the Third Reich.

The end of World War II in Quedlinburg looked very different from the utter destruction of similar-sized historical centers in the Harz region. The town was spared the air raids that decimated other nearby historical monuments in Halberstadt, Hildesheim, and Magdeburg. Artillery fire slightly damaged the roofs of the towers and the westwork—the only destruction done to the church as a direct result of war. The mayor had committed suicide after destroying many photographs and documents, and the SS officials stationed in Quedlinburg to oversee activities at the church moved out in the spring. American troops reached Quedlinburg first on April 19, 1945. On July 1, Quedlinburg became part of the Soviet sector along with the entire province of Saxony.

On June 3, 1945, the congregation of St. Servatius, which had been forcibly expropriated by the SS in 1938 and resettled in the Church of St. Blasius not far from the main town square, decided to resanctify the structure and held their first service since Easter 1938. While the sparse literature on the SS appropriation of the church situates St. Servatius as a site of Protestant resistance to the Nazi regime, the church's staffing choices after the war reveal a much more complicated narrative.[6] The Protestant church's provincial building office in Magdeburg commissioned Robert Hiecke as advisor for the rebuilding and renovation project immediately after the war.[7] The congregation and church officials saw Hiecke as a professional with decades of experience and firsthand knowledge of the church. However, his intimate familiarity with St. Servatius came while working on the SS-led alterations. As the chief Prussian conservator of monuments from 1918 to 1945, leader of the monuments division of the Reichsbund Volkstum und Heimat (Reich Association for Folklore and Home) until its dissolution in 1935, and NSDAP member, Hiecke formed the crucial link between the SS and historic preservation and wielded a heavy hand in the decision-making process on both sides.[8]

Hiecke oversaw a group of middle managers from various organizations during the alterations. A certain SS-Untersturmführer Schmidt oversaw the Quedlinburg SS *Arbeitsstab* (work branch) and needed to have all decisions and actions approved by Hiecke. Schmidt often acted as the mediator between the preservationists and Himmler. Hermann Giesau, the provincial conservator from Halle from 1930 to 1945, coordinated much of the work with Hiecke and often represented him at on-site meetings that Hiecke could not attend personally. In contrast to Hiecke,

Giesau expressed certain reservations about the SS-instigated alterations. Although he had been a member of the NSDAP since 1937, Giesau remained unconvinced by the alterations and often withdrew from public events at the church. He was not able to continue working under Hiecke after the war, however, as he was sent to an internment camp for a year, after which he received a *Berufsverbot* (order of professional disqualification) and was forbidden from further work in 1946.[9]

Nevertheless, Hiecke and Giesau orchestrated a radical aesthetic transformation of the sacred space of St. Servatius (figs. 1 and 2). One of the most apparent SS adjustments in the nave was the removal of overtly Christian elements—the pews, the altars, the pulpit, and the abbesses' tombs that had filled the center of the main nave aisle. The chairs that replaced the pews were built in the workshops of the Dachau concentration camp. Obersturmführer-SS Dr. Höhne, who was also heavily involved in the archaeological excavation at the castle hill to locate the bones of Heinrich I, noted in a letter to Giesau the economic advantage of ordering the chairs from Dachau, a chilling calculation when considering the fate of the majority of the carpenters at the camp.[10]

There were also more subtle renovations in the nave that were nevertheless crucial to SS ritual and ideology. Militaristic processions required wider stairs leading up to the choir. The decorative stone banisters were removed to streamline the ascent to the choir. The platform between the stairs and above the entrance to the crypt provided a speaking stand from which Himmler and other leaders could address assembled SS men in the nave during rituals. Himmler's taste for the Romanesque also necessitated the removal of the electric lighting system and its replacement by wrought iron light fixtures.

The largest architectural modification was the removal of the Gothic vaulting and lancet windows in the choir in favor of a highly simplified, smaller apse with a round stained glass window depicting the German eagle perched atop a swastika.[11] At Himmler's request, a dividing wall spatially separated the apse from the choir.[12] The flat wooden ceiling of this addition emulated the Ottonian building tradition. The exterior of the choir retained the lancet windows and buttresses of the vaulting with the insertion of a circular opening for the new window, creating a stylistic disjunction between interior and exterior.

There are various explanations for the removal of the Gothic elements of St. Servatius and the continued absence of the Gothic after 1945. German scholars had long understood the Gothic as French in origin, part

Fig. 1. St. Servatius, twelfth-century nave with the Gothic east choir. Photo from early twentieth century. (Photo: Landesamt für Denkmalpflege und Archäologie Halle.)

of the reason for the preference for the Romanesque as an ur-Germanic style. Especially those Nazi elites particularly captivated by St. Servatius (Himmler, Darré, Frick, Rosenberg) who came from the *völkisch* branch of the party sought a more conservative cultural policy rooted in what they saw as inherently historical German traditions. General trends in postwar historic preservation practices also dictated a unified aesthetic in a structure, even if it meant the destruction of original building material. The Hallerian Way in historic preservation was granted its name after 1945 for Giesau's influential role in the development of this mode of thinking.[13] The Hallerian Way favored early medieval architecture of the Ottonians and Salians and allowed for the guiltless removal of later additions to such structures, especially nineteenth-century renovations. While preservationists saw little artistic value in baroque and nineteenth-century altars, frescoes, and ornamentations, they nevertheless sought to complete histori-

Fig. 2. St. Servatius, nave after the SS-led reconstructions. 1938. (Photo: Landesamt für Denkmalpflege und Archäologie Halle.)

cally significant buildings with their own modern alterations to create a unified early medieval aesthetic.

The turn to Romanesque also speaks to contemporary Nazi-sponsored architectural projects. Although scholars tend to focus on the Nazi use of stripped neoclassicism, the solid, severe Romanesque aesthetic—with bulky masonry and streamlined expanses of space—offered even more stylistic correlation with several of the key monumental buildings of such architects as Albert Speer and Wilhelm Kreis than with the architecture of antiquity. Kreis's Soldiers' Hall in Berlin specifically reveals striking similarities with the crypt of St. Servatius, in which a neo-Romanesque secular eagle-motif window replaced the circular Gothic stained glass window and officials allowed the stark repetition of columns and groin vaults to remain. Similarly, the Soldiers' Hall consists of a matrix of rounded arches framing the focal point at the end of an axial hall.

Although Himmler never returned to Quedlinburg after the outbreak of war and so support for the development of the shrine diminished, Hiecke continued to devise plans for future renovations and even drew potential designs for the SS shrine in late 1944, while his Berlin office was constantly threatened by air raids and the encroaching front. These drawings express a jarring juxtaposition of medieval and Christian elements with modern Nazi symbolism and austerity. Hiecke's odd introduction of overt Christian symbolism, such as the cross suspended in the crossing and the Chi-Rho symbol on the altar in the nave, would have been blasphemous to Himmler. At this late stage in the war, though, he was never able to see these drawings. For Hiecke, however, there was no contradiction inherent in this mixture of symbolism, for he anticipated the reintroduction of Christian worship services at St. Servatius after the war.[14] The twin towers of the westwork illustrated his diametrically opposed ideology: throughout the Third Reich, one tower was adorned with a cross, while the other was outfitted with the Nazi eagle—also the choice of adornment for the towers after their restoration in the late 1940s. In Hiecke's redesign of the choir, the eagle window retained its prominent position. Underneath the window is the insignia of Heinrich I: a large *H* with the rest of the letters of his name placed around it. Hiecke also added the *Heinrichsmal*, a small altar placed in front of the apse as the focus of rituals. Hiecke intended for the side wall to include inscriptions of the places in Germany that shared a connection to King Heinrich I and were part of the foundation Himmler established for the memorialization of the medieval German ruler.[15]

Unlike Giesau, who began to reflect on the moral implications of the alterations even before 1945, Hiecke never exhibited any similar self-criticism or inner struggles with his own Nazi past. Not only did he transition seamlessly into postwar plans for St. Servatius, but he also completely rearranged his own attitude toward the alterations of St. Servatius. In a letter to Giesau's successor, Wolf Schubert, he brazenly offered his guidance in reversing the changes made to the building during the Third Reich.

> I am especially thankful that I still now have the opportunity to contribute to the work at the Quedlinburg minster. In the course of the past ten years (or maybe more?) this task has become very dear to me. It was often very difficult for me to carry out Himmler's ideas, which were often very adventurous, ad absurdum—or at least deviate from them enough that no disaster occurred. However some things hap-

pened on their own against my own will, which Mr. Giesau and I were not able to approve.[16]

Perhaps because he had escaped indictment and imprisonment, Hiecke was never forced to confront his involvement in the Nazi regime. Yet there were many professionals in cultural fields who managed to avoid any loss of position or overt denazification procedures. What is different about Hiecke's stance is not only the continuity in his involvement at St. Servatius but also the practice of historic preservation itself. The principles of the Hallerian Way encouraged free license with the destruction and recreation of historical building material, which adhered to the skewed perspective of German history promoted not only by the SS but also later by the party officials in the German Democratic Republic.

During the postwar era, the Hallerian Way easily reflected the larger post-1945 phenomenon of repression of recent history and the desire for a politically neutral national identity. The unwillingness or inability on the local level to confront St. Servatius's unsavory past exemplifies the silence surrounding the crimes of the Third Reich on the larger East German political stage. When the Federal Republic declared itself to be the heir of the Nazi regime, East Germany declared itself the antifascist state and focused on the persecution of Communists in its Nazi-era narratives.[17] The Holocaust was subsumed under party rhetoric and ideology as the GDR refused to pay reparations to Israel or survivors, purged party members who sought to give Jewish persecution greater prominence, and supported Israel's enemies. East Germany distinguished between fighters of fascism and victims of fascism, creating a hierarchy of survivors, elevating the Communists and marginalizing the Jews, Jehovah's Witnesses, Roma, and homosexuals. The suppression of the Holocaust in East German historical narratives ultimately transformed Germans into the victims of a fascist regime. In turn, government officials legitimated their own rule, since the Socialist path was seen as the only viable alternative to the Western capitalism and imperialism that had spawned fascist rule in Germany.

The medieval masonry of St. Servatius, as a remnant of a more distant, idealized past, was inserted into the new historical lineage of the GDR and circumvented a direct confrontation with East Germany's recent past. The cultural and historical amnesia that befell both German states in the immediate postwar years was not a complete turning away from history but, instead, the selective highlighting of particular histories that involved less painful soul-searching. Compared to other like-sized towns in the area that had experienced the almost total destruction of their medieval architecture, Quedlinburg was a gleaming bastion of German medieval heritage. There were also a mere handful of prewar Jewish families, no major Nazi military compounds or concentration camps in Quedlinburg to complicate the historical erasure. Consequently, the preservation of St. Servatius could be used as an important project for national identity rooted in a whitewashed, distant past. Because these other centers of early medieval German history had been completely leveled, the significance of the medieval material culture of Quedlinburg was heightened, and this material culture became the symbol of the past grandeur of the early medieval empire for a wider audience of German scholars and historic preservationists.

After the removal of the eagle and swastika tracery of the east choir window and other SS cult objects, the first goal for St. Servatius was stabilizing its westwork towers. Not only did both spires succumb to direct artillery hits, but the southwest tower proved especially problematic for the structural integrity of the entire building. Prussian conservator of monuments Ferdinand von Quast meant for this tower (built between 1872 and 1882) to complete the westwork ensemble, but two decades later, it had already separated itself from the church because of the unstable foundation on the sandstone cliffs. Originally, discussions centered around dismantling the tower not simply for structural concerns but also because the tower represented what Hiecke and others still saw as a nineteenth-century blemish on the medieval facade.[18] While the tower remained, the spires, in need of repair, were redesigned significantly. Instead of the taller, narrower spires constructed by von Quast's team and more characteristic of medieval tower terminations from the Rhineland, both towers were capped by squatter tetrahedron roofs modeled after the oldest surviving visual representation of the St. Servatius done by Braun and Hogenberg in 1582.[19] This was not the first time Hiecke raised this suggestion; in 1941, he also pushed for the removal of the nineteenth-century spires and their replacement with the local, Lower Saxon tradition of tetrahedron roofs.[20] On the surface, it appears as if there is nothing inherently intertwined with Nazi ideology in this decision. Because Hiecke had thought about the jarring stylistic disjunction in 1941 and again in 1946 does not immediately reveal a lingering SS agenda at St. Servatius. Yet this emphasis on using local building materials and local building traditions stemmed from a very *völkisch* mode of thinking in which building materials reflect the very attributes of the German civilization that ideologues believed made them superior to other cultures.²¹ Combined with the Hallerian Way of historic preservation, which destroyed as much historical material as it created in the name of stylistic unity, it served the needs of not only the Third Reich but also the fledgling German Democratic Republic.

The dedication festivities for the southeast tower on June 11, 1948, also exposed the Quedlinburg public's inability to work through the larger implications of the SS appropriation of St. Servatius. The speech of City Council Chairman Stolze is particularly striking in its aggressive nationalism at what was presented as the dedication of a reconstruction project at a resanctified Lutheran house of worship. Besides using this opportunity to call for a single German unity a few months before the founding of the German Democratic Republic in October, Stolze also stressed the erasure of St. Servatius's dark past "in order to create the new from the old and shape the *necessary newness.*"²² He concluded by proclaiming, "I thank God, who elected me German; I thank the mother who bore me German; I thank the ground, which kindles my Germanness; I thank the *Volk,* which raised me German; Germany, my fatherland!"²³

After structural work was finished on the westwork and spires, reconstruction of the interior of the choir, an ideologically more complicated task, started in the early 1950s. The eagle and swastika masonry had already been removed from the choir window in 1945, before the first postwar Lutheran service in St. Servatius. In 1953, the window in the choir was completely removed and walled over, but the masonry of the now bare apse reveals clearly the outline of where it once was (fig. 3). Pulpit and altars restored the Christian appearance of the interior. The altars not only served liturgical functions but were strategically placed to diminish the monumentality of the streamlined Romanesque interior. In 1953, one altar was placed in the apse specifically to divert attention away from the bareness. A late sixteenth-century triptych altarpiece added in the mid-1970s contributed to this effect. Another altar and crucifix were placed in front of the crypt entrance in the late 1950s to remove some of the visual focus from the crypt, which had been the nexus of SS rituals.

Other Nazi alterations, such as the staircases to the choir, were retained after the war, due partially to the dire economic situation in the eastern sector in the early years after the war and partially to what appeared to be the minor, purely formal nature of some of the Nazi renovations. The rebuilding of the Gothic choir came into debate after World War II, when reconstruction of the westwork towers began. After German reunification in 1990, the question of rebuilding the Gothic choir arose

Fig. 3. St. Servatius, nave after the first wave of postwar renovations. (Photo: Landesamt für Denkmalpflege und Archäologie Halle.)

again, but inspectors expressed concern about the structural integrity of the church.[24] Officials declared the project unnecessary at a historical moment when demand for housing and the rebuilding of urban infrastructure overrode most other building concerns. After World War II, conservators also decided that the neo-Romanesque style better suited a unified aesthetic in the church. In 1989, Hans Berger, architect by training and Giesau's ideological successor in the provincial preservation office, even commended the SS-led renovations, stating that the reinstitution of the Gothic choir would "contradict the wish for a building with a unified atmosphere and coherence in the artistic impression, toward which the conservators in the 1930s strived, *regardless* of whether they achieved this with questionable means."[25] Thus, the political connections between Himmler's choice of the Romanesque aesthetic and SS ideology were ignored blatantly in the name of a unified style. Giesau seems to have been the lone voice of dissent when writing, in 1946, "the complete removal of the NS-undertakings is an act of honesty and historical cleanliness."[26]

Indeed, even Giesau, the official most conflicted about the SS-instigated reconstruction, used the medieval masonry of St. Servatius—as a remnant of a less-burdened painful past—to construct a new kind of national historical narrative in the wake of the Third Reich and to circumvent a direct confrontation with (East) Germany's Nazi past. His desire to "cleanse" the events of the Nazi era is a prime example of the selective amnesia present in both Germanys immediately after World War II. Instead of a complete rejection of history, it represents an orchestrated selection of particular histories that involved less painful soul-searching, similar to the selective preservationist practices of the Hallerian Way.

From the beginning, Giesau expressed major reservations about the SS appropriation of a sacred object for its own propagandistic purposes. The medieval treasury was of particular concern for him. In spring 1938, he described to Hiecke his deep disappointment with the removal of the treasury objects from the church, noting, "I must say that this mere thought deeply disturbs me, that these things could move from their location."[27] Yet he admitted in the very next passage, "I was able to adjust myself to everything and went along somewhat voluntarily, because it can really be a *considerable win* for the entire undertaking."[28] While it is clear that Giesau was not unequivocally executing the will of Himmler or Hiecke, anyone who joined the SA in 1933 and the NSDAP in 1937 and thought of the profanation, destruction, and reconstruction of an almost eight-hundred-year-old church as a "considerable win" is a far cry from a resistance fighter. It is unclear if Andreas Stahl's claim that Giesau belonged to the resistance group centered around Theodor Lieser in Halle can be trusted.[29] The only definitive conclusion we can find for Giesau's position is the one he provided when he labeled himself an "onlooker and aesthetic complainer."[30]

As the crimes of the Nazi past were overshadowed by cold war concerns in West and East Germany, conservators on both sides of the iron curtain mobilized the medieval grandeur of St. Servatius to express resentment and sorrow over the breakup of the German state. Berger reminded the county commission in Halle of St. Servatius's significance not only for all of Germany but for European art and architectural history.[31] In an October 1957 article in *Neues Deutschland,* City Councilwoman Ilse Günther exploited the medieval history of St. Servatius both to fan the flames of cold war rhetoric and to give an open plea for building materials.

> Many ancient cities lost their monuments during the imperialist war, but Quedlinburg remained preserved save for the smallest damage. During the "thousand-year Reich" the city received very little care. . . . In order to prevent the threat of continued dilapidation, we quickly need material assistance. We know that the cost for the maintenance of our thousand-year-old city is large. In the interest of our residents, there is only one possibility—to begin quickly with the restoration work.[32]

By claiming that the city received no attention between 1933 and 1945, Günther did not acknowledge the annual Heinrich celebrations of 1936–45 and the SS's involvement in them. Both Günther and Berger pointed to the medieval history of St. Servatius in order to counter what they saw as crimes of the present, such as the Allies' division of Germany.

In 1962, West German conservators toured major sites of reconstruction in the GDR, establishing solidarity with their eastern compatriots. In Heinrich Kreisel's report on the excursion, he praised conservation efforts in East Germany and noted how the preservation of monuments drew both nations spiritually and culturally closer: "The tour and also our visit last but not least should express how much we, [the East Germans'] West German colleagues, value their work, how much we are thankful for them, and how much we stand behind them as conservators and as people."[33] When describing his stay in Quedlinburg, Kreisel became perceptibly emotional in his description of "the greatness of the architecture from the zenith of the German imperial era." He expressed grief knowing that St. Servatius was separated from medieval monuments in nearby West German towns, such as Hildesheim or Goslar, but no grief concerning the crimes that led to the division of Germany. Besides sidestepping Quedlinburg's conspicuous connection to the SS and the Third Reich, Kreisel did not acknowledge the connection between the destruction of these medieval monuments in World War II and the cause of that war: "We were all deeply moved and overjoyed that these famous monuments are reconstructed and partially ashamed that *a crazy political separation* has allowed us to forget that to some extent our best lies 'over there.'"[34]

When West Germany officially reunited with "over there" in 1990, another narrative of loss and retribution took precedence in Quedlinburg. The mysterious disappearance of a collection of medieval manuscripts and reliquaries from St. Servatius's treasury at the end of the war also expressed a narrative of German victimhood. The miraculous return of these treasures has diverted scholarly focus away from a reconsideration of the SS activity at St. Servatius until only very recently. The priceless gold-scripted medieval manuscripts and ivory reliquaries had been transferred from the church to a cave in the nearby foothills of the Harz Mountains during the war.[35] In the chaos and confusion in the spring and summer of 1945, a few of the carefully inventoried boxes went missing without drawing much attention. The culprit, Lieutenant Joe Tom Meador of the U.S. Army's Eighty-seventh Armored Field Artillery Battalion, remained unidentified for the rest of his life, quietly enjoying the treasures as a dilettantish art aficionado in northern Texas. After his death in 1980, his siblings first tried to sell the precious works at a garage sale, completely unaware of their value and provenance. After coming into contact with an art dealer in Dallas, however, they sold the ninth-century Samuhel Gospels in Switzerland in 1982. Although scholars and buyers easily recognized the piece as one of the missing Quedlinburg manuscripts, they were only able to sit by and observe. In 1990, the West German governmental organization Kultur Stiftung der Länder (Culture Foundation of the Provinces) was able to purchase the Samuhel Gospels for a finder's fee of three million dollars, and the treasures' journey back to Quedlinburg followed in rapid succession.

As Germans tore down the Berlin Wall with pickaxes and sledgehammers, the Meador family was uncovered in northern Texas by a West German lawyer and a *New York Times* reporter, and the remaining medieval treasures were found. For various legal reasons, the treasures were displayed publicly for the first time in almost fifty years at the Dallas Museum of Art. Shockingly, the accompanying catalog mentioned nothing of the dubious context for the exhibition.[36] The congregation of St. Servatius, the rightful owners, received the manuscripts and treasures in an official ceremony in St. Servatius on September 19, 1993. In the speech of Klaus Maurice, general secretary of Kultur Stiftung der Länder, the reunification of the treasury objects with St. Servatius became a parallel to the fledgling reunified German Republic. Maurice stated: "[T]he treasure is unified again with the place, which is connected to the foundation of the German Empire 1,150 years ago. Therefore, the return of the treasure became a sign of the unity of this state."[37] Maurice went on to draw parallels between the disappearance of the treasures and the forced expulsion of millions of ethnic Germans from Eastern Europe following the Nazi defeat: "In contrast to the unending throngs of people, who in the process of German history were driven out and failed to receive acknowledgment of their forced foreign status after involuntary emigration, the treasure returns."[38] Here, Maurice's reference to Germans driven from their homes throughout the course of history was a thinly veiled allusion to a specific group of *Vertriebene* (expellees)—the ethnic Germans in Poland, Czechoslovakia, Romania, Hungary, and elsewhere forcibly removed from their homes in the quest to create purely ethnically homogeneous states after World War II. The celebration of the return of key pieces of the St. Servatius treasury after an almost fifty-year absence became a stage on which to reflect on other injustices done to Germans after World War II.

While expellee organizations are not active in the region around Quedlinburg, other forms of right-wing extremism exploded in the former East Germany in the early 1990s. Neo-Nazi visits to St. Servatius demonstrate how these groups continue to capitalize on the history of the building in their self-definition. In July 1991, a group of twelve men dressed in boots and black leather bomber jackets and carrying a flag with the imperial eagle arrived at St. Servatius for a guided tour with the deacon, Werner Bley.[39] They rolled up the flag in the church and attentively listened to Bley's tour. An incident took place in the crypt, at the grave of King Heinrich I, when they photographed the interior, despite the restriction on photography due to the delicate condition of the Romanesque frescoes. While the visit remained an isolated occurrence that year, it represents one of many confrontations between right-wing extremists, repressed history, and difficult transitions in Quedlinburg in the early 1990s.[40]

Given the sociopolitical situation, a confrontation with the SS past at St. Servatius has been slow to develop in Quedlinburg. When I first visited the church as a tourist in 2001, I found only the most cursory mention of the Heinrich celebrations and no indication of what parts of the building were remnants of the SS-instigated alterations. With a 2003 symposium and the 2004 opening of a permanent exhibition on the propagandistic abuse of medieval history and architecture in Quedlinburg, however, there has been a productive start to serious memory work. Cosponsored by the Heinrich-Böll-Foundation of Sachsen-Anhalt, the castle museum of Quedlinburg, and the Museum Association of Sachsen-Anhalt, the symposium assembled an interdisciplinary group of scholars to discuss publicly for the first time ever the Nazi past of St. Servatius. Antje Vollmer, vice president of the Bundestag, declared in her opening words at the symposium, "The working through of Quedlinburg's NS history, which has barely happened up until this point, represents a 'white spot' in German historiography."[41] In detailing the exhibition concept, Christian Mühldorfer-Vogt explaining that some in Quedlinburg felt the musealization of the topic would lead to further visits to the site by right-wing extremist groups.[42] However, the exhibit History and Propaganda: The Ottonians in the Shadow of National Socialism opened without incident and is now a component to the castle museum's permanent exhibit. Part of the larger exhibit Tracking the Ottonians, it is contained in one of the smallest rooms in the entire exhibit, a cellar of about thirty-six square meters. An interactive CD-ROM in the exhibit provides more in-depth information on various topics, from the reception of Heinrich I in the nineteenth century to the texts of Himmler's speeches given at St. Servatius, thus more fully utilizing the cramped space. Perhaps the final panel of the display, which chronicles the persecution, deportation, and murder of a Roma girl from Quedlinburg, is the most effective element of the exhibit. In a small town that had no large Jewish population and was far removed from large concentration camps and the death camps further east, drawing this connection between the SS appropriation and alteration of St. Servatius and the genocidal policies of the Nazi regime elevates this exhibit to a deeper, more significant confrontation with the past.

However, Quedlinburg is a rural town left physically unscathed in the war and now consists of an aging, dwindling population. Working through the city's unsavory history remains on a restrained level, in the form of small exhibitions and brief allusions in tourist-oriented texts on city history. The most indelible marks of the Third Reich remain confined to St. Servatius, although the SS also expropriated the eleventh-century crypt of the St. Wiperti chapel to use it as a shrine. Hence, the broader geography of memory in Quedlinburg remains sparse and barren, with only the occasional neo-Nazi demonstration or World War II commemoration bubbling up to the surface of the public consciousness. Yet St. Servatius still stands on the castle hill looking down on the city's winding cobblestone lanes and half-timbered facades. Thus, the challenge of *Vergangenheitsbewältigung* in Quedlinburg means incorporating the complicated historical layers of St. Servatius into the city's larger fairy-tale image of medieval German building traditions (preserved in the city since Quedlinburg was made a UNESCO World Heritage Site in 1994). The inclusion of new exhibitions in the castle museum points toward this direction of an informed awareness of the processes of renovation, reassessment, and redemption in St. Servatius.

NOTES

1. The most extensive survey of the architecture of the church is Klaus Voigtländer's *Die Stiftskirche St. Servatii zu Quedlinburg: Geschichte ihrer Restaurierung und Ausstattung* (Berlin, 1989).
2. Josef Ackermann, *Heinrich Himmler als Ideologe* (Göttingen, 1970), 60; Reinhard Heydenreuter, *Kunstraub: Die Geschichte des Quedlinburgers Stiftsschatzes* (Munich, 1993), 186.
3. Stadtarchiv Quedlinburg, XI 363 V 1–3.
4. Heydenreuter, *Kunstraub*, 181.
5. Voigtländer, *Die Stiftskirche St. Servatii*, 53.
6. Franz Hildebrandt, "Die Gewaltsame Inbesitznahme der Stiftskirche in Quedlinburg," in *Ich glaube eine heilige Kirche: Festschrift für D. Hans Asmussen zum 65. Geburtstag*, ed. Walter Bauer, Hellmut Heeger, Friedrich Hübner, and Walter Zimmermann (Stuttgart, 1963), 105–14; Willi Schultze, "Der Quedlinburger Dom als Kultstätte der SS," in *Jahrbuch für Wirtschaftsgeschichte* 4 (1966): 215–34.
7. The subsequent discussion is based primarily on the following sources: Landesamt für Denkmalpflege und Archäologie (hereafter LDA), AA Quedlinburg Schlosskirche 1945–53; LDA AA Quedlinburg Stiftskirche 337 1953–60; Hans Berger, "Die denkmalpflegerischen Maßnahmen seit 1945," in Voigtländer, *Die Stiftskirche St. Servatii*, 136–40.
8. There is no mention of Hiecke's past political involvements in Voigtländer's *Die Stiftskirche St. Servatii*.
9. Andreas Stahl, "Der Provinzialkonservator Hermann Giesau," in *"Es thun iher viel Fragen . . .": Kunstgeschichte in Mitteldeutschland, Hans-Joachim Krause gewidmet* (Petersburg, 2001), 263.
10. Stadtarchiv Quedlinburg, XI 363 I 192.
11. Heydenreuter, *Kunstraub*, 187.
12. Voigtländer, *Die Stiftskirche St. Servatii*, 54.
13. Stahl, "Provinzialkonservator Hermann Giesau," 249–51.
14. Voigtländer, *Die Stiftskirche St. Servatii*, 57–58.
15. Voigtländer, *Die Stiftskirche St. Servatii*, 55 (with n. 146), 57.
16. LDA AA Quedlinburger Schlosskirche 1945–53, 379.
17. The following discussion is drawn from Jeffrey Herf, *Divided Memory: The Nazi Past in the Two Germanys* (Cambridge, MA, 1997).
18. File notes from Hermann Wäscher, June 13, 1946, LDA AA Quedlinburg Schlosskirche 1945–53, 12.
19. Hiecke's drawing from December 1944 illustrates the shorter spires that were realized a few years later (Heinrich's cathedral in Quedlinburg, view from the east, December 1944, LDA AA Quedlinburg Schlosskirche 1945–53, 190).
20. Landeshauptarchiv Sachsen-Anhalt, MG, Rep C 28 II, 8813, 37-front, quoted in Voigtländer, *Die Stiftskirche St. Servatii*, 135.
21. Christian Fuhrmeister, *Beton, Klinker, Granit: Material, Macht, Politik; Eine Materialikonographie* (Berlin, 2001).
22. Address at the dedication of the second westwork towers on June 11, 1948, LDA AA Quedlinburg Schlosskirche 1945–53, 114 (emphasis mine).

23. Ibid.
24. I am grateful to Friedemann Gosslau for providing me with this information.
25. Berger, "Die denkmalpflegerischen Maßnahmen," 138 (emphasis mine).
26. Stadtbauamt Gernrode, Sammlung Gernrode, quoted in Andreas Stahl, "Provinzialkonservator Hermann Giesau," 258.
27. Letter from Giesau to Hiecke, May 2, 1938, LDA AA Quedlinburg Schlosskirche 1935–1938, 65.
28. Ibid. (emphasis mine).
29. Stahl's own source for this information is a letter from Professor Günther Schmid of the University of Halle. Writing in 1946, perhaps as a way to retrofit a less complicated narrative on to the past, his description of Giesau's work is full of hyperbole.
30. LDA AA Quedlinburg Schlosskirche 1945–53, 60. Unlike Hiecke, Giesau was arrested in August 1945 and spent a year in an internment camp. After he received a *Berufsverbot* in 1946, scholars from the West German zones of occupation found him a position as instructor for historic preservation at the Technical School of Aachen in 1949. Giesau survived his new appointment only by six months.
31. LDA AA Quedlinburg Stiftskirche 337 1953–60.
32. "Stadtbild bleibt erhalten," *Neues Deutschland*, no. 245 (October 16, 1957), LDA AA Quedlinburg Stiftskirche 337 1953–60.
33. Heinrich Kreisel, "Die Tagung und Besichtigungsfahrten der Denkmalpfleger im Juni 1962 in Niedersachsen und Mitteldeutschland," *Kunstchronik* 15 (September 1962): 242.
34. Ibid., 244 (emphasis mine).
35. Here, I am only able to provide a rudimentary overview of this fascinating story. See Friedemann Gosslau, *Verloren, Gefunden, Heimgeholt: Die Wiedervereinigung des Quedlinburger Domschatzes* (Quedlinburg, 1996); William H. Honan, *Treasure Hunt: A New York Times Reporter Tracks the Quedlinburg Hoard* (New York, 1997).
36. Dallas Museum of Art, *The Quedlinburg Treasury* (Dallas, 1991).
37. Quoted in Gosslau, *Verloren, Gefunden, Heimgeholt*, 70.
38. Quoted in ibid., 68.
39. "Hier herrscht seit '33 Diktatur," *Der Spiegel*, no. 46 (1992).
40. At that time, the National German Party (NPD) and Republicans garnered 15 to 20 percent of the votes in local elections.
41. Antje Vollmer, "Grußwort," in *Geschichte und Propaganda: Die Ottonen im Schatten des Nationalsozialismus*, ed. Christian Mühldorfer-Vogt and Heinrich-Böll-Stiftung Sachsen-Anhalt (Halle, 2005), 9.
42. Christian Mühldorfer-Vogt, "Die Ausstellungskonzeption von 'Geschichte und Propaganda' im Quedlinburger Schlossmuseum," in Mühldorfer-Vogt and Heinrich-Böll-Stiftung, *Geschichte und Propaganda*, 11.

PART 4

Jewish Sites:
Commemorating the Holocaust

The Politics of Antifascism
Historic Preservation, Jewish Sites, and the Rebuilding of Potsdam's Altstadt
Michael Meng

In June 1970, East Germany's Association of Jewish Communities sent a letter to the mayor of Potsdam requesting funds for the preservation of the city's historic Jewish cemetery and the erection of a small Holocaust monument on the cemetery's grounds. City officials responded that they could not afford any preservation efforts at the cemetery; the ongoing rebuilding of Potsdam's Altstadt (Old Town) had to take priority over any other building projects. Moreover, since the cemetery's location one mile outside of town was too "remote," it made little sense to erect a monument there. Rather, the proposed memorial to the German Communist and "antifascist" hero Karl Liebknecht would suffice. Placed in the heart of Potsdam's center, this monument would stand for "all the victims of Nazi persecution."[1] City officials left unexplained how a memorial to a Communist leader who was killed by a paramilitary group in 1919 could possibly represent the victims of racial genocide.

The city's rejection of the Jewish community's request was hardly surprising. Since the founding of the German Democratic Republic (GDR) in 1949, East Germany's Socialist Unity Party (SED) paid little attention to Jewish sites and developed an antifascist interpretation of the Nazi era that largely marginalized the Holocaust.[2] Beginning in the late 1970s, mostly for foreign policy reasons, this approach began to change as the SED gradually supported the preservation of Jewish sites, but throughout much of East Germany's existence, the SED generally showed little interest in their condition. In Potsdam, city officials initiated a major project to restore the city's bombed-out Altstadt under the heading "We're building a Socialist Potsdam." The plan combined an emphasis on historic preservation with Socialist architecture, restoring historic buildings and constructing new ones that reflected the "humanist," "progressive," and "antifascist" traditions of the German past and of the new Socialist dictatorship. But preserving Jewish sites did not fit into any of these aims, nor were they included in any of Potsdam's rebuilding plans: officials tore down its war-damaged synagogue in 1958 and left its cemetery unpreserved for nearly four decades.

After 1945, the main traces of Jewish life left in Germany were synagogues, districts, and cemeteries. Since so few Jews survived the Holocaust and many of those who did decided not to return to Germany, the physical remnants of buildings were all that was left of Jewish life in most places. In Potsdam, a Jewish community never reemerged until after the fall of the Berlin Wall. Postwar Germany became a place of empty and abandoned Jewish spaces scattered across the landscape from the smallest village to the metropolis. These Jewish sites—broken, fractured, ruined—were arguably the most visible reminders of the lowest and most tragic moment in the history of German-Jewish relations. When Germans rebuilt their bombed-out cities after the war, they had to deal with the legacies of confiscated, vandalized, and bombed Jewish property. They faced a complex question: what should be done with the ordinary spaces of Jewish life—the synagogues, Jewish cemeteries, Jewish districts left behind in the wake of mass murder?

This chapter attempts to examine this central question by looking at how SED officials and East German historic preservationists dealt with Potsdam's two main Jewish sites from 1945 to 1989—its synagogue located in the city center and its Jewish cemetery.[3] It analyzes the treatment of Potsdam's Jewish sites against the backdrop of wider debates about urban reconstruction and historic preservation, paying attention to how authorities dealt with two other, non-Jewish buildings, the Stadtschloss and the Garnisonkirche. It is largely within these broader discussions about urban reconstruction and historic preservation that the city's general policy of neglect and indifference toward Jewish sites must be seen. In the SED's attempt to transform Potsdam from a Prussian *Garnisonstadt* (garrison city) into an antifascist, Communist city, the SED placed little emphasis on historic preservation and tore down those historic sites that contradicted its antifascist understanding of the Nazi past. It was not until the late 1970s that this official interpretation of the past became contested, when ordinary citizens attempted to restore those few remaining signs of Jewish life still left in Potsdam.

Transforming Potsdam's Altstadt into an Antifascist City

Throughout much of East Germany's history, the SED faced the difficult task of attempting to establish the GDR as a legitimate Communist state. In contrast to the Soviet Union, the GDR was the product not of a Communist revolution but, rather, of the collapse of a fascist regime and foreign occupation. The absence of a "real" Communist revolution meant that the SED had to reach back into German history and find a Socialist past that it could use to justify the existence of its state.[4] The SED stressed the earlier traditions of the Communist Party of Germany, idolized such German Communists as Rosa Luxemburg and Karl Liebknecht, and emphasized the proletarian and antifascist origins of German Socialism. But while the SED espoused the "progressive" legacies of German history, it claimed that the formation of the Communist state had eliminated the darker sides of the German past, such as fascism, war, capitalism, and anti-Semitism.[5] In order to propagate this selective view of German history, the SED developed a broad cultural program that involved the utilization of film, literature, monuments, and historiography.[6] Historic preservation and urban reconstruction formed an important part of this effort, but they proved difficult to use for ideological purposes in a way that other forms of cultural media did not. The SED often confronted buildings that reflected some "bourgeois," "militaristic," "fascist," or "capitalist" style; it had to deal with historical buildings that did not easily fit into the image of the German past that it wished to fashion.

In few other East German cities did this dilemma emerge more acutely than in Potsdam. Located just on the outskirts of Berlin, the city's grandiose buildings of Prussian glory and its symbolic ties with the Nazi movement hardly represented a Socialist city of workers or an ideal model of antifascism. The Hohenzollerns had left behind a rich architectural heritage of towering churches, ornate palaces, and baroque-styled houses. In 1933, it was precisely this overt Prussian heritage that attracted Hitler to Potsdam when he used the city's famous Prussian church, the Garnisonkirche, to celebrate the Nazi rise to power, during a grand ceremony dubbed the Day of Potsdam. After the war, an obvious question emerged: how was one to build an antifascist, Communist city among Prussian ruins and Nazi symbolism? The SED and its urban planners responded by embarking on an extensive rebuilding of Potsdam's Altstadt that tore down most of the city's historic buildings (many of which were damaged during World War II) and replaced them with new, Socialist buildings. One of the central elements of this transformation into a "Socialist city" was the formation of a wide city square. In East German urban planning, the city square, named usually in honor of a Communist hero, served as the city's central point both architecturally and ideologically: it stood in the heart of the city and was used to stage huge political demonstrations.[7] In Potsdam, SED officials moved quickly to build a square and searched for a local Communist leader to honor. But while Potsdam's history had an abundance of Prussian kings to offer, it had little in the area of Communist heroes with one minor exception. In 1912, the city elected Karl Liebknecht to the Reichstag, where he emerged as an outspoken opponent of World War I. Five decades later, Liebknecht's connections to Potsdam became key to the city's reconstruction as SED officials decided to build a *Platz* in his honor, located in the heart of the city center.[8]

Although discovering Liebknecht's "local" ties signaled a triumph for the SED's project to build a Socialist, antifascist Potsdam, the party still confronted the problem of what to do with the city's many historic buildings that, while damaged, still remained prominent markers of the urban landscape. The SED gradually realized that constructing a Socialist Potsdam inherently conflicted with historic preservation. As the city council put it in 1958, "those buildings that were turned into ruins by the terror attack of Anglo-American bombers in April 1945 will be restored only when they are of extraordinary cultural-historical significance, when they do not interfere with all of the demands associated with developing a modern urban traffic system, and when their reconstruction is economically sound."[9] Key here is the phrase "extraordinary cultural-historical significance." The SED did not provide a clear definition of the term but, rather, assigned cultural value to buildings that either complimented or at least did not hinder the practical and ideological demands of building the Socialist city. It is within this broader conception of historic preservation—of what the SED deemed cultural and what it did not—that the treatment of Potsdam's Jewish sites must be placed.

Relics of the Prussian Past

In January 1949, Peter Scheib, the local chairman of the SED in Potsdam, used the local newspaper to address the mayor in an open letter that opposed plans to rebuild the war-damaged Stadtschloss, a majestic eighteenth-century Prussian castle that stood in the heart of Potsdam and was designed by the famed architect Georg Wenzeslaus von Knobelsdorff (fig. 1). He argued that its reconstruction would be too expensive and would obstruct projected plans to widen a street. But Scheib's chief complaint rested on less practical concerns; he opposed the reconstruction of the Stadtschloss because it symbolized the militaristic and exploitative tendencies of the Prussian past: "The actions of the Hohenzollerns toward our people were not worthy enough to warrant the rebuilding of a destroyed castle. It was not coincidental that Hitler's henchmen implemented their criminal activities in line with the methods of Frederick II."[10] By connecting the Stadtschloss to Prussian militarism and fascism, Scheib rejected the notion that the castle could possibly represent a monument of "cultural-historical significance." But not everyone agreed with Scheib's assessment. In the winter of 1949, a flurry of letters from citizens, politicians, and architectural historians strongly criticized his position.[11] Several days later, Potsdam's city council declared that the "the ruins of the Stadtschloss will be preserved" and used for "a museum and picture gallery or for some other cultural purpose."[12] It appeared as if historic preservation had triumphed over Scheib's call to "clear away this rubble of history," and for nearly a decade it had: all of Potsdam's plans included the reconstruction of the Stadtschloss until 1956, when top local SED leaders opposed its preservation for the first time. Reflecting Walter Ulbricht's order to construct cheap, prefabricated apartment complexes, they argued that its reconstruction would cost too much money and take away resources from the building of affordable housing.[13] A year later, the destruction of the Stadtschloss appeared increasingly certain. Party officials continued their argument about cost and the need for apartment buildings, but they now employed a more overtly political approach, arguing that the historical symbolism of the Stadtschloss prevented it from fitting into the "Socialist" city.[14] When the SED announced its decision to tear down the castle, it received intense criticism from citizens, academics, and politicians who argued for rebuilding the war-torn Stadtschloss.[15] East Germany's Institute for Historic Preservation even prepared an extensive report on the castle, concluding that it must be preserved "as the best example of baroque architecture in the German Democratic Republic," but the SED ignored its advice and tore it down in 1960.[16]

In the same year that the SED tore down the Stadtschloss, it moved to demolish Potsdam's Garnisonkirche (fig. 2). In 1933, Hitler used this towering, baroque church to open the newly elected Reichstag of 1933.

Fig. 1. The Stadtschloss, designed by Georg Wenzeslaus von Knobelsdorff, Potsdam, begun in 1743. Photo from 1900. (Photo: Neue Photographische Gesellschaft A.G. BPK.)

With some one hundred thousand spectators lining the streets of Potsdam, Hitler and Field Marshal Paul von Hindenburg paraded through the city before giving speeches at the church, where they both spoke of the "eternal connection" between National Socialism, imperial Germany, and Prussia.[17] Despite these clear connections to the Nazi past, the Garnisonkirche at first did not appear problematic for the SED. In the early 1950s, the SED even assured its religious community that the church would remain intact, and in 1956, the Institute for Historic Preservation officially placed the building under historic preservation.[18] But by 1960, the future of the Garnisonkirche increasingly appeared less certain. In a design competition announced that year, the SED for the first time omitted the church's reconstruction from its plans.[19] Throughout the early 1960s, it appeared as if the Garnisonkirche would eventually be destroyed, but nearly seven years elapsed before the SED finally decided to tear it down. The order came most likely directly from Ulbricht, who visited Potsdam that year and indicated to city officials that the church should be removed.[20] Potsdam's city council agreed, citing plans for a new street and the political symbolism of the church as reasons for its decision: "In our

Fig. 2. The Garnisonkirche, designed by Johann Philipp Gerlach, Potsdam, 1735. Photo from 1911. (Photo: Friedrich Seidenstücker. BPK.)

opinion, destruction is necessary in order to erase this symbol of Prussian militarism from the memory of local citizens. . . . The former Garnisonkirche was designed to be a museum for the military rather than a place of worship. The Day of Potsdam, the alliance between Hitler and Hindenburg, is likewise associated with the former Garnisonkirche."[21]

Jewish Sites in a Socialist Potsdam

Unlike in the cases of the Stadtschloss or the Garnisonkirche, the postwar fate of Potsdam's synagogue was complicated first by legal matters (fig. 3). Before the SED was able to consider what to do with the building, it first had to confront the complex problem of returning the property that had been confiscated by the Nazis to its original owners in a city where an official Jewish community (*Gemeinde*) no longer existed. Once an organi-

Fig. 3. The Potsdam synagogue designed by J. Otto Kerwien, pictured on November 10, 1938, after Kristallnacht. The synagogue was located in the heart of the city's Wilhelmplatz. (Photo: Hans Weber. Potsdam Museum.)

zation of six hundred members, Potsdam's Jewish community totaled a mere two after the war.[22] The absence of an official *Gemeinde* did not, however, mean that returning the synagogue was legally impossible. On April 29, 1948, the Soviet Military Administration (SMA) issued Decree No. 82, which ordered the "return of property confiscated by the Nazi state to democratic organizations." Although intended mainly for Communist organizations, the decree allowed the return of property to "church or humanitarian" institutions.[23] In theory, Jewish communities in the Soviet zone had a legal basis to reclaim their confiscated property, but doing so was hardly easy, not least because Soviet authorities demanded that all organizations submit their claims within a mere two months. Since most Jewish communities lacked the organizational resources to file the paperwork themselves, the newly formed State Association of Jewish Communities of the Soviet Occupied Zone (Landesverband der Jüdischen Gemeinden in der Sowjetischen Besatzungszone) was forced to do much of the legal work. Established in 1947 and directed by the Holocaust survivor Julius Meyer, the Landesverband sought the return of as much property as possible, but its own scarce resources severely limited its efforts. Without any Jewish community to assist in gathering the necessary paperwork, the Landesverband had to submit an incomplete list for the state of Brandenburg and ultimately recovered a mere four properties in the entire region. In 1949, the Landesverband was able to secure the return of additional property in Brandenburg, but Potsdam's synagogue and Jewish cemetery were not among the properties given back.[24]

Thus the city of Potsdam remained the official owner and caretaker of both Jewish sites after the war. At first, city and party officials decided to rebuild the synagogue, which had been damaged during the war and Kristallnacht. In an issue commemorating the sixth-year anniversary of Potsdam's destruction, the *Märkishe Volksstimme* reported that the reconstruction of the synagogue's facade had begun. A three-sentence byline underneath a picture of the synagogue enclosed with scaffolding read: "The facade of the synagogue on Platz der Einheit is being restored. It went up in flames during Kristallnacht of 1938. The work of fascist cultural barbarism was only continued by British and American air force squadrons on April 14, 1945."[25] As this short report suggests, the synagogue was seen as part of the larger destruction of Potsdam. It suffered from the "cultural barbarism" of fascism and war just like any other building in the city. Restoring the synagogue would not fulfill any religious purpose (city officials clearly knew that the Jewish community no longer existed); rather, its reconstruction would reinforce the antifascist message of the GDR: the East German state was restoring what the fascists and Western Allies had destroyed.

The fact that city officials initially supported the reconstruction of the synagogue should be of little surprise. Including the memory of the Jews in the Communist, antifascist project of the GDR proved common in the immediate postwar years even if it was not a major priority for SED leaders. Just a month after the war ended, in a now famous "appeal" (*Aufruf*) to the German people of June 1945, German Communist leaders confronted openly the need for accepting responsibility for the "consequences" of the Third Reich: "awareness and shame must burn in every German person, for the German people carry a significant part of the shared guilt and shared responsibility for the war and its consequences."[26] Commemorations of Kristallnacht, scholarly investigations into the origins of German anti-Semitism, and a dialogue about financial restitution for the Jews built on the political message of the appeal.[27] But such solidarity with Jews did not last long. By early 1952, the situation for East German Jews turned highly repressive. As part of a broader wave of Stalinist purges across the Soviet bloc that had strong anti-Semitic overtones, the SED carried out a campaign against "cosmopolitanism" that targeted veteran Communists of largely Jewish origin. Employing an overtly nationalist tone about the "enslavement and destruction of the German *Volk,*" the SED purged a number of Jews from the government and charged them with harboring an international conspiracy against the state.[28] Although the purge ended ten months later during the period of de-Stalinization, it had a lasting impact on the interpretation of the Nazi past that the SED fashioned in East Germany. The attention once given to the Nazi persecution of the Jews in the Soviet Zone vanished after 1952. East Germany's antifascist ideology, with its understanding of fascism as a dictatorial and imperialist form of finance capital, now left little room for the remembrance of the Jews; rather, the German Communists—those who fought against Hitler's regime—were commemorated and celebrated. They were the victims of "fascism."[29]

In the wake of the 1951–52 purge, it became increasingly impossible to include the reconstruction of Potsdam's synagogue in the GDR's antifascist memory politics. After 1951, no other mention of the synagogue's rebuilding can be found, and by 1956, Potsdam's city council moved to tear the building down. City officials began discussions with the Institute for Historic Preservation (Institut für Denkmalpflege, or IfDP) to destroy three structures on the eastside of Platz der Einheit—two eighteenth-century buildings and the synagogue. Citing Ulbricht's demand to increase the number of apartment buildings, the council proposed to use the space to erect a housing complex.[30] The IfDP protested the proposal, since it had just put the two buildings next to the synagogue under historic preservation, though it had left out any plans for the synagogue. In a letter to the IfDP, Potsdam's chief architect referred specifically to the synagogue to support his argument against restoring all three buildings, suggesting that reconstructing the two eighteenth-century buildings "would also mean that the synagogue . . . would have to be restored as well." Since the synagogue was "in general of no architectural value," he asked the institute to "clarify" its position.[31] The institute responded by proposing to tear down the synagogue while restoring the two other buildings.[32] City officials rejected this proposal and, two years later, decided that all three buildings should be torn down. As Potsdam's local party newspaper reported, the decision signaled a clear triumph for the city: "Buildings protected under historic preservation often stand in the way of Potsdam's current building projects. One only has to think of the facade next to the post office, which from the beginning was to remain absolutely preserved. . . . [Now] this motto will be followed: What's valuable will be preserved! What's of no value will be cleared away!"[33] What this article referred to as the "facade next to the post office" was Potsdam's synagogue.

How should the destruction of the synagogue be understood? The city's decision must first be seen within the wider context of Potsdam's reconstruction. Similar to the Stadtschloss and the Garnisonkirche, the city's definition of "cultural-historical buildings" did not include the synagogue. Restoring it would have precluded the city from its aim of building a Socialist Potsdam. By the mid-1950s, constructing apartment complexes had become an important ideological element of East German urban reconstruction: it showed the party's commitment toward economic equality by providing affordable housing for all citizens. In Potsdam, one of the central areas targeted for an apartment complex was Platz der Einheit itself.[34] Moreover, rebuilding the synagogue, again in a way similar to both the Stadtschloss and the Garnisonkirche, did not fit clearly into the memory of the Nazi past that the SED sought to develop. In 1951, when the SED still remained open to including the memory of the Jews in its conception of antifascism, the city planned the reconstruction of the synagogue as part of its effort to repeal the "cultural barbarism" of fascism and war. The purge of cosmopolitanism closed off this opening. The SED now developed a memory politics around the "sacrifice" of the Communist, antifascist resistance fighter. Restoring the synagogue would simply not have fit into this interpretation of the Nazi past that the SED hoped to fashion.

Yet one of the most intriguing aspects of this case is the sheer silence surrounding the synagogue's destruction. Extensive archival searches found no attempts by citizens, politicians, or architectural historians—not even one attempt by one single person—to save the synagogue. Even the Institute for Historic Preservation, which at the time was arguing vigorously for the protection of Potsdam's historic buildings (including the Stadtschloss and Garnisonkirche), made no effort to preserve the synagogue but, rather, suggested its destruction. In all probability, the IfDP simply did not perceive it to be a site worthy of preservation. East German historic preservationists mainly advocated preserving either buildings designed by well-known architects or those constructed before the mid-nineteenth century. Built in 1900 in neo-baroque style by the local and relatively unknown architect J. Otto Kerwien, the synagogue was not considered to be a monument of "extraordinary cultural-historical significance." But on another, perhaps deeper level, city officials, party leaders, and historic preservationists saw little significance in the synagogue partly because of what it represented—a site of Jewish culture. In 1952, the East German state established the IfDP in order to preserve the "cultural heritage of the German people."[35] In an earlier law, the SED defined clearly what it meant by "cultural heritage." It called for the development of a "progressive" democratic culture that stood in direct opposition to cultural developments in West Germany.

> The provisional government of the German Democratic Republic wishes to point out to the entire German people the development of a new, progressive German culture that demands a resolute and ruthless fight against all manifestations of neofascist, reactionary culture and decadence, against the penetration of the cultural barbarism of American imperialism in West Germany. The struggle for this culture requires a determined resistance against all cosmopolitan tendencies.[36]

This passage is striking in several ways. By 1951–52, the SED increasingly identified Jewish culture as one of the central manifestations of "cosmopolitan tendencies." In the early GDR, Jewish culture had become one of the central foil characteristics of East German culture. A distinctly nationalist tone permeated this conception of *Kultur:* the GDR remained the true bearer of German culture, its only defender against the "penetration" of foreign elements. In this sense, historic preservation became a key way for the GDR to emphasize the distinctly "German" aspects of its regime. In 1956, the director of the IfDP linked historic preservation with the preservation of the *Heimat* (homeland): "After Germany's collapse and subsequent national catastrophe in 1945, the GDR created the conditions necessary for a powerful development of national consciousness. [Historic preservation] seeks to bring the worker closer to our national tradition by preserving those monuments of our national heritage and thereby arousing love for the *Heimat*."[37] As the debates about Potsdam's Prussian heritage clearly showed, the choice of buildings that comprised the idea of the *Heimat* was highly politicized and selective.[38] But some relics of the Prussian past were included in it, and it is here that the difference between the fate of the synagogue and other historic buildings in

Potsdam lies. Although the destruction of the Stadtschloss and Garnisonkirche are the most well-known aspects of Potsdam's urban reconstruction, the SED did not always show disregard for historic preservation; not all relics of the Prussian past were seen as negative symbols of German history. In Potsdam's center, the party restored three main Prussian buildings that it claimed reflected the "progressive" and "humanist" traditions of German history: Potsdam's nineteenth-century Nikolaikirche; its eighteenth-century Rathaus; and the Marstall, an elaborate late eighteenth-century building used originally as a royal stable. But while East German urban planners did reconstruct some Prussian buildings, they did not preserve any Jewish sites in Potsdam until much later, when it became expedient to do in the midst of shifting cold war realities.

Preserving Jewish Sites in the 1970s and 1980s

Beginning in the 1970s, the exclusion of Jewish sites from East German conceptions of historic preservation started to change somewhat in the wake of broader cultural and foreign policy shifts during the reign of Erich Honecker. In a radical revision of its understanding and presentation of German history, the SED developed a policy of "heritage and tradition" (*Erbe und Tradition*) that aimed to nationalize the GDR's development in previously taboo historical periods. In such figures as Frederick the Great and Martin Luther, it saw legacies that could ground the Communist project in a distinctly German past.[39] This new approach also included a recovery of Jewish culture. With support from the state, the Jewish communities in Berlin, Leipzig, and Dresden developed an array of cultural programs, from lectures on Jewish literature to concerts featuring synagogue music.[40] But the SED did not support the recovery of Jewish culture only because it worked well with the party's new conception of the German past. Honecker and other top party leaders also had a clear political agenda: supporting East Germany's small Jewish community was a way to project a more positive image of the GDR abroad, which became particularly important in the 1980s, when Honecker wished to secure "most favored nation" status from the United States.[41] Indeed, foreign policy concerns largely account for Honecker's most elaborate attempt to recover the Jewish past: the plan to restore the Neue Synagoge in East Berlin at a cost of eighty-five million marks. A synagogue that remained in bombed-out form for nearly four decades, the Neue Synagoge, a towering, ornate building constructed in Moorish style in the late nineteenth century, became the centerpiece of the GDR's massive 1988 celebration of the fortieth anniversary of Kristallnacht.

Sitting just outside East Berlin and away from Western observers, Potsdam, like many other smaller East German cities, benefited from these changes in SED policy toward Jewish culture in a much more limited way. The city's last remaining Jewish site—the cemetery located about a mile outside the city center—suffered from a general policy of neglect and indifference. In 1949, the city officially accepted responsibility for maintaining the cemetery but paid almost no attention to it for nearly two decades. In city records, the first mention of the cemetery's condition does not even appear until 1970. In a letter to city officials, the Landesverband solicited funds for the preservation of the cemetery and the erection of a small monument in remembrance of the Nazi persecution of the Jews. An official in the mayor's office rejected the request, explaining: "In its perspective plan for the period of 1971–80, the city of Potsdam has a number of tasks that it must take care of, above all the building of the city center. At the heart of the city center will be the Karl Liebknecht Forum with a monument dedicated to all the victims of the Nazi regime."[42] The building of Potsdam's center and the politics of East German antifascism once again emerged as a reason for not preserving a Jewish site. Although the association's request would not have required much money, city officials still remained ambivalent about preserving Jewish sites and remembering the plight of the Jews (fig. 4).

Nearly a decade elapsed before the city returned to the issue of the cemetery again. In 1978, Theodor Goldstein, a Jewish resident of Potsdam who survived the Holocaust, met with city officials to discuss the cemetery's current state. Goldstein found it to be in "unsatisfactory" condition and asked city officials to provide money for its restoration.[43] Ten months later, Potsdam's interior ministry agreed to supply a limited amount of funds for "small repairs" at the cemetery.[44] But how genuine the city's commitment was to preserving the cemetery remained questionable. In 1983, Potsdam's city council received two letters from concerned citizens that clearly put the intentions of city officials in doubt. Heidi Merkel, a local resident, explained that when she went to visit the Jewish cemetery, a woman who lived next door said that Potsdam's city council had issued an order prohibiting citizens from visiting the cemetery given its "disorderly condition." Merkel candidly expressed to city officials how much hearing this disturbed her.

Fig. 4. Memorial plaque placed on the front side of the apartment building that was erected after the Potsdam synagogue's destruction in 1958. At the suggestion of Theo Goldstein, a local Potsdam resident and Holocaust survivor, the city unveiled this plaque on November 9, 1979, in a small ceremony commemorating Kristallnacht. (Photo: Michael Meng.)

The reasoning behind such a prohibition is not at all satisfactory since everyone knows that today there are no Jewish citizens who can see to the regular upkeep of this cemetery because of the Nazis' complete annihilation [*Vernichtung*] of the Jewish people. But still this place should be left open to the people as a place of remembrance for this terrible genocide [*grausamer Völkermord*]. The fact that state institutions have prohibited visitations to it can easily be associated with anti-Semitic tendencies.[45]

Another letter, written by a local Christian pastor after a recent trip to the cemetery with his youth group, indicated that the cemetery was in poor condition, with a number of tombstones damaged or destroyed.[46] In response, city officials publicly maintained that the cemetery was in fine condition but privately agreed with both accounts, acknowledging that the cemetery was in fact in a state that visitors should not see. In a letter to the publisher of *A City Guide to Potsdam*, officials requested that future editions of the guidebook not include a passage about the Jewish cemetery, in light of its "current condition."[47] In the late 1970s and 1980s, the SED had officially loosened its policy toward the Jews and had become more supportive of Jewish culture, but as the case of Potsdam suggests, that change did not run very deep.

Conclusion

The SED saw the rebuilding of Potsdam's Altstadt as a way to legitimize its rule; it hoped, above all, to transform Potsdam into a Socialist city of wide streets, demonstration squares, and apartment complexes—a new Potsdam centered around the progressive legacy of Karl Liebknecht. Reverting back to earlier periods of German history through an extensive program of historic preservation was simply out of the question. East German urban planners emphasized historic preservation much less than their counterparts either west or east of the GDR. Modernist approaches to urban reconstruction were more influential in the rebuilding of such cities as Potsdam than in either West Germany or Poland, where old towns were meticulously rebuilt on a scale simply not seen in the GDR.[48] This disregard for historic preservation rested on a broader teleological sense of time that generally emphasized the future over the past; the East German regime confronted the Nazi past simply by moving away from it, removing physical markers of the past in its pursuit of building a new, Socialist future. When East German urban planners did incorporate historic buildings in their reconstruction plans, they selected buildings that emphasized what they believed fit into the "progressive, humanist" traditions of German history, which in the early GDR excluded Jewish sites. Yet the SED's general disregard for Jewish sites reflected not simply a disinterest in things old but also a deliberate attempt on the part of the party to develop a selective interpretation of the Nazi past that evaded confronting the Nazi persecution of the Jews. In Potsdam, SED leaders created an antifascist memory politics around the figure of Karl Liebknecht and tore down any historic buildings that hindered this broader effort. The synagogue—a site that conjured up memories of the Holocaust by its sheer emptiness—was such a building, and its destruction underscores the basic indifference to the Holocaust that defined the GDR. Even into the 1970s and 1980s, SED leaders remained ambivalent about how best, if at all, to incorporate the persecution of the Jews in the party's antifascist interpretation of the Nazi past. An important exception was East Berlin, which became the main site of Honecker's effort to rehabilitate the image of the GDR abroad.[49]

The degree to which this official, SED marginalization of the Holocaust represented how ordinary East Germans thought about, reflected on, and remembered the Nazi past is difficult to gauge. But the case of Potsdam does offer some plausible conclusions. One of the most startling aspects about the postwar handling of Potsdam's Jewish sites is the lack of any protest against the SED's approach toward them in the early decades of the GDR. Or perhaps such silence is not that startling at all. To protest the SED's general policy of neglect and destruction—to argue, for instance, that the synagogue must be preserved—would mean keeping alive the memory of a minority group to whose persecution the majority of Germans responded with either active complicity or passive indifference.[50] German attempts to comprehend the Nazi past after 1945 cannot be separated from that past; the Holocaust profoundly fractured German-Jewish relations, and that shattered symbiosis shaped how Germans interpreted the meaning of the Nazi era. In the early decades of the GDR, it is likely, then, that the SED's antifascist memory politics actually served a broader social desire to forget an uncomfortable past and remember a fictitious one of resistance and antifascism. Historians have long seen East German memory as orchestrated from above,[51] but what has been overlooked is the significant support that it received from below, in a way not entirely different from how most West Germans accepted Adenauer's *Vergangenheitspolitik* (at least until the late 1960s and 1970s).[52] On an official level, the memory of the Nazi past was divided in the two Germanys, but below the surface of high politics, both societies struggled to deal with a past that so clearly reminded them of their own human fragility, of their own capacity to become involved in a dictatorship of war and genocide. In the 1950s and 1960s, the SED doubtlessly knew that less was more—that avoiding a thorough discussion of the Nazi past was best for a population that had overwhelmingly supported the Third Reich. In this sense, the destruction of the synagogue and neglect of Potsdam's Jewish cemetery become less and less surprising. It would have been surprising, in fact, had they been preserved.

This stark indifference toward Jewish sites did, however, start to change somewhat in the latter decades of the GDR's history. Beyond the ranks of the SED, some voices suggesting alternative approaches toward Potsdam's Jewish sites did exist. Theo Goldstein and other local citizens who expressed concern about the maintenance of the Jewish cemetery recognized—in a way that the SED simply did not—the urgency of preserving the last remnants of Jewish culture in East Germany. For these residents, the fact that Potsdam had no Jewish community only reinforced the point that the city must accept responsibility for maintaining its Jewish sites. It is difficult to gauge how deep interest in Jewish sites penetrated East German society, but the case of Potsdam suggests that at least some in the GDR, partly in opposition to the policies of the SED and partly as a result of a growing consciousness of the Holocaust, did show increasing concern about their condition. Preserving Jewish sites became a concrete way to confront, reflect on, and work through the loss and absence of Jews in Germany, while also expressing discontent with a regime that was increasingly becoming less popular. If the SED's antifascist understanding of the Nazi period resonated with many East Germans in the 1950s and 1960s, it had less and less appeal by the late 1970s and 1980s, to the point that some even began to move beyond it and to think more critically about Germany's past.

NOTES

1. Letter to Association of Jewish Communities, August 31, 1970, 4508, Potsdam Stadtarchiv (hereinafter PSA).
2. Jeffrey Herf, *Divided Memory: The Nazi Past in the Two Germanys* (Cambridge, MA, 1997).
3. This essay extends themes discussed in Michael Meng, "East Germany's Jewish Question: The Return and Preservation of Jewish Sites in East Berlin and Potsdam, 1945–1989," *Central European History*, no. 4 (2005): 606–36.
4. Eric D. Weitz, *Creating German Communism, 1890–1990: From Popular Protests to Socialist State* (Princeton, 1997), 357–86.
5. Alan Nothnagle, *Building the East German Myth: Historical Mythology and Youth Propaganda in the German Democratic Republic* (Ann Arbor, 1999); Sigrid Meuschel, *Legitimation und Parteiherrschaft: Zum Paradox von Stabilität und Revolution in der DDR, 1945–1989* (Frankfurt am Main, 1992); Martin Sabrow, ed., *Verwaltete Vergangenheit: Geschichtskultur und Herrschaftslegitimation in der DDR* (Leipzig, 1997).
6. Sabrow, *Verwaltete Vergangenheit;* Brian Ladd, *Ghosts of Berlin: Confronting German History in the Urban Landscape* (Chicago, 1997).
7. Werner Durth, Jörn Düwel, and Niels Gutschow, *Architektur und Städtebau der DDR* (Frankfurt am Main, 1999), 58–60, 72–75.
8. Meeting of November 24, 1958, Rep. 530/1264, Brandenburgisches Landeshauptarchiv (hereinafter BLHA).
9. Decision of February 4, 1958, 382, PSA.
10. Peter Scheib, "Offener Brief an den Herrn Oberbürgermeister," *Märkische*

Volksstimme, January 11, 1949, 3.
11. Rep. 332, BLHA.
12. City council protocol, January 31, 1949, 480, PSA.
13. Notes on the meeting about the Stadtschloss, April 23, 1956, Rep. 530/1271, BLHA.
14. Meeting of November 21, 1958, Rep. 530/1264, BLHA.
15. Christina Emmerich-Focke, *Stadtplanung in Postdam 1945–1990* (Potsdame: Stadtwerk, 1999), 24–25.
16. "Argumentation des Instituts für Denkmalpflege zur Wiederherstellung des Stadtschlosses in Potsdam," Rep. 530/1269, BLHA.
17. Quoted in Werner Schwipps, *Garnisonkirche Potsdam* (Berlin, 2001), 90.
18. Institut für Denkmalpflege, "Objektliste der künstlerischen und historischen Baudenkmale (Einzelobjekte)," 1956, 388, PSA.
19. "Ideenwettbewerb zur sozialistischen Umgestaltung des Zentrums der Bezirkhauptstadt Potsdam 1960," *Deutsche Architektur* (1960): 534–41.
20. Emmerich-Focke, *Stadtplanung,* 160.
21. Letter to GDR Cultural Ministry, December 27, 1966, 264, PSA.
22. Letter from Landesverband to Brandenburg Ministry of Finance, December 27, 1948, Rep. 204A, no. 2631, BLHA.
23. SMA Decree No. 82, April 29, 1949, Rep. 203, no. 1830, BLHA.
24. 5B1, no. 107, Centrum Judaicum Archiv.
25. *Märkische Volksstimme,* April 14, 1951, 6.
26. "Aufruf des SK der KPD vom 11. Juni 1945," reprinted in *Dokumente und Materialien zur Geschichte der deutschen Arbeiterbewegung* 3, no. 1 (1959): 15.
27. Herf, *Divided Memory,* 69–105.
28. Thomas Haury, "'Finanzkapital oder Nation': Zur ideologischen Genese des Antizionismus der SED," *Jahrbuch für Antisemitismusforschung* (1996): 149–69; *Antisemitismus von Links: Kommunistische Ideologie, Nationalismus und Antizionismus in der frühen DDR* (Hamburg, 2002).
29. Herf, *Divided Memory,* chaps. 5–6.
30. City council presentation, June 25, 1956, 381, PSA.
31. Letter to Institute for Historic Preservation, June 27, 1956, 381, PSA.
32. Letter from Potsdam Interior Ministry, May 29, 1957, 381, PSA.
33. "Der Wohnungsbau steht weiter im Vordergrund," *Brandenburgische neuste Nachrichten,* February 2, 1958, 2.
34. Decision of the Potsdam District (Bezirk), February 14, 1958, 381, PSA.
35. Gründung des Instituts für Denkmalpflege, DR 1/8026, BA-Berlin (SAMPO). See also "Verordnung zur Erhaltung und Pflege der nationalen Kulturdenkmale (Denkmalschutz) vom 26. Juni 1952," Gesetzblatt No. 94, July 2, 1952, in *Gesetzblatt der Deutschen Demokratischen Republik* (Berlin, 1952).
36. "Verordnung zur Entwicklung einer fortschrittlichen demokratischen Kultur des deutschen Volkes und zur weiteren Verbesserung der Arbeits—und Lebensbedingungen der Intelligenz vom 16. März 1950," Gesetzblatt No. 28, March 23, 1950, in *Gesetzblatt der Deutschen Demokratischen Republik* (Berlin, 1950).
37. Minutes of the meeting of the Institute for Historic Preservation in Potsdam, October 25, 1956, 3553, PSA.

38. On the *Heimat* in the GDR, see Jan Palmowski, "Building an East German Nation: Construction of a Socialist *Heimat*, 1945–1961," *Central European History*, no. 3 (2004): 365–99.

39. Alan Nothnagle, "From Buchenwald to Bismarck: Historical Myth-Building in the German Democratic Republic, 1945–1989," *Central European History*, no. 1 (1993): 91–113; Helmut Meier and Walter Schmidt, eds., *Erbe und Tradition in der DDR: Die Diskussion der Historiker* (Berlin, 1988).

40. Jutta Illichmann, *Die DDR und die Juden: Die deutschlandpolitische Instrumentalisierung von Juden und Judentum durch die Partei- unde Staatsführung der SBZ/DDR von 1945 bix 1990* (Frankfurt am Main, 1997), 239–50.

41. Lothar Mertens, *Davidstern unter Hammer und Zirkel: Die Jüdischen Gemeinden in der SBZ/DDR und ihre Behandlungen durch Partei und Staat, 1945–1990* (Hildesheim, 1997), 275–88.

42. Letter to Association of Jewish Communities, August 31, 1970, 4508, PSA.

43. Letter from Potsdam Interior Ministry to GDR Cultural Ministry, May 31, 1978, 4508, PSA.

44. Letter to Goldstein, December 19, 1978, 4508, PSA.

45. Letter to Potsdam Interior Ministry, May 31, 1983, 4508, PSA.

46. Letter to Potsdam Interior Ministry, May 8, 1983, 4508, PSA.

47. Letter to VEB Verlag, June 14, 1984, 4508, PSA.

48. Jeffrey M. Diefendorf, *In the Wake of War: The Reconstruction of German Cities after World War II* (New York, 1993); Gavriel D. Rosenfeld, *Munich and Memory: Architecture, Monuments, and the Legacy of the Third Reich* (Berkeley, 2000); Bohdan Rymaszewski, *Klucze ochrony zabytków w Polsce* (Warsaw, 1992); Gregor Thum, *Die fremde Stadt: Breslau 1945* (Berlin, 2003).

49. Meng, "East Germany's Jewish Question."

50. David Bankier, *The Germans and the Final Solution: Public Opinion under Nazism* (Cambridge, MA, 1992); Robert Gellately, *Backing Hitler: Consent and Coercion in Nazi Germany* (New York, 2001).

51. Herf, *Divided Memory*.

52. Norbert Frei, *Adenauer's Germany and the Nazi Past: The Politics of Amnesty and Integration*, trans. Joel Golb (New York, 2002).

Marking Absence
Remembrance and Hamburg's Holocaust Memorials
Natasha Goldman

Recent Holocaust memorialization in Germany has embraced the visual trope of the countermonument, or memorials conceived to "challenge the conventional premises of the monument."[1] While traditional memorials often displace memory with figural representations aiming to either console or redeem viewers, countermonuments request the viewer's direct conceptual involvement in interpreting voids and/or a minimalist rhetoric. A case study is the constellation of memorials in Grindel, a neighborhood once central to Jewish life in Hamburg. Alfred Hrdlicka's unfinished *Countermonument* (1985–86) stands on Dammtordam directly across from and in deliberate opposition to Richard Kuöhl's 1936 Monument to the Seventy-sixth Infantry Regiment, known as the 76er Monument or Kriegsklotz (war monstrosity). Ulrich Rückriem's minimalist Memorial to the Deported Jews, erected in 1983, stands in a small triangular park near the University of Hamburg, and Margrit Kahl's Joseph-Carlebach-Platz Synagogue Monument, built in 1988, traces the outlines of a destroyed synagogue's vaulting in Grindelhof.[2] Until 2005, the only public monument dedicated to all Jewish citizens of Hamburg who were murdered during the Holocaust was installed by the Jewish community in 1951 in Ohlsdorf Cemetery, far from the monuments around the university or Dammtor. Reflecting the needs of the Jewish community in the seclusion of a Jewish cemetery, the monument does not attempt to address Holocaust memory for the city as a whole.[3]

While Hamburg is often seen as a city that turned a cold shoulder to Hitler and National Socialism, recent historical scholarship resists the myth of a liberal Hamburg and instead lays bare the Nazi activities of Hamburg citizens and officials. Memorialization dedicated to the Hamburg victims of Allied bombing (known as the Hamburg Feuersturm) was

251

common. Some individuals in Hamburg, however, have accepted the difficult challenge of remembering Nazi atrocities. Cultural Senator Wolfgang Tarnowski was especially active in realizing several memorials, sometimes under tight budgetary constraints. Most recently, the Grindelhof Citizen's Initiative has been active in the upkeep of the Joseph-Carlebach-Platz Synagogue Memorial.

The countermonuments at Dammtor are stylistically either postmodern or minimalist. While traditional interpretations of high modernist works of art (minimalism in particular) stress the materiality of the object or its aggressive positioning in relation to the viewer, revisions to this thinking posit that modernism can also seek to address memory and the Holocaust.[4] In the United States, some postwar modernist works of art, although alluding to the Holocaust via their titles, were rarely analyzed, at least in the early years, in terms of this seemingly blatant meaning.[5] Cases in point include Frank Stella's series of black paintings, including *Arbeit Macht Frei* (1958), and Morris Louis's *Charred Journal: Firewritten* (1951). Comparably, Louis Kahn's proposed Holocaust memorial (1966–72) for Battery Park in New York City consisted of nine glass cubes that made an outright association between modernism and the Holocaust (the memorial was never built).

More recent reinterpretations of high modernist works turn to the possibility of their attempt to locate a post-Holocaust position that requires a certain activation of memory on the viewer's part. Mark Godfrey, for example, provokingly suggests that Barnet Newman's *Stations of the Cross* (1958) activates a space of memory for the viewer. In contrast, Jill Bennett contributes a transformative analysis to trauma studies in elucidating the relationship between the work of art and the viewer as one that produces "affect." She claims: "Trauma related art is transactive, not communicative. It often touches us, but it does not communicate the 'secret' of personal experience."[6] More broadly, James Young's vital historical analyses of Holocaust memorials concern the ways in which collective memory is activated in the planning, commissioning, and reception of memorials. Young first analyzed the memorials at Dammtor in his 1993 study *The Texture of Memory*. To his analysis, I add reflections on German postwar attitudes to the Holocaust, particularly in relation to the representations of victims of Allied bombing.

Other scholars, such as Lisa Saltzman and Paul Jaskot, place national identity, postmodernism, and politics in the foreground of their research. While Saltzman locates Gerhard Richter's works in the social context of

German religious cycles of commemoration, Jaskot resists the myth that there was "silence" in art criticism regarding the analysis of artwork and its relationship to the Holocaust in the postwar period in Germany.[7] Emphasizing both Hamburg's political association with its National Socialist past and the role of the countermonument, I will contribute to this dialogue a political rethinking of postmodernism and memorials. Located in an area bordering on or in Grindel, the works in Hamburg can be better understood if the people, buildings, and empty spaces of that neighborhood are explained. A short summary of Jewish life in Hamburg is therefore one step in providing a conceptual framework for the analysis of memorials located in and around that neighborhood.

A Brief History of Jews in Hamburg

Four hundred years ago, Sephardic Jews fleeing the Inquisition in Spain and Portugal sought out the Hanseatic city on the Elbe as a home.[8] At the time, Altona (now a neighborhood in Hamburg) was part of Denmark and was less dismissive of the Jews and other minorities than the city of Hamburg. Many Jews lived in Altona but had their businesses in Hamburg.

In 1671, individual Ashkenazic communities united to form the Altona-Wandsbek-Hamburg community, which existed up until Napoleon's occupation of the city in 1812. At this time, the Jewish population numbered 6,429, or 4.87 percent of the total population.[9] Intolerant of a religious community that ignored French borders, Napoleon demanded that the group disband. Still, under Napoleon's rule, the freedoms of Hamburg Jews greatly increased, with Jews living in various parts of the city that had previously been closed to them. After Napoleon's reign, newly won freedoms were lost and prompted Jewish communities to work for emancipation. A Jewish Reform movement became active, gathering at the Israelite Freischule and the first "temple" on Alte Steinweg.

In the middle of the nineteenth century, many Jewish families improved their social standing and prosperity and could afford to move to the Neustadt and the new suburb at Grindel and around the Alster Lake. These new Jewish neighborhoods led to the building of the Orthodox synagogue at Bornplatz and the Neue Dammtor Synagogue. However, the relationship between the Reform and Orthodox communities was fraught with difficulty. At the turn of the century, when there were 17,949 Jews in Hamburg (2.34 percent of the population), a Conservative movement was founded that attempted to bring both traditions together at the Neue Dammtor Synagogue (near what is now Allende Platz), which was completed in 1895.[10] When the Bornplatz Synagogue was opened in 1906, with Joseph Carlebach as rabbi, the Neue Dammtor Synagogue lost many of its members. Home to twelve hundred members and located on a main street, the Bornplatz Synagogue was a symbol of Jewish self-confidence in the neighborhood known as Grindel (fig. 1). Regardless of community affiliation, all Jews in Hamburg encouraged education and participation in social and economic spheres. A Jewish life blossomed in Grindel; Jews were well integrated in Hamburg life and were accepted, for the most part, by Hamburg's citizens.

During the Weimar Republic, full and legal Jewish emancipation was available to all 19,904 Jews living in Hamburg but was coincident with a rise in anti-Semitism.[11] Hamburg became a new center for learning in Germany, with the help of such assimilated and emancipated Jews as Ernst Cassirer, president of the university, and Aby Warburg, art historian and founder of the Cultural Studies Library on Heilwigstrasse. The National Socialists would thoroughly destroy this vision of emancipation and assimilation.

Shortly after January 30, 1933, the systematic persecution of Hamburg's Jews began.[12] In 1933, there were 16,973 Jews living in Hamburg. In April 1945, there were 647.[13] The NSDAP gauleiter in Hamburg, Karl Kaufmann, was responsible for ensuring that *Reichspolitik* in Hamburg was total. The details of Jewish persecution in Hamburg are made clear in the 2005 anthology *Hamburg im "Dritten Reich,"* a very comprehensive investigation of Hamburg during National Socialism.[14]

Hamburg's status as a *Führerstadt* also deserves mention. In 1937, Hitler planned to completely redesign Hamburg, Berlin, and three other cities as *Führerstädte,* in which the power of the Third Reich would be spectacularly displayed through architecture and urban planning. As a port city of 1.7 million people, Hamburg's architectural task was to represent itself as a gateway to the world of modernity, proving the productivity of the Third Reich. Not least, it was to trump the United States and its famed Golden Gate Bridge with a suspension bridge planned for the Elbe made of one hundred eighty-meter pillars.[15] Further plans included a tower two-hundred fifty meters high, for the NSDAP gauleiter; a two-thousand-meter boulevard on the Elbe; a newly situated university in Flottbek; and a meeting center to seat 150,000 people. None of these were built.[16] In light of these facts, it is clear that Hamburg was hardly the moderate Hanseatic city that supposedly gave Hitler a cold shoulder.

Fig. 1. Bornplatz Synagogue for the Deutsch-Israelitischen Gemeinde (Synagogue of the German Israelite Community), designed by Ernst Friedmann and Semmy Engle, Hamburg, 1906. (Photo: Hamburg Kulturbehörde.)

The fact that, today, many claim it was "not so bad" in Hamburg during National Socialism demonstrates repression in the postwar period.[17] As Werner Johe puts it, in the postwar period, no one really wanted to remember the connection between the words *Hamburg* and *Hitler*.[18] Hamburg was considered a refuge for liberal traditions since the Middle Ages,[19] the "capital of Socialism,"[20] and a city of liberal merchants. The agents of the Nazi regime were seen as foreign elements who did not hail from the middle of the Hanseatic society.[21] In 1947, Rudolf Peterson, Hamburg's first postwar mayor, declared that the citizens of Hamburg had moderated the elements of the radical Right in Hamburg as a result of their Hanseatic worldview of trade and openness. This opinion was quickly disseminated, making it easy to forget the actions of citizens and officials during the Third Reich.[22] In this supposed guilt-free environment, Hitler evaded Hamburg because it was either too "Red" or too "Hanseatic."

This opinion was so entrenched in both academic and popular discourse that research into Hamburg and National Socialism did not even begin until 1960, with the opening of the Forschungsstelle für die Geschichte des Nationalsozialismus in Hamburg (Research Institute for the History of National Socialism in Hamburg). In the 1980s, this institute turned its attention to the Nazi persecution of Hamburg citizens. Additionally, in 1985, Geoffrey Giles argued that students in Hamburg were just as active in the Nazification of their university as were students in any other German institution of higher education.[23] In 1997, the Forschungsstelle für Zeitgeschichte in Hamburg (Research Institute for Contemporary History) opened, becoming an official part of the university in 2000.[24] Recent scholarship, much of it published by the Forschungsstelle, attempts to rectify the picture of a "moderate" Hamburg. Hitler visited the city thirty-three times from 1915 to 1929, more than any other city in Germany with the exceptions of Berlin, Munich, and Nuremberg. In the September 1930 Reichstag election, 18.3 percent of the voters voted for Hitler. In Hamburg, 19.2 percent voted for him, above the national average. Hamburg was not a *Mustergau* (model region), but it was also not the moderate Hanseatic city that supposedly gave Hitler a cold shoulder.[25] The more details about Hamburg's activities during National Socialism come to light, the clearer it becomes that Hamburg has been forgiving its myth of "moderation."[26]

Memorials to the Victims of World War II, 1945–85

If Hanseatic moderation clouded Hamburg's participation in National Socialism, the city's memorials to the victims of World War II demonstrate ambivalence toward its murdered Jewish citizens. The visual motifs employed in these memorials range from a stripped-down aesthetic resembling concentration camp smokestacks, to funerary urns, to mausoleums with figural representations. The memorials do not question the viewer's relationship to National Socialism. Instead, they offer the viewer comfort in easily recognizable iconography. If anything, responsibility remains absent.

The early memorials include Heinz Jürgen Ruscheweyh's Memorial for the Victims of Nazi Terror, installed at the entrance of Ohlsdorf Cemetery in 1949; the Jewish community's Memorial for the Murdered Jews of Hamburg (1951); Gerhard Marcks's Monument for the Victims of Bombing (1952); and the naming of the Nikolaikirche ruins as a memorial site in 1973.[27] The official death statistics reported in 1946 by the Staatistische Landesamt Hamburg include neither those killed at the concentration camp (KZ) Neuengamme, located southeast of Hamburg, nor the murdered Jews: of the 112,000 listed dead, 55,000 were victims of bombing, 35,000 were war dead, and 33,000 were missing or dead.[28]

In 1946, KPD (Communist Party) senator Franz Heitgres, chairman of the Association for the Persecuted of the Nazi Regime, initiated a memorial dedicated to National Socialist victims, which resulted—either directly or indirectly—in two separate memorials: the memorial for the "KZ dead" at Ohlsdorf Cemetery and the urn at the Jewish cemetery in Ohlsdorf. In 1946, architect Heinz Jürgen Ruscheweyh created the first memorial for the "KZ dead," Memorial to the Victims of Nazi Terror, that installed at the entrance of Ohlsdorf Cemetery in 1949. The inscription on the sixteen-meter-high concrete frame reads "1933–1945 / Wrongs brought us death. The living: recognize your duty." Within the frame are 105 urns with earth from twenty-six concentration camps, the names of which, in turn, are inscribed on a plaque in front of the monument. On the verso, an inscription reads, "Contemplate our hardship, consider our death, humans are brothers of humans." The thousands of Jews and others murdered at Neuengamme are not mentioned except as an implied part of the collective. In response, the Jewish community installed a memorial in 1951 in Ohlsdorf Cemetery. An urn with ashes from Auschwitz stands on an area of flat stones. On the wall behind it are words from Jeremiah 9:1: "my eyes a fountain of tears, that I might weep day and night for the slain of my people!"

Contemporaneously, Gerhard Marcks, a sculptor and former Bauhaus teacher, was commissioned to create a memorial for Allied bombing victims, installed in 1947–52 in Ohlsdorf Cemetery. According to Peter Reichel, one of the foremost historians of National Socialism and Hamburg,[29] the dedication of Marcks's work was the most important postwar memorial event in the city, drawing some twenty thousand participants.[30] The memorial consists of a cuboid shape with smooth, intersecting walls that create a cruciform enclosure to represent a mass grave: a simple mausoleum. Each arm of the cross is inscribed with the names of city neighborhoods that were bombed: Wandsbek, Eilbek, Borgfelde, and so on. In the middle of the cross is a square masonry form with a sculpture depicting

Charon, the pagan allegory of death, steering a boat of the living. Also as a memorial to the destruction, the city decided in 1973 that the ruins of the Nikolaikirche would be preserved and named a *Gedenkstätte* (memorial place), a move not unlike the decision to keep the ruins of the Kaiser Wilhelm Memorial Church as a memorial to the bombing of Berlin.[31] After long debate regarding the form the ruins might take, a mosaic after the design of Oskar Kokoschka's *Ecce Homo* (1972) was installed in 1974.

In 1978, the director of the Institute for the History of German Jews, Peter Freimark, approached the director of the City Office for Historical Preservation to create a list of Jewish buildings in Hamburg and put them on the city conservation list; he also recommended that bronze plaques be installed at their sites. In July 1979, Cultural Senator Wolfgang Tarnowski gave his support to this program. A list of sixteen buildings was created, including the site of the former Bornplatz Synagogue, and the Office of cultural Affairs granted between 1 and 1.5 million deutsche marks for the project, which included a new Heinrich Heine memorial (to replace one originally installed in 1926 and destroyed by the National Socialists in 1933). By November 9, 1983, eight bronze plaques were installed. But problems ensued with the plaque program: not all owners of private homes on the conservation list consented to the installation of bronze plaques. By 1985, only nine plaques had been installed. In 1982, the Heine Memorial was re-created.

Of the memorials discussed in this section, only the funerary urn installed by the Jewish community was dedicated to the murdered Jews of Hamburg. Funerary urns, stelae, and mausoleums are traditional forms used for memorials. Utilizing an easily recognizable visual vocabulary, they leave the viewer untouched by an engagement with works that affect the viewer, without insisting on identification with the victim—unlike the kind of position that the countermonument might provoke.[32] In contrast, the memorials in the Dammtor vicinity, by forgoing the visual vocabulary of modernism in favor of postmodernism, question the roles and forms of memorials, the viewer's engagement with them, and the commissioning bodies' attitudes toward the past.

The Dammtor Memorials

Richard Kuöhl's 1936 monument on Dammtordam has been a troublesome presence in Hamburg's public space and has sparked much debate:

should a monument from the fascist era be destroyed, or should it be recontextualized to address current attitudes? Neither Kuöhl's monument nor Hrdlicka's *Countermonument* at the site address the Holocaust directly, but together they constitute a paradigm for the city's representation of its history in public space (figs. 2–3). The *Countermonument* does not pay tribute to its former Jewish citizens; instead, it attests to the victimization of Germans.

The monument on Dammtordam honors the 76th Infantry Regiment, which participated in the German-French war in 1870–71 and subsequently was mobilized in World War I in 1914. It is a sculptural block with eighty-eight marching soldiers, arranged in groups of four and dressed in uniforms of the then-contemporary Wehrmacht. The nationalist tone of the inscription is impossible to ignore: "Germany must live, even if we must die" (Deutschland muss leben, und wenn wir sterben müssen).

Kuöhl's monument was first installed as a critical response to Klaus Hoffmann and Ernst Barlach's War Victims Memorial of 1931, located in front of city hall (*Rathausmarkt*). It is a tall stele with a relief of a pregnant mother and mourning child by Ernst Barlach. On its verso, an inscription reads, "Forty thousand sons of the city lost their lives for you."[33] After World War I, a controversy began over remembrance of war victims. Soldiers on the political right supported a cemetery honoring the dead, while those on the political left lobbied for an antiwar memorial. The war victims' alliance, in the meantime, suggested using the funds for social housing for the war widows and orphans. As a result, the city senate initiated a competition for a modern, inner-city memorial, resulting in Hoffmann and Barlach's design.[34] The 76er Association, the representative group of the 76th Infantry Regiment, successfully lobbied against the Hoffmann/Barlach monument, and in 1933, the senate finally gave the association a space on Stephansplatz for its own memorial.

The famous inscription on the 76er Monument is selected from Heinrich Lersch's poem "Soldier's Goodbye": "Let me go Mother / let me go. / Your last greeting I want to kiss you: / Germany must live, even if we must die!"[35] Because the poem dates from before the Nazi period and because the monument itself is for the dead soldiers of World War I, the monument is not easily defined as National Socialist. It is, however, designed in a style commensurate with National Socialism. Visually, the monument fits with the Nazi architecture of Albert Speer in its massive form; and conceptually, its unquestionable patriotism would have been familiar to National Socialist rhetoric.

Fig. 2. Monument to the 76th Infantry Regiment, designed by Richard Kuöhl, Hamburg, 1936. In the background is Alfred Hrdlicka's unfinished *Countermonument* from 1985–86. (Photo: Courtesy of Gersche-M. Cordes.)

After World War II, Allied directives required the destruction of all Nazi memorials. To save the 76er Memorial, the Office for the Preservation of Historical Monuments (Denkmalschutzamt) used a rule of exception—that memorials that served the dead, individuals, and regular military individuals should not be destroyed—a decision that was controversial.[36] A local citizen wrote in the *Hamburg Free Press* in 1946 that "the monument should be removed . . . [since] the Germany that 'should live, even if we die,' is already dead."[37] In 1957, the city installed a plaque "for the fallen of World War II."[38] The monument remained in place and continues to be a conceptual stumbling block to this day.[39]

In the 1970s, citizens demanded the inscription's removal, instigating the formation of a radical right group in defense of the monument, which had come to be called the Kriegsklotz (war monstrosity). In 1979, Representative Ibs (Social Democratic Party) supported a public competition to convert the militarist monument into a pacifist one.[40] A 1982 competition called for a countermonument to disrupt the 76er Monument's message of the glorification of war.[41] Alfred Hrdlicka, a jury member, submitted the

Fig. 3. *Countermonument,* designed by Alfred Hrdlicka, unfinished, Hamburg, 1985–86. On the left is the section entitled "Verfolgung und Widerstand"; on the right, "Hamburg Feuersturm." (Photo: Courtesy of Gersche-M. Cordes.)

winning proposal. The four-part work was to be installed in proximity to Kuöhl's monument without obscuring or altering it.

When completed, Hrdlicka's monument was to depict a broken swastika. Only two of the planned four parts have been installed. The first two parts—"Verfolgung und Widerstand" (Persecution and Resistance), dedicated on September 29, 1986; and "Hamburg Feuersturm" (Hamburg Firestorm), dedicated on May 8, 1985—memorialize the victims of the July 1943 Allied bombing of Hamburg and the Allied bombing of the ship Cap Arcona in May 1945, when it housed Neuengamme internees.[42] The focus on the Hamburg bombing is revealing. In the aftermath of World War II, Germans often accepted their cities' destruction as a price for the hubris of the Third Reich, while in public—and in private—they defined themselves as victims of Allied bombing. Neither Hamburg nor Hrdlicka's memorial were exceptions.

Like Gerhard Marcks's Monument for the Victims of Bombing and the Nikolaikirche ruins, Hrdlicka's *Countermonument* does not mention the missing Jews. Instead, the victimization of Germans takes center stage. The installation's two missing pieces (not built due to lack of financial support from the city) were not exceptions and were to be titled "Soldier's Death" and "The Image of Women in Fascism." Neither the monument nor the plaque placed by the city in its vicinity mention the word *Holocaust*.

Visually, Hrdlicka's memorial practically disappears against the background of trees on Stephansplatz. The melting bronze forms of "Hamburg Feuersturm" and "Verfolgung und Widerstand" look almost transparent next to the 76er Memorial. In the evening, while the 76er Memorial is lit up by spotlights, Hrdlicka's monument is left in darkness. Hrdlicka chose forms that have a one-to-one relationship between image and meaning: a broken swastika, melting bronze, flames of fire, figures writhing. Such figural representations are often associated with conventional monuments, such as Nathan Rapoport's Warsaw Ghetto Monument (1948), which might provide a figural precedent for Hrdlicka were it not for the melting, writhing forms created by the latter, whose figures contrast with the voluminous, muscle-bound figures of the former.[43] Hrdlicka's unfinished memorial speaks of the city's reticence to engage in an ongoing discussion of Holocaust memorialization.

While Hrdlicka's *Countermonument* seems to fade into the background of Dammtordam, Ulrich Rückriem's Memorial to the Deported Jews stands out as a minimalist work in a lonely triangular park near the university (fig. 4). Among the places of deportation in Hamburg were the Jewish school on Karolinenstrasse, the community center on Hartungstrasse, and the building of the Provinzialloge of Niedersachsen on Moorweidenstrasse. In front of the last, on a triangular plaza, Jews waited in lines for deportation. Cultural Senator Tarnowski supported a memorial on this site and commissioned Rückriem to create it. The memorial was dedicated on January 21, 1983. Standing alone in the park, the memorial consists of a granite block cut into seven stones and then reassembled. The entire park was to be the memorial. According to the artist, the rear side, facing toward Edmund-Siemers-Allee, was meant to evoke the Western Wall in Jerusalem. The front side suggested a protective house, from which the Hamburg Jews were forced to leave.[44]

This minimalist monument did not, however, fulfill the didactic goals of the city. In an effort to more clearly define this site of perpetration, two information plaques were installed. In a strange way, the two plaques reiterate one another. While one describes the thousands of lives lost and the necessity to beware in the present, the other provides a specific population

Fig. 4. Memorial to the Deported Jews, designed by Ulrich Rückriem, granite, Moorweidenstrasse, Hamburg, 1983. (Photo: Courtesy of Gersche-M. Cordes.)

of Jews in Hamburg and more vaguely states that thousands of those lives were destroyed in death camps. Rückriem's memorial did not "depict" the facts of deportation—such are the pitfalls, perhaps, of countermonuments. In refusing figural representations, countermonuments forgo figural representation in favor of visual metaphors that demand emotional and conceptual work on the part of the viewer.

Rückriem is not the first artist to employ minimalism to create works about the Holocaust. For example, Frank Stella gave works in his series of black paintings such individual titles as *Arbeit Macht Frei;* still, he claimed that these were about paint and nothing but paint.[45] More recently, ever since Maya Lin's Vietnam Veteran's Memorial (1987), minimalism has become the visual vocabulary par excellence for Holocaust memorials. This is the case at the U.S. Holocaust Memorial Museum. Sol Le Witt's *Consequence* (1993–95) for instance, is meant for contemplation between floors of historical documentation, its title prompting the viewer to engage in his or her own role in historical events. So, too, Joel Shapiro's *Loss and Regeneration,* an outdoor sculpture at the museum, is meant to be a minimalist, nonpolitical work that should direct the viewer toward memory.[46] These works complement the historical exhibition; they are deemed "appropriate" because the historical exhibition takes precedence over the work of art.

Such aesthetic choices have different valences in postwar Hamburg. Margrit Kahl's Joseph-Carlebach-Platz Synagogue Monument in Grindelhof (fig. 5) is just a few steps away from Rückriem's memorial and has witnessed a similar history of bronze plaque additions. In addition, it is a countermonument that refuses the monumental forms of traditional memorialization. In 1906, the Bornplatz Synagogue was the first synagogue open to the street in Hamburg. With twelve hundred seats and a forty-meter-high cupola, it was a symbol of the self-confidence of Hamburg Jews. On Kristallnacht, November 9 and 10, 1938, the synagogue was damaged but was not burned to the ground—in fact, it could have been rebuilt with its original walls intact.[47] In 1939, the Jewish community was forced to sell the land to the city, well under value, and was responsible for financing its final demolition, which took place in 1940. During the war, a bunker was installed next to the plaza, which still exists today. After 1945, the University of Hamburg used the plaza for extra parking and the bunker as office space. In 1957, a modest plaque was installed on the back of the bunker. In part, the plaque reads: "Here stood the main synagogue of the German-Israelite community of Hamburg at the time of National Socialist tyranny. It was destroyed by a despotic act on Novovember 9, 1938." While the plaque dates the destruction of the synagogue to Kristallnacht, it does not name that anti-Semitic event outright but, rather, refers to it as a "despotic act," thereby masking anti-Semitism completely.[48] Furthermore, the statement is a historical half-truth: the complete destruction of the synagogue did not take place on Kristallnacht but, rather, was enforced by the city of Hamburg and paid for by Jewish citizens. The institutionalized anti-Semitism of the era is not fully addressed.

The Office for the Preservation of Historic Monuments and Office of Cultural Affairs (with Cultural Senator Tarnowski once again leading the movement) expressed the need to make visible this history of the site. It

Fig. 5. The Joseph-Carlebach-Platz Synagogue Monument, designed by Margrit Kahl (artist) with Bernhard Hirche (architect), granite and black polished marble, Hamburg, 1988. (Photo: Courtesy of Gersche-M. Cordes.)

was suggested that the buried foundations of the synagogue could be laid bare. However, the Jewish community did not support that proposal and explicitly requested that the ruins remain buried. A committee formed by the city administration then suggested that the footprint of the synagogue should be "redrawn" on the ground. The District Office (Bezirksamt) and Planning Department and Building Control Office (Baubehörde) were not interested; the Office of Scholarly Affairs (Wissenschaftsbehörde), prioritizing the university's needs, lobbied for converting the area into a parking lot.[49] It was only in 1983, when the city's Arts Commission became active, that Margrit Kahl, a German sculptor, was chosen to design a memorial on the plaza; the city assigned Bernhard Hirche, an architect, to help realize her design.

Kahl suggested a stone mosaic that would project the vanished synagogue's vaulting schema on the ground. In 1986, the forty-eighth anniversary of Kristallnacht, Cultural Senator Helga Schuchardt put forth a proposal to the city senate for the memorial, and Kahl's monument was installed in 1988. The ground mosaic indicates the synagogue floor and the vaulting in its original scale. On November 11, 1988, the plaza was newly named Joseph-Carlebach-Platz for Dr. Joseph Carlebach, the last chief rabbi in Hamburg, who served in that capacity until his deportation to Theresienstadt in 1941.

Following the commission's concept, the artist expressed the footprint and vaulting of the synagogue in black and gray granite imported from Israel, converting the plaza into a kaleidoscopic design. The visitor must imagine the height and depth of the original building and is encouraged to walk over the space where it once stood, thereby conceptually participating in the memorial. In its insistence on the two-dimensionality of a drawing in stone, the memorial makes visible the absence of the destroyed building.

The lack of a conventional memorial with a clear message, however, prompted the city to install informational plaques. Shortly after the memorial's completion in 1988, a plaque was placed on the back of the former bunker. The text of the plaque concludes: "The monument memorializes the form of the house of god; it should be a warning that the irrational destruction is a crime against humanity. May the future put the descendants out of harm's way." If the viewer is looking for information, the full text of the plaque provides the year the synagogue was built, the number of seats, and the fact that it was severely damaged during Kristallnacht in 1938.[50] The reasons the synagogue was destroyed are not mentioned. In addition, the text's last statement is mysterious in its lack of clarity: are the "descendants" meant to mean all Hamburg citizens or only the descendants of Jews? The lack of clarity about the future underscores an unwillingness to fully elucidate the ramifications of the synagogue's history.

After the memorial was built, the plaza was ignored. Neither the District Office nor the Office of Cultural Affairs saw themselves as responsible for its care. The plaza was strewn with litter, and weeds grew over the stones, making the architectural lines illegible. The Grindelhof Citizen's Initiative, founded in 2001, responded to this state of affairs. According to member Christine Harff, the Citizen's Initiative was formed to protest a new traffic plan from the city, under governance of the CDU (Christian Democratic Party), FDP (Free Democratic Party), and "Schill Party."[51] The initiative thereafter became active in other aspects of life in Grindel, including the memorial on Bornplatz. With support of the City Garden Department and as suggested by the initiative, a movement metaphorically titled "Lasst kein gras drüberwachsen" (Don't let grass grow over it) was founded in April 2003. Starting with this effort, the cleaning of the plaza could begin. Since October 2003, the plaza is cared for as part of the Sozial-Macht-Schule program of the Arbeiter-Samariter-Bund. For three years, groups from different schools in Hamburg will be responsible for the care of the plaza via social internships. Its future thereafter is unknown.

Abandoned by the city but supported by the Grindelhof Citizen's Initiative, the memorial is telling for the understanding of the Holocaust in the present. The city's willingness to allow a memorial to reach a state of disrepair is a sad indicator of Holocaust memory in Hamburg. It also demonstrates, however, the ways in which individuals can impact memory. The Citizen's Initiative, for instance, proved important for the upkeep of the memorial: memory is kept alive on an individual and group level for the Grindel community.

In September 2004, a new, double-sided placard, providing photographs of the original synagogue and information about its history, was installed and sponsored by the Hamburg affiliate of the advertising agency JCDecaux, in conjunction with the Grindelhof Citizen's Initiative. Lit up from inside at night, shining with a light blue color, it is the first Hamburg memorial that mentions the murdered Jews of the city.

> ... In the Pogromnacht of November 9, 1938, the National Socialists made this plaza a showplace for Jewish persecution. They damaged the synagogue and forced its demolition. . . . In the memory of the persecuted and murdered Hamburg Jews fifty years after the Pogromnacht of November 9, 1938, this plaza was officially named Joseph-Carlebach-Platz.

JCDecaux will be responsible for the placard's upkeep. It may be necessary that every generation add its own plaque, board, or memorial. In a post-postmodern setting, it is perhaps not ideal, but not surprising, that a private corporation has sponsored a memorial. Nonetheless, each act of memory certainly demonstrates the active role that local citizens play in their neighborhoods.

Memorialization in Hamburg continues. In the summer of 2005, Gunter Demnig, the artist of the European-wide Stolpersteine Project, visited Hamburg and installed his bronze "stumbling stones" on Hamburg's streets (fig. 6). The *Stolpersteine* are bronze plaques that are placed in the sidewalks in front of homes where victims of Nazi atrocities lived. "A per-

Fig. 6. Two bronze plaques from the Stolpersteine Project, designed by Gunter Demnig, Hamburg, 2005. (Photo: Courtesy of Gersche-M. Cordes.)

son is only forgotten when his name is forgotten," says Demnig.[52] On each plaque is inscribed the name of a person, date of birth, date of deportation, date of murder, and location of death. For ninety-five Euros, one can sponsor the creation and installation of a *Stolperstein*. Perhaps the artist realizes what it has taken so long for others to understand: individuals can be powerful recorders of public memory. Thus a simple minimalist work of art declares the absence of victims of Nazi atrocities. This section of this essay began with one gigantic, over-life-sized "stumbling block" (the 76er Memorial, or Kriegsklotz) and ends with thousands of tiny *Stolpersteine*. Perhaps it is only in stumbling over memorials that memory is kept alive.

A rethinking of history (of Hamburg's reputation as a moderate city) is parallel to a reconsideration of traditional forms of remembrance in public space (the countermonument). Hrdlicka's *Countermonument* questions the modernist monument but fails to address the murdered Jews of Hamburg and opts to emphasize the victimization of Hamburg's citizens. Rückriem's Memorial to the Deported Jews presents a worked-on minimalist surface that was deemed "not enough" in light of the facts of history; informational plaques had to be added to make sure the facts of the story were told. Margrit Kahl's Joseph-Carlebach-Platz Synagogue Monument refuses to be an object of remembrance and instead impresses the towering cupola of the former synagogue into the ground by delineating its architectural structure in two-dimensional granite and marble lines. Public art must be commissioned with an eye to future restoration, and in this regard, Hamburg has failed in its duty to upkeep this last site. Instead, private funds from an advertising agency, a project initiated by private citizens, clearly reference the murdered Jews of Hamburg on JCDecaux's placard. In the end, each memorial is not enough on its own. More can always be told. Individuals from each generation add their voices, in visual form, to a memorial landscape. Those additions should be seen not necessarily as addressing a supposed lack of a former monument but, rather, as evidence of changing attitudes toward the past. The historical view of the past will continue to revise itself in the hands of artists, historians, and citizens who refuse to see the past as static and unchanging. Just as memorial plaques have been added to monuments in Hamburg in order for viewers to better "see" the past, so this essay is an addendum to the histories to which it is indebted.

NOTES

1. James E. Young, "Memory/Monument," in *Critical Terms for Art History*, ed. Richard Schiff (Chicago, 1996), 240.

2. James E. Young's work on the topic of Holocaust memorials and collective memory has been groundbreaking. However, his book *The Texture of Memory: Holocaust Memorials and Meaning* (New Haven, 1993) gives the works at Hamburg Dammtor only cursory analysis (104-12), as the details of the commissions and the problems encountered are not fully analyzed. Other Hamburg memorials to the Holocaust include Gloria Friedman's 1997 Hier + Jetzt—den Opfern nationalsozialistischer Justiz in Hamburg (Here and Now—the Victims of National Socialist Justice in Hamburg); Jochen and Esther Shalev Gerz's Mahnmal gegen Faschismus, Krieg, Gewalt—für Frieden und Menschenrechte (Memorial against Fascism, War and Violence—for Peace and Human Rights), completed in 1986-93; Sol LeWitt's Black Form—Dedicated to the Missing Jews (1987-89); and Lili Fischer's 1985 Rosengarten für die Kinder vom Bullenhuser Damm (Rose Garden for the Children of Bullenhuser Damm).

3. Volker Plagemann, *Vaterstadt, Vaterland—Denkmäler in Hamburg* (Hamburg, 1986), 163. See also Frank Kürschner-Pelkmann, *Jüdisches Leben in Hamburg* (Hamburg, 1997), 95.

4. For the traditional interpretation of modernism, see Clement Greenberg, "Modernist Painting," *Arts Yearbook* 4 (1961): 101-8. On minimalism's aggressivity, see Anna Chave, "Minimalism and the Rhetoric of Power," *Arts Magazine* 64 (January 1990): 44-63.

5. The case is different in Germany, as Paul B. Jaskot points out in "Gerhard Richter and Adolf Eichmann," *Oxford Art Journal* 28, no. 3 (2005): 457–78.
6. Jill Bennett, *Empathic Vision: Affect, Trauma, and Contemporary Art* (Stanford, 2005), 6.
7. Lisa Saltzman, "Gerhard Richter's Stations of the Cross: On Martyrdom and Memory in Postwar Art," *Oxford Art Journal* 28, no. 1 (2005): 27–44; Jaskot, "Gerhard Richter."
8. Kürschner-Pelkmann, *Jüdisches Leben in Hamburg.*
9. Frank Bajohr, "Von der Ausgrenzung zum Massenmord Die Verfolgung der Hamburger Juden 1933–1945," in *Hamburg im "Dritten Reich,"* ed. Forschungsstelle für Zeitgeschichte in Hamburg (Hamburg, 2005), 477.
10. Ibid.
11. Ibid., 472, 477.
12. Ibid., 471–518.
13. Ibid., 477.
14. Forschungstelle für Zeitgeschichte in Hamburg, *Hamburg im "Dritten Reich".*
15. Frederic Spotts, *Hitler and the Power of Aesthetics* (Woodstock, 2003), 373–75.
16. Peter Reichel and Harald Schmidt, *Von der Katastrophe zum Stolpersteine* (Hamburg, 2005), 53.
17. Joist Grolle, "Percy Ernst Schramm—ein Sonderfall in der Geschichtsschreibung Hamburgs," *Zeitschrift des Vereins für Hamburgische Geschichte* 81 (1995): 22–60.
18. Werner Johe, *Hitler in Hamburg* (Hamburg, 1996), 7.
19. Susanne Rau, "Holsteinische Landesstadt oder Reichststadt? Hamburgs Erfindung seiner Geschichte als Freie Reichstadt," in *Nordlichter: Geschichtsbewusstsein und Geschichtsmythen nördlich der Elbe,* ed. Bea Lundt (Cologne, 2004), 159–77.
20. *Arbeiter in Hamburg: Unterschichten, Arbeiter und Arbeiterbewegung siet dem ausgehenden 18. Jahrhundert,* ed. Arno Herzig, Kieter Langewiesche, and Arnold Sywottek (Hamburg, 1983).
21. Axel Schmidt, "Von der Kaufmann-Legende zur Hamburg-Legende: Heinrich Heffters Vortrag 'Hamburg und der Nationalsozialismus' in der Hamburger Universität am 9. November 1950," in *Zeitgeschichte in Hamburg: Nachrichten aus der Forschungsstelle für Zeitgeschichte in Hamburg 2003* (Hamburg, 2004), 10–46.
22. A sociological study of Hamburg's citizens' attitudes toward a "moderate" Hamburg in the postwar years has, to this author's knowledge, not been conducted to date.
23. Geoffrey J. Giles, *Students and National Socialism in Germany* (Princeton, 1985).
24. http://www.zeitgeschichte-hamburg.de.
25. Johe, *Hitler in Hamburg,* 8, 20.
26. Curiously missing in the most recent literature on Hamburg and National Socialism is the debate begun between Christopher Browning and Daniel Goldhagen about Reserve Battalion 101 from Hamburg. See Christopher Browning, *Ordi-*

nary Men: Reserve Battalion 101 and the Final Solution in Poland (New York, 1992); Daniel Jonah Goldhagen, *Hitler's Willing Executioners: Ordinary Germans and the Holocaust* (New York, 1996).

27. Reichel and Schmidt, *Von der Katastrophe*, 57.
28. Ibid., 49. Neuengamme was opened in 1938 as an *Aussenlager*—a peripheral concentration camp—of Sachsenhausen.
29. Since 1983, Reichel has been a professor in the Institute for Political Science at the University of Hamburg. He is the author of *Politik mit der Erinnerung: Gedächtnisorte im Streit um die nationalsozialistische Vergangenheit* (Munich, 1995) and edited *Das Gedächtnis der Stadt: Hamburg im Umgang mit seiner nationalsozialistischen Vergangenheit* (Hamburg, 1997), an interdisciplinary anthology that addresses National Socialist memory in Hamburg.
30. Reichel and Schmidt, *Von der Katastrophe*, 58.
31. Brian Ladd, *The Ghosts of Berlin* (Chicago, 1997), 177.
32. Bennett, *Empathic Vision*, 4.
33. Reichel and Schmidt, *Von der Katastrophe*, 61.
34. Peter Paret, *German Encounters with Modernism* (Cambridge, 2001), 176–84.
35. Heinrich Lersch (1889–36) was an autodidactic writer commonly referred to as an *Arbeiterdichter* (proletarian poet). After World War I, Hamburg was the largest "Red" city in Germany next to Berlin; therefore, the excerpt of this poem would have made sense to the 76th Infantry Regiment, a largely working-class regiment. See Reichel and Schmidt, *Von der Katastrophe*, 52.
36. Plagemann, *Vaterstadt, Vaterland*, 155; stated in Reichel and Schmidt, *Von der Katastrophe*, 61.
37. Plagemann, *Vaterstadt, Vaterland*, 158.
38. Ibid., 158.
39. Reichel and Schmidt, *Von der Katastrophe*, 62.
40. "Ideenwettbewerb, um dem Platz so umzugestalten, dass aus einer Kriegsverherrlichung ein Mahnmal gegen den Krieg wird," in Plagemann, *Vaterstadt, Vaterland*, 171.
41. Plagemann, *Vaterstadt, Vaterland*, 172.
42. In the last days of war, inmates of the Neuengamme concentration camp were sent on a death march to the Lübeck Bucht and there put on the floating concentration camp Cap Arcona, only to be bombed by the British on May 3, 1945.
43. Young, *Texture of Memory*, 164–74.
44. Plagemann, *Vaterstadt, Vaterland*, 176.
45. Chave, "Minimalism and the Rhetoric of Power," 48–51.
46. For an analysis of modernism and its supposed neutrality in relation to U.S. identity and the Holocaust, see Ken Johnson, "Art and Memory," *Art in America* 81 (November 1993), 90–99.
47. Kürschner-Pelkmann, *Jüdisches Leben*, 111.
48. Reichel and Schmidt, *Von der Katastrophe*, 65.
49. The area was already being used for extra parking for the university during the 1970s. Historical placards with pictures and text, organized by the Sociology Department of the University of Hamburg, are now in the archive of the Museum

für Hamburgische Geschichte. Information concerning the history of the area is drawn from the author's interview with Christine Harff, member of the Grindelhof Citizen's Initiative, December 2005.

50. The full text of the plaque reads:

Hier am Bornplatz stand bis 1939 die größte Synagoge Norddeutschlands / Sie wurde 1906 nach dem Planen der Architecten Friedheim und Engel / errichtet.

Bis zur ihrem Zwangsabbruch durch die Nationalsozialisten im Jahr 1939 / war die Synagoge ein Mittelpunkt des religiösen jüdischen Lebens in Hamburg; / in ihr fanden über 1100 Gläubige Platz.

In der Pogromnacht vom 9. / 10. November 1938 machten die Nationalsozialisten / diese geweihte Stätte zu einem Schauplatz der Judenvervolgung; die Synagoge / wurde in Brand gesteckt und schwer beschädigt. Nach dem Abbruch des Gotteshauses / wurde der Bunker errichtet.

Für den Ort der ehemaligen Hauptsynagoge der Deutsch-Israelitische Gemeinde / ist ein Monument entworfen worden. Es soll ein Abbild des Deckengewölbes der / Zerstörten Synagoge auf ihrer ehemaligen Stätte erscheinen lassen.

Das Monument soll an die Gestalt des Gotteshauses erinnenen, es soll eine Mahnung / sein, daß sinnlose Zerstörung ein Verbrechen gegen die Menschlichkeit gewesen ist. / Möge die Zukunft die Nachfahren von Unrecht bewahren.

51. Interview with Christine Harff, November 2005.
52. http://www.stolpersteine.com.

The New Börneplatz Memorial and the Nazi Past in Frankfurt am Main

Susanne Schönborn

Frankfurt am Main presents itself to visitors as a bustling commercial and banking center. The city's economic dynamism is reflected in its glass and steel skyscrapers, all of which give shape to an urban silhouette unlike any other German city. Already in the early postwar years, Frankfurt, as the base of the American armed forces and as the unofficial capital of the Western occupation zones, quickly developed into one of the most important economic centers of the young Federal Republic. During this period, Frankfurt made economic recovery its highest priority. Oriented firmly toward the future, Frankfurt took hardly any time for a backward glance, and the city administration used nearly all available resources to pursue a reconstruction program that was more consistently modern than any embraced by other, comparable German cities. Aside from the Paulskirche, which ranked as the "cradle of German democracy" and whose reconstruction was intended to symbolize West Germany's democratic new beginning, nearly all the salvageable ruins of historically significant buildings in the inner city were demolished.[1] The few historic-looking buildings that one sees in Frankfurt's city center today are mostly reconstructions or historically inspired works of new architecture from the 1980s.

    This essay takes readers on a virtual walk through Frankfurt in order to show how the city's confrontation with the Nazi past is reflected in its urban space. It focuses primarily on the strategies of commemoration visible in the city's memorials. Within Frankfurt's memorial landscape, one of the most important commemorative sites is the New Börneplatz Memorial to the Third Jewish Community Destroyed by the National Socialists (Gedenkstätte am Neuen Börneplatz für die von den Nationalsozialisten vernichtete Dritte Jüdische Gemeinde). By examining this memorial's history, especially the speeches given at its opening in 1996, this essay analyzes how city representatives have positioned themselves with regard to Frankfurt's Nazi past. It concludes with a look at the site of the former Grossmarkthalle (central market)—from which the Jews of Frankfurt were deported between 1941 and 1945 and where the European Central Bank (Europäische Zentralbank [EZB]) is currently building its new headquarters—and raises the question of how much space the memory of the Nazi past will eventually find in Frankfurt's urban image.

If one seeks out reminders of the National Socialist past during a walk through Frankfurt, one easily encounters the city's many "stumbling stones" (*Stolpersteine*), brass slabs ten centimeters square that have been installed in the pavement in different locations throughout the city in front of former apartment buildings of people who were persecuted and murdered by Germans during the Nazi era. On any given "stumbling stone," one reads, "Here lived," and then the name, birth date, and fate of the individual. Frankfurt currently has 101 of these "stumbling stones," which the artist Gunter Demnig has installed in numerous German cities since 1992.[2] The individual stones have been initiated and financed by citizens who wish to preserve the memory of the murdered in the neighborhoods where they once lived.

Frankfurt has other reminders of the Nazi past in its urban landscape as well. One site of note is the former I.G.-Farben-Haus—the "House of the Executioners," as Micha Brumlik has put it.[3] I. G. Farben was active in the war economy during World War II and recruited and exploited forced laborers, foreign laborers, and concentration camp inmates. A plaque and extended exhibition recalls the history of the building, whose name was deliberately preserved following a 2001 debate in Frankfurt on the subject of crafting an appropriate memory culture in the city.[4] Today, the Fritz Bauer Institute is located in the I.G.-Farben-Haus. It is also worth briefly mentioning the research group Topographie des NS-Terrors in Frankfurt am Main, which is currently working through Frankfurt's history during the National Socialist years.[5]

Official, city-sponsored commemoration efforts in Frankfurt are visible in more than seventy plaques that recall the sites of persecution and victims of the Holocaust. The first plaques were erected just over a year after the end of World War II, on March 20, 1946, at the suggestion of the Allied Military Government. Black granite slabs were erected at the former sites of the demolished Hauptsynagoge on the Börnestrasse, the Conservative synagogue on the Börneplatz, and the synagogue of the Jewish community (*Israelitischen Religionsgemeinschaft*) on the Friedberger Anlage. Each of these slabs noted the former presence of a synagogue "that was destroyed by Nazi criminals on November 9, 1938." As the mayor, Kurt Blum, stated at the dedication ceremony, the plaques were to be an admonition for all time about the scandalous deeds of the Nazi regime.[6]

From the end of the 1940s until the middle of the 1960s, further plaques were installed, mostly in cemeteries and the sites where synagogues once stood. One of the most important, due to both its location and its proximity in time to the Frankfurt Auschwitz Trials, was the unveiling of a monument to concentration camp victims at the Paulskirche on October 24, 1964.[7] Designed by the artist Hans Wimmer and erected on a red sandstone foundation, the monument was a statue of a man forced to his knees and trying to free himself of his chains.

In Frankfurt, the 1970s were a somewhat ambiguous time as far as the memory of World War II and the Holocaust is concerned. On the one hand, the student protest movement, which was very active in Frankfurt, pushed for a critical debate about the Nazi past. On the other hand, the small number of monuments erected during this period suggests that it was one of amnesia. After the middle of the 1980s, however, new memorial sites were created. Just as before, these recalled the victims of National Socialism, but they now did so at the scattered sites of persecution themselves. Thus, plaques were erected in 1987 at the site of the former Gestapo headquarters and at the former work education camp (*Arbeitserziehungslager*) of Heddernheim. The actual perpetrators of the crimes, however, remained unnamed, one of the defining features of Frankfurt's relation to its Nazi past. Remembrance in Frankfurt meant recalling the victims of Nazi crimes without concretely defining the perpetrators.

Against this backdrop, it is hardly surprising that the crimes committed during the Nazi years by the city of Frankfurt have remained undocumented at the Römerberg city hall complex. It appears to have been forgotten that on March 13, 1933, the swastika flag was hoisted there as a sign of the beginning of the Third Reich. Mayor Ludwig Landmann, who was Jewish, was then forced to resign and was replaced by Nazi Party member Friedrich Krebs. Under Krebs's leadership, Frankfurt tried to shake off the image of being a city contaminated by "Jewish and liberal influences." One of Krebs's first legislative measures, for the "removal of city employees of Jewish background," was passed on March 28, 1933—even before the passing of the Law for the Restoration of the Professional Civil Service at the national level on April 7, 1933. Business relationships between the municipal authorities and Jewish firms were dissolved, and no new ones were established. Krebs's measure went so far beyond the subsequent national law that certain features of it had to be rescinded. This was only the beginning of Frankfurt's persecution of its twenty-nine thousand Jewish citizens, fifteen thousand of whom ended up emigrating and eleven thousand of whom ended up being murdered, including, most famously, Anne Frank.[8]

The Memorial on the New Börneplatz

If one walks from the Römerberg to the east, one quickly arrives at the Börneplatz, somewhat set back from the heavily trafficked Kurt-Schumacher-Strasse and the Battonstrasse. A modern office building, the customer service center of Frankfurt's municipal utility, dominates the site. Next to it, between the office building and the old Jewish cemetery, is an almost empty, gray plaza with a few trees. Only at second glance does it become clear that the site is a memorial—the New Börneplatz Memorial for the Third Jewish Community Destroyed by the Nazis.

The most conspicuous element at the New Börneplatz Memorial, designed by architects Nicolas Hirsch, Wolfgang Lorch, and Andrea Wandel, is the newly formed wall for the thirteenth-century Jewish cemetery. The outer cemetery wall, more than three hundred meters long, is covered with gray cement, into which have been embedded five rows of 11,134 stainless steel blocks (fig. 1). Closer inspection of the blocks reveals the names of Frankfurt Jews who were deported and murdered; dates of birth and dates and locations of death are included to the extent they are known. At the top of each block is a Star of David. The blocks are arranged in such a way that small stones, like the ones that cover the plaza, can be placed on them (fig. 2). In the middle of the square, surrounded by sycamore trees, is a three-meter-high cube composed of reddish stones from the medieval ghetto's main street, known as Judengasse, or Jews' Lane (fig. 3). The stones still display their excavation numbers. The perimeter outline of the Börneplatz synagogue, which was destroyed on November 9, 1938, is marked on the ground by a basalt-ringed steel band. The outline ends at the customer service center, indicating that large sections of the synagogue were located where that building now stands. At the edge of the memorial, five street signs document the changing name of

Fig. 1. Newly formed wall of the Jewish cemetery at the New Börneplatz, Frankfurt am Main, 1999. (Photo: Janine Burnicki, Frankfurt am Main.)

the site: Judenmarkt (sixteenth century–1885), Börneplatz (1885–1935), Dominikanerplatz (1935–78), Börneplatz (1978–87), and New Börneplatz (since June 6, 1999). They are intended to document the fluctuating history of the square. A data center, containing the biographies of deported Frankfurt Jews, also belongs to the memorial and is located in the customer service center.[9]

The memorial at the New Börneplatz is the city's most prominent site of memory, not only because of its special place within Frankfurt's memorial landscape, which is otherwise comprised of small plaques, but also because of its relevance to the city's self-image. Mayor Petra Roth (CDU) described the unveiling of the memorial as "one of the most important events in the postwar history of the city." According to her, the creation of the memorial at the New Börneplatz made it "Frankfurt's main commemorative site for the victims of National Socialist mass murder."[10] Given the memorial's prominent status, a closer analysis of it is in order. Such an analysis reveals that the site's history and postwar aesthetic reconfiguration reflect the city's substantial difficulties in dealing with its Nazi past and German-Jewish history in general.

Fig. 2. Memorial stones placed on the cemetery wall for the murdered Jews of Frankfurt, Frankfurt am Main, 1999. (Photo: Janine Burnicki, Frankfurt am Main.)

The Börneplatz had been the center of Jewish life in Frankfurt since 1462. It witnessed the greatest achievements of Frankfurt's Jewish community, as well as its greatest sufferings—for example, the 1614 expulsion of the Jews from the city for a period of two years.[11] In 1935, the Nazis renamed the Börneplatz the Dominikanerplatz. The National Socialist municipality claimed that the well-known nineteenth-century journalist Ludwig Börne had been a Jew who had polemicized against Germandom in his writings. In November 1938, the Börneplatz synagogue was burned down along with all of Frankfurt's other synagogues. The ruins of the scorched synagogue were carted off at the expense of the Jewish community.

Immediately after the end of the war, the fourth Jewish community of Frankfurt was established. During this early period, the Dominikaner/ Börneplatz was largely forgotten as a site of special Jewish historical relevance. Although the Allied Military Government helped bring about the erection of a plaque on the former site of the synagogue on the Börneplatz, there were no signs that pointed to the site's history. Only at the end of the 1970s did the square become the object of public attention. Paul Arnsberg,

Fig. 3. The New Börneplatz Memorial, Frankfurt am Main, 1999. (Photo: Janine Burnicki, Frankfurt am Main.)

then the director of the Kirchheimische Stiftung, directed attention, in several articles, to the Jewish traditions of Frankfurt and especially to the significance of the Börneplatz and suggested creating a memorial park there.[12] This project remained unrealized, but he did succeed in bringing about the renaming of the square back to Börneplatz in 1978.[13]

In 1984, Frankfurt's magistrate decided to use the site for a new customer service center for its municipal utility. After discussions with the Jewish community and the Kirchheimische Stiftung, the municipality decided to leave the south side of the square free of construction so that a Jewish memorial and a worthy entrance to the Jewish cemetery could be built. In excavation work conducted in early 1987, foundations and cellar remnants of nineteen houses from the former Judengasse were exposed, including two *mikvot* (ritual baths). One of the *mikvot* was from the original ghetto, founded in 1462 (fig. 4).[14] Many discussions ensued about what to do with the archaeological evidence, the site, its history, and its meaning for the city of Frankfurt. A newly formed citizens' initiative, Save the

Fig. 4. Excavation on the Börneplatz, Frankfurt am Main, 1987. (Photo: Andreas Pohlmann. Jüdisches Museum Frankfurt am Main.)

Börneplatz (Aktionsbündnis—Rettet den Börneplatz), joined with the SPD, the Greens, and the Jewish community to demand the preservation of the "irreplaceable monuments of Jewish life" at the site.[15] The Börneplatz was to be maintained as an authentic site of remembrance.

The CDU-run municipal government of Frankfurt, however, insisted on building the planned customer service center. The mayor at the time, Wolfram Brück (CDU), decided in favor of the economic interests of the city utility and cited the Jewish community's earlier agreement to the building project as sufficient grounds to proceed with it. In response to this decision and in order to prevent the further demolition of other cellar walls

Fig. 5. Demonstrators on the Börneplatz, Frankfurt am Main, 1987. (Photo: Klaus Malorny. Institut für Stadtgeschichte Frankfurt am Main.)

and to bring about an immediate halt to the building activity, a group of non-Jewish and Jewish demonstrators occupied the square (fig. 5). They pointed to the site's cultural and historical value and noted that since there were hardly any existing reminders of Jewish life in Frankfurt, the remains of the Judengasse were predestined, by virtue of their authenticity, to testify to the common history of Jews and Christians in the city. They accused the mayor of repressing recent German history.

In analyzing the lines of conflict in the debate over preserving the historical remnants of the Börneplatz, it would be inaccurate to describe it as a debate pitting Jews against Germans. The debate was much more of a clash between differing identities and memories. Within the Jewish community itself, there was no consensus about how German-Jewish history should be remembered in the wake of Auschwitz. There was tension between those young Jews who had consciously decided to live in Germany and those Holocaust survivors who had been stranded in postwar Germany as displaced persons (DPs). The young generation wanted to gaze back once more to German-Jewish history prior to 1933, searching for possible roots. The former DPs, some of whom have described their lives in Germany as "sitting on packed suitcases" for decades, disavowed any connection to German-Jewish history prior to 1933. The community was divided, in short, about which identity they wanted their children to inherit. This ambivalence of the Jewish community and its roots in different traditions—one German-Jewish, the other Eastern European—were reflected in the fact that the community did not unanimously come out in favor of preserving the ghetto's remnants.[16] There was also tension between the non-Jewish citizens of Frankfurt about how to interpret German-Jewish history before 1933—as a successful story of a German-Jewish symbiosis or as the way to Auschwitz.

On September 2, 1987, the mayor responded to the sit-in on the Börneplatz by sending in the police to clear the plaza of the roughly forty protesters. Shortly thereafter, the demolition of archaeological remnants proceeded.[17] In the end, the customer service center was built in altered form. Instead of conserving the remnants of the former Judengasse, parts of it were reconstructed in the cellar of the building, and an exhibition was created documenting the fate of the eleven thousand deported Jews. Moreover, the municipality held an artistic competition for a memorial, which was constructed on the Börneplatz nine years later.

With its decision not to preserve the Judengasse, the city of Frankfurt made a fundamental choice about how it wanted to represent its German-Jewish history. The remnants of the Judengasse—which told of a centuries-old relationship and which, as an unexpected inheritance from a bygone era, were not oriented to the future—were replaced by a Holocaust memorial site that mainly is an expression of present interpretations of that history. This decision reveals that in Frankfurt, as in many other parts of Germany, German-Jewish history was primarily thought of as Holocaust history.

Aside from the unprecedented violence of the Nazi-era persecutions, which lent them a special status in memory, it must be asked what motives underpinned the decision to destroy the authentic remnants of German-Jewish history in favor of a customer service center and a Holocaust memorial. The Frankfurt municipal government argued that the destruction of the ruins was necessary for economic reasons. In doing so, city administrators utilized a line of argumentation from the early postwar years, when historic preservation was regarded as blocking the city's reconstruction. Just as then, economic factors were cited in the 1980s. The remains of the Judengasse would have threatened a stable self-image and raised questions about the existence of continuities between anti-Jewish and anti-Semitic sentiment in Frankfurt's history.

In 1987, such questions were sensitive. Only two years earlier, Frankfurt had been shocked by the scandal surrounding the performance of Rainer Werner Fassbinder's play *Garbage, the City, and Death.*[18] Frankfurt's Jewish community had considered the play to be anti-Semitic and had prevented its opening by occupying the stage. During the ensuing debate, questions about the continuity of anti-Semitism in Frankfurt had been raised. The Fassbinder debate is the political background that needs to be considered in judging how the discovery of the Judengasse remnants threatened Frankfurt's self-image and why it was so important to the municipality to limit the discussion of anti-Semitism to the Nazi era. Yet, as we shall see, precisely by erecting a memorial site on the spot of the ghetto's historic remnants, the city paradoxically made its confrontation with its German-Jewish history a major theme.

The Holocaust in German-Jewish History

Memorial sites document—if sometimes unintentionally—the interests, historical interpretations, and self-image of those who erect them. As a result, they are documents of a double-historical era, since they speak to a bygone event as well as its representation in the present. Depending on where monuments are erected and by whom, their iconography (and their resulting representation of the past) is shaped by various myths, ideals, and political interests.[19] In the case of the memorial at the New Börneplatz, its location and the debate it sparked about preserving its archaeological remnants highlighted an essential aspect of Holocaust remembrance in Germany—namely, the need to interpret the Holocaust by placing the Nazi era within German-Jewish history both before 1933 and after 1945. Of particular interest is the question of whether the Nazi era should be regarded as a period in which certain traditions of German anti-Semitism were continued or not.

The memorial at the New Börneplatz made reference to the history of German Jewry before 1933 in several ways—by virtue of its location, the embedded outline of the synagogue destroyed in 1938, and the cube of stones from the former Judengasse in the middle of the square. Similarly, the street signs with the changing names of the square placed the memorial into the larger context of German-Jewish history and thus also referred to the continuity of anti-Jewish and anti-Semitic excesses in Frankfurt. A glance at the speeches delivered at the June 16, 1996, dedication of the memorial also reveal how the Holocaust was interpreted as a part of Frankfurt's larger German-Jewish history.[20]

Salomon Korn, then a member of the Frankfurt Jewish community's board of trustees, interpreted the memorial as "compensation for the destruction of historic original building material" at the square.[21] For Korn, it was clear that "the Frankfurt municipal government in the year 1987 regarded Jewish history not as a component of Frankfurt's history, but, rather, as the separate history of a special minority"—a belief that led it to conclude that "the remnants of the Judengasse . . . did not deserve a place in the cityscape."[22] Korn further pointed out that the visible outline of the Börneplatz synagogue "superimposed two chronologically distinct acts of destruction upon one another: the destruction of the Jewish house of worship on the so-called Reichskristallnacht and the more recent partial removal of the retaining walls and foundations of the synagogue, which had withstood all of the destruction not only from the original night of arson but also from the war years themselves."[23] Korn thus argued that "it was important not only to commemorate the Nazi crime but, for the sake of historical truth, to separate the different layers of destruction, before and after 1945, from one another."[24] Korn regarded the cube composed of stones from the Judengasse and set in the middle of the square as embodying the destructive approach to German-Jewish history: "The destruction of original historic Jewish building material in Frankfurt am Main, visible in the stone cube, will prevent the immensity of the Nazis' crimes from becoming a screen memory for the shameful dealing with the Jewish dimensions of local urban history in 1987."[25] To be sure, whether the stone cube, in its strongly abstract character, is really capable of realizing this goal is questionable, especially since the cube did not provoke Korn to address the Frankfurt Jewish community's own role in the conflict surrounding the Börneplatz. While young community members had occupied the construction site together with non-Jewish protesters, the leadership of the Jewish community had approved the construction of the city building.

The ambiguity of the cube's symbolism—indeed, the possibility that it was promoting a prettified view of German-Jewish history—is further suggested by the speech of Mayor Roth. Roth spoke before Korn at the dedication and, in her speech, emphasized exactly what Korn feared: the use of the Holocaust as a screen memory. There was no mention in her presentation of the 1987 destruction of the stone remains and the concomitant debate concerning the site's authenticity. She took the cube as an opportunity for a seemingly critical remark about the coexistence of Jewish and Christian Frankfurters during the Middle Ages. In this comment, though, she nevertheless revealed the true colors of her idealized interpretation of German-Jewish history: "The cube made out of the stones of the Frankfurt Judengasse reminds us that this cohabitation existed for almost 350 years under the shadow of the ghetto, a walled and closed residential district in which the Jews had to live at night as well as during the Christian holidays."[26] Contrary to how Roth saw it, the main problem of the Judengasse was not merely the closing of the ghetto gates but living with the permanent insecurity of anti-Jewish riots and expulsions. In Mayor Roth's speech, the persecutions and discriminations faced by the Jews in Frankfurt before 1933 were ignored, with possible continuities and responsibilities unnamed.

Roth's speech indicates that the abstraction of embodying the archaeological remnants in the form of a cube does not necessarily question an idealized picture of German-Jewish history. It remains an open issue as to whether preserving the ruins of the Judengasse would have produced a visibility that would have more clearly called this view into question. In any case, Roth's speech was characterized by emphasis on the positive sides of the relationship of the Jews to the city of Frankfurt: "There is no German city which was influenced by its Jewish citizens in the nineteenth and first third of the twentieth centuries as much as Frankfurt."[27] According to Roth's representation, this harmonious coexistence between Jews and non-Jews was destroyed solely through the persecutions during the Nazi era. With that, she legitimated the erection of a memorial for the Frankfurt Jews murdered during the National Socialist era.

Perspectives of Holocaust Memory

Memorials that commemorate the Holocaust are bound up with special implications in Germany—as the land of the perpetrators and victims.[28] To remember the Holocaust in Germany means to be confronted with both the particular history during National Socialism and the postwar generational question. This confrontation is different for non-Jewish Germans and for Jews, and it is different for those who lived at the time and those born after 1945. For Jews in Germany, remembering the Holocaust means facing the loss of family members and mourning.[29] For non-Jewish Germans, remembering the Holocaust means, as the historian Reinhart Koselleck argues, the double task of memorializing the victims and simultaneously naming the crimes and deeds of the perpetrators. Koselleck states that recalling negative memories that do not attempt to get around the guilt of one's own ancestors is the formula for an enlightened memory culture.[30] This double task generally leads to a variety of reactions, ranging from a defensive form of denial to an acknowledgment of one's guilt. These reactions often exist parallel to each other, both in the public sphere of the Federal Republic and also within each individual. Although the historical responsibility has been more strongly expressed since the middle of the 1990s, the specific naming of guilt often plays only a small part in the government's public commemoration. The debate concerning a central Holocaust memorial in Berlin, for example, never produced an answer to the question of how the nation of perpetrators regards its guilt.[31]

The New Börneplatz Memorial in Frankfurt is explicitly dedicated to the remembrance of the victims of the Holocaust. This is reflected in the symbolism of the monument, with its wall of commemorative stones, which Roth saw as the central element of the memorial. In the mayor's opinion, these stones should make the individual fate of the murdered Jews visible and "connect [the Jews] symbolically with the city and the long tradition of Jewish life in Frankfurt."[32] In saying this, Roth displayed an attitude toward the genocide that was widespread after the broadcast of the American television series *Holocaust* in the Federal Republic in 1979. With this series, the nameless Jewish population whose fate had been merely presented in abstract death statistics was given a face and was made personally comprehensible. The empathy with the victim evoked by the miniseries led many German cities to the search in local history for traces of the Jewish victims. Concomitantly, federal memorialization in the 1980s and 1990s also increasingly referred to single persons, with the goal of individualizing the victim and of connecting their commemoration to the community, the region, the city, or the neighborhood in which the murdered had once lived. Parallel to this trend, in her speech at the unveiling of the memorial, Rita Süssmuth, president of the German parliament at the time, also interpreted the wall with the commemorative stones as "giving [the murdered] a home . . . and getting them right into the heart of the city."[33]

In Salomon Korn's speech, it became clear that the desire to bring the victims home was not unproblematic. He interpreted the commemorative stones quite differently from the speakers who came before him: "Indeed, the blocks of names are part of the cemetery, but they remain on its exterior. They belong to the cemetery, and yet, because they are placed in the outer wall, they do not quite belong to it. In this sensitive balance between reconciliation (namely, the symbolic return home of the deported) and their last rejection lies one of the greatest qualities of the memorial."[34] For Korn, ambivalence predominates and lies fixed in the symbolism of the blocks of names: bringing the victims metaphorically back home and yet being quite clear that this is no longer possible. Making this ambivalence visible avoids the danger of taking on the victims' role, of evading the appropriation of their history that can be part of the attempt to bring them symbolically home. Indeed, the appropriation of the victim's history is a tendency that is widespread in the Federal Republic; the consequence of this trend is that broad areas of National Socialist history appear as identical to the history of the Jewish persecution. In Frankfurt, this tendency can be seen if one considers that this central site of memory commemorates exclusively the persecution of the Jews during National Socialism, reducing a complex history to this one event.

In particular, while the New Börneplatz Memorial lists all the murdered Frankfurt Jews by name, the perpetrators remain anonymous; they are only abstractly referred to in passing. The perpetrators were named as "the Nazi criminals" (die Nazi-Verbrecher) only on the old 1946 memorial plaque that was integrated into the new memorial. This corresponds to the designation of the memorial as "for the third Jewish community in Frankfurt am Main destroyed by the National Socialists." With the description of the perpetrator as National Socialists, a distance from guilt is explicitly created. Even in Mayor Roth's speech, this distancing remains. Although she had chosen Frankfurt as the natural frame for her speech, she did not name the concrete guilt of the responsible parties within Frankfurt's municipality or what role they played for the crimes committed during the National Socialist. While her view of victims of the Holocaust focused on single individuals, the perpetrators as well as other city officials remained faceless. She did not position herself—either personally or as a representative of the city—as a descendant of the Nazi past.

President Süssmuth discussed her own relationship to the past quite differently in her speech. As the president of parliament, she understood herself as "acting on behalf of many towns in Germany in which Jews were excluded, persecuted, deported out of the midst of our communities, and murdered."[35] With this statement, she put herself personally and, as the representative of the German people, expressly in the line of succession from the perpetrators. Drawing on this responsibility, the memorial's opening ceremony was, for her, "not only [about] remembering murder and incomparable events" but also an occasion to challenge the listener: "we should admit our guilt for that which happened because of us and, as I say less and less, not in the name of the Germans but, rather, through the Germans." With this naming of responsibility, Süssmuth broke through the distance to the perpetrator. She referred neither to the abstract "National Socialists" nor to murder "in the name of the Germans"; rather, the murderers were quite explicitly Germans. She consciously described herself and all Germans as the Nazis' successors and consequently invited her audience to take up the responsibility. For her, responsibility stood, on the one hand, for the duty to resist vehemently every attempt "to relativize [the crime] because others have also persecuted" and, on the other hand, for a heightened attentiveness "so that we perceive the origins [of criminality in our own society] in order to check what is to be averted."[36]

This motif of the contemporary lesson cut through Süssmuth's entire speech. Time and again, she linked the memory of the Holocaust to actual experiences in and questions about the society of the Federal Republic. She turned her gaze quickly from the memorial and toward current political conditions: "Most importantly, what must come from this memorial [is] that living together is made easier for those who have come back, [an act] that indeed is anything but expected—yes, perhaps not even comprehensible."[37] By referring to those who had returned, she meant not only the Jews who lived in Germany before 1933 but also explicitly those from the Commonwealth of Independent States (CIS) in the former Soviet Union, whose emigration to Germany in the 1990s was the cause of much public debate. For Süssmuth, to be a descendant of the perpetrators meant the obligation to come up with a positive solution to the problem of Jewish refugees. Süssmuth's speech represented an extension of another widespread strategy used to deal with the National Socialist past in Germany: using the Holocaust to legitimate contemporary political actions. On the one hand, this allowed for the possibility of drawing lessons from the Holocaust. On the other hand, within this strategy exists the danger of politically instrumentalizing and relativizing the Holocaust. It can easily be forgotten that the Holocaust did not happen in Germany by chance and that Auschwitz was an explicitly German extermination project.

The Holocaust as an Emotional Experience

Both Roth's and Süssmuth's speeches ascribed emotional content to memories from the perpetrators' perspective. The only time that Roth spoke of pain, she meant "the painful questions [for descendants of the Nazis] about individual guilt and collective responsibility, about destroyed synagogues and the murder of so many people; questions [such as] where the path to the Holocaust began and why we heard so little about indignation and a refusal to go along."[38] This description of the emotional experience of the descendants of the perpetrators as painful is especially notable given the fact that Roth completely avoided discussing the issue of continuity. In her speech, postwar generations were isolated from any specific relation to Nazi history, irrespective of whether the responsibility for the descendants was described as burdened and painful.

This description of the emotional experience was also shared by Süssmuth. In an answer to the question of how to deal with the past, she stressed "that suppression burdens, remembering liberates."[39] With this phrase, she touched on a typical German trope for handling the Holocaust: remembering brings redemption. Above all, in his May 8, 1985, speech establishing that date as the Day of Liberation, Richard von Weizsäcker cited the Talmudic saying that "the secret of redemption is memory."[40] Since then, this sentence has become the explicit consensus of official thinking about the Holocaust. By one means or another, this motif found its way into each of the opening-day speeches in Frankfurt.

In contrast to Roth and Süssmuth, Mordechai Breuer's speech documented a quite different emotional experience. Coming from a Frankfurt family that immigrated to Israel and remained there after the war, Breuer spoke as a representative of the former Frankfurt Jews. He did not speak of abstract feelings but let the listener sympathize with his personal experiences. In the context of Breuer's speech, the trope of "redemption" was taken back to its religious origin. As a deeply religious person, Breuer attempted, for himself and others, to place the catastrophe of the German Jews in the tradition of the prophecies and, in the process, to almost find comfort in that. For him, history is not without purpose but, rather, is a revelation of God's will. Because Breuer spoke from the distance of one who no longer lived in Frankfurt, his access to the National Socialist past of the city was more direct and more emotional. His speech did not stand in for the city's handling of its past and yet revealed indirectly much about this process. While Breuer's speech represented a religious and emotional access to the National Socialist past, it also made the emotional deficit of the other speeches clear. It spoke to the entangled nature of memory discourse in Germany, which Alexander and Margarete Mitscherlich already described in the 1960s as "the inability to mourn."[41]

Future Confrontation with the National Socialist Past: The Grossmarkthalle

Thinking about the Holocaust in Germany always means tackling the problem of the special relationship between Jews and non-Jewish Germans. This special relationship is determined by the shared history of the Holocaust, which bound both groups to each other but also inscribed their different historical and emotional experiences. Decisive for the success of a collective memory is dealing with these differences—that is, perceiving their existence and not experiencing them exclusively as a division but, rather, using them to bind the two respective efforts at commemoration and mourning into a dialogue.

It remains an open question how much space in the future built environment of Frankfurt will be allowed for sites of memory. However, the land of the former Grossmarkthalle (central market) in the eastern section of the city indicates a potential direction for further developments. The Grossmarkthalle was the assembly point for the deportation of Jews from Frankfurt and the surrounding area, and a plaque commemorating the site was put up in 1997. Since then, the European Central Bank (EZB) bought the land in order "to use the architectural monument [Grossmarkthalle] as the 'lobby' for its new headquarters in Frankfurt."[42] The 185-meter-high double skyscraper that will rise along both sides of the Grossmarkthalle, according to the understanding of the city, should "become an emblem for the Euro and the financial position of Frankfurt."[43]

Given the fact that the site has been identified as a defining one for the city in the twenty-first century, the question of how the National Socialist past will be handled here is quite significant. In the fall of 2004, a working group representing members of the EZB, the city of Frankfurt, and the Jewish community was called together to prepare a competition for a future memorial addressing the Nazi past. Besides considering whether the memorial should also have an information center, the question of the exact location (and hence the authenticity) of the potential monument has, up until now, remained unclear. Most important to the question of authenticity is whether the cellar and tracks (from which the Frankfurt Jews were deported) should be preserved and made part of the memorial. The competition was planned for the summer of 2005, although nothing had happened as of the end of 2006.[44] It remains to be seen whether economic considerations will lead to the destruction of the site's historical remains, a move that would be typical of Frankfurt's handling of its National Socialist past. In any case, the future memorial on the land of the EZB will influence subsequent attempts to handle the traces of the National Socialist past and will indicate how successful Frankfurt will be in making commemoration of the Holocaust an integral part of a European transnational culture of memory.[45]

NOTES

I would like to thank Paul Jaskot and Gavriel Rosenfeld for translating my essay from German into English.

1. See Georg Heuberger, *Stationen des Vergessens* (Frankfurt am Main, 1992), 114–17.
2. Statistics from the Cultural Affairs Office, Frankfurt, September 23, 2005. Cf. http://www.stolpersteine.com.
3. Micha Brumlik, "Rede an der Gedenkveranstaltung anlässlich des 100. Geburtstag von Fritz Bauer im Kasino des IG Farben-Hauses in Frankfurt am Main," July 16, 2003.
4. Irmtrud Wojak, "'Gerichtstag halten über uns selbst . . .': Geschichte und Wirkung des ersten Frankfurter Ausschwitz-Prozesses" (Frankfurt am Main, 2001).
5. http://www.frankfurt1933–1945.de (accessed November 10, 2006).
6. Hans-Otto Schembs, *Der Börneplatz in Frankfurt am Main* (Frankfurt am Main, 1987), 123.
7. The first of the so-called Auschwitz Trials took place in 1963–65, initially beginning in the Plenarsaal of the Frankfurt City Council at the Römerberg but then moving to the Haus Gallus. A plaque commemorating the trial was later placed at the Haus Gallus (but not at the Römerberg). See Jürgen Wilke, *Holocaust und NS-Prozesse: Die Presseberichterstattung in Israel und Deutschland zwischen Aneignung und Abwehr* (Cologne, 1995); Fritz Bauer Institut and Staatliches Museum Auschwitz-Birkenau, eds., *Der Auschwitz-Prozeß: Tonbandmitschnitte, Protokolle, Dokumente,* DVD-ROM (Berlin, 2004).
8. Monica Kingreen, ed., *"Nach der Kristallnacht": Jüdisches Leben und antijüdische Politik in Frankfurt am Main 1938–1945* (Frankfurt am Main, 1999), 319–56.
9. Amt für Wissenschaft und Kunst, Stadt Frankfurt am Main, ed., *Gedenkstätte am Neuen Börneplatz für die von Nationalsozialisten vernichtete dritte*

jüdische Gemeinde in Frankfurt (Frankfurt am Main, 1996); Janine Burnicki, "Steine der Erinnerung: Der Konflikt um den Frankfurter Börneplatz und 'Die Gedenkstätte am Neuen Börneplatz für die von den Nationalsozialisten vernichtete dritte jüdische Gemeinde in Frankfurt am Main'" (master's thesis, University of Frankfurt am Main, 1999).

10. Petra Roth, "Rede von Petra Roth anlässlich der Einweihung der Gedenkstätte am Neuen Börneplatz," June 16, 1996, Protokollamt der Stadt Frankfurt am Main.

11. Jews are first mentioned in Frankfurt in a letter of ca. 1150 from the Rabbi Elieser ben Nathan. In 1614, during the so-called Fettmilch rebellion, the Judengasse, to which Jews had been relegated, was plundered, and the Jews were expelled. Only in 1864 did the Jews of Frankfurt get full emancipation.

12. The Kirchheimsche Stiftung was devoted to the promotion of the traditions of the old Frankfurt Jewish community.

13. Dieter Bartetzko, "Ihr Juden gehört uns mit Leib und Gut," in *Der Frankfurter Börneplatz,* ed. Michael Best (Frankfurt am Main, 1988). See also Heuberger, *Stationen,* 130n.

14. Museum für Vor- und Frühgeschichte, Archäologisches Museum, der Stadt Frankfurt am Main, ed., *Die Judengasse in Frankfurt am Main: Ergebnisse der archäologischen Untersuchungen am Börneplatz* (Frankfurt am Main, 2000).

15. "Resolution der Jüdischen Gemeinde," August 9, 1987, in Heuberger, *Stationen,* 156.

16. Micha Brumlik, "Erinnern und Erklären: Unsystematische Überlegungen eines Beteiligten zum Börneplatz-Konflikt," *Babylon,* no. 3 (1988).

17. Best, *Der Frankfurter Börneplatz.*

18. Heiner Lichtenstein, ed., *Die Fassbinder-Kontroverse oder das Ende der Schonzeit* (Königstein, 1986); Susanne Schönborn, "'Ein reinigendes Gewitter': Die Fassbinder-Debatte 1984/85 als Markstein deutsch-jüdischer Nachkriegsgeschichte," in *Juden in der Bundesrepublik. Trumah: Zeitschrift der Hochschule für Jüdische Studien* (Heidelberg) 14 (2005): 109–28.

19. Peter Reichel, *Politik mit der Erinnerung* (Munich, 1995), 49n.

20. At the unveiling of the memorial on June 16, 1996, the biographies of some deported Frankfurt Jews were read aloud. Speeches followed from Mayor Roth, Prof. Rita Süssmuth (president of the German parliament), Hans Eichel (prime minister of Hesse), Ignatz Bubis (head of the Zentralrates der Juden in Deutschland and of the Frankfurt Jewish community), Dr. Salomon Korn (a member of the Frankfurt Jewish community's board of trustees), Roni Milo (mayor of Tel Aviv), and Prof. Mordechai Breuer (Jerusalem). Unfortunately, there is no copy of Bubis's speech, which was delivered without notes.

21. Salomon Korn, "Rede von Salomon Korn anlässlich der Einweihung der Gedenkstätte am Neuen Börneplatz," June 16, 1996, 3, Protokollamt der Stadt Frankfurt am Main.

22. Ibid., 4.

23. Ibid., 3.

24. Ibid., 1.

25. Ibid., 4.

26. Roth, "Rede von Petra Roth," 2.
27. Ibid., 2.
28. I consciously use the phrase "land of perpetrators and victims" instead of the more commonly employed "land of perpetrators." My view is that it makes more explicit the issue that the relational history between Jews and non-Jews in Germany after 1945 needs to be thematized.
29. See, for example, Kurt Grünberg, Trauma-Transfer: Überlebende der Shoah und ihre Nachkommen im Land der Täter," in *Zwischen Erinnerung und Neubeginn: Zur deutsch-jüdischen Geschichte nach 1945,* ed. Susanne Schönborn (Munich, 2006).
30. Reinhart Koselleck, *die tageszeitung,* March 25, 2005.
31. Miriam Haardt, *Zwischen Schandmal und nationaler Sinnstiftung: Die Debatte um das Holocaust-Mahnmal in Berlin* (Bremen, 2001); Jan-Holger Kirsch, *Nationaler Mythos oder historische Trauer? Der Streit um ein zentrales "Holocaust Mahnmal" für die Berliner Republik* (Cologne, 2003).
32. Roth, "Rede von Petra Roth," 1.
33. Rita Süssmuth, "Rede von Rita Süssmuth anlässlich der Einweihung der Gedenkstätte am Neuen Börneplatz," June 16, 1996, Protokollamt der Stadt Frankfurt am Main, 1.
34. Korn, "Rede von Salomon Korn," 2.
35. Süssmuth, "Rede von Rita Süsmuth," 1.
36. Ibid., 2.
37. Ibid., 2.
38. Roth, "Rede von Petra Roth," 3.
39. Süssmuth, "Rede von Rita Süsmuth," 1.
40. The key Talmudic sentence that is also used to explain the Holocaust memorial at Yad Vashem in Jerusalem states, "Forgetting extends the exile; memory is the secret of redemption."
41. Alexander and Margarete Mitscherlich, *Die Unfähigkeit zu trauern: Grundlagen kollektiven Verhaltens* (Munich, 1968).
42. Mitteilung des Presse- und Informationsamtes der Stadt Frankfurt am Main, *Frankfurt im 21. Jahrhundert* (March 15, 2005).
43. Ibid.
44. Pressemitteilung der EZB, *Gedenk- und Informationsstätte zur Erinnerung an die Deportation jüdischer Bürgerinnen und Bürger von der Großmarkthalle* (November 5, 2004).
45. On the approaching paradigm shift in memory, see Daniel Levy and Natan Sznaider, *Erinnerung im globalen Zeitalter: Der Holocaust* (Frankfurt am Main, 2001).

Epilogue: The View from Berlin
Brian Ladd

Two centuries ago, German intellectuals, grasping for solid ground amid fearful upheavals, persuaded much of the world of the power of group identities rooted in place by ancestral traditions. In nineteenth-century Central Europe, many of these local identities were put in the service of German nationalism. Even after Germany went a long way toward destroying itself in the twentieth century, its national identity has persisted, albeit in a troubled form. Efforts to shape a usable identity in the face of the Nazi past have made Germany a laboratory of collective memory. Many foreigners find any expression of German national pride to be repugnant, and increasing numbers of Germans have also come to believe that the stain of Nazism demands a new kind of attitude toward the German nation and its history. This new identity is far from settled, however; so far, it mixes shame with pride to produce dissonance, anguish, and, at best, humility.

Painful national debates about identity have been complemented—and often shaped—by a wide array of initiatives to incorporate the Third Reich into local histories. Local memory attracts attention because of the extent to which people find that memories either persist or can be revived when they attach themselves to familiar buildings, monuments, or places. The Third Reich was a national institution, and World War II and the Holocaust were international catastrophes, but they make themselves felt most viscerally in the experience of particular places, whether Anne Frank's house in Amsterdam, the Auschwitz camp in Poland, or many of the German sites described in this volume.

Many urban sites carry all the more power because of their layers of memory: they have served widely different purposes at different times and, crucially, there are often incompatible demands for their continued use. Conflicts between commemorative and more quotidian functions—as, for example, in the case of the Frankfurt Jewish quarter described by Susanne

Schönborn in her essay in this volume—draw attention, spark debate, and thus make places meaningful to their users as well as to a larger public. Above all, attention to the Third Reich's remnants challenges a quiet postwar consensus that has separated the national catastrophe of the Third Reich from local memories that were implicitly understood to have been essentially innocent.

Some ruins cannot deny their Nazi provenance, notably the hulking bunkers of Bremen (described by Inge Marszolek and Marc Buggeln in this volume) or the Nuremberg complex. The fame of the latter (especially its enduring portrayal in Leni Riefenstahl's film *Triumph of the Will*) might lead outsiders to think that its singular meaning is unambiguous and undeniable, but Paul Jaskot reminds us in his essay in this volume that the site has a longer history and that its more mundane uses before and after the Third Reich loomed larger in the daily lives of local residents. Still, fame and size make the Nuremberg Reich Party Rally Grounds a relic that locals have to face up to, even as they wince at the recognition that their city will henceforth have not one but two claims to enduring fame and thus will have to come to terms with a historical reputation reaching "from Dürer to Führer."

Such enormous Nazi monuments are not rare, but neither are they typical. The Third Reich left its imprint everywhere in Germany; and in most places, its traces are intertwined with older as well as newer buildings and fragments, making it all the more difficult to frame an appropriate response. The Nazi component of a site becomes important when local activists call attention to it, as has happened in many cases discussed in this volume. Once the troubling legacy has been brought to light, it becomes hard to ignore. It can be acknowledged with the words of a plaque or the physical presence of a memorial, or it can somehow be made part of an old or new building.

Design solutions can take many forms, as in the case of Hamburg's varied Holocaust memorials described in Natasha Goldman's essay in this volume. They can engage elite opinion and attract wide (if sometimes brief) attention. A design's effects are more profound, if less noticeable, when it shapes people's daily lives. It is this power that leads Kathleen James-Chakraborty and Jan Otakar Fischer to argue in their essays that architecture can tell us things that archival verbiage cannot. Certainly there is a sense in which architecture reaches a broader public than any written text, whether in a book, an official proclamation, a museum exhibit, or a plaque. Yet architecture can conceal as well as reveal history.

Just as local histories can depict a town's innocence, so, too, can designs be read selectively. Fischer and James-Chakraborty remind us, for example, that the architectural establishment long avoided confrontation with the Nazi past by proclaiming the democratic purity of modernist architecture. In short, physical designs intended to resolve verbal disputes, just like verbal debates about place and memory, reach different publics, in different ways, and offer partial but sometimes illuminating truths.

Another design strategy emphasizes historic preservation, which has become a well-established vehicle for remembrance, for making statements about local identity—and also for forgetting histories deemed inessential. Take the remarkable story of the Church of St. Servatius in Quedlinburg, as told in this volume by Annah Kellogg-Krieg. In such a venerable building, it was easy to pretend that the Nazis had not been there or at least that they did not leave any traces. The profession of historic preservation gave a respectable imprimatur to this repression of memory. Preservation is always selective, as a matter of practice, since not every building or feature can be preserved; and the selection has traditionally served established narratives of local and national identity. When the Nazis were in power, they fit the story line; afterward, they did not. More recent preservationist practice (less apparent in Quedlinburg than in other places) has tried to complicate the story, but at the risk of diluting any message a building might bear.

Collective identity, like historic preservation, depends on a precarious combination of remembering and forgetting. (We think of "forgetting" as accidental, whereas accusations of the "denial" of history imply an intentional suppression of memory; but in matters of collective memory, it usually proves impossible to separate one from the other. The psychoanalytic term *repression,* suggesting an unconscious desire to forget, may thus be apropos in this context.) The very reuse of a building or site, even if for entirely practical reasons, makes an implicit statement about the significance of what came before. Forgetting is all the easier where a building has been destroyed, as was so often the case in German cities after 1945. The desire to restore a place to its undamaged prewar appearance has been apparent in many German cities from the 1940s to the 2000s, with both Dresden and Berlin as late examples. The intent is to proclaim that the destruction of war has been overcome; the effect, all too easily welcomed, is to make it appear as if the Third Reich never happened.

Thus, selective memories that reinforce traditional forms of local as well as national identity are open to challenge from those who point an accusing finger and demand an end to the denial of uncomfortable truths. That has been happening all over Germany. Recent, unconventional memorials point the way to new local and national narratives that challenge accepted stories.

Many of the controversies discussed in this volume resemble better-known battles in Berlin. By dint of political and cultural authority, Berlin has been the center of discussion about diplomatic, pedagogical, and artistic responses to Germany's troubled past. This book raises the question of whether studies of German memorials and other urban responses to the Nazi past have been too Berlin-centered. The focus on Berlin is especially striking among works by non-German scholars. Trivial reasons have undoubtedly played a role: since 1990, scholars and intellectuals have flocked to the ferment of the reunified capital (many historians by necessity, as federal archival holdings have been centralized here), and for the first time, local studies of Germany have begun to exhibit a little of the centripetal tendency that has long been so pronounced in France and England.

More important to the Berlin memory boom has been what visitors (as well as residents) have observed here: vigorous public debates and lengthy battles over the fate of crumbling buildings, abandoned lots, and dusty corners. Long before the Federal Republic's official representatives relocated from Bonn at the end of the 1990s, architects and sculptors had joined hands with scholars, intellectuals, and neighborhood activists to call attention to sites deemed to have historical significance. The resulting turmoil, as well as the subsequent memorials, exhibitions, and acts of preservation, have deserved the recognition they have received. What has been lacking has been comparable attention to other cities.

How special is Berlin? A single book can offer only some tentative answers. Perhaps Berlin is special indeed. Rostock is not like Berlin, according to Susan Mazur-Stommen's essay in this volume. Nor, even more clearly, is the Dresden described by Susanne Vees-Gulani in this book. Dresden, indeed, seems to stand at the opposite pole from Berlin. Even the foreign image of Dresden, the shattered "Florence on the Elbe," diverges dramatically from that of Hitler's former capital. There is a widespread popular consensus in former Allied lands that the bombing of Dresden in February 1945 was a mistake, if not a crime. If, for Westerners, Berlin is still the fallen capital of Nazi aggression, Dresden is the innocent victim of a necessary war, and in both cities, local citizens have taken their reputations to heart. In Vees-Gulani's telling, the citizens of Dresden have been able to embrace their victim status with little audible dissent at home or abroad. The contrast with Berlin is striking: here, claims of German victimhood never go unchallenged.

Berlin and Dresden might thus illustrate the contrast between center and periphery. It would be a mistake, however, to see their differences exclusively in those terms. Another crucial element lacking in Dresden (and Rostock) was the Federal Republic's political culture of the 1980s. Many of the case studies in this book reveal the legacy of Germany's decades-long division. There were, of course, notable similarities between the two German states' excruciating inattention to their immediate past in the postwar years. As Michael Meng notes in his essay on postwar Potsdam, the German Democratic Republic's "antifascist" ideology legitimized a widespread desire to forget one's own complicity in the Third Reich. By the 1970s and especially the 1980s, however, a younger generation was busy calling attention to local Nazi legacies in many West German cities. The essays here reveal a decisive turn in the 1980s toward pitiless revelation of painful memories in Cologne, Wolfsburg, Nuremberg, Munich, Frankfurt, and Hamburg.[1] The absence of a comparable public sphere in the German Democratic Republic (GDR) has left a legacy that emerges clearly from this collection.

It is too simple, yet far from false, to observe that East German cities have had more pressing problems engaging the attention of politicians and citizens. Not the least of those problems has been the disposition of monuments and sites associated with their more recent dictatorship. They share that fate with the formerly divided Berlin, which is in the unique position of having been both a West German and an East German city, with West German intellectual culture as well as East German detritus ripe for reinterpretation.

There is probably also some unquantifiable truth in the common belief that Berlin has bred an antiauthoritarian culture and an eagerness to embrace alternative identities. In one of the recent studies of Berlin, sociologist Jennifer Jordan has enumerated four forces that drive the creation of memorial spaces.[2] The initial two—the existence of "memorial entrepreneurs" and the resonance of their efforts with a broader public—suggest reasons why Berlin's concentration of critical intellectuals and their institutions might set the capital apart. However, the essays collected in this volume show us would-be memorial entrepreneurs demanding attention to sensitive sites across Germany—and finding resonance, if to greatly varying degrees. Although Berlin probably boasts a larger core of engaged citizens, there is little reason to believe that Berlin's population as a whole is any more open-minded than that of other cities. Jordan's other two criteria, landownership and land use, help explain successes and failures of memorial efforts in Berlin and in other cities as well. Certainly the spatial reorganization and redistribution of property in Berlin after the dismantling of the Wall has created extraordinary, but not unparalleled, opportunities to dust off neglected sites.

Berlin's status as capital (or as a capital in mothballs, as one might characterize West Berlin during the decades of division) has also made it relatively easy to make local sites part of a national story. Sites of obvious national significance that have been scrutinized in recent years include Hitler's bunker, Göring's ministry, Himmler's and Eichmann's headquarters, and the villa where the notorious Wannsee Conference laid out plans for the murder of millions of Jews. Still, Berlin's much scrutinized synagogues (as places of vanished Jewish life and as places of persecution and desecration), SA prisons, and deportation ramps have their equally important but generally more neglected counterparts elsewhere (although it is worth noting that Berlin's prewar Jewish population was far larger than that of any other German city).

While Berlin's local history has long been viewed through a national lens, other cities have been better able to detach their local traditions from the national ones. Cologne, for example, in the words of a postwar mayor quoted by Jeffry Diefendorf in his essay in this volume, was a peaceful city shaped by traditions antithetical to Nazi racism and militarism. Similarly, Natasha Goldman cites Hamburg's first postwar mayor assuring his citizens that their Hanseatic moderation had set them apart from the fanatical Nazis.

Berlin, of course, can and sometimes does point to its strong Communist and Socialist traditions to claim that it, too, was a city conquered by the Nazis, rather than one that bred them—indeed, that was the GDR's position. That view has gone out of fashion in Berlin, and things are not really so different in Germany's next-largest cities, as we see in the changing local responses to the Holocaust in Hamburg and in the varied forms of commemoration at the EL-DE-Haus and other sites in Cologne. As in Berlin, the change over the decades has been enormous, if gradual and uneven. Gavriel Rosenfeld's account herein of recent developments in Munich (a city that arguably did, more than any other, breed Nazis) reveals that even in this place with a reputation for reluctance to confront its Nazi past, we are now far beyond any simple battles of memory versus denial. The city, the Bavarian state, and many other institutional actors are negotiating complicated choices for the treatment of many sites—hoping, perhaps, that the Nazi legacy does not loom too large, but mainly deciding whether attention should be centralized or decentralized and if it should take the form of memorials, museums, or documentation centers. As in Berlin, the conflicts are never-ending, as are the accusations of denial and neglect, but so is the public debate, as well as the recognition that there are different kinds of remembrance, different ideas about local identity, and conflicting demands on urban space. Perhaps this messy state of affairs is a kind of new German normality.

NOTES

1. One might similarly characterize the final sections of the story in Harold Marcuse's *Legacies of Dachau: The Uses and Abuses of a Concentration Camp, 1933–2001* (Cambridge, 2001), as well as some of the case studies in Klaus Neumann's *Shifting Memories: The Nazi Past in the New Germany* (Ann Arbor, 2000).

2. Jennifer A. Jordan, *Structures of Memory: Understanding Urban Change in Berlin and Beyond* (Stanford, 2006), 11–14.

Contributors

Marc Buggeln is working on his Ph.D. at the University of Bremen with a grant from the Heinrich-Böll-Stiftung. His dissertation is entitled "The Satellite Camp System of the Concentration Camp Neuengamme." He is a member of the editorial boards of the journals *WerkstattGeschichte* and *Sozial.Geschichte.*

Jeffry M. Diefendorf is a professor of history at the University of New Hampshire. His publications include *In the Wake of War: The Reconstruction of German Cities after World War II* (Oxford, 1993) and, as editor, *Rebuilding Europe's Bombed Cities* (New York, 1990) and *Lessons and Legacies,* volume 6, *New Currents in Holocaust Research* (Chicago, 2004).

Jan Otakar Fischer is an architect, journalist, and critic living in Berlin. He has written widely on architecture and urbanism for such publications as the *Harvard Design Magazine,* the *New York Times,* the *International Herald Tribune, Architectural Record,* and *Architecture* magazine. He is cofounder of the Lexia International Berlin Architecture Program.

Natasha Goldman received her Ph.D. in visual and cultural studies from the University of Rochester in 2002. She teaches at the University of Texas, El Paso, as an assistant professor of art history. Her research and teaching concentrate on contemporary art, theory, and public space, specifically examining post-Holocaust aesthetics and Holocaust memorials. She has published in exhibition catalogs and has a forthcoming article in *Art Journal* entitled "Israeli Holocaust Memorial Strategies at Yad Vashem: From Silence to Recognition." She currently is revising her manuscript "Missing Absence: Trauma and National Memorials to the Holocaust" for publication.

Kathleen James-Chakraborty is a professor and Head, School of Art History and Cultural Policy, University College Dublin in Ireland. Her books include *German Architecture for a Mass Audience* (London and New

York, 2000), *Erich Mendelsohn and the Architecture of German Modernism* (Cambridge, 1997), and the edited collection *Bauhaus Culture: From Weimar to the Cold War* (Minneapolis, 2006).

Paul B. Jaskot is an associate professor of modern art and architectural history at DePaul University. He is the author of *The Architecture of Oppression: The SS, Forced Labor, and the Nazi Monumental Building Economy* (London and New York, 2000), as well as many essays on art and politics during the Nazi period. His current project focuses on the political reception of the Nazi past and postwar German art.

Annah Kellogg-Krieg is a Ph.D. candidate in the Department of the History of Art and Architecture at the University of Pittsburgh. Her upcoming dissertation is on architecture, historic preservation, and medievalism in the city of Breslau/Wroclaw from 1860 to 1960.

Brian Ladd is a research associate in the Department of History at the State University of New York at Albany. He is the author of *The Ghosts of Berlin: Confronting German History in the Urban Landscape* (Chicago, 1997) and *The Companion Guide to Berlin* (Suffolk, UK, 2004).

Inge Marszolek is a professor in the Department of Cultural Studies at Bremen University. She is the author of many studies on such themes as popular culture and media history in Germany, power and society in the National Socialist and postwar eras, and wartime exchanges of letters and photography. Her many publications include, coedited with A.v. Saldern, *Radio zwischen Lenkung und Ablenkung,* volume 1, *Radio in the Third Reich,* and volume 2, *Radio in the Early GDR* (Tübingen, 1998).

Susan Mazur-Stommen is a research associate at the University of California, Riverside, where she completed her Ph.D. in cultural anthropology in 2002. Her book *Engines of Ideology: Urban Renewal in Rostock, Germany, 1990–2000* (Berlin, 2005), an ethnography of a small city in former East Germany, is now available in the United States from Transaction Publishers. She can be reached via her Web site, http://www.susanmazur.com.

Michael Meng is a Ph.D. candidate in the Department of History at the University of North Carolina at Chapel Hill, working on a dissertation entitled "From Destruction to Preservation: Jewish Sites in Germany and Poland after the Holocaust." He has published essays in *Central European History* and *Contemporary European History.*

Gavriel D. Rosenfeld is an associate professor of history at Fairfield University. He is the author of *Munich and Memory: Architecture, Monuments, and the Legacy of the Third Reich* (Berkeley, 2000), which appeared in German translation in 2004 as *Architektur und Gedächtnis: München und Nationalsozialismus, Strategien des Vergessens* (Munich, 2004). He is also the author of *The World Hitler Never Made: Alternate History and the Memory of Nazism* (Cambridge, 2005) and over a dozen articles on the history and memory of the Nazi era.

Susanne Schönborn is completing her Ph.D. at the Center for Antisemitism Research in Berlin. Her dissertation is entitled "Jewish Identities Reflected in Political Debates of the Federal Republic of Germany." Among her publications is "'Juden reden über Gefühle, und die anderen über Kunst'—Konstruktionen jüdischer Identität nach 1945," *Transversal: Zeitschrift des David-erzog-Centrums für Jüdische Studien an der Universität Graz* 6, no. 2 (2005).

Susanne Vees-Gulani is an assistant professor of German and comparative literature in the Department of Modern Languages and Literatures at Case Western Reserve University. She is the author of *Trauma and Guilt: Literature of Wartime Bombing in Germany* (Berlin and New York, 2003) and several articles on German postwar rebuilding, W. G. Sebald, Dieter Forte, psychiatry and literature, and science and literature.

Index

Aalto, Alvar, 102, 106–7, 110, 111
Adenauer, Konrad, 50–51, 58, 247
African refugees, 198–99
Agora, 106
Air-raid shelters: in Bremen, 185–87, 188–90, 197–201, 204, 206, 296; in Hamburg, 264, 266
Aldi grocery store, 173
Aller Valley, 89
Allgemeine Elektrizitäts-Gesellschaft (AEG), 122
Amsterdam, 295
Anderle, Walter, 153–54
Andriessen, Mari, 58
Antifascism, 73, 120, 133, 200
  as articulated in GDR, 32, 34, 41–43, 217, 231–34, 239–40, 241, 246–47
Anti-Semitism, 27–28, 32–33, 59, 80, 177, 188, 233, 239–40, 254, 264, 283–84, 285
Arado and Heinkel Company, 73
Architecture, 3, 5, 8, 11, 12–13, 27–30, 34, 36, 40, 42–44, 60–61, 70, 71, 81–82, 90, 101–12, 143–44, 147–48, 186, 205–6, 218–19, 233–35, 265–66, 269, 276, 290
  building in Nazi period, 2, 3, 5, 8, 13, 51, 68, 77–78, 90, 91, 94, 98, 102–5, 119–20, 125–27, 129, 147, 164–65, 185, 188–90, 212–15, 241–42, 254, 259
  industrial, 12–13, 15, 16, 17, 18, 68, 91, 94–95, 98, 101, 102, 103–5, 116, 118–34
  military, 15, 68, 76–77, 80, 185, 188–90
  Plattenbau, 76
  postwar competitions, 56, 105, 153–58, 168, 172
  style: baroque, 29, 214, 235; deconstruction, 120; Gothic architecture, 3, 55, 143, 209, 210–11, 213, 215, 219–20; *Heimatstil* (vernacular style), 8, 102–3, 124; historicism, 8, 34, 40, 125, 133; modernism, 5, 8, 77–79, 103–7, 110, 119–20, 124–25, 128, 130, 133–34, 149, 153, 192, 246, 296; Moorish, 27, 244; neo-baroque, 242; neoclassical, 3, 8, 103, 120, 130, 147, 149, 152, 164, 215; neo-Gothic, 189; neo-Romanesque, 27, 48–49, 215, 220; postmodern, 1, 120, 130–31, 133; Romanesque, 51, 53, 209, 213–15, 219, 224
Armaments industry, 73
Arnsberg, Paul, 278–79
Aryan, 147
Asylum seekers, 72–73, 198–99, 206
Auschwitz, 99, 257, 275, 281, 282, 289, 295
Austria, 95, 153
Autobahn, 89, 91, 94
Autostadt (Wolfsburg), 108–9, 110

Bähr, Georg, 26
Baltic Sea, 67
Band, Karl, 56, 58
Barlach, Ernst, 259; *Angel of Death*, 55, 56
Bauhaus, 79, 96, 103, 118–19, 121–25, 127, 128, 130, 132, 133–34, 257
Bäumler, Klaus, 169
Bavaria, 13, 144, 147, 148, 149, 150, 164, 166–68, 169–75, 177–80, 301
Bavarian Jubilee Exhibition, 147
Bavarian Landtag, 170, 172
Becher, Bernd and Hilla, 129

308 Index

Beer Hall Putsch, 165
Behrens, Peter, 122
Belgium, 57, 58, 129
Bennett, Jill, 252
Berger, Hans, 220, 221–22
Berlin, 1–2, 4, 5, 6, 8, 9, 11, 13, 16, 50, 55, 67–68, 82, 84, 89, 120, 121, 123, 125, 133, 143–44, 151, 158, 159, 173, 180, 205, 216, 233, 243, 254, 256, 297–301
  Jewish Museum, 155, 170, 175
  memorials in, 11, 18: Kaiser Wilhelm Gedächtniskirche, 81, 258; Memorial to the Murdered Jews of Europe, 2, 9, 144, 151, 170, 178; Neue Wache, 151; Soviet memorial on Unter den Linden, 146
  Nikolai Quarter, 68
  Oranienburgerstrasse Synagogue (Neue Synagogue), 16, 243–44
  Soldiers' Hall, 215
  Speer's office of the Generalbauinspektor, 91
  Technische Hochschule, 91
  Topography of Terror, 9, 15–16, 68, 150, 169, 170, 178–79
Berlin Philharmonic, 107
Berlin Wall, 8, 9, 16, 76, 133, 223, 232
Bernard, Josef, 56
Berringer, Gustav Wilhelm, 77–78
Berchtesgaden, 170–71, 173
Bestelmeyer, German, 164
Bitburg Affair, 9, 150
Bley, Werner, 224
Blum, Kurt, 275
Bochum, 133
Bode River, 209
Böll, Heinrich, 48–49, 61–62
  Billiards at Half-Past Nine, 48–49
  Heinrich-Böll-Foundation, 224
Bonn, 298
Börne, Ludwig, 278
Boyer, M. Christine, 5
Bradley, Richard, 81
Brandenburg, 74, 239
Braun, Hildebrecht, 167
Braun and Hogenberg, 218
Braunschweig, 91
Brazil, 58
Bremen, 13, 16, 17, 70, 185–206
  after reunification, 204
  architecture of
    air-raid shelters, 185–87, 188–90, 197–201, 204, 206, 296: Admiralstrasse, 199–200; Diakonissenhaus, 189; use of forced labor to construct, 189–90
    Liebfrauenkirche, 192
    submarine bunkers, 15, 187, 206, 296: Hornisse, 190, 197, 203; use of forced labor at, 197, 202–3; Valentin, 185–86, 190, 195–96, 202–3, 204–5
    synagogue, 202
  Bremen-Gröpelingen, 190
  Bremen School of Arts, 191
  Bremen-Vegesack, 190
  Bremer Stadtwerke, 194
  Bürgerpark, 185, 198
  Cathedral Square, 198
  Farge, 190, 195, 203
  Freikorps in, 192–93
  FRG era, 190–204
  Friedensinitiative Ostertor, 201
  Gerstenberg Division, 192
  Friedrich-Karl-Strasse, 199
  Jewish life in, 188, 202
  local history workshops, 199–201
  memorials in: Kriegerdenkmal Altmannshöhe, 191–92, 201; Sterbende Jüngling, 192–93, 201–2; submarine shelters, 202–3
  Nazi era, 185, 188–90
  visit from Hitler, 193–94
  Oberfinanzpräsidenten, 196
  Port Building Authority, 197
  Radio Bremen, 196, 202
  Scharnhorststrasse, 199
  Soviet Republic of Bremen, 192
  University, 203
  Wall-Anlagen Park, 193
  Weimar Republic, 187–88, 190, 192
  Zwinglistrasse, 199
Breuer, Mordechai, 289–90
Brown House (Munich), 13, 165, 167, 172, 177–78
Brück, Wolfram, 280–82
Brühlsche Terrasse (Dresden), 27, 33
Brumlik, Micha, 274
Bubis, Ignaz, 10
Buggeln, Marc, 13, 296

Bundestag (Federal Parliament), 99, 224, 286, 287
Bundeswehr (Federal Armed Forces), 185, 196, 202
Burauen, Theodor, 58
Bürgerbräukeller (Munich), 164, 167
Buschmann, Walter, 128–29
Buxloh, Friedrich Wilhelm Schulze, 122

Carlebach, Joseph, 254, 266
Cassirer, Ernst, 254
Catholic Center Party, 50, 121
Catholic Church, 49, 56
Cemeteries, 80, 81, 99–100, 231–32, 239, 244–46, 247, 251, 257, 259, 276, 279, 287
Center against Expulsion, 10
Chicago, 128
Christian Democratic Union (*Christlich-Demokratische Union* [CDU]), 54, 150, 191, 266, 277, 280
Christian Social Union (*Christlich-Soziale Union* [CSU]), 144, 151–52, 156, 158, 172, 174
Christians, 49, 57, 211, 213, 216, 219, 236, 245, 279, 281, 285
  All Saint's Day observation of, 54
  Easter observation of, 212
Claasen, Hermann, 53, 60
Cobain, Kurt, 185
Cold war and Germany, 6, 8–9, 16, 30–31, 33, 148, 198, 221–23, 242–43
Cologne, 12, 15, 17, 48–63, 180, 299, 300
  Altstadt, 49
  anti-Semitic attacks, postwar, 59
  architecture of: cathedral, 51; Church of Gross St. Martin, 51; *Haus der Arbeit,* 51; synagogue, rebuilt, 58–59
  carnival, 49, 55–56
  celebration of 1900th anniversary of city's founding (1950), 50, 56
  City Council, 50–51, 53
  City Planning Office, 51
  Cologne-Deutz, 50, 51
  Eigelsteintorburg, 53
  Gauforum, 51
  Germania Judaica, 58–59
  Jewish life in, 52–53, 54, 58–59
  memorials in, 15
    Antoniterkirche, 55
    Else-Falk-Haus, 58
    Hansaring tablet, 58, 59
    monument in Hindenburg Park, 61–62
    St. Alban and the Gürzenich, 12, 55–58, 60–61: memorial competitions, 56
    St. Maria im Capitol, 53–55, 60
  Nazi era, 48–53, 58, 59–60
    EL-DE-Haus used as Gestapo Headquarters, 51–52: as documentation center, 59, 63, 180, 300
    forced labor in city area, 51–52
    visit from Hitler, 50
  Neumarkt, 60
  Neustadt, 61
  Niehl (northern suburb), 52
  postwar FRG era, 48–50, 53–63
  Rhine bridge, 50
  synagogues, destruction of, 52
  University, 51
  Zollstock (suburb), 58
Communists, 75, 231, 233–34, 238, 239–40, 241, 300
  persecution under National Socialists, 32, 50, 188, 217
Concentration camps, 32, 52–53, 59, 99, 102, 197, 202, 218, 225, 257, 263, 274, 275
  Arbeitsdorf, 109
  Auschwitz, 99, 257, 275, 281, 282, 289, 295
  Buchenwald, 51, 59, 175
  Dachau, 167, 171, 173, 213
  Dora-Mittelbau, 175
  Laagberg, 99, 100
  memorialization at, 6, 8, 32
  Neuengamme, 74, 190, 203, 257, 261
  Ravensbrück, 74
  Sachsenhausen, 74
  Theresienstadt, 266
  See also names of individual concentration camps
Crimes of the Wehrmacht exhibition, 9
Critical reconstruction, 2, 133
Cubism, 118, 119, 126, 130
Czechoslovakia, 224

310 Index

Dachau, 167, 171, 173, 213
Dahm, Volker, 172–74
Dahmen, Leopold, 51, 59
Dainat, Leo, 79
Dallas, TX, 223
Dallas Museum of Art, 223
Darré, Walter, 214
Dearborn, MI, 90
Death marches, 73
Demnig, Günter, 180, 267–68, 274
Denmark, 73, 253
Dessau, 118
Deutsche Arbeitsfront (German Labor Front [DAF]), 16, 90–91, 98, 102, 105
   Kraft durch Freude (strength through joy), 90–91, 102
Deutsche Reichspartei, 59
Deutsche Werkbund, 122–23, 132
Diefendorf, Jeffry M., 12, 300
Die Zeit, 199
Displaced persons, 281–82
Documentation Center for the History of National Socialism (*NS-Dokumentationszentrum*, Munich), 13, 15, 164, 167–80
Dokumentation Obersalzberg (Berchtesgaden), 170–71, 173
Dokumentationszentrum Reichsparteitagsgelände (Documentation Center of the Reich Party Rally Grounds, Nuremberg), 15, 152–54, 155–56, 158, 170–71, 173
Domenig, Günther, 153
Dora-Mittelbau, 175
Dortmund, 129
Dresden, 12, 15, 16–17, 25–44, 76, 297, 298–99
   after reunification, 25–26, 34–44
   Altmarkt, 29
   architecture of
      Frauenkirche, 12, 25, 42–43: reconstruction of, 26, 36–40; ruins as postwar monument, 30–31, 33
      Hofkirche, 29, 43
      Kulturpalast, 30
      New Synagogue, 12, 15, 38–40, 42–44
      Schloss, 43
      Semper's Synagogue, 12, 25–29, 33–34, 39–40, 42
      Zwinger, 25, 29
   GDR era, 25–26, 28–34, 35, 36–38, 41–43
   Jewish life in, 25–28, 38, 40, 42–43
   memorials in, 30–31, 33
      Ehrenhain memorial park at Heidefriedhof, 32
   Nazi era, 25–26, 28, 30, 42–43, 243
   neo-Nazi activity in, 38–39
   Neumarkt, 30, 35–36
   Prager Straße, 29, 35
   Rathenauplatz, 33
Duisburg: Küpersmühle museum, 133; Landschaft Park, 133
Dürer, Albrecht, 143, 296
Durth, Werner, 5

East Prussia, 112
Economic Party (*Wirtschaftspartei*), 75
Eichmann, Adolf, 300
Eiffel Tower, 118
Eisenman, Peter, 144, 151
Elbe, 27, 40, 42, 43, 253, 254, 298
EL-DE-Haus (Cologne), 51–52, 59, 63, 180, 300
Elstner, Reinhold, 177
Erbs, Martina, 155
Essen, 13, 15, 17, 18, 116–34
   after reunification, 118–19, 127–28, 130–34
   architecture of
      Red Dot Design Museum conversion, 131–32
      synagogue, 116–17, 121
      Zeche Zollverein Pithead XII, 13, 116, 118–34: and IBA Emscher Park, 127–28, 129–31, 133; miners' attitudes toward, 119
   Folkwang, 131, 132
   FRG era, 128–29
   Katernberg, 121
   memorials in Jewish community
      memorial in reconstructed synagogue, 117
   Nazi era, 117, 126–27
   Ruhrlandmuseum, 132
   Weimar Republic, 121–25
European Central Bank, 274, 290–91

European Union, 70, 122, 132
Expressionism, 107

Falk, Bernard, 58
Falk, Else, 58
Fascination and Terror (*Faszination und Gewalt*) exhibition, 151–52, 153, 155
Fassbinder, Rainer Werner, *Garbage, the City, and Death*, 283
Fischer, Jan Otakar, 12, 296–97
Florence, 298
Folkwang Museum (Essen), 131, 132
Foote, Kenneth, 5
Ford, Henry, 90, 109
Ford Motor Company, 90
  and forced labor, 52
  Model T, 90, 96
Foster, Norman, 130, 131
Foucault, Michel, 187
Four-Year Plan, 147
Fox, Thomas C., 32
France, 50, 95, 99, 100, 129, 202–3, 213
Franco-Prussian War (German-French War), 54, 259
Frank, Anne, 276, 295
Frankfurt am Main, 14, 16, 17, 273–91, 295–96, 299
  after reunification, 274, 284–91
  architecture of
    Customer Service Center, 276, 279–82
    demonstration against to protect historical ruins, 280–82
    Grossmarkthalle, European Central Bank Headquarters, 274, 290–91
    I.G.-Farben-Haus, 274
    Paulskirche, 273, 275
    Rathaus Römerberg, 275, 276
    synagogues, 274–75, 278: conservative synagogue, Börneplatz, 274, 276, 278, 283, 284; Hauptsynagogue, Börnestrasse, 274; Jewish Community synagogue, 274–75
  FRG era, 273–75, 278–84
  Fritz Bauer Institute, 274
  Jewish cemetery, 276, 279, 287
  Jewish life in, 274–83, 284–91
  Judengasse, 276, 279–83, 284–85
  memorials in, 15
    former Gestapo Headquarters, 275
    Goethe House, 9
    Grossmarkthalle memorial addressing Nazi past, 290–91
    Hedderheim work camp, 275
    monument to concentration camp victims (Paulskirche), 275
    New Börneplatz Memorial, 14, 273–74, 276–90: competition for, 282; dedication of, 284–90
    Stolpersteine, 274
  Nazi era, 274–78, 290–91
  Save the Börneplatz citizens' initiative, 279–80
  Topography of NS Terror group, 274
Frankfurt Auschwitz Trials, 275
Frauenkirche (Dresden), 12, 25–26, 30–31, 33, 36–40, 42–43
Frederick II (the Great), 235, 243
Free Democratic Party (*Freie Demokratische Partei* [FDP]), 167, 191, 266
Frei, Norbert, 144, 175
Freikorps, 192–93
Freimark, Peter, 258
French Revolution (1789), 49
Frick, Wilhelm, 214
Friedrich, Jörg, 10
Fritz Bauer Institute, 274
Führerstädte (Hitler Cities), 12, 16, 17, 51, 254
Fulbright Fellowship, 70

Galicia, 112
Ganser, Karl, 131
Garnisonkirche (Potsdam), 232, 233, 235–37, 241
Gdansk (Danzig), 76, 112
German Communist Party (*Kommunistische Partei Deutschlands* [KPD]), 75, 121, 257
German Democratic Party (*Deutsche Demokratische Partei* [DDP]), 75
German Democratic Republic (East) (GDR), 1, 2, 3, 8–9, 14, 16, 25, 28–34, 35–38, 41–43, 67–69, 76, 77, 82, 211–12, 216–23, 231–48, 299, 300

German Democratic Republic (East) (GDR) (*continued*)
commemoration of victims of, 68
State Association of Jewish Communities, 231, 238–39, 244
German National People's Party (*Deutschnationale Volkspartei* [DNVP]), 50, 75
German People's Party (*Deutsche Volkspartei* [DVP]), 75
Germania Judaica (Cologne), 58–59
Germany, Federal Republic of (West) (FRG), 1, 2, 3, 5, 8–9, 15–16, 48–50, 53–63, 89, 95–108, 116–18, 128–29, 147–51, 165–68, 190–204, 217, 222–23, 242, 246, 247, 251, 256–66, 273–75, 278–84, 299
  after reunification, 9–11, 25–26, 33, 34–44, 67–70, 72–73, 75, 76–84, 90, 108–12, 118–19, 127–28, 130–34, 151–59, 168–81, 203, 219–20, 223–25, 251, 266–69, 274, 284–91, 298
  Turkish population of, 131
Germany, National Socialist, 2, 3, 5, 8, 12–14, 16–18, 25–26, 28, 30, 32–34, 42–43, 48–53, 55, 59–60, 68, 73–75, 77–79, 82, 89–95, 102, 116–18, 124–27, 129, 147, 152, 164–65, 173, 185, 188–90, 199, 202, 209–11, 212–17, 233, 251, 254–56, 264, 274–78, 290–91
  and forced labor, 13, 51–52, 75, 95, 98–101, 109, 117, 118, 125, 189–90, 197, 202–3, 206, 213, 274, 275
Germany, Weimar Republic of, 13, 17, 27, 50, 74–75, 77–79, 103, 107, 116, 121–25, 129, 132, 133, 147, 187–88, 190, 254, 259
Germany, Wilhelmine, 5, 27, 50, 122, 187, 253–54, 264
Gerz, Esther and Jochen, 9
Gestapo, 51, 58, 59, 180, 275
Gestapo Headquarters (Berlin), 9, 15–16, 169
Giesau, Hermann, 212–13, 214, 216–17, 220–21
Giles, Geoffrey, 256
Glaser, Hermann, 151
Godfrey, Mark, 252

Goebbels, Joseph, 103
Goering, Hermann, 127, 300
Goethe, Johann Wolfgang von, 3, 4
Goethe House (Frankfurt), 9
Golden Gate Bridge, 254
Goldenbogen, Nora, 28
Goldman, Natasha, 14, 296, 300
Goldschmidt, Mortiz, 54
Goldstein, Theodor, 244, 247
Görlinger, Robert, 54–55
Gorsemann, Ernst, 191, 201
Goslar, 222
Götterdammerung, 185
Grass, Günter, 10
Great Depression, 75
Greece, ancient, 147
Green Party, 99, 151, 170, 191, 280
Grieger, Manfred, 101
Grindelhof Citizen's Intitiative, 252, 266–67
Gropius, Walter, 110, 118–19, 122, 123, 125, 128, 132
Grosche, Robert, 54
Grossmarkthalle (Frankfurt am Main), 274, 290–91
Günther, Ilse, 221–22
Gürzenich (Cologne), 55–58, 60–61
Güstrow Cathedral, 55
Guthardt, Wolfgang, 109
Gutschow, Niels, 5
Gymnasium am Goetheplatz, 77–80

Hadid, Zaha, 110
Halberstadt, 212
Halbwachs, Maurice, 4–5
Halle, 211, 212, 221
Hamburg, 6, 14, 16, 17, 74, 205, 251–69, 299, 300
  after reunification, 251, 266–69
  Allende Platz, 254
  Alster Lake, 253
  Alte Steinweg, 253
  Altona, 253
  architecture of
    Rathaus, 259
    synagogue, 251, 252: Neue Dammtor Synagogue, 253–54; synagogue at Bornplatz, 253–54, 258, 264–66, 269
  Borgfelde, 257
  Cultural Studies Library, 254

Dammtor, 251, 252, 258–64
Edmund-Siemers-Allee, 262
Eilbek, 257
Flottbek, 254
Forschungsstelle für die Geschichte des Nationalsozialismus in Hamburg, 256
Forschungsstelle für Zeitgeschichte in Hamburg, 256
FRG era, 194–95, 251, 256–66
Grindel, 251, 253–54
Grindelhof, 251, 264
Grindelhof Citizen's Intiative, 252, 266–67
Hartungstrasse, 262
Heilwigstrasse, 254
Institute for the History of German Jews, 258
Israelite Freischule, 253
Jewish life in, 251, 253–54, 257, 263, 265, 267
Karolinenstrasse, 262
Memorials in, 15, 180, 256–58, 296
  Countermonument (Alfred Hrdlicka), 251, 259, 260–62, 268: competition for, 260
  Countermonument (Jochen and Esther Gerz), 9
  Heinrich Heine memorial, 258
  Joseph-Carlebach-Platz Synagogue Monument, 251, 252, 264–67, 268–69
  Memorial for the Murdered Jews of Hamburg, 257, 262–63
  Memorial for the Victims of Nazi Terror, 256–57, 261
  Memorial to the Deported Jews, 251, 268
  Monument to the Seventy-sixth Infantry Regiment, 251, 258–62, 268
  Nikolaikirche Memorial, 257, 258, 261
  Ohlsdorf Cemetery, 251, 257
  Stolpersteine, 267–68
  War Victims Memorial, 259: competition for, 259; Moorweidenstrasse, 262
Nazi era, 188, 194, 251, 254–56, 258, 264
Neustadt, 253
Stephansplatz, 259, 262
University, 251, 256, 264, 265
Wandsbek, 257
Weimar Republic, 254, 259
Hamburg Free Press, 260
Hamburg im "Dritten Reich," 254
Harff, Christine, 266
Hartl, Lydia, 176
Harz, 89, 209, 223
Hayden, Dolores, 5
Heidegger, Martin, 69
Heimannsberg, Barbara, 34
Heine, Heinrich, 258
Heinkel, 73
Heinrich I, 16, 209–10, 213, 216, 222, 224, 225
Heitgres, Franz, 257
Hennig, Silke, 201
Herf, Jeffrey, 144
Herzog, Roman, 9
Herzog and De Meuron, 133
Hiecke, Robert, 212–13, 216–17, 218, 221
Hildesheim, 212, 222
Himmler, Heinrich, 3, 14, 16, 99, 212, 300
  interest in Heinrich I and Quedlinburg, 209–10, 213–14, 225
Hindenburg, Paul von, 49, 61–62, 236–37
Hirche, Bernhard, 265
Hirst, Ivan, 95
Historian's Debate, 9, 176
Historical Monuments, Office for the Preservation of (Hamburg), 260, 264–65
Historic preservation, 1, 5, 8, 11, 13, 14–15, 30, 36, 38, 58, 60, 70, 77, 79, 82, 116–18, 122, 127, 149, 151, 154–55, 167–68, 211, 212–13, 218–22, 231–35, 239–40, 246, 258, 273, 279–83, 290, 297
  "Hallerian Way," 211, 214–17, 219, 221
  Institute for Historic Preservation (GDR), 235–36, 240–43
Historic Preservation Bureau (Rostock), 67–68
Historic Preservation Law, Bavaria, 149

Index

Hitler, Adolf, 3, 12, 13, 16–17, 28, 49, 60, 90–91, 94, 112, 125–26, 143–44, 147, 150, 151, 154, 159, 165, 167, 170, 193–94, 210, 233, 235–37, 240, 254–56, 296, 298, 300
Hobsbawm, Eric, 68
Hoffmann, Klaus, 259
Hofkirche (Dresden), 29
Hohenzollern, 233, 235
Hohlmeier, Monika, 172
Holocaust, 2, 14, 25, 33, 40, 52–53, 73–74, 117, 145, 148, 188, 217, 239, 244–45, 246–47
  memorialization, 6, 14, 17, 26, 32, 33, 54, 59, 116–17, 120, 144, 200, 225, 231–32, 251–53, 256–58, 259, 261–69, 274–75, 276–91, 295–96, 300
  Stolpersteine, 180, 267–68, 274
Holocaust miniseries, 286
Homosexual, 217
Honecker, Erich, 243, 247
Hrdlicka, Alfred, Countermonument (Hamburg), 251, 259, 260–62, 268
Hungary, 224

I.G.-Farben-Haus (Frankfurt), 274
Illinois Institute of Technology, 128
Innere Mission, 199
Institut für Zeitgeschichte, 172
International Building Exhibition (IBA) Emscher Park, 127–28, 129–31, 133
International Federation of Resistance Fighters, 32
Iraq, 110
Israel, 217, 266, 289
Italian Industrial Workers Association, 98

James-Chakraborty, Kathleen, 13, 296–97
Jaskot, Paul, 13, 252–53, 296
JCDecaux, 267
Jehovah's Witnesses, 217
Jerusalem, 262
Jewish Museum (Berlin), 155, 170, 175
Jews, 12, 14, 25–28, 32–33, 40, 42–43, 52–53, 54, 58–59, 80, 81, 116–17, 145, 188, 200, 202, 217, 218, 225, 237–238, 242, 243–46, 251, 253–54, 257, 258, 263, 265, 267, 275–83, 284–90, 300
  Aryanization of Jewish property, 52, 59, 232, 237, 264
  boycott of Jewish businesses, 52
  Central Council of Jews in Germany (FRG), 10
  conditions in GDR, 240
  deportation of, 148, 188, 262, 266, 274, 276, 287, 290–91, 300
  postunification immigration from East, 38, 288
  State Association of Jewish Communities of the Soviet Occupied Zone, 231, 238–39, 244
Johe, Werner, 255
Jordan, Jennifer, 299–300
Judengasse (Frankfurt am Main), 276, 279–83, 284–85

Kahl, Margrit, Joseph-Carlebach-Platz Synagogue Monument (Hamburg), 251, 264–67, 268–69
Kahn, Louis, Holocaust Memorial for Battery Park (unbuilt), 252
Kaiser Wilhelm Gedächtniskirche (Berlin), 81, 258
Kansas State University, 71
Kastner, Wolfram, 180
Kaufmann, Karl, 254
Kellogg-Krieg, Annah, 13–14, 297
Kerwien, J. Otto, 242
KGB, 68, 82
Kier, Hiltrud, 59–60
Klemperer, Victor, 25
Klotz, Clemens, 51
Kluge, Alexander, *Brutalität in Stein*, 149
Knigge, Volkhard, 175
Knobelsdorff, Georg Wenzeslaus von, 235
Kohl, Helmut, 150, 151–52
Kohlbecker, Karl, 91
Kokoschka, Oskar, 258
Koller, Peter, 89, 91–94, 95, 96, 98, 102, 109, 112
Kollwitz, Käthe, 56–57, 60–61
Königsberg, 75
Königsplatz (Munich), 164–69, 171
  Ehrentempel, 165–66, 168, 169

Führerbau and Verwaltungsbau der NSDAP, 164–65
Plattensee, 165–67
Koolhaas, Rem, 132
Korn, Salomon, 284, 286–87
Koselleck, Reinhart, 286
Koshar, Rudy, 5
Kraus, Karl, *The Last Days of Mankind*, 203
Krebs, Friedrich, 275–76
Kreis, Wilhelm, 215
Kreisel, Heinrich, 222
Kremmer, Martin, 91, 118, 122–23, 125, 127, 128, 130
Krier, Rob, 130
Kristallnacht Pogrom, 33, 244
  Bremen, 202
  Cologne, 52, 59
  Dresden, 12, 26, 28, 33–34, 39, 40, 42
  Essen, 117
  Frankfurt am Main, 275, 276, 278, 283
  Hamburg, 264, 265–67
  Potsdam, 239
Kronawitter, Hildegard, 170
Krupp, Deschimag AG Weser (Bremen-Gröpelingen), 190
Krupp von Bohlen und Halbach, Alfried, 118
Kubicka, Herbert, 192
Kugelmann, Cilly, 175
Kulturpalast (Dresden), 30
Kulturzentrum (Wolfsburg), 106
Kuöhl, Richard, Monument to the Seventy-sixth Infantry Regiment (or Kriegsklotz) (Hamburg), 251, 258–62, 268
Kurdish refugees, 199

Ladd, Brian, 18, 67, 68
Lafferentz, Bodo, 91, 112
Lambek, Michael, 79
Landmann, Ludwig, 275
Latz, Peter, 133
Law for the Restoration of the Professional Civil Service, 275–76
Leipzig, 243
Lersch, Heinrich, 259
Le Witt, Sol, 264
Lexzau, Scharbau & Co., 197, 203
Ley, Robert, 90–91, 94, 105, 109, 112

Libeskind, Daniel, 155
Lidice, 202
Liebknecht, Karl, 231, 233, 234, 244, 246
Lin, Maya, 263–64
London, UK, 110, 125
  Tate Modern, 133
Louis, Morris, *Charred Journal: Firewritten*, 252
Lowenthal, David, 5, 134
Lower Saxony, 91, 95, 218, 262
Ludwig I, King of Bavaria, 164
Luftwaffe, 32
Luther, Martin, 243
Lutheran Church, 81, 219
Luxemburg, Rosa, 233
Lynch, Kevin, 69

Magdeburg, 212
Mainzer, Udo, 118–19
Maly, Ulrich, 157–58
Marcks, Gerhard, 257–58, 261
  Angel of Death, 53–55, 56, 60
Marcuse, Harold, 6
Marineamt Barracks (Rostock), 68, 76–77, 80
Märkische Volksstimme, 239
Marszolek, Inge, 13, 296
Mathilde, Queen, 209
Maurice, Klaus, 223–24
May, Ernst, 122
Mayer, Fritz, 147
Mazur-Stommen, Susan, 12, 298
McCloy, John, 196
McDonald, Merlin, 68
Meador, Joe Tom, 223
Mecklenburg, 74
Mecklenburg-Vorpommern, 67, 77, 79, 81
Meinertz, Erik, 155
Memorial to the Murdered Jews of Europe (Berlin), 2, 9, 144, 151, 170, 178
Memory Studies, 4
Mendelsohn, Erich, 122
Meng, Michael, 14, 299
Merkel, Heidi, 244–45
Messerschmidt, Willy, 103
Mewes, Emil, 91
Meyer, Julius, 239
Mies van der Rohe, Ludwig, 128

Minimalism as choice for memorialization, 251, 262–64, 268
Mitscherlich, Alexander and Margarete, 290
Mittelland Canal, 89, 91, 104
Mittig, Hans-Ernst, 5
Modernism, 5, 8, 77–79, 103–7, 110, 119–20, 124–25, 128, 130, 133–34, 153, 191, 246, 252, 258, 267, 297
Mommsen, Hans, 95, 99, 100–101
Monument in Hindenburg Park (Cologne), 61–62
Mühldorfer-Vogt, Christian, 225
Munich, 6, 13, 16, 17, 120, 144, 150, 158, 159, 163–81, 205, 256, 299, 300–301
  after reunification, 164, 168–81
  architecture of
    Brown House, 13, 165, 167, 172, 177–78
    Deutsches Museum, Kongressaal, 164
    Feldherrnhalle, 177
    Haus der Deutschen Kunst, 164
    Königsplatz, 164–69, 171: Ehrentempel, 165–66, 168, 169; Führerbau and Verwaltungsbau der NSDAP, 164–65, 177; New Synagogue, 177, 180; Plattensee, 165–67
  Bürgerbräukeller, 164, 167
  City Council, 167–68, 169, 170, 173–74, 175–77
    Documentation Center for the History of National Socialism (*NS- Dokumentationszentrum*), 13, 15, 164, 167–80
    Initiativkreis für ein NS-Dokumentationszentrum, 170
  FRG era, 163, 165–68
  Institut für Zeitgeschichte, 172
  Jakobsplatz, 177, 180
  Maxvorstadt, 169, 171, 176
  Nazi era, 164–65, 173
  neo-Nazi activity in, 177
  Olympic Games, 172
  Riem airport, 164
  Stadtarchiv München, 173
  Stadtmuseum, 176
    Bauen im Nationalsozialismus: Bayern, 1933–1945 exhibition, 169

Hauptstadt der Bewegung exhibition, 169
Technical University, 171, 175
  Bürokratie und Kult exhibition, 169
  Ort und Erinnerung exhibition, 181
Münsterland, 124
Mussolini, Benito, 132

Napoleon, Bonaparte, 253
National Democratic Party (*Nationaldemokratische Partei* Deutschland [NPD]), 39
National Socialist German Workers Party (*Nationalsozialistische Deutsche Arbeiterpartei* [NSDAP]), 13, 51, 74–75, 96, 124, 164, 165–66, 169, 185, 188, 195, 198, 212, 213, 221, 254, 275
Neo-Nazis, 10, 38–39, 72–73, 75, 80, 82–83, 177, 224
Nerdinger, Winfried, 5, 127, 171, 175–77
Netherlands, 99, 132
Neuengamme, 74, 190, 203, 205, 257, 261
Neues Deutschland, 221
Neue Wache (Berlin), 151
Neue Zürcher Zeitung, 171
Nevada, and atomic testing, 198
New Börneplatz Memorial to the Third Jewish Community Destroyed by the National Socialists (Frankfurt am Main), 14, 273–74, 276–90
Newman, Barnet, 252
New York City, 125, 252
New York Times, 95, 110, 223
Niehl, 52
Nikolai Quarter (Berlin), 68
Nipperdey, Thomas, 5
Nishizawa, Ryue, 132
Nora, Pierre, 187
Nordhoff, Heinrich, 96
Normandy, Allied invasion of, 189
North Atlantic Treaty Organization (NATO), 30, 61
North Rhine-Westphalia, 131
Nuremberg, 13, 16, 17, 120, 143–60, 180, 205, 256, 296, 299

after reunification, 151–59
architecture of
  Convention Center, 149, 150, 153, 154, 155, 158
  Deutsches Stadion, 149, 154
  Dokumentationszentrum, 15, 152–54, 155–56, 158, 170–71, 173
  Grosse Strasse, 147, 149, 155
  Kongresshalle, 147, 149, 151, 153, 155
  Luitpoldhain, 147
  Märzfeld, 148–49
  Reich Party Rally Grounds, 13, 15, 102, 144, 146–60, 170, 180, 296
  Zeppelinfeld, 148–49, 150, 151
City Council, 144, 149, 150–52, 154, 156, 157–58
competition of ideas for former Reich Party rally grounds, 153–58
Dutzendteich, 146, 148, 155
Fascination and Terror (*Faszination und Gewalt*), 151–52, 153, 155
FRG era, 147–51
hosting of World Cup, 144, 158
Langwasser, 148–49
Nazi era, 147
Nazi Party rallies at, 143, 147
Silbersee, 149
Weimar Republic, 147
Nuremberg racial laws, 147
Nuremberg Tribunals, 118, 180

Obersalzberg, 170, 173
Office of Metropolitan Architecture, 132
Olympic Games, 172
"Ostalgie," 70
Ostfriesland, 77
Ottonian Empire, 16, 213–14, 225

Papen, Franz von, 60
Paris, 125
Petersen, Rudolf, 195, 255
Petrikirche Turm (Rostock), 80, 81–82
Pfotenhauer, Angela, 58
Phæno (Wolfsburg), 109–10
Plattenbau, 76
Poland, 28, 75–76, 99, 224, 246, 295
  Jews of, 28

Porsche, Ferdinand, 90–91, 94–95, 96, 99, 100, 103, 105
Porsche motor company, 111
Porschestrasse (Wolfsburg), 96, 98, 105, 106, 109
Portugal, 253
Postmodernism, 1, 120, 130–31, 133, 253, 258
Potsdam, 14, 15, 17, 231–48, 299
  Altstadt, 231–34, 246
  architecture in
    Garnisonkirche, 232, 233, 235–37, 241
    Stadtschloss, 232, 234–35, 237, 241
    Synagogue, 14, 232, 237–43, 246, 247
  City Council, 234, 235–37, 240, 244
  GDR era, 231–48
  Jewish life in, 231–32, 237–39, 243–46
  memorials in
    Jewish cemetery, 231–32, 239, 244–46, 247
    Liebknecht memorial, 231, 234
  Nazi era, 233, 235–36, 239
  Platz der Einheit, 239, 240–41
Prager Strasse (Dresden), 29, 35
Prinz-Albrecht-Strasse (Berlin), 9, 15, 169
Prisoners of war, 54, 57, 99
Pritzker Prize, 132
Protestant Church, 189, 212
Prussia, 49–50, 75, 212, 218, 232, 233–34, 235, 242–43
Pyramids, Egypt, 118

Quast, Ferdinand von, 218
Quedlinburg, 14, 15, 16, 17, 209–25, 297
  after reunification, 219–20, 223–25
  architecture of
    Rathaus, 209
    St. Blasius, 212
    St. Servatius, 14, 209–25, 297: connected to Heinrich I, 209–10, 216, 222, 224, 225
    St. Wiperti chapel, 225
  City Council, 219, 221
  GDR era, 211–12, 216–23
  medieval period, 209
  Nazi era, 209–11, 212–17
  visit by Himmler, 209–10, 216, 225

Quedlinburg (*continued*)
"History and Propaganda: The Ottonians in the Shadow of National Socialism" exhibition, 225
Jewish life in, 218, 225
neo-Nazi activity in, 224–25
treasures of, 221, 222–24

Rapoport, Nathan, 262
Ravensbrück, 74
Reagan, Ronald, 150
Red Army, 10
Red Dot Design Museum (Essen), 131–32
Reich Association for Folklore and Home (*Reichsbun Volkstum und Heimat*), 212
Reichel, Peter, 6, 257
Reich Party Rally Grounds (Nuremberg), 13, 15, 102, 144, 146–60, 170, 296
Reichsbahn, 198
Reichstag, 27
elections to, 50, 74–75, 234, 235–36, 256
Reimann, Siegfried, 38
Republikaner, 73
Reunification of Germany, 2, 9, 11, 25, 33, 34, 38, 67, 68, 72, 76, 80, 82, 152, 298
Rhine, 50, 118
Richter, Gerhard, 252–53
Riefenstahl, Leni, 177
Triumph of the Will, 296
Riemenschneider, Tilmann, 123
Ring architectural group, 124–25
Roehm, Ernst, 176
Roman Empire, 147
Romania, 199, 224
Roma/Sinti, 51, 59, 198–99, 217, 225
Rome, 132
Rosenberg, Alfred, 214
Rosenfeld, Gavriel, 13, 300–301
Rossi, Aldo, 5, 130
Rostock, 12, 15, 17, 67–84, 298, 299
after reunification, 67–70, 72–73, 76–84
architecture of
Gymnasium am Goetheplatz, 77–80

Marineamt Barracks, 68, 76–77, 80
Neptun Werft, 68
Petrikirche Turm, 80, 81–82
Plattenbau, 76
bomb damage (*Bombenlücken*), 80–81
Budapester Strasse, 70
Bürgerhaus, 70
Café Waldemar and Margarete, 70
GDR era, 68, 76, 77, 79, 82
Hansaviertel, 76–77
Jewish cemetery at Lindenpark, 80, 81
Kopernikus Strasse, 77
Kröpeliner Strasse, 80
Kröpeliner Tor Vorstadt, 76
Lichtenhagen (suburb), 73, 75
memorials in, 70
Opfer deutscher Diktaturen, 68
Nazi era, 68, 73–75, 77–79, 82
neo-Nazi activity in, 72–73, 75, 80, 82–83
Neptun Schwimmhalle, 77
Office of City Marketing, 69–70
Ostsee Stadion, 77
Schmarl, 76
Toitenwinkel (suburb), 75
University, 68, 70, 73, 80
Weimar Republic, 77–78
Rostock Society for Urban Renewal, Development and Housing (*Rostocker Gesellschaft für Stadterneuerung, Stadtentwicklung und Wohnungsbau GmbH* [RGS]), 70, 79
Roth, Petra, 277, 284–86, 287, 289
Rowlands, Michael, 81
Rückriem, Ulrich, Memorial to the Deported Jews (Hamburg), 251, 262–63, 268
Ruff, Ludwig and Franz, 147, 153
Ruhrgebiet, 89, 117–18, 120, 124, 125, 127, 129, 133
Ruscheweyh, Heinz Jürgen, 256–57

Sachsen-Anhalt, 224
Sachsenhausen, 74
Sächsische Zeitung, 42
Sagebiel, Ernst, 164
Salians, 214

Saltzman, Lisa, 252
Samuhel Gospels, 223
San Francisco, Exploratorium, 110
Saxony, 27, 39, 76, 212
Scharoun, Hans, 102, 106–7, 109–10, 111, 112
Scheib, Peter, 234–35
Schilling, Hans, 56
Schinkel, Karl Friedrich, 151
Schloss Wolfsburg, 91, 95, 96, 98, 109
  Stadtmuseum at, 101
Schmitthenner, Paul, 123
Schnatz, Helmut, 41
Schneider-Bönninger, Birgit, 101
Scholz, Ludwig, 152
Schönborn, Susanne, 14, 295–96
Schröder, Kurt, 60
Schubert, Wolf, 216
Schuchardt, Helga, 265
Schultze-Naumburg, Paul, 3
Schupp, Fritz, 91, 118, 122–23, 125, 127, 128, 130
Schutz, Brigitte, 176
Schütz, Erhard, 97
Schutzstaffel (SS), 14, 16, 99, 209–13, 216, 217, 218–25
Schwarz, Rudolf, 56–58
Schwerin, 74
Schwering, Ernst, 54–55, 58
Schwering, Max Leo, 59
Seamon, David, 71–72
Sebald, W. G., 10
Sejima, Kazuyo, 132
Semper, Gottfried, 12, 27–28, 34, 39–40, 42
76er Association, 76th Infantry Regiment (Hamburg), 259
Sexuality, 4
Shapiro, Joel, 264
Siegfried, Klaus-Jörg, 100–101
Siegfried Line, 189
Sievert, Thomas, 133
Silesia, 112
Social Democratic Party (*Sozialdemokratische Partei Deutschlands* [SPD]), 54, 74–75, 99, 121, 133, 144, 150–52, 157–58, 170, 174, 187–88, 190–91, 193, 199, 260, 280
Socialist Unity Party (*Sozialistische Einheitspartei Deutschlands* [SED]), 16, 17, 231–37, 239–44, 246–48
Sonnenberger, Franz, 152–53, 156, 159
Spain, 253
Speer, Albert, 91, 94, 105, 124, 130, 144, 147, 149–50, 152, 154–55, 159, 215, 259
Spengler, Oswald, 124
Stadtkrone, 94, 96, 102, 105
Stadtler, Martin, 155
Stadtschloss (Potsdam), 232, 234–35, 237, 241
Stadtverband Kölner Frauenvereine, 58
Stahl, Andreas, 221
St. Alban's (Cologne), 12, 55–58, 60–61
Stalin, Josef, 68, 240
Stankowski, Martin, 61
Stasi (*Staatssicherheit*), 68, 82
Steimker Berg housing estate (Wolfsburg), 94, 98, 102–3
Stella, Frank, 252, 263
Sterilization, 60
St. Maria im Capitol (Cologne), 53, 60
St. Peter's (Rostock), 80, 81–82
Strasbourg Cathedral, 3
St. Servatius (Quedlinburg), 14, 209–25, 297
Stunde Null, 98
Sturmabteilung (SA), 28, 50, 176, 221, 300
Stuttgart, 90, 123
Submarine Bunkers (Bremen), 15, 187, 206, 296
  Hornisse, 190, 196, 203
  Valentin, 185–86, 190, 195–96, 202–3, 204–5
Süddeutsche Zeitung, 171, 178
Sudetenland, 112
Sullivan, Louis, 118
Süssmuth, Rita, 286–89
Sweden, 73
Switzerland, 133, 171, 223
Sydney Opera, 107
Synagogues
  Berlin, 16, 243–44, 300
  Bremen, 202
  Cologne, 58–59
  Dresden, 12, 15, 25–29, 33–34, 38–40, 42–44
  Essen, 116–17, 121

Synagogues (*continued*)
  Frankfurt am Main, 274–76, 278, 283, 284
  Hamburg, 251, 252, 253–54, 258, 264–66, 269
  Munich, 177, 180
  Potsdam, 14, 232, 237–43, 246, 247

Taeschner, Titus, 89, 105
Talmud, 289
Tarnowski, Wolfgang, 252, 258, 262, 264
Tessenow, Heinrich, 91
Theresienstadt, 266
Thyssen, Bremer Vulkan AG (Bremen-Vegesack), 190
Topography of NS Terror (Frankfurt am Main), 274
Topography of Terror (Berlin), 9, 15–16, 68, 150, 169, 170, 178–79
Tourism, 4, 14, 16, 36, 39, 90–91, 108–9, 127, 143, 145, 152, 171, 224, 246
"Tragedy of a City" exhibition, 53
Troost, Gerdy, 125–26
Troost, Paul Ludwig, 164
Turks, 131

Ude, Christian, 176, 180
Ulbricht, Walter, 235–36, 240
UNESCO World Heritage Site
  Dresden, 38
  Quedlinburg, 225
  Zeche Zollverein Pithead XII (Essen), 118–19
Ungers, O. M., 130
Union of Soviet Socialist Republics (U.S.S.R.), 9, 28, 31, 38, 68, 75, 76, 95, 99, 123, 146, 212, 233, 240, 288
  influence on postwar building in East Germany, 29–30
  Soviet Military Administration (SMA), 238
  West German attitudes toward, 49
United Kingdom, 43, 95, 129, 189, 239
  military in Germany, 195
United States, 5, 31, 41, 43, 49, 80, 82, 94, 95, 96, 134, 198, 254, 286
  and East German attitudes toward Allies, 82, 239, 242
  military in Germany, 195, 212, 222–23
  zone of occupation in postwar era, 147–49, 273
United States Holocaust Memorial Museum, 74, 156, 178, 264
Urban Planning, 3, 4, 25–26, 29–30, 33, 34–36, 51, 70, 90, 91–94, 96, 107, 109, 116–17, 132, 147, 165–67, 188, 231–34, 240–41, 246, 254
  influence of garden city movement, 93–94, 96, 121
Utzon, Jørn, 107

VEB-Foto-Verlag Erlbach, 34
Vees-Gulani, Susanne, 12, 298–99
Venturi, Robert, 5
Vereinigte Stahlwerke AG, 119, 122, 124
Vergangenheitsbewältigung ("coming to terms with the past"), 1–2, 6–11, 12, 15–16, 18, 90, 144–46, 150, 158–59, 164, 180, 187, 211, 247
"*Vernichtung durch Arbeit,*" 99
Vögler, Albert, 119, 121, 124
Vogtland, 34
Völkisch racial theories under Nazis, 3, 102–3, 218
Volkswagen automobile company, 89–101, 108–9, 111
  Beetle, 89, 95–96
  factory building, 91, 94, 98, 101, 102, 103–5, 112
  and forced labor, 95, 98–101
  Kübelwagen, 94–95
Vollmer, Antje, 224–25
V1 rocket, 99, 101

Waffen-SS, 148
Wagner, Herbert, 39
Waigel, Theodor, 178
Walhalla, 102
Waller, Jürgen, 200, 202
Walser, Martin, 10
Wandel, Höfer, Lorch, and Hirsch 12, 40, 276
Wang, Wilfried, 106
Wannsee Conference, 300
Warburg, Aby, 254
Warnemünde, 78
Warnow, 68
Warsaw Ghetto Memorial, 262
Washington, DC, 178
Weizsäcker, Richard von, 99, 289

Weser, 185, 190
Westdeutscher Beobachter, 50
Westphalia, 126
Widera, Thomas, 30
Wilhelmshaven, 77
Wimmer, Hans, 275
Wirtschaftswunder (Economic Miracle), 90, 96, 106, 149
Wolf, Markus, 70
Wolfsburg, 12–13, 15, 16, 89–112, 299
  after reunification, 90, 108–12
  architecture of
    Autostadt, 108–9, 110
    City Theatre, 106–7, 109, 112
    Kulturzentrum, 106
    Rathaus, 89, 105–6
    Schloss Wolfsburg, 91, 95, 96, 98, 109: Stadtmuseum at, 101; Documentation about the Victims of National Socialist Tyranny, permanent exhibition, 100–101
    Steimker Berg, 94, 98, 102–3
    Tullio-Cianetti-Halle, 98, 106
    Volkswagen Autostadt, 108–9
    Volkswagen factory, 91, 94, 98, 102, 103–5, 112: Hall 1, 101
  Ausländerfriedhof, 99–100
    renaming as Memorial to the Victims of National Socialist Tyranny, 100
  FRG era, 89, 95–108
    postwar labor from east, 97
  Klieversberg, 92, 94, 96, 98, 106, 109, 111
  Laagberg, concentration camp, 99
  memorials in,
    Laagberg, 100
    Memorial to the Victims of National Socialist Tyranny, 100
    Place of Remembrance of Forced Labor in Volkswagen Factory, 101
    war memorial, 112

Nazi era, 90–95, 98–101
  development as center of Volkswagen works, 89, 91–94
  Jewish forced labor, 99
  Porschehütte, 112
  Schillerteich, 103
  Stadtarchiv, 100–101
  Stadtkrone, 94, 96, 102, 105
  Wellekamp, 103
Women, 58, 75, 99, 189, 262
  and rape during and after war, 10
World Cup Soccer Championship, 144, 158
World War I, 54–55, 57, 61, 75, 105, 122, 125, 191, 234, 259
World War II, 10, 36, 48, 68, 75–76, 94–95, 98–99, 116, 123, 124, 133, 163, 185, 189–90, 219–21, 222–23, 224, 234, 264, 274, 278, 295
  bombing of German cities, 1, 3, 8, 10, 11–12, 25–26, 28–32, 33–34, 39–42, 49, 53, 58, 80–82, 95, 101, 189–90, 212, 231–32, 234, 239, 251, 257, 261, 298
  "Tragedy of a City" Exhibition, 53
  Commemoration of, 9, 39, 54–55, 57, 61–62, 99, 112, 150–51, 169, 192, 204, 256, 289
  Occupation of Eastern Europe, 188
Wulf, Harms, 155

Young, James, 6, 179, 252
  The Texture of Memory, 252
Yugoslavia, 199

Zec, Peter, 131–32
Zeche Germania, 129
Zeche Zollern (Dortmund), 129
Zeche Zollverein Pithead XII (Essen), 13, 116, 118–34
Zell am See, 95
Zwinger (Dresden), 25, 29